Futures Markets

Futures Markets

Modelling, Managing and Monitoring Futures Trading

Edited by

MANFRED E. STREIT

Published in cooperation with
the European University Institute, Florence

Basil Blackwell

First published 1983
Basil Blackwell Publisher Limited
108 Cowley Road, Oxford OX4 1JF, England

British Library Cataloguing in Publication Data

Futures markets: modelling, managing and
monitoring futures trading.
1. Commodity exchanges
I. Streit, Manfred E.
332.64'4 HG6046

ISBN 0-631-13294-5

Typesetting by Unicus Graphics Ltd, Horsham
Printed in Great Britain by T.J. Press Ltd, Padstow

Contents

List of Contributors

BRENDAN BROWN, Lecturer, Graduate School of Business, London, and Amex Bank Ltd, London

JOSEPH M. BURNS, Senior Economist, Antitrust Division, US Department of Justice, Washington DC

DANIEL FRIEDMAN, Assistant Professor, Department of Economics, University of California, Los Angeles

GORDON T. GEMMILL, Senior Research Fellow, the City University Business School, London

GLENN W. HARRISON, Assistant Professor, Department of Economics, University of Western Ontario, London, Canada

DAVID LEVHARI, Professor, Faculty of Social Sciences, Hebrew University of Jerusalem

DAVID M. NEWBERY, Chief, Public Economics Division, Development Research Department, World Bank, Washington DC

JACQUES ROLFO, Chief, Investment Strategy Division, World Bank, Washington DC

MICHAEL ROTHSCHILD, Professor, Department of Economics, University of Wisconsin, Madison

DAVID J. S. RUTLEDGE, Chief Executive, Sydney Futures Exchange Ltd

JON W. SALMON, Graduate Student, Department of Economics, University of California, Lod Angeles

RICHARD L. SANDOR, Director, Conti Financial, Chicago, and Visiting Professor of Finance, Northwestern University, Evanston, Illinois

HOWARD B. SOSIN, Partner, MP Industrial Traders and MPH Partners, and Associate Professor, Columbia Business School, New York City

JOSEPH E. STIGLITZ, Professor, Department of Economics, Princeton University

MANFRED E. STREIT, Professor, Department of Economics, European University Institute, Florence

STEPHEN J. TAYLOR, Lecturer, Department of Operational Research, Lancaster University

BASIL S. YAMEY, Professor, Department of Economics, London School of Economics and Political Science

Acknowledgements

The present volume contains a set of contributions that emerged out of an international colloquium organized by myself as member of the Department of Economics of the European University Institute at Florence, while on leave from the University of Mannheim (Germany). I would like to join the other delegates in thanking those staff members of the Institute who helped to make the conference such a success. I myself am particularly grateful to Barbara Bonke, who acted with graceful efficiency as conference secretary and undertook most of the related secretarial work. I also wish to thank Peter Versteeg, who helped in the editing and proofreading of the papers. Scientifically, I am most indebted to my paternal friend, Basil S. Yamey, whose encouragement and advice was very helpful when planning the colloquium and writing the introductory paper. With respect to financial support, the Institute provided a solid basis which was further broadened by the German Marshall Fund whose contribution is gratefully acknowledged.

Manfred E. Streit
Florence

1

Modelling, Managing and Monitoring Futures Trading: Frontiers of Analytical Inquiry

MANFRED E. STREIT

The more we learn about the world and the deeper our learning, the more conscious, specific, and articulate will be our knowledge of what we do not know, our knowledge of our ignorance.

(K. R. Popper, 1960)

1 Introduction

1.1 The key questions

The last one and a half decades have witnessed an acceleration of the growth of trading in most conventional futures and the spectacular success of some new ventures, particularly financial futures. The expansion of futures trading is also reflected in the successful launching of new markets away from the traditional centres in the United States and England. So far, however, initiatives in this field cannot be recorded for continental Europe. Possible explanations are: (a) a reduction of potentially tradable commodities as a consequence of the price controls executed via the Common Agricultural Policy; (b) limitations of potential market participation of the banking sector owing to public regulation; (c) barriers to entry of speculators because of adverse legislation as in the case of the German Exchange Act, which largely inhibits speculative trading in commodities; and (d) perhaps even more deep-rooted than elsewhere, a widespread contempt for and misinterpretation of speculation, one of the vital elements in any futures market.

But the aforementioned obstacles to futures trading in continental Europe have not completely prevented the business community from using the markets in London and the United States.[1] Whether the new markets in financial futures in London (London International Financial Futures Exchange, LIFFE) will attract sufficient European users and market-makers for it to become more than a satellite market to Chicago is still uncertain. This uncertainty is rather underlined by the poor performance of trading of financial futures at the New York Futures Exchange (NYFE), which itself also points to the difficulty of predicting the success or failure of new markets and new contracts.

As far as the scientific analysis of futures markets is concerned, the growth of futures trading has been well matched by corresponding research. Particularly in the United States, major advances in both empirical and purely theoretical research have been recorded. And both types of research have converged, especially in the analysis of information-processing via markets. European contributions, although quite important in content from the very beginning, have so far been comparatively few and largely restricted to English scholars. From this point of view, a volume like the present one may perhaps stimulate research in futures trading, not least as a market approach to imperfect information and uncertainty. And it is the major purpose of this introductory essay to point to frontiers of analytical inquiry which partly are revealed by the contributions to this volume and partly became apparent during the proceedings of the colloquium at which the contributions were initially presented.

The studies of the present volume basically deal with three interrelated issues, which can be summarized by the following questions:

(a) *Modelling:* to what extent do economic models of futures trading cover those aspects of these markets that are considered salient in the light of what is known empirically about these markets?
(b) *Managing:* taking into account the answer to the first question, what advice can be given to private economic agents using futures markets, and to governments trying to assess such markets as an allocation device that may be a substitute for, or a complement of, some instruments of public policy?
(c) *Monitoring:* to what extent does the performance of futures markets depend on their institutional framework, properties of the underlying commodities, the design of the traded contracts and the monitoring of trading via private and public regulation?

1.2 The contributions in perspective

Although most contributors to this volume go beyond addressing themselves to a single one of the aforementioned questions, from their main focus the following assignments to the three issues suggest themselves.

Dealing with the first issue, B. S. Yamey (chapter 2) confronts some major postwar contributions to the theory of futures trading with earlier views. He traces the process of trial and error in the development of basic concepts that so far have not even led to definite answers to a number of basic questions, such as the relevance of the various forms of hedging, the need for and existence of a risk premium, the interpretation of convenience yield, and the analytical value of futures markets statistics. J. M. Burns (chapter 3) demonstrates the necessity to reduce the degree to which institutional aspects of futures markets are abstracted from in theoretical studies. As one important consequence, the presently dominant concept of informational efficiency turns out to be only a part, although an important part, of a wider concept of market efficiency. Within the context of informational efficiency, J. E. Stiglitz (chapter 4) shows that the conditions for a revealing full communication equilibrium are even more stringent than has been believed. However, his major results concern the evaluation of an equilibrium model of futures trading, with which he analyses the possibilities of producers and users of a non-storable commodity adjusting to both price and quantity risk. The contribution by D. Levhari and M. Rothschild (chapter 5) basically consists of an attempt to discuss futures trading in a wider macroeconomic context. Hedging via futures as a market response to the observable increase in the variability of interest rates is linked with investment behaviour. This allows speculation on possible reactions in terms of changes in the interest rate elasticity and the structural properties of investment. As far as tests of the validity of theoretical propositions are concerned, D. Friedman, G. W. Harrison and J. W. Salmon (chapter 6) belong to the comparatively small number of economists who try to employ the experimental method. The results obtained for a still narrowly defined experimental situation demonstrate sufficiently the potential of this method to single out the relative importance of the various determinants of futures prices, which can hardly be disentangled by using conventional econometrics.

Related to both the first and the second question is the contribution by S. J. Taylor (chapter 7). The trading rules with which he analyses price series of some London commodity futures and of currencies traded in Chicago produce new empirical evidence concerning the informational efficiency of futures markets. But they can also be considered as more sophisticated methods which may help operators to explore profitable trading opportunities. J. Rolfo and H. B. Sosin (chapter 8) go beyond the analysis of the riskiness of simple hedges by considering a trader who wants to lock in both the cost of inputs and the value of outputs. The analysis of the five strategies that they discuss is designed to take into account, in addition, potential margin calls and interest rate risk. Price volatility as a problem of public policy is taken up by D. M. Newbery (chapter 9). He offers a model that ultimately allows one to deal with the question of whether futures markets promise to perform better than a marketing board in protecting producers against price variations. The answer is shown to depend, last but not least, on whether it is also possible to take into account quantity risks. B. Brown (chapter 10) looks at forward and futures trading in currencies in order to establish which arbitrage constraints a domestically oriented policy may have to face depending upon the convertibility of the currencies. It is shown that there are more arbitrage opportunities than are usually accounted for in the theory of foreign exchange.

The contributions by R. L. Sandor and H. B. Sosin (chapter 11) and by D. J. S. Rutledge (chapter 12), are primarily related to the third question. These chapters analyse the experience of the introduction of interest rate futures at two different exchanges. They provide first-hand information on the art of contract design and on the criteria that may be useful in evaluating proposals for the introduction of new futures. Attention is also paid to the structure of membership and to the prudential control of brokers as possible factors determining success or failure of a new futures market. Finally, G. T. Gemmill (chapter 13) looks into differences between public surveillance and regulation of futures markets in the United States and England, and assesses the validity of arguments in favour of public regulation in general. This also leads to an investigation of the effectiveness of both the existing regulation by public authorities and by the exchanges themselves.

2 Modelling futures markets: positive knowledge and adequate abstraction

Among those aspects of futures trading that represent a challenge when trying to model those markets, at least three still seem to require further attention: trading motives and the corresponding variety of transactions; price formation and the extent to which it is governed by expectations; and the importance of information for trading and as an element in the efficiency of futures markets.

2.1 *Trading motives and transactions variety*

From the very beginning of the analysis of futures markets, and quite in line with the views of the users of these markets, attitudes towards risk were considered to be central. Futures trading was essentially a risk-shifting operation. At least inasmuch as it was not possible in practice to pool risks within the group of hedgers, those who wanted to shed risks had to pay a premium to speculators who were prepared to take them but were also risk-averse on average. When modelling futures markets, this view allowed the dichotomization of market participants accordingly into hedgers and speculators. As discussed by B. S. Yamey (chapter 2), in the postwar period the view gained ground that the pursuit of profit, rather than the shifting of risk, was the governing motive. The dialectics of the propagation of new ideas by now seem to have converged to a synthesis in the sense that the theory of hedging has become more sophisticated and accommodates both risk and return.

The recognition of the profit motive in hedging at the same time required the laying of stress on the information aspect of futures trading. Given the standardization of contracts and the organized, highly competitive trading, only an informational advantage could serve as a second potential source of systematic returns, besides the scarcity rent possibly obtainable by risk-bearers. Even if they were on average risk-neutral, and no scarcity rent was distributable, speculators would still have an opportunity to gain from the acquisition and use of informational advantages. The implication for hedging is that the price to be paid for unloading risk on to the futures market can, in principle, be reduced by information activities. The least a potential hedger can do in this respect is to use the information he acquires in the course of his business in actuals as a basis for forming his own expectations. They in turn allow him to assess the hedging situation, i.e. the current futures price. This approach contrasts with a notion of hedging that for a long time dominated the theoretical interpretation of futures markets. It implied that hedgers always content themselves with locking in a futures price.[2] What remains unsettled, however, is essentially an empirical problem: the relative importance of discretionary forms of hedging as opposed to routine hedging still has to be established.

In terms of modelling, a further departure from the comparatively simple concept of routine hedging should be mentioned. It refers to the recognition that the quantity to be hedged is a decision variable, instead of always assuming completely hedged positions. Particularly in the case of agricultural commodities, it is evident that a producer has to face not only a price risk but also a quantity risk. And, as demonstrated by J. E. Stiglitz (chapter 4), deviations from a completely hedged position are rational and depend on the kind of relationship between output and price variability. Although the practice of incomplete hedging was well known, its recognition as a theoretical issue was related mainly to attempts to apply portfolio theory to hedging behaviour (e.g. Johnson, 1960; Rutledge, 1972).

The easy conceptualization of a futures market in terms of the simple dichotomy between hedging and speculation probably also encouraged abstraction from all other types of transactions observable on futures markets. And again, these differ in a characteristic way from routine hedging and straightforward speculation when considering the risks involved and the related information activities. There are, first, the possibilities of profiting from differences between (a) prices of the same contract at different exchanges and (b) prices of a futures contract and the corresponding spot prices – i.e. pure inter-market arbitrage and, in the case of storable commodities, inter-temporal arbitrage. These transactions are practically riskless if the arbitrageur manages to lock in the relevant costs of inter-locational and inter-temporal substitution (i.e. transport and storage costs). Second, effective arbitrage in turn opens up possibilities for speculating in futures but limiting the risk, i.e. intra-commodity, inter-commodity and inter-market spreads in futures as opposed to straightforward speculation by holding a completely open futures position. The reduction of potential losses results from the price link between the two positions of a spread. The link is stabilized via arbitrage based on the corresponding costs of substitution (i.e., again, transport and storage costs and, in the case of inter-commodity spreads, for example the processing or transformation costs).

The difficulties in extending the analysis of futures markets to such transactions are reflected in at least two shortcomings of most available models of futures markets: (a) they are one-market models, abstracting from the interrelations between those actuals and futures markets that are firmly linked via substitution possiblities; (b) they are comparative static models, abstracting from inter-temporal relations and from the actual trading process. Tentative efforts to overcome this limitation (e.g. Peston and Yamey, 1960) clearly demonstrate the price that most probably would have to be paid in terms of highly complex or even indeterminate solutions if the analysis were to be extended. But as will be argued here, unless such extensions or elaborations were attempted, the speculative element in all futures transactions as well as the processing and conveying of information would probably have to remain inaccessible or elusive.

A discussion of the motives for futures trading would be incomplete without reference to tax considerations.[3] Although taxation-induced market participation does not lead to new forms of transactions worthy of exploration, it does affect the volume and structure of trade. The tax implications of futures trading may differ for non-speculative and speculative transactions. Tax implications of futures trading can be taken into account by traders in basically a passive way in their decisions to enter the market. However, they may also be used actively to try to manipulate the tax burden resulting from other activities. In particular, spreading can offer an opportunity to manipulate the time structure of taxable revenues to the advantage of the taxpayer. Depending on the relevant rules of taxation and particularly changes in the rules, incentives and disincentives to use futures markets for tax purposes may produce additional difficulties for the empirical analysis of these markets.

2.2 *Expectations and price formation*

The modelling of futures trading predominantly within a comparative static framework definitely facilitates the analysis, but it fails to capture a characteristic feature of trading on these and other speculative markets: the specific time structure that futures transactions normally have. As emphasized more recently again by Hirshleifer (1975, 1977), trading usually consists of two stages. In a first round a trader establishes a position that he hopes to revise at a profit in a later round. The obvious but basic conclusion then is that traders tend to be induced to take an open position in futures in a discretionary way if they anticipate that the current futures price or, in the case of hedgers, the difference between two prices (the basis), will change, i.e., if they in fact consider the current price to be a wrong forecast of the price at maturity of a contract and hence of the future spot price (or the futures price at any earlier date at which they intend to close out).

If some traders are able to establish, say, a positive position at a futures price they consider to be a wrong forecast, the above reasoning, equally, suggests that those who are prepared to hold the opposite position must have expectations that diverge both from those implicit in the traded price and those held by the other side of the market. In this case it can be demonstrated (c.f. Streit, 1983) that, during the period before the maturity of a contract, trading at 'false' prices determined by divergent beliefs or expectations is the rule. Only at the maturity of a contract is a transient consensus imposed upon traders by the facts of the spot market.

This view has interesting implications both for the interpretation of futures prices and also for the modelling of their formation. According to this view, prices at which transactions have taken place before the maturity of a contract represent wrong forecasts of future market conditions to traders who have made transactions at those prices. The implicit forecasts have been acceptable only to those who refrained from trading at those prices. As far as price changes indicate changes in information situations, those who trade tend to disagree that the observable price changes reflect accurately the changes in information. This has a further implication. Suppose it turns out, empirically, that the futures prices in a particular market over a particular period prove to have been good forecasts and that the market has to be judged efficient in the informational sense. This observed result would have been brought about by the actions of market participants who in fact disputed the forecasts implicit in the various futures prices. Thus the favourable 'performance' of the market would be the unintended outcome of numerous decisions of the many participants who traded precisely because they considered various prices to be inappropriate and unjustified, not least in the light of the information available to them, and who intended to profit from the mistakes. The rationale for active market participation differs completely from the observable market result. The modelling problem that has to be solved conforms to Popper's general description of the task of theoretical social sciences: 'to trace the unintended social repercussions of intentional human actions' (Popper, 1948, p. 342).

To fulfil this task seems to be particularly difficult in the case of futures trading or, more generally, speculative trading. If divergent beliefs are essential for such trading, Hawtrey's early verdict on the conventional method of bridging the gap between individual decisions and market results still holds: namely, that divergent beliefs represent 'a fatal objection to the introduction of any aggregates or averages of expectations into economic reasoning' (Hawtrey, 1939–40, p. 203). This also means that the usual econometric approach of inferring from the aggregate performance of such markets how expectations are actually formed is basically invalidated. It remains to be explored whether it is an adequate approximation to segment a futures market according to types of transactions and positions taken and to analyse the consequences of correspondingly segmented expectations (as done, e.g., by Goss and Giles, 1981).

2.3 *Information-processing and market efficiency*

The difficulties of comparative static equilibrium analysis in capturing salient features of speculative markets also apply to the information activities on these markets. They are particularly well demonstrated by the link between the conveying of information and the informational efficiency of markets, which has been established by an impossibility theorem (e.g., Grossman and Stiglitz, 1980). The theorem is based on a free-rider problem which leads to an erosion of futures markets as a means for processing and disseminating information.[4] If the conditions are such that prices convey all information that informed traders collect, other traders can get the information free by just observing market prices. Hence speculative markets can exist only if they are not informationally efficient. This can be modelled by adding sufficient noise to the price signals.

In the meantime, and as demonstrated by J. E. Stiglitz (chapter 4), it has become clear that the assumptions necessary to establish the theorem are even more stringent than originally thought. However, it can be argued that modelling information activities in the conventional (neoclassical) way raises a more fundamental problem. The problem results from the abstraction from time. Given the time structure of transactions, the informational externality created via trading can only endanger the existence of a speculative market if an informed trader has no opportunity of trading before his new informational situation has become general. This opportunity to trade at a price that is false in the light of his information-based beliefs, and to re-trade at a profit if his beliefs turn out to be correct, is the greater the smaller is the market weight of his transaction and the less he initially has to share his informational advantage with others.

The dynamic view also leads to the conclusion that speculative markets cannot be completely efficient at every point in time. But whereas in the case of the theorem of informational inefficiency is a necessary condition for the existence of such markets, inefficiency in this view is part of the process of discovery and communication of information when considering market dynamics. Furthermore the incentive problem is seen differently. In the static analysis, it is noise that guarantees a rent distributable to informed traders. It must be high enough to cover their information costs. In a dynamic context, however, inefficiency is the result of some traders being able to trade at a temporary informational advantage. The derivable profit is a premium for being faster in the acquisition and correct reading of new information, and also for re-interpreting already available information more quickly. The premium is highly uncertain, and is exposed to the competitive information activities of other traders. It is the competition for a temporary informational monopoly that determines not only the informational quality of prices, but also the speed at which changes in beliefs and underlying information are disseminated.

If the above interpretation of the market process from an informational point of view comes closer to reality, a further modelling problem results. It concerns the relationship between informational efficiency and competition. Inefficiency from a static point of view reflects in a competitive market the generated incentives that are the source of its dynamic efficiency. What in the static approach is interpreted as a deviation from Pareto optimality (e.g. Grossman, 1976, p. 584; Figlewski, 1978, p. 581) is in the dynamic approach a source of virtue as emphasized by Hayek (1937 and 1945).

Permanent efficiency in a Paretian sense is not only 'at best an irrelevant fiction' (Lachmann, 1977, p. 37) but would also be undesirable if it could be achieved. If the state of permanent Pareto efficiency were to be used as a (fictitious) reference point, it would be necessary to establish a kind of optimum degree of inefficiency. For the market to fulfil its function of collecting and disseminating information, the optimum would refer to a balance that had to be struck between the access to information premia and their erosion through competition. The same applies to the function of facilitating transactions. In order to recruit sufficient support from potential market-makers, they have to be offered an incentive. But at the same time they have to be threatened by competition. Two points emerge out of these considerations, which are raised by J. M. Burns (chapter 3): (a) in view of the functions a market has to fulfil, informational efficiency is only one, although an important, element of a wider concept of market efficiency; and (b) the institutional framework of trading and the design of the tradeable contracts can be considered as controlling variables with respect to the effectiveness of competition.

To assess competing theoretical propositions empirically has proved to be difficult. First, the available statistical information is partly inadequate, as explained by B. S. Yamey (chapter 2). Second, the inference from the observable price, volume and participation data to the unobservable expectations and information of traders has to overcome analytical obstacles (section 2.2 above). Third, the application of econometric methods has problems of its own, as demonstrated by S. J. Taylor (chapter 7). Given these difficulties, the experimental method presented by D. Friedman, G. W. Harrison and J. W. Salmon (chapter 6) could help to improve the empirical assessment of rival theories. The improvement would result primarily from the characteristic property of the experimental method of allowing individual influences to be isolated. This is already demonstrated by the aforementioned contribution, inasmuch as it shows that within a stationary environment results can be observed that come quite close to those of the conventional equilibrium analyses. It would now be particularly interesting to trace the consequences of a change in the experimental design by allowing for event uncertainty and a stochastic inflow of information.

3 Managing futures trading: the perspectives of business and government

3.1 Investment strategies and risk management

Futures markets can be approached from two basic business perspectives, which, however, can be and are frequently merged, as emphasized in the discussion of trading motives (section 2.1 above):

(a) the search for unexploited profit opportunities, including tax considerations, and
(b) the attempt to manage risks that are predominantly multidimensional.

The first perspective can be described by asking whether it is possible and necessary to forecast prices in order to profit from an investment in futures. If the first part of the question is reduced to the possibility of forecasting short-term price movements from past futures prices, the link between investment opportunities and informational efficiency of the weak variety becomes visible. The second part of the question concerns the skills of market participants to forecast medium-term price developments by considering 'fundamentals', and the existence of a risk premium that would reduce the value of such skills.

As far as short-term price-forecasting is concerned, the random walk, introduced into futures markets analysis more than 40 years ago (Working, 1934, 1942, 1949), still serves as the basic, negative proposition. The statistical models and methods that have been developed in the meantime, and to which S. J. Taylor (chapter 7) has something to add, primarily helped to reveal the structure of the, on average, small and unexploitable deviations from the proposition that consecutive price changes are basically unpredictable.

Even if short-term price movements do not deviate in an exploitable way from the random walk, investors may still be able to profit from longer-term price changes. The simplest possibility would be to exploit price trends with a buy-and-hold strategy. But if such trends exist, do investors, or for that matter speculators, profit merely from bearing the price risks that hedgers may want to unload on to the futures markets, or do speculators earn profits because they successfully forecast prices? The attempts to settle the question of the relevance of a risk premium have been numerous and have been made with persistently improved statistical methods. But the results have to be qualified, at least on the following grounds. First, there is the aforementioned identification problem. Second, even if one accepts the test's performance so far, the available evidence is inconclusive because it varies between commodities, contracts, trading periods and exchanges. Third, in the case of (temporarily) thin and hence imperfect markets, speculators may equally well be risk-neutral but earn a scarcity rent. Fourth, even sizeable premia are not necessarily a sufficient indicator of a risk premium, because if speculators were to be averse to risk, they would probably also consider the risk related to a risk premium, i.e. its variability.

The last point leads to a more general qualification, also made by S. J. Taylor (chapter 7), so far as the results presented in his contribution are concerned. The risk premium is necessarily a highly subjective concept. As such, and from a modelling point of view, it must also refer to expectations on the variability of the premium. Hence efforts to model price formation on futures markets in the tradition of Kaldor (1939–40) tend to obscure the issue because they rely upon the notions of quasi-objective 'representative' price expectations and a (constant) risk premium to accommodate speculators.

Turning to the second business perspective, risk management, the gap between its oversimplified theoretical conceptionalization and sophisticated business practice has been narrowed somewhat in recent years. This concerns particularly the move away from the one-dimensional price risk and the inclusion of quantity risk, as also exemplified by J. E. Stiglitz (chapter 4) and D. M. Newbery (chapter 9). And that there are even more dimensions of risk worth being considered, and dependent upon the specific situation of a potential hedger, is clearly demonstrated by J. Rolfo and H. Sosin (chapter 8). The hedging strategies that they discuss also partly serve as a reminder that, via cross-commodity hedges, developments on various futures markets and the underlying spot markets can be directly linked, thus increasing the complexity of their price determination. But a look at the conditions underlying the various strategies equally supports the verdict that 'the differences of opinion and practices as well as the intricacies of the variables involved make it all but impossible to reduce the outcomes to general rules for the improvement of trading effectiveness' (Teweles *et al.*, 1977, p. 43).

3.2 Futures trading and public policy

At least four public policy issues can be identified in addition to the need for an effectiveness of the regulation of futures markets (section 4.2 below):

(a) trading in financial futures as a feedback mechanism relevant to monetary policy and debt management;
(b) trading in futures as a substitute for interventions in the underlying commodity markets;
(c) interventions in futures markets as a substitute for interventions in the underlying commodity markets;
(d) interventions in futures markets in order to improve some of the functions of these markets.

Regarding the first issue, hardly any empirical conclusions have been established so far. If, for example, futures markets were to add to the variability of interest rates, they could create a problem for monetary policy to the extent that such signals from the financial markets are used for the scaling and timing of policy. Similarly, if the monetary theory of exchange rate determination contained realistic propositions, and if, again, currency futures tended to increase the variability of spot exchange rates, an undesirable side-effect of futures trading would have to be taken into account. But as far as the latter point is concerned, there is also the argument put forward by B. Brown (chapter 10) that currency futures are not likely to add very much to the responsiveness of currency markets, given the dominant and comparatively efficient interbank forward market.

In any case, the possible undesirable feedbacks on monetary policy depend on the relationship between the presence of futures trading and the volatility or variability of spot prices. The question has received considerable attention with respect to both commodity and financial futures. There are good *a priori* grounds for supposing that futures trading does not increase price volatility; and the empirical evidence seems to bear this out.[5] But the question cannot be definitely settled with the help of conventional (non-experimental) econometric methods. However, the policy problem also has to be assessed from a wider cost–benefit point of view. Against possible but hardly substantiated negative feedbacks on monetary policy have to be set the private and public benefits provided by futures markets, emphasized, for example, by J. M. Burns (chapter 3). And last but not least, it seems reasonable to ask whether the problem would not become negligible in any case if there were to be a changeover from the observable, partly erratic, monetary policy and the monetary shocks resulting from fiscal activism to a more steady conduct of macroeconomic policy.

The second issue – futures trading as a substitute for interventions in commodity markets – is of particular importance as regards various price stabilization schemes put forward in the discussion of a new international economic order. In this context, the results obtained by D. M. Newbery (chapter 9). have to be emphasized. He shows that, in general, futures markets are likely to offer better insurance to producers than price stabilization schemes, as long as, and to the extent that, futures markets can be made and kept highly competitive. And this condition, quite contrary to widespread prejudice, requires sufficient speculation. The comparative advantage that futures trading has over price stabilization schemes largely results from (a) the discretion it gives to the potential hedger, also allowing him to take into account a possible quantity risk, and (b) the production incentives, which may become distorted with the operation of price stabilization schemes. A normative implication of using futures markets instead of price stabilization schemes may also be worth pointing out: namely, that producers of the commodities in question should take care of the marketing side of their business themselves like any other producer, trader of manufacturer.

The remaining two policy issues – intervening in futures markets either as a substitute for interventions in the underlying commodity markets or in order to improve the functioning of futures markets – are particularly well exemplified by two proposals made by Houthakker (1967, p. 51) and McKinnon (1967, p. 851). The proposals serve well to demonstrate that even well-intended interventions in futures markets are likely to be counter productive.

According to Houthakker, a Commodity Stabilization Agency would be established to operate in futures markets under the following rules.

– Interventions would be guided by a so-called 'indicator price', representing a three-year moving average of commodity spot prices.

- Interventions via buying or selling of futures contracts are supposed to induce private storage to the extent that spot prices are kept within a range to be established around the indicator price.
- Interventions would be restricted to contracts six to nine months from maturity.

The scheme would operate as follows. If the spot price tended to fall below the floor of the price range, the Agency would have to buy futures contracts. Such purchases would have to produce a positive difference between futures and spot price (contango) large enough to induce a withdrawal of supplies via short carrying-charge hedging and and also to attract additional demand via arbitrage. Hence the spot price would be supported through induced private decisions to increase stocks. Conversely, if spot prices tended to rise above the ceiling, a negative difference between futures and spot price (backwardation) would have to be produced. By selling contracts, demand for stockholding purposes would be discouraged whereas additional supplies would be attracted, leading to a reduction of private stocks. The price incentives given through a manipulation of some more distant futures prices are supposed to produce private storage decisions similar to those that a buffer stock authority would have to make in order to stabilize spot prices; consequently, the financial burden of the stockholding operations would be shifted to private market participants.

A first limitation of this proposal is rather obvious. Like buffer stock arrangements, it is applicable only to continuous inventory markets and inapplicable to non-inventory markets. With respect to discontinuous inventory markets, qualifications would be necessary in respect of the period during which practically no stocks are held. Furthermore, the possibility of attracting, if necessary, additional supplies is rather limited towards the end of the storage season. The latter point leads to a more general argument. The possiblity of putting pressure on spot prices is limited by the size of private stocks held. In terms of the proposal, this means that, against its original intentions, the Agency might be drawn into holding stocks in order for it to be able to step in with spot sales, should insufficient private supplies not be coming forward when needed (Richardson and Farris, 1973, p. 229).

A further problem results from the declared intention to restrict interventions to contracts six to nine months from maturity. There are side-effects to be taken into account. These result from the interdependence among the prices of all the contract maturities traded.

Those prices that are directly manipulated may easily induce hedging, arbitrage and spreading operations affecting contracts of other maturities as well. Basically, such transactions would be profitable as long as intertemporal price spreads prevail that differ from the corresponding costs of storage. But such transactions would also affect the spot price. This could mean that consecutive interventions in the selected contracts would be required; however, these might not be sufficient to control spot prices (Tomek and Gray, 1970, p. 379). As a consequence, interventions would have to be spread to other contracts as well, making the job of the Agency difficult if not impossible.

Doubts can also be raised as to the predictive quality of the indicator price. If the likely price trend could be detected so easily by using the suggested or any similar method of extrapolation, it is very likely that private market participants would already be using it successfully. In this case interventions along the same lines would hardly pay. But there are also some technical problems involved. The smoothing effect of the moving average depends upon how well deviations from the trend even out over the period considered. And from this point of view the length of the period required is very likely to differ among commodities. Furthermore, it is uncertain whether the pattern of fluctuation would remain the same in the future. As to the trend that has to be isolated by this method, the results are different for a linear trend and a non-linear trend. In the latter case, the method can provide only a linear approximation. The quality of the approximation tends to vary according to the polynomial applicable to the trend. Finally, the predictive quality also depends upon how speedily changes in the trend are indicated. A lagged response is practically unavoidable, and it will be greater the more observations of past spot prices are included. Hence the requirements as to smoothing can conflict with those conducive to signalling a change in the trend.

It is also uncertain how private market participants will behave, given the Agency's planned interventions. They could continue to adjust to the now manipulated market conditions. Alternatively, speculators could find it profitable to anticipate likely future interventions to the Agency according to the market information available to them. In this case, one possibility is that the amount of intervention would be reduced, although it would hardly be in a foreseeable way (Richardson and Farris, 1973, p. 229). But, *a priori*, it is also possible that the amount of intervention registered would increase. If, for example, the indicator price follows trend changes with a noticeable lag, informed speculators would have almost riskless opportunities to take advantage of the lagged response of the Agency which would have to defend its indicator price.[6] Furthermore, it can be argued that traders in the actual commodity would be inclined to economize their stocks and reduce or even stop hedging, given the announced stabilization of spot prices (and confidence that it would be achieved). Consequently, commercial transactions in futures, i.e. hedging, might decline. However, according to the available evidence, they appear to be the basis for financial transactions, i.e. speculation.[7] Hence the market volume attributable to private participants might shrink even further. This tendency could be aggravated if Keynes (1930, vol. 2, p. 141) were to be proven correct in expecting that only relatively large variations of spot prices attract a sufficient amount of speculation. All this could mean that, if the Agency proved to be successful in stabilizing spot prices, it would serve eventually to destroy, or at least debilitate, the basis for its own interventions, viz. the futures market.

Whether Houthakker's stabilization scheme would at least have a successful start can also be questioned. *Ex post* simulations of the market for soybeans over a period of 14 years led to the conclusion that the volatility of spot prices would tend to be increased under a Houthakker regime,[8] changes in private market participants' behaviour being excluded. According to this study, the main reason for the failure of the scheme seemed to be that the three-year moving average imposed 'backward-looking trends' of futures prices and quantities.

Turning to McKinnon's proposal, it would be the task of the Commodity Authority to ensure that 'distant futures prices are stable and do reflect the long-term trend in spot prices' (McKinnon, 1967, p. 857), leaving spot prices and near-term futures prices free to vary. Any stabilizing effect on spot prices is considered to be only a welcome side-effect, and not the major objective of interventions in futures trading. Hence one of the criticisms raised against Houthakker's proposal does not apply here. The Authority is not likely to be drawn into any storage operations against its original intentions. However, again, reservations have to be made according to the storability of the commodities in question. In the case of continuous inventory markets, the interdependence of futures and spot prices has to be taken into account. If the Authority simply controlled distant futures prices, probably mainly by taking long positions, this would block any feedback of spot price developments on those futures prices. Only near-term futures contracts would be affected, with the risk of causing distortions in the intertemporal price spreads.

And this would add to the volatility of spot prices via induced private transactions. Under these circumstances the proposal is more applicable to discontinuous and non-inventory markets, where the relationship between spot and futures prices is less stringent.

As in Houthakker's proposal, it is uncertain how private market participants will react to the activities of the Authority. But an even more important problem appears to be how the Authority would make sure that it inserted the 'right' long-term trend. McKinnon assumes that the Authority could solve this information problem. With growing experience, it is supposed 'to learn to discern a secular trend in distant futures prices by the size of the net long position it had to take in order to support a target price'. And 'secular changes in prices will be modest in size to which the Authority should accommodate itself to avoid supporting any longterm disequilibrium price' (McKinnon, 1967, p. 859). The first expectation is hardly justified in the case of continuous inventory markets. Because of the interrelatedness of spot and futures prices, the Authority could easily be misled by developments in the spot market spilling over into the futures market; admittedly, this can be assumed away by attributing sufficient experience to the Authority. The second expectation cuts both ways. Even if secular price changes were modest, it could prove difficult to isolate them because of this very property. Hence the Authority could hold on too long to a wrongly estimated price trend.

The last point leads to the question of the kind of information the price trend should be based on, apart from the size of the net long position. It can at least be doubted whether a public agency would be able to achieve more than is done by numerous private market participants in collecting and using information relevant to the future. Or to put it in more general terms, 'the real issue which is thereby posed is whether speculation should be done by private traders or official agencies, or by some combination of the two' (Gray and Rutledge, 1971, p. 81).

Finally, a policy that involves the establishment of more distant futures contracts than those currently available can be questioned altogether. First, it may be doubted whether there really is a strong demand for longer-term contracts. To be able to lock in one single price over a long period may be counter-productive in view of the fact that market participants are unable to control in a similar way all, or at least many, of the other input and output prices that help to determine the profitability of their economic activities. Second, even if it could ever be shown that private risk aversion is greater than desired by society, with the likely effect of shortening the average time span covered by futures contracts, the priorities for economic policy can be considered to be different. Instead of trying to intervene in futures markets with highly dubious success, it may be worthwhile to explore possibilities that could lower the risk burden. And a considerable part of this burden is imposed by the multitude and unpredictability of changes of government interventions at large.[9]

4 Monitoring futures trading: issues of promotion and regulation

4.1 Promoting futures trading

The successes and the failures in launching new and sustaining old futures contracts and in opening new and expanding traditional exchanges with diverging institutional infrastructures during the past 15 years invite us to ask again what are the preconditions for successful futures trading. Besides adding to positive economic knowledge, the answers to the question are important from two points of view.

(a) Futures trading has definitely passed the stage of predominantly spontaneous development and has become an industry with 'products' introduced, managed and diversified by the exchanges. Hence the answers are of instrumental value to the competitors, actual and potential, in this comparatively new industry.
(b) Futures markets have grown to a size that in many cases is of considerable importance to the underlying spot markets and which involves a wide-ranging market participation. As a consequence, governments have been induced to consider and reconsider the regulation of such markets, an activity that requires sufficient knowledge if the markets are not to be inadvertently and unnecessarily crippled by public policy.

The answers relevant to the two points of view basically refer to the two sides of the same coin, liquidity of the market and effective competition. The need for public regulation is largely a question of how to induce and to safeguard effective competition in futures trading (cf. section 4.2 below); and it becomes redundant when this has come about. For the futures industry, the success of a contract depends on whether it is possible to attract and sustain sufficient liquidity. And as already indicated (section 2.3 above), the system of incentives to trade can be considered a controlling variable.

The incentive system can be split into two components: the underlying commodity or financial instrument and its properties, and the institutional infrastructure provided by the futures contract and the trading arrangements. As pointed out by D. J. S. Rutledge (chapter 12), both components have received different analytical attention in the past, with the emphasis moving towards the institutional characteristics of futures markets. Rutledge also demonstrates that, on an international scale, the characteristics show a remarkable diversity. Furthermore, and as reported by R. L. Sandor and H. B. Sosin (chapter 11), the method of trial and error still ranks high when it comes to determining the provisions of a contract such as contract size, 'tick' size, daily price limit, position limit size and deliverable grades. It may well be that the choice of the most attractive provisions is one of the areas where technical and hence systematic knowledge has to be combined with ingenuity and possibly flair.

A further unsettled question concerning the incentive system is the assessment of floor trading. There seems to be a consensus that floor brokers add liquidity to a market. Their presence or absence serves, for example, at least as a partial explanation of differences in liquidity and - possibly - informational efficiency between American and English markets for the same commodity. But this additional liquidity comes at a price. As argued by J. M. Burns (chapter 3), floor brokers find themselves in a priviledged position compared with other market participants when it comes to the speed at which orders can be executed. Hence they enjoy an institutionally determined competitive advantage in the exploitation of trading opportunities arising out of new information. Furthermore, a minimum return is provided to them depending, as shown by R. L. Sandor and H. B. Sosin (chapter 11), on the 'tick' size. It may well be that these selective incentives, on balance, still create net benefits by attracting additional trade and trading skills, given the present organization of exchanges. But it remains to be explored whether an organizational innovation like electronic trading may not allow the striking of an even more favourable balance between incentives to trading and the strength of competition.

4.2 Regulation and market performance

As with all other economic activities, the performance of futures markets can be assessed on allocative and distributive criteria. Even if the result of such an assessment were to support government regulation in principle, rationality would require us to weigh carefully the likely benefits of regulation against the cost to be incurred. Assessment requires the following:

(a) an operational reference system that allows a comparison between actual performance and possible performance;

(b) solid empirical evidence to establish deviations between actual and possible performance;
(c) courses of regulatory action which, according to *a priori* reasoning and relevant experience, are likely to be effective in terms of reducing or removing such deviations;
(d) estimates of the direct costs of regulation in terms of resources required as well as an evaluation of possible side-effects of regulatory action.

Only too frequently, one or even several of these requirements for a rational policy conduct are violated.

To date, public opinion on the functions and the performance of futures markets seems to reveal even more contempt for these markets than for stock exchanges. Hence arguments for their regulation, or even prohibition, receive widespread support only too easily. Among arguments put forward in favour of regulation three are particularly popular: (a) dangers of price manipulation, (b) additional price volatility owing to speculation, and (c) losses imposed upon inexperienced traders. While the last argument is purely distributive, the first two suggest market failure with allocative and distributive consequences.

As far as manipulation and price volatility are concerned, it is important to note at the outset that it proved to be extremely difficult to muster unambiguous empirical evidence. As regards manipulation, the results presented by G. T. Gemmill (chapter 13) reaffirm previous findings. They can be summarized in terms of the verdict of Cagan (1981, pp. 173, 174) referring to interest rate futures markets: (a) 'the bugaboo of corners should be laid to rest. Although their possibility always seems to cast an ominous shadow over futures markets, corners are almost never achieved'; (b) 'Most squeezes probably reflect fortuitous developments rather than intended manipulation.'

Turning to the alleged additional volatility of futures and spot prices owing to speculation on organized futures markets, the proposition has already been questioned when dealing with the more general issue of whether futures trading has a destabilizing impact on prices (section 3.2 above). Furthermore, destabilizing speculation is difficult to reconcile with the predominant finding that prices on liquid futures markets can be reasonably closely described in terms of the random walk model. If price changes turn out to be basically unpredictable, they indicate that the market participants have not missed significant opportunities to profit from informational advantages. As an unintended (external) effect of their competitive trading, prices tend to become informationally efficient. Any trading effort to drive prices off this efficiency 'walk' would simply invite losses, except when such efforts turn out to be consistent with future developments so far unknown to anybody. This does not exclude the possibility that the efforts themselves may be undertaken at random (Cagan, 1981, p. 178). But it is difficult to see them as a major but still random component in price determination. Even the proposition of overshooting, which refers to a sequence of price changes as a whole and not to individual consecutive changes, has less empirical force than a simple inspection of futures prices may frequently suggest. As shown as early as 1934 by Working, a random walk can be quite consistent with a price series that seems to suggest a systematic cyclical component.

As far as inexperienced but nevertheless avaricious market participants are concerned, they may well be responsible for some of the random changes in prices, and may have to take losses that necessarily must be profits to others. But it is difficult to see that such redistribution should require any regulation going beyond protection against criminal acts like fraud. First of all, the possible implication that experience is a sufficient safeguard against losses cannot be reconciled with imperfect information and uncertainty. Second, nobody has forced inexperienced market participants to engage in trading. Hence they may well be left to bear the full responsibility of that freedom of action as is done in other cases of economic activity. Third, losses resulting from poor decisions can be a better teacher than paternalistic regulation.

But even if it is accepted that market participants should be protected from their own imprudence, what form should such protection take? In order to be effective, more than public warnings and the provision of information would be required. Most likely, such regulation would have to assign to brokers the task of protecting customers. But how should the requisite rules be defined? Where is the borderline to be drawn between prudent and imprudent trading decisions? Who is to supervise the performance of brokers, and who is to audit the supervisors? The likely outcome would be a regulatory chain of little effectiveness in terms of protection but with stifling consequences for futures trading. If there is to be any protection of inexperienced traders, it has to come from the brokers themselves acting in their own interest. And it can well be argued that they have an interest in advising their customers well, particularly as they have to offer their services, including their advice, under competitive conditions. Furthermore, the exchanges have an interest in orderly relationships between their members and the members' clients.

Hence feasible safeguards have been introduced over time into the self-regulation of the exchanges.

Self-regulation and public regulation are also substitutes when it comes to preventing manipulation. This is demonstrated by G. T. Gemmill (chapter 13), who compares the British and American practice. And both substitutes seem to be equally ineffective in view of the practical difficulties of excluding completely (temporary) concentration as a precondition for manipulation. However, particularly in view of the competition between the various exchanges, which no longer stops at national borders, it can be argued that exchanges and their members have an interest in maintaining orderly trading conditions in general and in protecting their clients in particular. This does not exclude, on the other hand, the possibility that they are inclined to tolerate monopolistic elements in the trading organization and in contract design as a source of revenues for their members – as is argued, for example, by J. M. Burns (chapter 3). But it is difficult to see that frequent and substantiated complants of monopolistic trading practices on an exchange would leave its volume of transactions unaffected.

If, however, there exists an incentive for self-regulation, the exchanges are unlikely to extend regulation beyond codifying and generalizing common practice, because such extension would merely increase the costs of using these markets. Similar restraint cannot be expected from government regulation, where an extension of regulation is more compatible with the production incentives of bureaucracies weakly checked by budget constraints. And given the limited effectiveness of both private and public regulation, the harsh verdict of Stigler (1975, p. 177) may serve as a useful reminder whenever one is tempted to strive for perfection through regulation: 'Public regulation, for all its enormous momentum, lives by its goals and not by its achievements, and surely we ought eventually to tire of promising preambles and unpromising achievements.'

Notes

1 Corresponding evidence has been provided, for example, for the International Monetary Market (IMM) in Chicago by the 1977 survey of the Commodity Futures Trading Commission (CFTC) (cf. International Commodities Clearing House, 1979, Appendix V).

2 Notable exceptions are quite early contributions like the one by Hoffman (1932), who emphasizes (p. 407): 'that hedging is something more than simply setting up counter future transactions and hoping for the best'.

And his definition of hedging (pp. 405ff) correspondingly includes expectations as to basis changes as a constitutive element.

3 For a discussion of the taxation aspects of futures trading with reference to US laws and regulations, cf. Powers and Vogel (1981, chapter 19).

4 For a more detailed discussion see Streit (1982).

5 For a summary, cf. Streit (1981, pp. 495ff).

6 To skilled chartists, such technical shortcomings of the intervention scheme would be quickly revealed. If the Agency tried to frustrate speculative trading by frequently changing the scheme, this would presumably be counter-productive to the stabilization objective.

7 Studies relating hedging and speculation suggest that, when measured in terms of open contracts, the total amount of business done on a futures market tends to vary fairly closely with the amount of hedging contracts outstanding and not so much according to those open contracts attributable to speculation (e.g. Working, 1970, p. 14). In addition, according to the history of individual futures markets, no cases are known where speculative motives rather than the desire to shift commercial risks were the driving force to open such a market.

8 According to Richardson and Farris (1973), who claim to have used as indicators for the total market the values for the elasticity of demand and supply that are even rather favourable when taking into account the operation of the scheme.

9 For a wider discussion of the time horizon in futures markets and of government interventions, cf. Streit (1981, p. 500).

References

Cagan, P. (1981), 'Financial Futures Markets – Is more Regulation Needed?' *Journal of Futures Markets*, 1.

Figlewski, S. (1978), 'Market "Efficiency" in a Market with Heterogeneous Information', *Journal of Political Economy*, 86.

Goss, B. A. and Giles, D. E. A. (1981), 'Comparative Modelling of Price Determination and Storage in United States and Australian Commodity Markets: Soybeans and Wool', paper presented to the Western Economic Association International Conference, San Francisco, 2–6 July.

Gray, R. W. and Rutledge, D. J. S. (1971), 'The Economics of Commodity Futures Markets – A Survey', *Review of Marketing and Agricultural Economics*, 39.

Grossman, S. J. (1976), 'On the Efficiency of Competitive Stock Markets where Traders have Diverse Information', *Journal of Finance*, 31.

Grossman, S. J. and Stiglitz, J. E. (1980), 'On the Impossibility of Informationally Efficient Markets', *American Economic Review*, 70.

Hawtrey, R. G. (1939–40), 'Mr Kaldor on the Forward Market', *Review of Economic Studies*, 7.

Hayek, F. A. (1937), 'Economics of Knowledge', *Economica*, 4.

Hayek, F. A. (1945), 'The Use of Knowledge in Society', *American Economic Review*, 35.

Hirshleifer, J. (1975), 'Speculation and Equilibrium: Information, Risk and Markets', *Quarterly Journal of Economics*, 89.

Hirshleifer, J. (1977), 'The Theory of Speculation under Alternative Regimes of Markets', *Journal of Finance*, 32.

Hoffman, W. G. (1932), *Futures Trading upon Organized Commodity Markets in the United States*, Philadelphia.

Houthakker, H. S. (1967), *Economic Policy for the Farm Sector*, Washington DC.

International Commodities Clearing House Ltd (1979), *Financial Futures in Britain?* London.

Johnson, L. L. (1960), 'The Theory of Hedging and Speculation in Commodity Futures', *Review of Economic Studies*, 27.

Kaldor, N. (1939–40), 'A Note on the Theory of the Forward Market', *Review of Economic Studies*, 7.

Keynes, J. M. (1930), *A Treatise on Money*, 2 vols, London.

Lachmann, L. M. (1977), 'Austrian Economics in the Present Crisis of Economic Thought', in L. M. Lachmann (ed. with Introduction by W. E. Grinder), *Capital, Expectations and the Market Process, Essays on the Theory of the Market Economy*, Menlo Park, California.

McKinnon, R. I. (1967), 'Futures Markets, Buffer Stocks, and Income Stability for Primary Producers', *Journal of Political Economy*, 75.

Peston, M. H. and Yamey, B. S. (1960), 'Inter-temporal Price Relationships with Forward Markets: A Method of Analysis', *Economica*, 27–29.

Popper, K. R. (1948), 'Prediction and Prophecy in the Social Sciences', Library on the 10th International Congress of Philosophy, vol. 1, 1948; reprinted in K. R. Popper, *Conjectures and Refutations – The Growth of Scientific Knowledge* (4th ed.), Henley-on-Thames, reprinted 1976.

Popper, K. R. (1960), 'On the Sources of Knowledge and Ignorance', Proceedings of the British Academy, 1960; reprinted in K. R. Popper, *Conjectures and Refutations – The Growth of Scientific Knowledge* (4th ed.), Henley-on-Thames, reprinted 1976.

Powers, M. and Vogel, D. (1981), *Inside the Financial Futures Markets*, New York.

Richardson, R. A. and Farris, P. L. (1973), 'Farm Commodity Price Stabilization through Futures Markets', *American Journal of Agricultural Economics*, 55.

Rutledge, D. J. S. (1972), 'Hedgers' Demand for Futures Contracts: A Theoretical Framework with Applications to the United States Soybean Complex', *Food Research Institute Studies*, 10.

Stigler, G. J. (1975), 'Regulation: The Confusion of Means and Ends', in G. J. Stigler, *The Citizen and the State – Essays on Regulation*, Chicago.

Streit, M. E. (1981), 'On the Use of Futures Markets for Stabilization Purposes', *Weltwirtschaftliches Archiv*, 116.

Streit, M. E. (1982), 'Information Processing in Futures Markets – An Essay on the Adequacy of Abstraction', European University Institute, Working Paper no. 9.

Streit, M. E. (1983), 'Heterogene Erwartungen, Preisbildung und Informationseffizienz auf spekulativen Märkten' (Heterogeneous Expectations, Price Formation and Informational Efficiency on Speculative Markets), *Zeitschrift für die gesamte Staatswissenschaft*, 139.

Teweles, R. J., Harlow, C. V. and Stone, H. L. (1977), *The Commodity Futures Game – Who Wins? Who Loses? Why?* (abridged ed.) New York.

Tomek, H. G. and Gray, R. W. (1970), 'Temporal Relationships Among Prices on Commodity Futures Markets: Their Allocation and Stabilizing Roles', *American Journal of Agricultural Economics*, 52.

Working, H. (1934), 'A Random Difference Series for Use in the Analysis of Time Series', *Journal of the American Statistical Association*, 29.

Working, H. (1942), 'Quotations on Commodity Futures as Price Forecasts', *Econometrica*, 1.

Working, H. (1949), 'The Investigation of Economic Expectations', *American Economic Review*, 39.

Working, H. (1970), 'Economic Functions of Futures Markets', in H. B. Bakken (ed.), *Futures Trading in Livestock*, Chicago.

2

The Economics of Futures Trading: Some Notes and Queries

BASIL S. YAMEY

1 Introduction

Books and articles on the economics of futures trading were sparse before 1945. In the English language there was a mere handful of books, including the highly informative and now somewhat neglected monograph by Hoffman (1932). Marshall had a chapter on the subject in his *Industry and Trade* (1920). Both Keynes and Hicks devoted a few pages to futures in their famous books, respectively the *Treatise on Money* (Keynes, 1930) and *Value and Capital* (Hicks, 1939). The journals included articles by H. S. Irwin, N. Kaldor, J. C. R. Dow, R. G. Hawtrey and G. Blau, among others.

Since the end of the Second World War the literature on the economics of futures trading has proliferated, notably in the journals. And that the subject has 'arrived' as a specialized branch of study has been recognized, in the familiar way, by the establishment of a specialist journal devoted to it.

In this paper I consider some of the developments that are reflected in the postwar publications.[1] The four sections that follow deal with hedging (sections 2 and 3), price forecasting (section 4) and some aspects of the statistics of futures markets (section 5).

In sections 2 and 3, I discuss certain postwar contributions to the economics of hedging, and view them in the light of the earlier literature and what might be called the traditional approach. My purpose is not so much to criticize the new or to defend the old as to see where the progress of the subject has brought us. If, in the process, some of the points I make will show that earlier contributors saw and understood more than is now sometimes acknowledged, the aim is neither to dredge up antiquarian relics nor to propound that there is nothing new under the sun. Much in the postwar literature has been enlightening and stimulating. Even when some of the more recent developments can be criticized on fairly basic grounds, these developments have helped to provoke useful inquiry and to clarify obscurities. For example, although I am critical of some of the work of Holbrook Working, it is evident that his contributions, made over several decades, and ranging as they do over all aspects of futures trading, have profoundly enriched our understanding of the working of futures markets and their economic significance.

2 Hedging: risk-shifting versus profit-making

2.1 The traditional approach and Working's criticisms

The traditional approach to hedging in futures markets was both simple and clear-cut. In the writings of economists before 1945 the message is plain. In the words of a subheading in Hoffman's treatise, 'Hedging is Shifting of Risk' (1932, p. 382). Kaldor wrote succinctly and pointedly of what by then was the standard view of those few economists who had written on the subject (1939b, p. 197): 'It is the speculators who assume the risks and the hedgers who get rid of them.' And Gerda Blau, whose article was published during the last year of the war and marked the end of an era in the study of futures markets, was bold enough to assert that 'commodity futures exchanges are market organisations specially developed for facilitating the shifting of risks due to unknown future changes in commodity prices; i.e. risks which are of such a nature that they cannot be covered by means of ordinary insurance' (1944, p. 1). In fact, economists were saying about hedging in futures markets precisely what businessmen and commodity dealers have almost invariably said, and still say, about the practice.

Holbrook Working was to change the emphasis altogether in a series of articles in the first two postwar decades. He expounded the notion that the shifting or reduction of price risks by hedgers was unimportant, or at most incidental. The important or central feature of hedging was not the reduction of risk, as in the traditional approach: rather, it was the pursuit of profit through the exploitation of changes or expected changes in the basis, that is, the exploitation of opportunities for profit presented by the prospective movement of prices in the futures market relatively to the movement of prices in the cash (or physical or actuals) market. In this view, hedging was primarily a sort of arbitrage, to be engaged in only when the hedger perceived a promising opportunity for profit, for example when the basis was large relatively to the costs of carrying a stock of commodity over the relevant period. Hedging was therefore a form of speculation – speculation on the basis, not the price; and with some futures – actuals price constellations, the speculative element could be minute.

Hedgers had been transformed. They were not the timid, risk-averse characters typified in the traditional approach. Instead, they were, in their hedging operations, entrepreneurs on the lookout for opportunities to make profits. The lambs were not lambs. They were lions, or at least mini-lions.

It seems as if Working fairly soon came to realize that he, or some of his followers, may have overstated the new view and gone too far in his revisionism. By 1962 he had acquainted us with a variety of types of hedging. In the catalogue of hedging types, risk reduction or risk avoidance hedging appears rather prominently in the guise of 'selective hedging', although in its description Working tried hard, but unsuccessfully, to avoid the use of the notion of risk or risk avoidance (1962, p. 440). Moreover, both he and his distinguished follower, Roger Gray, not infrequently referred in their writings to hedging in situations in which risk reduction of the traditional kind evidently was involved, rather than profit-making on changes in the basis. Thus Working has referred to the 'price at which hedged stocks will be carried' and to the rendering of a 'service for which hedgers are willing to pay' (1960, pp. 207, 209). And Gray has written: 'Coffee hedgers who require a short hedge have paid a price for it, as have short hedgers in Minneapolis wheat futures' (1960, p. 76).

Eventually Working seems to have renounced his earlier position altogether. In a paper published in 1967, he asserted that hedgers (in the context, short hedgers) tend to lose money to speculators on their hedge transactions in the futures markets; and that they do so even during periods in which futures prices in the market in question have fallen (so that long speculators would tend to lose money) (Working, 1967, p. 5). The explanation was, in effect, that the reported series of market closing or opening prices, used in statistical studies, naturally did not record the price 'dips' or 'bulges' that tend to occur when hedgers sell or buy futures contracts. And according to Working, the profits accruing from this source to floor traders, an important subset of speculators, are substantial but are not reflected in calculations of profits or losses based on reported prices.

It is not relevant here whether Working was correct in his assessment of the importance of the price dips and bulges. What is relevant is that the notion that income tends to be transferred systematically from hedgers to speculators runs directly counter to the notion that short hedgers tend to profit on their hedging by taking advantage of arbitrage opportunities, expanding their inventories and hedging whenever by so doing they expect to profit from a narrowing of the basis. The willingness of Working's new-style hedgers to pay a price to speculators – in his words, to incur an 'execution cost' for the prompt carrying-out of their sale or purchase orders – makes them near-relatives of the cautious hedgers of the traditional literature, willing to pay a price, if necessary, to escape the worst risks of adverse price changes. Indeed, the most likely reason for hedgers wishing to have their orders executed expeditiously is to reduce the interval in which their inventories (or forward sales in actuals) are left uncovered, exposed to the risk of price change.

2.2 *Why arbitrage hedging was neglected in the traditional approach*

Working's signal contribution in his postwar papers up to the mid-1960s was to emphasize that not all hedging in practice was concerned primarily with risk avoidance, and that in particular there was arbitrage or carrying-charge hedging as a quite different category.[2]

One may ask why arbitrage hedging was neglected in the earlier literature on futures trading. In fact, earlier writers were considering the position of operators whose business it was to trade in or use the (actuals) commodity, so that they were 'obliged' to enter into actuals commitments in order to carry out their 'principal' merchanting, processing or manufacturing activities. If and when they hedged they did so in connection with the commitment in actuals, itself subject to the risk of price change. Within their self-imposed terms of reference, the earlier writers naturally did not concern themselves with the possibilities of profit-making through arbitrage between the actuals and futures market (though arbitrage between different futures markets for the same commodity was discussed).

Sometimes earlier writers were explicit on the point that their hedgers became involved in hedging because of their necessary involvement in the actuals market. This is clear in Hicks (1939, p. 137):

> The ordinary business man only enters into a forward contract [futures] if by so doing he can 'hedge' – that is to say, if the forward transaction lessens the riskiness of his position. And this will only happen in those cases where he is

somehow otherwise committed to making a sale or purchase at the [future] date in question; if he has already planned such a sale or purchase, and if he has already done something which will make it difficult for him to alter his plan.

But even when they were not as explicit as Hicks, it is evident that other authors had a similar position in mind. They were apt to distinguish between two aspects of a trader or a manufacturer's operations: one aspect was his value-adding operations, in which the inputs were transformed into outputs of higher value (disregarding changes in the prices of the inputs themselves); the other was his concomitant exposure to changes in prices over his 'production' period. The existence of a futures market enabled him to specialize on the former, and to leave it to other specialists to relieve him of the need to cope with the latter. The matter is expressed effectively in this passage in Emery (1896, p. 159):[3]

The trader is primarily concerned with getting a profit from differences of price in different markets. He buys in the producer's market and sells in the consumer's. In a sense the same is true of the manufacturer. He buys material and labor, and attempts to sell his product for something more than the cost of production. The difference between markets is constant and normal, and constitutes the reward for the services of the middleman and manufacturer. To ensure such normal profits, their desire is to escape the risks of fluctuation within the same market. This, to a large extent, the speculative market enables them to do.

No doubt the early writers might have explained more clearly and precisely what they had in mind. And on occasion their chosen phraseology and formulations may strike one as odd. Thus Smith wrote that, if the middleman does not hedge, 'speculative loss or profit ensues; and the hedger [of an inventory] becomes a gambler instead of continuing to be an honest merchant' (1922, p. 86). Nevertheless, these writers focused on important phenomena; and they concluded that futures markets facilitated the division of labour between merchants and manufacturers on the one hand, and speculators on the other, a specialization of activities that enables, and through competition, forces the former to operate on narrower profit margins. But by focusing exclusively on merchants and manufacturers, the earlier writers failed to observe or to discuss the case of the 'pure' arbitrage hedger who engages in the actuals market only in order to take advantage of an anticipated favourable change in the basis, or of the ordinary hedger who on occasions might act like a 'pure' arbitrageur.

Kaldor was the notable exception. He clearly observed that there were two categories of (short) hedgers, the 'ordinary holders' of stocks of the commodity, and the arbitrageurs. The difference between them was that the latter derived no convenience yield at all from their stocks, while the former gained a convenience yield on certain amounts of the stocks they held (Kaldor, 1939a, p. 6; 1939b, pp. 198–9).

Working correctly criticized the traditional approach to hedging for its neglect of arbitrage hedging. But it was inappropriate for him and others to assert or assume that this approach implied that the hedger habitually, and as it were automatically, hedged or covered his entire actuals commitment, i.e., that he exercised no discretion or judgement. Hicks, for example, observed that in certain situations the price to be paid for risk avoidance could be too high, and 'potential hedgers will prefer not to hedge' (1939, p. 139). Blau concluded a longish discussion by saying that 'hedgers like speculators must undertake some weighing of chances [of price changes]; in other words, hedgers, too, must make some kind of a risk estimate although based on somewhat different factors' (1944, p. 14). Working's category of discretionary or selective hedging was not as novel as has sometimes been suggested. (To fall in this category, the hedger hedges only when he expects the price of the commodity to decline.)

2.3 The reinstatement of hedging as risk-shifting

The connection between hedging and risk has now been reinstated in the literature on the economics of futures trading. In an authoritative article Franklin Edwards has written that the 'second economic function of futures markets is to provide a market mechanism for the allocation of risk. This is their "hedging" function. There may be other ways to insure against risk, but none which is more flexible . . . ' (1981, p. 426). But the reinstatement of the risk-shifting element in hedging has not meant the sacrifice of the insights provided by Working and others. Revisionism has left its mark. We do not now speak about hedging in quite the same way as did our predecessors, even when risk reduction is being emphasized.

The widespread adoption of the portfolio theory approach to decisions in futures markets represents a further rehabilitation of the risk reduction notion in hedging practice. The emphasis in this approach on both risk and return nicely links the pre-Working approach with the Working approach.

One might question, however, whether the characteristic product of the portfolio theory approach – the concept of the optimal hedging programme or strategy – is useful, except perhaps as a neat encapsulation of features of basis values and basis changes in the markets and periods examined. It is extremely improbable that any short hedger (whether merchant, manufacturer or government of a primary product producing country) would adhere to a so-called optimal hedging strategy and sell futures when he was pretty certain that the price of the product was not going to fall; or that he would not fully hedge (or even over-hedge) his actuals position when he was confident that the price was going to fall, even if the optimal strategy called for only, say, 90 per cent hedge cover. In other words, the notion of the optimal hedge strategy turns the hedger into a routine hedger who exercises no judgement or discretion: his decision for the coming trading period is pre-determined, regardless of what may be his assessment of the market in the immediately future period. He would not indulge in Working's selective or discretionary hedging. This is altogether unrealistic – notably so when it is evident that the optimal hedge would have been estimated from data pertaining to some preceding period of years, the price experience of which cannot be expected to repeat itself. (Of course, if the optimal hedge were to be estimated from forecasts of prices and price relationships over a period of years yet to be experienced, the hedger would be even less likely slavishly to tie his decisions to the optimal strategy.)

3 Telser on futures markets and hedging

3.1 Risk-shifting and the need for futures markets

Are futures markets necessary for hedging as a form of protection against price changes? In recent papers Lester Telser has made much of the fact that one does not need futures market for hedging. 'Even if we accept the [price insurance] theory, it does not explain why an organized futures market is necessary in order to accommodate hedging. A merchant who wishes to avoid the price risks of holding inventories can do so without an organized futures market' (1981, p. 5). He can do so by entering into forward transactions in the actuals markets.

Now this is true, as was well known to those who studied the economics of futures trading in bygone decades. And they, like

Telser, know why it was that hedging in futures markets typically was better than hedging in forward (actuals) markets. It is true that they did not couch their explanation in such terms as market liquidity, search costs, transactions costs and default risk. But they were saying those same things that Telser has emphasized. Here is Marshall's account, relating to long hedging (1920, p. 260, n. 2):

It may be noted that the millar who contracts in advance to deliver flour of a specially fine quality is put in a better position by buying a future on the Exchange than he would probably be by contracting with individual dealers for the delivery to him of the sorts [of wheat] that he expects to need. Such a contract would be difficult to make, and it would be liable to uncertainty and friction in the execution.

And he makes the further point that the millar who hedged in futures 'possibly readjusts his combinations of various sorts [of wheat] according to their several conditions and current prices'. Smith, following Marshall, put the matter crisply (1922, p. 95): 'Contracts of the latter kind [forward contracts in actuals] are difficult to conclude and uncertain as regards fulfilment.'[4]

In any event, it is difficult to follow Telser when he states that, because there can be hedging without organized futures markets, 'it is not the demand for price insurance that explains why there is an organized futures market' (1981, p. 8). No doubt futures markets owe their origin and subsequent viability to various circumstances and forces. But it seems reasonably clear that the demand for hedging facilities or improved hedging facilities has been a major factor behind the establishment of new futures markets, in recent decades as well as in the last century. The fact that an available mechanism can satisfy a need does not mean that there can be no demand for an improved mechanism, and that the demand cannot serve to elicit a supply response.

3.2 Convenience yield and futures markets

Telser has deftly defined convenience yield from a stock of a commodity as 'the return that inventories yield their owner aside from an expectation of rising prices' (1981, p. 7).[5] The concept of convenience yield and recognition of its significance appear to be due to Kaldor (1939a, p. 6). It helps to explain why merchants and manufacturers may hold stocks when they expect its price to fall, and why they may hold and hedge stocks even when the basis is negative (i.e. when the 'price of storage' is negative).[6]

There is a substantial measure of agreement about the nature of the benefits to the stockholder that are subsumed in the term 'convenience yield'. There is also agreement that, while it may be relatively large when stocks are unusually small, the marginal convenience yield decreases rapidly with increases in stock, until it becomes zero.

The convenience yield arises because of uncertainty about the demands to be made on a merchant's or manufacturer's stocks and their resulting 'convenience', 'the possibility of making use of them the moment they are wanted' (Kaldor, 1939a, p. 6). Brennan attributes convenience yield for a producing firm 'to the advantage (in terms of less delay and lower costs) of being able to keep regular customers satisfied' (1958, p. 53). Yamey substitutes 'preferred customers' for 'regular customers': the merchant is better placed, by virtue of his uncommitted stocks, 'to satisfy the unpredictable requirements of his preferred, because more profitable, customers – more profitable, for example, because they are likely to offer opportunities for profitable dealings in the same or in other commodities, or because the costs of transacting business with them are relatively low' (1971, p. 419).[7] Cootner underlined the nature of convenience yield by noting that it 'would not exist in the absence of uncertainty or transactions costs', and 'is quite independent of any attitudes the inventory holder may have toward risk' (1967, p. 69).[8]

There has also been a general agreement that stocks hedged by the sale of futures produce a convenience yield, whereas stocks hedged by the sale of forward (actuals) contracts do not. The measure of agreement stems from the consideration that stocks that are committed or earmarked for the satisfaction of specific forward contracts cannot be sold to meet an unexpected requirement calling for a spot sale.

Telser has now challenged this general view. He writes (1981, p. 8):[9]

> A merchant can surely sell stocks on hand to any customer who appears and is willing to take immediate delivery. He must still honor his previous forward sales contract by delivering stocks of the proper kind to his forward customers. This requires him to arrange to have the stocks on hand for delivery when the time comes, which is equivalent to buying forward in order to offset his previous forward sale.

It is by no means clear what is involved here. If forward purchases are made successively to replace the stock as it is run down because of successive spot sales, then the traditional view has not been upset by Telser: the capacity to garner convenience yield declines because the uncommitted stock has been depleted. (There is no convenience yield on the forward purchases of actuals made in order to replace the stock that has been sold and in order to be able to discharge the obligations on forward sales contracts.) Alternatively, if stock is maintained at a given level by replacement purchases of actuals, and forward purchases are made wholly or partly to cover existing forward sales, then all or part of the constant stock is held unhedged. Forward purchases are part of the (gross) positive stock held by the merchant or manufacturer; and, other things being equal, the larger they are relative to forward sales, the smaller is the extent of the hedge cover provided by a given volume of such forward sales.

While Telser's explanation is flawed, it is nevertheless the case that, as regards convenience yield, the difference between the two modes of hedging may be exaggerated in general discussions of the matter. Thus the difference would not be present where the forward sale relates to a grade or description of a commodity of which supplies ordinarily are readily available at all times, and of which the degree of standardization is such that a forward seller has no need to earmark supplies to meet the specific obligations undertaken in a contract for forward delivery.[10] One would imagine that these conditions are satisfied in some metal markets, for example. Moreover, the more impersonal is the trading in the commodity in question, the less significant are considerations of convenience yield likely to be.

Telser is surely correct in emphasizing that hedging in futures contracts is preferred to hedging in forward contracts because of the high degree of liquidity, low transactions costs and low default risk in futures markets. Considerations of convenience yield, where present, are an added bonus. But Telser is as surely not correct when he writes of those economists who have invoked the concept of convenience yield that, 'in order to explain why there is an organized futures market', they have argued that it is only stocks hedged in futures that provide a convenience yield (1981, pp. 7–8).

4 Price forecasting on futures markets

4.1 Avoidable and unavoidable errors in forecasting

According to Franklin Edwards, 'futures markets provide two fundamental economic services.' The second of these – to facilitate the shifting of risk – has already been quoted in section 3 above. The following is the first of the economic services identified by Edwards (1981, p. 425):

> Futures contracts provide price signals which can be used by the producers, processors and distributors to allocate real resources. More specifically, futures prices may influence storage and inventory decisions and may exert an important influence on production decisions. This is their 'price discovery' function. Futures markets are seen as an efficient collector, processor, and disseminator of information.

Before 1945, the efficiency of futures markets in their pricing function was probably accepted by most economists as almost axiomatic. Since 1945 a number of attempts have been made to test their efficiency. Aspects of some of these tests are considered in this section.

How good are (forward) futures prices as forecasts of the eventual price of the commodity in question? Here the main attention has been focused on the predictive power of futures markets for seasonally produced agricultural commodities, and more notably on the predictive accuracy of futures prices at the time production decisions have to be taken. Do futures prices at this critical time of the agricultural year serve as reliable forecasts of the eventual market price at harvest time?

One test of the reliability or accuracy of such forecasts is based on a statistical analysis of the relationship between planting-time prices of futures contracts maturing at harvest-time and the prices of those contracts at harvest-time.[11] A regression equation in which the latter is the dependent variable would indicate efficient or accurate forecasting if the equation has high explanatory power (a high R^2), a zero intercept and a slope coefficient of one.[12] Thus, for example, a low value of R^2 implies that forward futures prices are worthless as forecasts of the eventual price; while slope coefficients significantly different from one indicate systematic bias in forecasting.

Studies based on this method assume implicitly that there are no purely random events, i.e., inherently unpredictable and unsystematic events which can cause the forecast price to differ from the eventual price (or else they assume that over the sample period these individual 'disturbances' cancel each other out). In practice there are such factors, the significance and incidence of which can be expected to differ from one period to another and from one market to another. Such random occurrences include transport strikes, the 'accidents' of international politics, particular acts of government intervention such as sales from the US government's stockpile of tin, and market manoeuvres such as those on the London tin market in early 1982.

The studies fail to take account of the important distinction made by Working in 1949 between 'necessary' and 'objectionable' inaccuracy (Working, 1949a, p. 158):

> The most perfect expectations possible in economic affairs must be subject to substantial error because the outcome depends on unpredictable future events. Market expectations, therefore, have a certain necessary inaccuracy. By necessary inaccuracy in market expectations I mean the irreducible minimum of inaccuracy which must result from response of prices to unpredictable changes in supply and in consumption demand schedules. An excess of inaccuracy over this minimum may be called objectionable inaccuracy.

In so far as normative implications are drawn from the results of these studies, they imply that all the inaccuracy is objectionable or avoidable. Unfortunately, it does not appear possible to allow for the irreducible or unavoidable errors so as to reveal the extent of the avoidable errors.[13]

4.2 Inventories and errors of forecasting

Tomek and Gray (1970) have shown that futures prices at planting time are much more accurate as forecasts of immediate post-harvest prices for commodities like wheat and corn, which have continuous inventories, than are those for potatoes, which do not have continuous inventories. They explain this difference largely in terms of a particular role played by inventories. Inventories 'provide a linkage between the springtime [planting time] prices of the post-harvest futures and the subsequent harvest-time prices, which helps to make the futures price a self-fulfilling forecast' (1970, p. 375).

Although the notion of self-fulfilling forecasts is unhelpful, it is likely that inter-seasonal stockholding performs some price-cushioning effect. Thus the effects on price of an unexpectedly large crop can be cushioned to the extent that the preceding year's inventory can be run down more rapidly once the previously prevailing 'error' has been realized, and also to the extent that a larger stock than had been 'planned' can be carried over from the bumper crop into the succeeding year. But the inevitable cushioning effect need not always be significant. Early forecasts of a bumper crop can lead to lower prices as well as to more rapid decumulation of stocks – and this would reduce the scope for correction of the error in forecasting when it transpires later that the crop is likely to be small.

However this may be, and disregarding the crucial consideration noted in section 4.1, one would be inclined to place more weight on inter-season stockholding as a factor in reducing errors in forecasting if it were the case that the futures prices of, say, potatoes performed no worse than those of, say, corn and soyabeans, within the season when inventories are held for all three commodities, that is, over the intra-season storage period.

The results reported by Gray (1972) for potatoes are poor, in the sense that the values of R^2 for two intra-season forecast test equations are low. Indeed, they are considerably lower than the R^2 of inter-season forecast test equations for wheat, corn, soyabeans and coffee prices eight months or six months before harvest.[14] Further, some simple statistics show, for the years 1954–68, that the intra-season forecasting 'error' was on the average much larger for potatoes than for corn and soyabeans in the United States.[15]

It is evident that any satisfactory explanation of differences in the forecasting performance of different futures markets is bound to be complex. This is so even if, as seems improbable, suitable allowance can be made for Working's 'necessary' errors.

4.3 Tests of market 'efficiency' in the semi-strong form

Another line of approach to the forecasting performance of futures markets may seem more promising. One could compare the forecasts implicit in (forward) futures prices with the forecasts yielded by an econometric model making use of publicly available data. This is the test for the efficiency of a market in the semi-strong form. Does a particular futures market do a better or worse job of price forecasting than the econometric model?[16]

Again, the value of this kind of test can be questioned – and this for a reason that does not depend upon the unpredictable impact of purely random events.

Suppose the participants in a market behave impeccably in economics textbook fashion, and typically get things right about supply and demand fundamentals. Futures prices will then tend to be good forecasts of eventual prices. What is more, a suitably designed econometric model which takes account of market fundamentals will also tend to yield good price forecasts.

Next suppose, by way of contrast, that the participants in the market behave irrationally and erratically, and tend to disregard market fundamentals. The course of prices will reflect this behaviour. Forward futures prices will tend to be poor forecasts of the eventual prices. A suitably designed econometric model which takes account of market fundamentals will also tend to perform poorly as forecaster of eventual prices. These prices will reflect only the immediate short-term market fundamentals and will, in any case, be affected also by the market's hypothesized irrational or erratic views of developments in the next period(s).

In short, the forecasting performance of the econometric model is likely to depend heavily on the behaviour and performance of market participants and is therefore not likely to provide an independent test of the efficiency of the market. There is no good reason to suppose that over a period of years a well-designed econometric model will do significantly better or significantly worse as price forecaster than futures prices: their performances in this respect are likely to be strongly interrelated.

There is a further difficulty in interpreting the results of a test of a market's efficiency in the semi-strong sense.

Suppose a market with futures trading has been found in such a test to have performed badly in the sample period studied. Can one then assume or infer that the market would have been more efficient (in the same sense) had there been no futures trading in it? To hold that it would have been more efficient is to suppose that market participants would have acted more closely in accordance with the information and functional relationships incorporated in the econometric model – but for the presence of the futures market and the trading in it. But even if they had access to the model's successive predictions, can it be assumed that the market participants would have taken them seriously enough to act upon them, given contemporary expectations, market activity and rumours concerning likely future developments? Market gossip, waves of sentiment and information often difficult to interpret are not peculiar to futures markets.

5 Futures market statistics

A feature of the study of futures markets since 1945 has been the efflorescence of statistical investigations into aspects of their operations. Before the war such investigations were few, although they include, for example, Hoffman's highly important study of the relationship between the volume of short hedging and the volume of commercial stocks in wheat (Hoffman, 1932, pp. 414–15).

By far the majority of statistical investigations are based on market data for the United States, the richness of its available statistical materials being an unambiguously beneficial effect of the official regulation of most futures markets in the United States. However, it may be useful to note some of the limitations of the commendably copious statistical series.

The categorization of market participants as hedgers and speculators has itself undergone changes, and the reliability of the underlying information is not always beyond question.[17] Again, statistics of the total volume of trading have their limitations for inter-market or inter-temporal comparisons, because they add together scalping and spreading as well as hedging and (longer-term) speculation. Difficulty of interpretation is reinforced by the fact that the use of futures trading simply for tax avoidance purposes is not the same in all commodities, and this component of the total has been influenced by changes in tax legislation.

As to reported prices, I have drawn attention to Working's implied criticisms (section 2.1 above) of these prices if they are taken to stand for transaction prices. His emphasis on price dips and bulges is important, even though their quantitative significance has not yet been established.[18] If these phenomena are as pronounced as Working has suggested, many of the studies based on recorded prices have to be reconsidered. And maybe, after all that has been said about it, something of Keynes's theory of normal backwardation can be salvaged in the sense of it being provided with satisfactory empirical under-pinning (if not with a satisfactory theoretical foundation): speculators are provided with a systematic source of income without having to act on their price forecasts in any serious sense of the term.

As a further example, the possible distorting effects of official limits on daily price movements may be noted. Whenever these limits affect trading directly, prices are recorded that are neither actual transaction prices nor indications of the level of such prices; and apparent trends may be introduced into recorded price series that are nothing more than artefacts produced by the rules and regulations. As the impact of these official limits is neither constant nor the same for all markets, they may well affect some studies of market efficiency.

But if price data for futures markets have their shortcomings, how much more problematical are the price series for commodities that are not the subject of futures trading? Spot and forward transactions in such actuals markets are not standardized in the sense that transactions are standardized in futures markets. And, since much trading is not conducted in public, reported prices are at best somewhat removed from the scene of buying and selling. And often they are seriously wrong. The use of published price series may effect some of the studies in which price behaviour in periods without futures trading is compared with price behaviour in periods with futures trading in the same commodity. I suspect that the stability of prices in the former periods might be exaggerated; but there is no way of knowing.

This is a pity. It would be interesting to be able to apply the same tests of efficiency as have been applied to futures-traded commodities to markets of commodities without futures trading. This may conceivably enable one to form a clearer view of the price effects of futures trading as such, although the problem of 'necessary' inaccuracy remains perplexing. As it is, in the absence of reliable comparisons of this kind, futures markets and futures trading are likely to continue to be judged in terms of absolute but unattainable standards of market performance. Economists have a penchant for comparing real-world situations and sequences with situations and sequences belonging to some model world: Pareto optimality, perfect competition, and, in the present context, the efficient market. However, the use of the experimental method in economics (one example of which is described in this book) may offer an ingenious way out.

Notes

1 I acknowledge the considerable help I have received from Valerie Brasse in many discussions in recent years.

2 The available statistical material does not enable one to determine or estimate the relative proportions of risk-shifting and arbitrage hedging in the various futures markets. No inference can be drawn, for example, from the relationship between the volume of hedging and the size of the basis, because both types of hedging may be expected to be positively associated with the size of the basis when hedges are placed. One study is of interest. In the 1950s, Johnson studied the New York coffee market. On types of hedging he concluded that arbitrage hedging was 'apparently a rare occurrence'. The futures market at the time was generally inverted (Johnson, 1957, p. 320).

3 See also Marshall (1920, p. 253), Smith (1922, pp. 81, 86) and Hoffman (1932, p. 380).

4 See also Blau (1944, pp. 2–3), who also stresses the importance of market liquidity.

5 See Blau (1944, p. 6) for a similar definition.

6 See Working (1949b, p. 1260).

7 Yamey also shows that the convenience yield from being open-to-sell (or open-to-use) has its analogue in the position of a manufacturer with a negative stock, i.e. one with uncovered forward sales commitments. He is open-to-buy, and has the opportunity of buying from preferred suppliers.

8 Cootner includes in convenience yield the economic rent to be derived from the sale of stocks if a local 'shortage' should develop (1967, pp. 68–9). This should not be included if one accepts the Telser definition quoted

in the text above. Brennan also goes against the definition when he includes in convenience yield the benefit of 'being able to take advantage of a rise in demand in price without resorting to a revision of the production schedule' (1958, p. 53). Kaldor similarly widens the scope of convenience yield when he includes in it 'the risk of having to pay more for the commodity at some unspecified date in the future, should it be wanted for immediate delivery' (1939b, p. 199, n. 2).

9 Telser subscribed earlier to the general proposition under consideration here (1967, p. 136).

10 There is some discussion of this point in Blau (1944, pp. 6–7).

11 The method is applicable also to futures prices as forecasts within the consumption year – prices that are likely to affect storage decisions.

12 See, for example, Tomek and Gray (1970), Kofi (1973).

13 This consideration undermines Stein's ingenious attempt to derive estimates of avoidable welfare loss from the results of regression analyses of the kind under discussion. See Stein (1981).

14 Compare Gray (1972, p. 333, Table 3) and Kofi (1973, p. 587, Table 2).

15 The forecasting 'error' has been calculated for each year as:

$$\frac{\text{May futures price (end April)} - \text{May futures price (mid-January)}}{\text{May futures prices (mid-January)}} \times 100$$

(with signs ignored). For corn, the median error was 3.7%; for soyabeans, 4.2%; for potatoes, 20.1%. The arithmetic mean error was 5.3%, 8.1% and 26.0% respectively. Two-thirds of the annual 'errors' for potatoes exceeded 15%, as against none for corn and one-fifth for soyabeans. Two-fifths of the 'errors' for potatoes exceeded 25%.

Calculations for potatoes using the mid-November price of the May futures as forecast show even greater errors: median, 27.2%, arithmetic mean, 29.7%. The forecast test equation for the latter series, for the period 1954–68, is as follows (standard errors in brackets):

$$\begin{array}{lll} x_1 = -0.2126 & + \; 1.0915x_2 & R^2 = 0.3971 \\ \quad\;\;(1.1447) & \quad(0.3730) & \bar{R}^2 = 0.3508 \end{array}$$

These values are closely similar to those in the corresponding equation reported by Gray for the period 1953–70 (1972, p. 333, Table 3). According to Gray, this would be a 'good' forecast in the sense that the slope and intercept are 'appropriate'. Yet the average 'error' in the period 1954–68 was over 25%.

16 An interesting study is Leuthold and Hartmann (1979).

17 See, for example, the exchanges of views and information in Gray (1980, pp. 78–100), Houthakker (1980, pp. 101–5), and the ensuing discussion.

18 But see Gray (1979, pp. 153–4).

References

Blau, G. (1944), 'Some Aspects of the Theory of Futures Trading', *Review of Economic Studies*, 12.

Brennan, M. J. (1958), 'The Supply of Storage', *American Economic Review*, 48.

Cootner, P. H. (1967), 'Speculation and Hedging', *Food Research Institute Studies*, 7, supplement.

Edwards, F. R. (1981), 'The Regulation of Futures Markets: A Conceptual Framework', *Journal of Futures Markets*, 1, supplement.

Emery, H. C. (1896), *Speculation on the Stock and Produce Exchanges of the United States*, New York.

Gray, R. W. (1960), 'The Importance of Hedging in Futures Trading', in *Futures Trading Seminar*, vol. 1, Madison, Wisconsin.

Gray, R. W. (1972), 'The Futures Market in Maine Potatoes: An Appraisal', *Food Research Institute Studies*, 11.

Gray, R. W. (1979), 'Commentary' [on 'A Re-Examination of Price Changes in the Commodity Futures Market', by T. F. Martell and B. P. Helms], *International Futures Trading Seminar: Proceedings*, vol. 5, Chicago.

Gray, R. W. (1980), 'The Emergence of Short Speculation', in *International Futures Trading Seminar: Proceedings*, vol. 6, Chicago.

Hicks, J. R. (1939), *Value and Capital*, London.

Hoffman, G. W. (1932), *Futures Trading upon Organized Commodity Markets in the United States*, Philadelphia.

Houthakker, H. S. (1980), 'Commentary' [on 'The Emergence of Short Speculation' by R. W. Gray], *International Futures Trading Seminar: Proceedings*, vol. 6, Chicago.

Johnson, L. L. (1957), 'Price Instability, Hedging and Trade Volume in the Coffee Futures Market', *Journal of Political Economy*, 65.

Kaldor, N. (1939a), 'Speculation and Economic Stability', *Review of Economic Studies*, 7.

Kaldor, N. (1939b), 'A Note on the Theory of the Forward Market', *Review of Economic Studies*, 7.

Keynes, J. M. (1930), *A Treatise on Money*, vol. 2, London.

Kofi, T. A. (1973), 'A Framework for Comparing the Efficiency of Futures Markets', *American Journal of Agricultural Economics*, 55.

Leuthold, R. and Hartmann, P. (1979), 'A Semi-Strong Form Evaluation of the Efficiency of the Hog Futures Market', *American Journal of Agricultural Economics*, 61.

Marshall, A. (1920), *Industry and Trade*, London.

Smith, J. G. (1922), *Organised Produce Markets*, London.

Stein, J. L. (1981), 'Speculative Price: Economic Welfare and the Idiot of Chance', *Review of Economics and Statistics*, 63.

Telser, L. G. (1967), 'The Supply of Speculative Services in Wheat, Corn and Soybeans', *Food Research Institute Studies*, 7, supplement.

Telser, L. G. (1981), 'Why there are Organized Futures Markets', *Journal of Law and Economics*, 24.

Tomek, W. G. and Gray, R. W. (1970), 'Temporal Relationships among Prices on Commodity Futures Markets', *American Journal of Agricultural Economics*, 52.

Working, H. (1949a), 'The Investigation of Economic Expectations', *American Economic Review*, 39, supplement.

Working, H. (1949b), 'The Theory of the Price of Storage', *American Economic Review*, 39.

Working, H. (1960), 'Speculation on Hedging Markets', *Food Research Institute Studies*, 1.

Working, H. (1962), 'New Concepts Concerning Futures Markets', *American Economic Economic Review*, 52.

Working, H. (1967), 'Tests of a Theory concerning Floor Trading on Commodity Exchanges', *Food Research Institute Studies*, 7, supplement.

Yamey, B. S. (1971), 'Short Hedging and Long Hedging in Futures Markets', *Journal of Law and Economics*, 14.

3

Futures Markets and Market Efficiency

JOSEPH M. BURNS

1 Introduction

Market development provides an appropriate setting for the study of futures markets. Futures markets grow out of efficient spot markets, usually become more efficient than the underlying spot markets (perhaps become the most efficient markets in the world), and in the process tend to make the underlying spot markets (and other related markets) more efficient than they otherwise would be.

Section 2 below presents some comments on the meaning of the terms 'market' and 'market efficiency'. The subsequent sections discuss aspects of futures markets involving market efficiency. Specifically, section 3 discusses factors contributing to the development of futures markets; section 4 examines the efficiency of futures markets; and section 5 analyses the effects of futures markets, especially those involving enhanced efficiency of related markets.

One final comment is in order. Governmental as well as private forces affect the development of futures markets; and the development of futures markets has effects on government policy as well as on private firms. The discussion in this paper focuses on private forces.[1]

2 Markets and market efficiency

2.1 The meaning of a market

A market is a mechanism for effecting purchases and sales of goods or services in a relatively public manner. Thus, a market entails a way of carrying out transactions and some means of collecting and disseminating information on the terms of transactions.

The two aspects of a market – transactions and information – are inherently interrelated. The economic demand for effecting transactions precedes the economic demand for information. This precedence is more a matter of logic than of actual sequence, inasmuch as the demand for effecting transactions immediately gives rise to demand for information concerning the terms of a transaction. The logical connection emphasizes an important point: the means of collecting and disseminating information are designed to facilitate the carrying out of transactions. For any asset, the ways of carrying out transactions are a product of commercial needs and practices, which in turn reflect real demand and supply capabilities.

Markets – whether they relate to real assets (such as land, machinery and commodities) or financial assets (such as bonds, common stock and futures contracts) – do not exist in a vacuum. They develop in response to persistent needs and economic demands for more efficient mechanisms to carry out transactions and to collect and disseminate information on the terms of transactions. The development of a market may refer to establishing a new market or to enhancing the 'efficiency' or expanding the size of an already existing one.

2.2 The meaning of market efficiency

The efficiency of a market simply refers to the efficiency with which a market performs its related functions of facilitating transactions and improving information on the terms of transactions (actual or potential). Thus, the efficiency of a market depends on the ease or difficulty of transferring ownership of a good or service (that is, 'transaction costs') as well as on the quality of information conveyed about the terms of transactions. The quality of information relates to both the liquidity of an asset and the efficiency with which an asset is priced.

Each of these aspects – transactions costs, liquidity and pricing efficiency – is important; however, none of them has received sufficient attention in economic literature. In part, this may reflect excessive concentration on the analysis of specific industry structures – such as perfect competition, monopolistic competition or pure monopoly – in which development in regard to many aspects of market efficiency is by definition subsumed away. Also, the neglect may reflect the conventional treatment of 'efficient markets' in finance literature – namely, 'efficient markets' are simply those 'in which prices always fully reflect' available information (Fama, 1970);

this concept diverts attention from the fact that efficiency of a market is a variable to be explained rather than a parameter that is given (implicitly or explicitly).

A broader concept of market efficiency is necessary for understanding how and why markets develop and what effects their development has on the general economy. In this connection, we must keep firmly in mind the distinction between the 'efficiency' of a market (which says nothing about whether or not there is a failure in the workings of a market) and the 'operating efficiency' of a market (which indicates whether or not a market failure exists). A market that has a high level of efficiency (in the sense of being highly developed) may be operating inefficiently (that is, there may still be a market failure); and a rather rudimentary market (from the standpoint of its degree of development) may be operating quite efficiently. For example, a Treasury bond futures market may be operating inefficiently, and a secondary mortgage market in Montana may be operating efficiently.

All markets are – to some degree – incomplete in their development. Uncertainty and transactions costs are facts of life. They can be reduced in one way or another, but they cannot be eliminated.

One final prefatory comment is in order – namely, the importance of the distinction between market efficiency and industry efficiency. It is possible that an improvement in industry efficiency (say, the gold-producing industry) may be accompanied by a worsening of market efficiency (say, the market on which gold is traded). In general, the paper does not deal with this possibility.

2.2.1 Efficiency

The several components of a market's efficiency are interrelated; for analytical purposes, they are discussed separately.

Transactions costs Transactions costs may be incurred both in transferring physical title or ownership and in searching for information about quality and/or price of prospective transactions. Costs of physical transfer refer to costs – such as packaging, delivery, brokerage and some part of a bid-asked price spread – that are incurred in transferring physical title or ownership. Search costs are that part of transactions costs that involve a search for information. Search costs may be considered in the context of imperfect information about transactions – the subject discussed in the following two subsections.

Liquidity Market liquidity, or liquidity of an asset traded on a market, has two related aspects: certainty of price (liquidity proper), and expected marketability.[2] Liquidity proper refers to the degree of certainty, or predictability, of an asset's underlying value. An asset's underlying value refers to its value if no time constraints were imposed on its disposal and if conditions in the market remained constant.[3] Thus, liquidity proper depends on how much is known about an asset's underlying value. Assets, such as securities, that are traded on organized exchanges are high in liquidity proper compared with assets, such as used cars, that are traded on highly segmented markets.

The expected marketability of an asset refers to the expected ease or difficulty of approximately realizing the asset's underlying value during the period of time allowed for its disposal. Expected marketability thus depends on expectations about the effect of transactions on the variance of price, which in turn depends on schedules of bid and asked price quotations.

Marketability is a multi-dimensional concept. With a constant demand schedule, a large volume of a given asset is, by definition, less marketable than a smaller volume – that is, the larger the volume of a given asset put up for sale, the lower the transaction price will tend to be (at least after a certain point), even if the asset's underlying value has not changed.

Marketability also has a time dimension. In particular, the more time allowed for the disposal of an asset, the higher its expected net sale price.[4] Thus, at a given point in time, an asset is likely to have different degrees of marketability depending on how much time is allowed for its disposal. A particular asset that is more marketable than another in a short disposal period might be less marketable in a long disposal period.

The two aspects of liquidity – certainty of price and expected marketability – are closely related. The more certain an asset's underlying value is expected to be, the greater should be its marketability. Indeed, the ease of realizing an asset's approximate underlying value is directly related to the certainty of that value. The converse – the more marketable an asset, the greater the degree of certainty of its underlying value – is also true.

It is relevant to observe here that narrow bid-asked price spreads, an indicator of liquidity, tend to generate more favourable price executions of orders. In this way, liquidity tends to beget greater liquidity.

Pricing efficiency Pricing efficiency refers to the degree to which an asset's price reflects demand–supply conditions in a market. There are at least two elements of pricing efficiency: the degree to which an asset's price is determined by competitive forces, and the speed with which an asset's price or price quotation incorporates information about changes in demand–supply conditions. The term 'pricing efficiency' seems preferable to the term 'price efficiency', inasmuch as it tends to convey better the notion of a process via which a price (or price quotation) is established.

As with market liquidity, pricing efficiency is a variable to be explained. It is frequently overlooked that a market with high pricing efficiency tends to develop out of a situation in which little information exists about transactions together with considerable market power by one of the market participants.[5] In a primitive economy, transactions are generally of a purely private nature and one of the parties to a transaction is likely to have considerable market power. Even in an advanced economy, many transactions take the form of private exchanges. However, as an economy develops, more and more transactions are conducted in public. In part, this reflects the emergence of goods of the second, third, and still higher orders, in which homogeneity or ease of standardization often exist. Such goods – by their nature – lend themselves well to public information and to competition among suppliers.

Interrelationships Pricing efficiency and market liquidity are closely related. Improvements in pricing efficiency – whether involving competition or communication – tend to promote market liquidity. Indeed, a greater number of avenues of demand and sources of supply tend to augment trading and thereby to improve liquidity. In addition, an enhanced speed and improved accuracy of transmitting new information tends to improve knowledge of demand–supply forces and to impair the viability of deliberately false rumours, thereby also improving liquidity.

In turn, improvements in market liquidity tend to foster pricing efficiency – both competition and communication. Competition (whether among participants on the same side of a market or between parties on opposite sides of a market) may be enhanced because of either a reduction of scale economies in the collection of information or a reduction of market power in information about demand–supply conditions on the part of some market participants. Innovations in communication tend to be induced because of the greater prospective profits that such innovations may then realize.

In addition, just as the two aspects of a market (transactions and information) are interrelated, so are the two aspects of a market's efficiency – transactions costs and quality of information. For example, improvements in liquidity serve to reduce transactions costs – by reducing search costs and perhaps by reducing transfer costs (through the realization of economies of scale from an increase in the volume of transactions). In turn, an increased volume of transactions serves to improve liquidity.

2.2.2 *Operating efficiency*

A market is operating efficiently – in a given economic environment, including the policies of government at the time – when the efficiency (development) of a market is at its optimal level.[6]

A market's operations embrace both trading conditions and market organization. Improvements in trading conditions or market organization tend to lower transactions costs and to improve market information (liquidity and/or pricing efficiency). However, such improvements may entail costs as well as benefits.[7]

Trading conditions Efficient trading conditions may be said to exist when trading is not hampered by artificial barriers to, or constraints on, market use (such as price-fixing agreements); inefficient trading conditions exist when trading is so impaired.

Market organization The organization of a market embraces the institutions that directly service a market – the brokers, dealers, exchanges, clearing houses and inspection services. Elements of a market's organization typically establish the framework within which trading takes place and information is collected and disseminated.

Typically, the more efficient a market, the more developed is the market's organization. An efficient market tends to enable the realization of economies of scale and attendant specialization of function in the carrying out of market-related tasks (whether actual transactions or information about transactions) by, for example, brokers. In turn, development of a market's organization (whether the emergence of brokers, dealers or an exchange) tends to improve market information as well as to reduce transactions costs.

Whether a market organization (say, an exchange) is operating efficiently or inefficiently in a given economic environment depends on whether artificial factors impede provision of new services or lowering of prices of existing services.

3 Factors contributing to the development of futures markets

Futures markets develop in response to persistent needs and economic demands of market participants in spot markets. Commercial demand for contracts negotiated today for transactions to be consummated in the future (that is, contracts for future transactions) tend to generate at first forward contracts and later, if conditions warrant, futures contracts.

A futures exchange may be viewed as the application of economies of scale to trading in forward contracts. When the volume of forward trading becomes sufficiently large, it tends to become advantageous for brokers and dealers to set up such exchanges, or centralized market places, with their standardized contracts, risk-reducing technology (clearing houses and adjustable margin requirements) and low carrying costs (low margin requirements). The principal objective of the founding brokers and dealers is to facilitate their trading in contracts for future transactions (whether for their own accounts or for those of their customers).

Most early futures exchanges were set up at exchanges for spot market transactions. Such exchanges were a natural location for the creation of a futures market: potential transactors in futures were located there, product quality and commercial practices in spot markets tended to be standardized there (which facilitated the design of futures contracts), and information relevant to futures traders (especially spot prices or price quotations) was easiest to obtain there.

The creation of a futures exchange requires some capital to finance the requisite plant and equipment (with plant and equipment defined broadly to include research and administrative costs associated with delineation of contract terms and conditions, and development of exchange rules and regulations). The founders supply (directly or indirectly) the necessary capital. In return, centralization of the market place, standardization of contracts, reduction of default risk and low carrying costs facilitate the transactions of member brokers and dealers in contracts for future transactions – in terms of both lower transactions costs of negotiating or transferring contracts and lower costs of search for information.

A crucial factor underlying the creation of futures markets is thus the expectation of a strong and reasonably persistent demand for futures contracts. Such an expectation tends to be formed on the basis of developments in underlying spot and associated forward markets (for the commodity, security or foreign currency in question), together with expectations concerning the role of a futures market organization in fostering the economic demand for futures contracts.

Section 3.1 below sketches some developments in spot markets that tend to foster the economic demand for contracts for future transactions (whether forward or futures). Section 3.2 examines comparative advantages of forward and futures contracts, including aspects of a futures market organization that contribute to advantages of futures contracts.

3.1 Developments in spot markets

An exposed position in a spot market together with uncertainty about spot prices is the foundation of economic demand for contracts for future transactions. Production, marketing and processing of goods require producers, dealers and processors to assume exposed positions in spot markets; and price uncertainty is inherent in a dynamic economy. The combination of an exposed position and price uncertainty creates an economic demand for ways to reduce the cost of exposure. Contracts for future transactions – whether forward or futures – are one way of meeting this demand.

In actual experience, the risk of price uncertainty attached to new output and inventory holdings served to limit the volume of output and inventory holdings. And this in turn limited the benefits that specialization of functions and attendant economies of scale could bring. There thus developed a tendency to diversify, rather than specialize, production and inventory holdings in order to reduce the risk of price uncertainty. Diversifying production and inventory holdings, however (especially at an early stage of economic development) tends to be less efficient operationally than does specializing. Further, diversification could not always appreciably reduce risk because of covariation of commodity prices. Thus, the price risk in specialized production and inventory holdings (actual or potential) became a prime factor in the economic demand for contracts for future transactions.

Contracts for future transactions may arise for any asset. They are most likely, however, to arise for assets that have large output and inventory holdings, together with extensive, unanticipated changes in price and limited market power of market participants. These conditions tend to be met in spot markets having a high liquidity and pricing efficiency.

3.1.1 Liquidity

Large output and inventory holdings tend to occur in liquid markets. Indeed, liquidity is a by-product of large output and especially of inventory holdings as well as a contributor to still larger output and especially inventory holdings.

A number of interrelated factors affect the development of a liquid spot market. The proximate determinants include the breadth and urgency of demand, the ease of ascertaining an asset's quality (as well as quantity), the quality of communication technology, the ease of carrying assets or holding inventories (which includes storage costs, risk of deterioration of quality, risk of fire or theft if not covered by insurance, financing costs, and the risk of price change), the portability of an asset (that is, the cost of transporting an asset in relation to its value), the ease of transferring (exchanging) an asset and the delineation and enforcement of rights to property.[8]

The comprehensiveness and urgency of demand are basic to a market's development. Indeed, for a market to exist, there must be the expectation of a strong and reasonably persistent demand generated by numerous entities. (To be sure, there must also be a positive cost of supplying the good in question.) Suffice it to say that the breadth and urgency of demand help explain the early development of spot markets for agricultural products, the development of spot markets for industrial raw materials in the eighteenth and nineteenth centuries, and the rapid development of foreign exchange markets for the increasingly interdependent national economies of the twentieth century.

The ease of ascertaining an asset's quality (either because of homogeneity or a low cost of standardization) has also been instrumental in the development of liquidity. This factor helps explain the development of liquid markets for staple raw materials and securities of well-known companies and stable governments, as well as for precious metals and certain foreign currencies. In this connection, the grading of agricultural commodities and the rating of corporate securities have played a major role.

Also, the portability of precious metals and the ease of holding inventories in them (in part, because of their durability and high value in relation to bulk) have fostered market development in gold and silver. In contrast, the difficulty of transporting other durables, such as bricks, whose value is low in relation to bulk, has inhibited market development in them. The practicability of holding inventories in non-durables, such as fresh fruit, is severely limited, thereby inhibiting the development of liquid markets.

In the case of securities, the low cost of carrying them over time, the ease of ascertaining their quality and the low cost of transferring them have contributed to the considerable speculative investment in them, and thereby to their high liquidity.

3.1.2 Pricing efficiency

Extensive and unanticipated changes in spot market prices as well as limited market power of spot market participants are also conducive to the inception of contracts for future transactions.

Price changes tend to be large for assets whose supply cannot be varied by rapid and extensive changes in the rate of production. The prices of such assets tend to fluctuate greatly with changes in demand. In addition, if the demand schedules for such assets are inelastic, their prices will also fluctuate extensively with exogenous changes in supply, as may occur, for example, with sharp changes in weather conditions. Thus, inelasticity of supply and demand schedules together with fluctuating and independent changes in demand and supply (from exogenous forces) tend to promote extensive changes in price.[9]

Extensive and unanticipated changes in price tend to occur in a number of goods, including agricultural ones and precious metals. For agricultural goods, large price changes often occur because of exogenous changes in supply (from weather conditions) in conjunction with rather inelastic demands. For precious metals, large price changes often occur because of frequent shifts in demand (occasioned by changed expectations about political and economic conditions) in conjunction with difficulty in short-run supply adjustments.

Speculative investors are attracted to spot markets in which the market power of any participant is very limited and in which large, unanticipated (in a free market sense) price changes tend to occur; they tend to avoid a market in which the underlying asset's price is subject unduly to the personal discretion of a market participant (whether private or governmental). This is not to say that it is easy for speculative investors to predict prices in highly competitive markets. However, whatever difficulties exist, they are faced more or less equally by all market participants. Those who are able to earn the highest return on their investments in such markets are able to do so through their superior insights and analyses, rather than through luck.

Participation of speculative investors in a spot market, in turn, tends to enhance market competition as well as to foster the rapid adjustment of prices to new information. Competition and rapid price adjustment in spot markets are conducive to speculative investment in forward and futures contracts of the corresponding asset. For a viable futures market, such investment is in fact a necessary condition.

One final point here is worth noting. The ease of ascertaining an asset's quality, which helps to promote liquidity, also helps to promote competition among producers. The reason is that it tends to discourage the development of brand names and thereby to reduce the possibility of market power. It is thus not surprising that futures markets tend to be established in homogeneous or easily standardizable assets.

3.2 Comparative advantages of forward and futures contracts

This section examines the comparative advantages of forward and futures contracts for commercial and speculative entities. Because commercial demand for forward and futures contracts precedes speculative demand for such contracts, we will first consider commercial demand. In the case of futures markets, the precedence of commercial demand is more a matter of logic than of sequence: all viable futures markets have both speculative and commercial entities.[10]

Commercial firms may demand contracts for future transactions as a substitute or a complement to spot market transactions. Either way, the contracts enable firms to secure a better position with regard to risk and rate of return. When a commercial firm takes a complementary position in such a contract, it will not necessarily be in a less risky position than previously: the contract may be the vehicle for extending the firm's operations, and this may result in expanded risk as well as in new profit opportunities. However, the firm's new risk exposure – even if extended – is likely to be less than it would have been without the offsetting contract. The reduction of risk exposure for a given spot market position (actual or anticipated) facilitates expansion of inventory holdings or commodity output or use, thereby making gains from economies of scale or from functional specialization possible.

Hedging tends to reduce the cost of exposure to price uncertainty if there is less uncertainty about the basis (or the difference between spot and forward prices) than about the level of the spot price. The expected benefits of hedging thus depend on the degree to which the basis is more predictable than the level of the spot price. The basis is likely to be more predictable when inventories can be carried over easily from one maturity date of a contract to another; this tends to occur for assets with low carrying costs (storage costs, deterioration of quality, etc.). Thus, inventories not only give rise to risk exposure, and thereby potential demand for contracts for future transactions, but also help effectuate this demand by enhancing the expected benefits of hedging.

For commercial firms, the gross benefits of hedging through futures contracts are likely to be somewhat smaller than those gained through tailor-made forward contracts. Because of the greater standardization of futures contracts, the futures price tends to have a lower degree of covariation with the spot price of specific assets than does the forward price of tailor-made contracts. However, the cost of hedging through futures is usually significantly lower. And it is in this area – cost reductions – that we must look to determine the comparative advantage of futures contracts.

The development of interrelated aspects of a futures market's organization (exchange, standardized contract, clearing house and low margin requirements) helps reduce the cost (commercial and speculative) of taking positions in contracts for future transactions. In particular, the market's organization helps reduce transactions costs, facilitates ascertainment of asset quality and helps lower costs of carrying a position over time (primarily default risk).

The ease of effecting transactions in futures contracts results in part from the centralization of the market-place at an exchange. This centralization is a by-product of, and contributor to, a large volume of impersonal transactions and thereby to a liquid market.

Standardization inherent in futures contracts may be viewed as an information-producing activity that makes it easier to ascertain the quality of the contract. The standardized futures contract is both a by-product of a large volume of contracts for future transactions and a contributor to a still greater volume of such contracts. It thereby facilitates economies of scale in the establishment of a futures exchange.

The standardization of futures contracts involves two elements: the specification of contract terms and conditions (typically done so as to maximize commercial use) and the specification of the other party (namely, a clearing house) to any contract position. Such specifications virtually eliminate the cost of ascertaining the quality of a futures contract (in contrast to the rather high cost for a forward contract).

The clearing house, by interposing itself between all short and long positions, virtually eliminates default risk (of an involuntary nature). The financial resources of the clearing house assure the integrity of both sides to all futures contracts. Clearing house settlement procedures are economically feasible because of the large volume of futures transactions made possible by the centralized market-place and the standardized contracts. Thus, the clearing house arrangement is both a by-product of, and a contributor to, market liquidity.

The cost of carrying a position in a futures contract is also very low – indeed, much lower than the carrying cost of a forward contract. The lower carrying cost is attributable primarily to the virtual elimination of default risk. (Both forward and future contracts have low opportunity costs because of their low margin requirements, or surety deposits.)

In a forward contract, there are two types of default risk that may be included in a hedging firm's carrying cost: the default risk facing the hedging firm, and that facing the other party to the forward contract. The cost of default risk facing the hedging firm depends on the perceived quality of the other party to the forward contract and on the prospective cost of contract enforcement. The cost of default risk of the other type may be included in the hedger's payment necessary to induce the other party to take a position in a forward contract; this payment takes the form of a premium embedded in the price of the forward contract. The premium (or discount) consists approximately of the difference between the forward price of a contract at a given point in time and the spot price of the corresponding transaction expected to be consummated in the future (when the contract matures). The magnitude of the premium (discount) is determined by demand–supply conditions in the market for contracts for future transactions.

For speculators, the lower costs of using futures contracts means that at the margin they will require lower prospective returns from their speculative investments. As a result, the premiums embedded in future prices will be lower than those that had been embedded in forward prices. A large speculative interest in futures markets is useful, since it serves, *inter alia*, to reduce the cost of hedging – particularly the size of the premiums that had been embedded in forward prices – by providing balance to a market characterized by unequal hedging strengths. In view of the fact that most futures markets are characterized by stronger hedging interests on one side of the market than the other over long periods of time, speculation is essential to the viability of such markets.

Speculators, then, through both their market participation and enhancement of the long-run stability of futures prices, increase liquidity. In addition, and of significance, speculation is likely to enhance the pricing efficiency of futures by improving the accuracy with which futures prices (for a given degree of price variability) predict future spot prices. Indeed, the business skill of speculators – in fact, their comparative advantage – lies in forecasting price developments.

Thus, because of cost reductions (transaction and carrying), commercial and speculative entities will tend to switch from forward markets to futures markets, and other entities that had not been using forward or futures markets may now be willing or eager to do so. The increased willingness of commercial and speculative entities to use futures markets makes these markets more liquid and the pricing more efficient, as activity of one group reinforces activity of the other. In short, the comparative advantage of futures markets in relation to forward markets lies in their higher efficiency.

It is not surprising that the sequence in the development of futures markets roughly parallels – with a time lag – that of organized spot markets. The earliest futures markets embraced agricultural commodities, industrial raw materials and precious metals. Later, futures markets developed for semi-processed products, such as plywood. More recently, futures markets have developed for foreign currencies and financial assets.

4 The efficiency of futures markets

The efficiency of futures markets varies from one market to another as well as for a given market over time. Taken as a group, futures markets are perhaps the most efficient markets in the world. It is not clear, however, that futures markets are operating efficiently.

Section 4.1 below presents briefly some aspects of the efficiency of futures markets. We have already described elements of the efficiency of these markets in considering their development. Section 4.2 examines aspects of their operating efficiency.

4.1 Efficiency

Because futures markets are of a multi-dimensional nature (involving a contract today for a spot transaction in the future), they have both an observed and unobserved element of information. The observed element relates to contract prices (or price quotations), volume of transactions in contracts, and open interest (contracts outstanding); the unobserved element relates to expectations about spot prices (and, more broadly, spot markets) in the future. Thus, the quality of information in futures markets involves not just the liquidity and pricing efficiency of the observed element, but also the quality of information that the observed element conveys about the unobserved element, particularly about expected spot prices.

The observed and unobserved elements of futures markets typically diverge; in particular, a futures price normally is different from the spot price expected to prevail in the future because of the typical predominance of hedging on one side of the market and the positive cost of speculation on the other. The observed and unobserved elements are, however, inextricably interrelated. Improvement of information about the unobserved element has fostered the development of information about observed elements of actual markets. In turn, development of actual markets (in size and efficiency) has served to convey information about the unobserved element.

Because of their multi-dimensional nature, futures markets have an additional aspect of market efficiency. Specifically, the greater the accuracy with which futures prices serve as estimators of future spot prices, the better is the quality of information imparted by futures markets and thus the more efficient are the markets.

The accuracy with which futures prices estimate future spot prices cannot easily be discerned by comparing futures prices with the corresponding subsequent (or realized) spot prices. With the passage of time, new information may appear and the evaluation of existing information may change. In view of the fact that a plethora of information is relevant to a futures price, that each item of information may be continually changing, and that the digestion of this information (which is spread among countless firms and individuals) is also continually changing, we must expect rather continual changes in prices and price expectations.

In addition, there may be instances in which a current futures price represents something of a compromise between two or more plausible modes of an expected distribution of future spot prices, each of which is predicated on a different assumption about a governmental policy decision that could be taken in a relevant area. For example, during the fixed exchange rate regime, futures prices were influenced by traders' expectations about the timing and magnitude of devaluation decisions.

Furthermore, to the extent that premiums are embedded in futures prices, such prices will change as the maturity date of the contract approaches. For all of these reasons, it is not surprising that there are usually wide discrepancies between current futures prices and the spot prices that later materialize.

4.2 *Operating efficiency*

For the optimal efficiency of futures markets to be realized, the markets must be operating efficiently.

4.2.1 Trading conditions

From the standpoint of trading conditions, futures markets appear to be operating quite well. Indeed, from this standpoint, futures markets do not appear to be beset by any serious artificial impediment either to competition or to information.

To be sure, manipulation or attempted manipulation of futures markets (together with the underlying spot markets) does occur from time to time. In particular, manipulation tends to occur more frequently in illiquid futures markets than in liquid ones, because of the higher probability of success.

When manipulations or attempted manipulations do occur, they may result from some market power in conjunction with special market conditions such as warehouse fires, strikes in transportation industries, or other impediments to storage or delivery of supplies. In addition, they may result from poorly designed contracts which enable a small group of traders to corner the relevant deliverable supply of a commodity.

The recent participation of foreign governments in futures markets (such as in coffee) is likely to create a more serious problem than temporary private manipulation. Without appropriate action by exchanges or a regulatory authority, such participation may impair competition among users of futures markets.

4.2.2 Market organization

In contrast to the competitiveness among users of futures contracts, market power appears to reside in the exchanges, the industry that produces (or designs) futures contracts and processes futures trading. In particular, exchanges appear to have market power in existing contracts.[11]

Within the exchanges, whose structure has not received much attention from economists, so-called 'floor brokers' (who are mostly dealers) appear to wield this market power. The market power of exchanges in existing contracts appears to have enabled independent floor brokers to charge more for transaction services than the costs of providing such services, as well as to impede the introduction of cost-saving transaction technology.

With manual trading, transactions costs appear to be higher than those warranted by costs of production. Under this trading system, executions of orders at most exchanges are bracketed in 30-minute intervals for purposes of time-stamping. When manual trading and 30-minute bracketing are combined with dual trading by independent floor brokers and brokerage firms, the potential for trading abuses by brokers exists. For example, an independent floor broker may insert his own order for a particular futures contract ahead of his customers' orders. Or he may allocate favourable executions (of orders) falling within a particular time bracket to himself and/or his favoured customers. With the current trading and bracketing system, allegations of trading abuse can be neither confirmed nor refuted.

Such actual or potential conflicts of interest generate an implicit transaction cost to market users. Thus, users' transaction cost, which includes not only a brokerage fee and part of a bid-asked price spread but also an implicit cost attributable to possible trading abuse, may exceed the cost of providing transaction services. The independent floor brokers are reportedly able to protect their position (market power) by keeping other exchange members, including representatives of brokerage houses, from doing much trading in the so-called 'pits',[12]

Another possible operating inefficiency may involve production technology. In particular, electronic trading appears to be technologically and economically feasible, but the influential floor brokers apparently have impeded its introduction.

Given today's state of telecommunications technology, the high volume of standardized trading in many futures contracts appears to provide a favourable climate for economies of scale through electronic trading. Indeed, just as futures markets may be viewed as the application of economies of scale to trading of forward contracts, so electronic trading of futures contracts may be seen as the application of economies of scale to manual trading of such contracts.

With electronic trading, market efficiency would be strengthened. In particular, transaction costs would be reduced and the quality of information would be improved. In addition, market integrity (actual or perceived) would be strengthened; and in view of the interrelationship of market equity and market efficiency, the efficiency of the market would be further enhanced.

The independent floor brokers have apparently been opposed to electronic trading. Since floor brokers would no longer have a 'floor' on which to perform, it is understandable that they would oppose electronic trading, and would seek to influence the exchanges to retain manual trading. Little, if any, empirical data exist on floor brokers' influence on exchange policies. However, they are reported to have considerable influence, especially in matters – such as trading technique – that have a critical bearing on their livelihood.[13]

Although existing exchanges have not yet seen fit to introduce electronic trading, they have been highly innovative in other areas, such as the development of new contracts (especially in financial futures). A possible reason for this difference is instructive. In the case of trading technique, automation would tend to dissipate the market power of the exchanges' influential floor brokers; in other operations, innovations may enable the given exchange (more precisely, the collective exchange membership) to attract more business in its current products and/or to extend its business to new products.[14]

It is quite possible that the continued introduction of new contracts, especially in financial futures, will increase the substitutability of contracts among market participants, thereby weakening the exchanges' market power in existing contracts and improving the prospects for innovation in trading technology.[15]

From a static point of view, it can be reasonably argued that manual trading of futures contracts constitutes an operating inefficiency. If, however, the market power of independent floor brokers is actually an important contributor to innovations in areas outside of trading technique (such as development of new contracts), then it is less clear that an operating inefficiency in fact exists. Thus, a crucial issue is whether, from a dynamic standpoint, the market power of independent floor brokers is necessary to secure such innovations.

5 Economic benefits of futures markets

Establishing a new futures market or enhancing the efficiency of an existing one brings both direct and indirect economic benefits. The direct benefits derive from the ability to carry out transactions more efficiently; the indirect benefits derive from the improvement in the quality of information about the terms of transactions (actual or potential).

The potential transactors in a futures market are the proximate contributors to such a market's establishment and organization. That role is not surprising in view of the benefits that the transactors expect to realize. However, all users of the market – indirect as well as direct – benefit from the improvement in information made possible by futures markets, as do users of related markets. In addition, any increase in the efficiency of a particular futures market encourages its use, as well as that of related markets, by both new and present users; and this expansion of use augments the economic benefits of the particular market's development.

Furthermore, as the level of market development in an economy advances, the beneficial effects of a particular market's improved efficiency tend to become cumulative; this is attributable to the greater variety and enhanced efficiency of related markets together with the improved integration among related markets. Since a futures market necessarily comes into existence at an advanced stage of market development (when a wide array of related efficient markets is already functioning), its emergence tends to generate pronounced beneficial effects.

In the rudimentary stages of an economy's development, the principal benefits of a market's development are direct ones. In the more advanced stages of market development, however, the indirect benefits are of greater significance than the direct ones. And, yet, the indirect benefits of market development – the principal benefits of futures markets – have received little attention.

The primary focus of this section is on the indirect benefits of improvements in futures markets. The direct benefits have already been discussed in the earlier examination of the development of futures markets. It is, however, important to recognize that the direct and indirect benefits are interrelated; the separate discussions are for analytical convenience.

5.1 Direct benefits

Establishing a new futures market (or enhancing the efficiency of an existing one) has an impact on the direct users – commercial firms and speculators – of that market.

For commercial firms, a futures market reduces the cost of hedging and thereby promotes their use of the market. Lower hedging costs foster the expansion of output (by producers and users of an asset) and facilitate the carrying of inventories (by producers, users and dealers); and this tends to promote functional specialization and attendant economies of scale in such activities.

In some instances, the reduction of hedging costs is so large that firms that had previously used a tailor-made forward contract, or had not previously hedged at all, will use a futures contract for a good that differs from, but is related to, the particular good that they produce or deal in. For example, some dealers in grain sorghum use corn futures for hedging purposes. This 'cross-hedging' also tends to foster an expansion of output and inventory holdings.

Futures markets also tend to augment the benefits of hedging. To the extent that futures markets enhance the volume of inventories, the basis tends to become more stable and thereby is likely to become more predictable. Thus, futures markets, which tend to emerge in part because of their beneficial effects on hedging costs, in the end also have a favourable impact on hedging benefits.

For speculative investors in actuals, the development of futures markets enables them to improve their risk return positions: futures contracts facilitate the temporary hedging of an exposed position in actuals. For the more speculative investors, the development of futures markets reduces greatly the cost of speculating in contracts for future transactions and thereby encourages a larger amount of such speculation.

Positions in futures contracts may also be used to facilitate purchases and sales of certain actuals. This effect has received little attention, but it may be important (at least for a period of time) in some spot markets that are relatively illiquid. In illiquid spot markets, large purchases and sales may cause wide price movements, which might be avoided by using futures contracts of a related good.

For example, several years ago (before the development of liquid spot and futures markets in certificates of deposit), some banks that had wanted to issue a large volume of certificates of deposit (CDs) were constrained from doing so by the illiquidity of this market. However, by taking initially a short position in Treasury bill futures and then unwinding this position gradually over time, in accordance with the volume and date of its CD issues, a bank was able to stretch out its sale of CDs and at the same time take advantage of its expectations about the prospective behaviour of interest rates.

In this example, the use of Treasury bill futures reduced the cost to a bank of issuing, at one time, a large volume of liabilities in an illiquid market. Such a use of Treasury bill futures is not, however, without its own cost. Transactions and carrying costs exist, and the price of those futures may not move in perfect unison with the price of Treasury bills, let alone CDs.

5.2 Indirect benefits

The development of a particular futures market has indirect benefits for firms that make use of the publicly available information about futures prices. In addition, improvement of information about future spot prices of a specific asset tends to improve the efficiency of related markets and to foster the integration of related markets (with the particular market in question and with one another); a futures market thereby is of benefit to all users – direct and indirect – of related markets. The indirect benefits are related; the separate discussions are for analytical convenience.

5.2.1 Effects on users of the particular market

Improved information (both liquidity and pricing efficiency) about futures prices of a specific asset, and especially the improved expectations about the asset's future spot price, will help commercial firms that produce or use this or related goods to make planning and pricing decisions. In particular, the improved information may help firms reach decisions about production (output, distribution and processing), marketing, or final use of a commodity. The greatest improvement in the decision-making process is likely to be in the early stages of production (output and distribution), inasmuch as the comparability of asset quality between actuals and futures – and thereby the potential for market use – is greatest there. Improved information about expected interest rates for securities may help firms reach decisions about issuing new securities, trading existing securities and processing (or transforming) existing securities through financial intermediaries. And improved information about expected exchange rates may help multinational firms (and domestic firms engaged in foreign trade) deal with foreign exchange risk.

Increased efficiency in the production, marketing or use of an asset (real or financial) tends to result in greater output of commodities or securities, together with lower prices or interest rates.

5.2.2 Effects on related markets as a whole

The development of a futures market tends to make related markets more efficient both by fostering transactions in them and by conveying more and better information to them. The resultant improved liquidity and pricing efficiency of related markets promotes their use, both directly and indirectly. This process tends to generate larger output and lower prices of the related goods.

A futures market in a particular asset (say, a futures market for gold) has many related markets: spot, forward and option markets for the underlying asset (gold); a similar set of markets, as well as futures, for assets (such as silver) bearing a complementary or substitutive relationship to the underlying asset; and in many of these markets a number of geographical trading centres. The spot markets include the markets for new assets as well as existing assets; and the forward, futures and option markets may embrace many different maturity dates of the assets (and, in the case of options, different striking prices).

Two of the markets most closely related to a specific futures market are the underlying spot market and the associated forward market in the same asset. We shall examine more closely some of the effects in these markets produced by the development of a futures market.

5.2.3 Effects on underlying spot markets

The development of a futures market is likely to improve considerably the efficiency of the underlying spot market because of the inherently close relationship between the futures and spot markets for the same asset. The close relationship between the efficiency of markets for spot and futures is very important, but has not, as far as I am aware, received much attention.

The development of a futures market is likely to have a beneficial effect on interrelated aspects of a spot market's efficiency – transaction costs, liquidity and pricing efficiency.

Liquidity We may expect the development of a futures market to reduce bid-asked price spreads, which are an indicator of liquidity. In part, this effect should result from the larger inventory holdings that a more efficient hedging mechanism tends to encourage. Larger inventory holdings tend to reduce the variability of prices over time and thereby to reduce price uncertainty; the resultant lower price risk enables dealers to reduce their bid-asked price spreads. In addition, the smaller bid-asked price spreads should result directly from the improved information about current demand–supply conditions that futures markets tend to generate (to be discussed further).

Evidence of changes in bid-asked price spreads for the Government National Mortgage Association (GNMA) securities after the emergence of a futures market for GNMA securities appears to lend support to this point. In the last two months of 1975, shortly after the introduction of the GNMA futures contract (October 1975), the spread between bid and asked prices on 8 per cent GNMAs was about 24/32 of a point. In January 1976 the spread narrowed to about 20/32 of a point, and by the spring of 1976 it had narrowed to about 16/32; in December 1976 the spread was even smaller (about 8/32). For at least two or three years thereafter, it fluctuated between 8/32 and 16/32 of a point.

To be sure, part of the 1976 reduction in the bid-asked price spread on GNMA securities may have been due to a reduction of uncertainty about underlying economic conditions, and some part of the reduction may have come from innovations in the dealers' market. But the introduction of the futures contract also appears to have played a role. The fact that bid-asked spreads on related securities, such as Federal National Mortgage Association securities and Treasury bonds, narrowed little (if any) during the 1976 period lends support to the idea that a futures market reduces bid-asked price spreads in the underlying spot market.

Pricing efficiency Improved information about the expected price of actuals tends to impart quicker and more accurate information to market participants about current demand–supply conditions of actuals. This tends to enhance the pricing efficiency of actuals – that is, the speed with which an actual's price (or price quotation) incorporates information about changes in demand–supply condition as well as the degree to which an actual's price (or price quotation) is determined by competitive forces.

An indication of increased pricing efficiency of actuals is the use by more and more companies (such as dealers in staple grains) of near-term futures prices to help set prices of actuals (often in a rather mechanical way). Transactions are typically far fewer in spot markets than in the associated futures markets. Near-term futures prices tend to give spot market participants useful information about changes in market conditions (which information may be often difficult, if not impossible, to obtain through other channels).

Because of the effects that futures prices have on pricing in spot markets, futures markets are likely to increase the day-to-day variation in the level of spot prices. Such increased price variability – to the extent it exists – might suggest (at first glance) that uncertainty about conditions in spot markets is now greater and that the efficiency of such markets has thus been impaired. Such an interpretation, however, does not appear to be correct. Futures markets improve the quality of information flowing to spot markets, and spot prices accordingly reflect more promptly changes that occur in demand–supply conditions. A lack of information leads to price inflexibility; such inflexibility prevents the immediate and continuing adjustment of resources in response to changes in demand–supply conditions and necessitates eventual larger price and resource adjustments.

Quicker and more continuous economic adjustments, with their smaller long-run price changes and smaller distant-term uncertainty, improve the allocation of resources. In particular, output, especially of a long-term investment nature, increases when there is less distant-term price uncertainty. This effect is significant for the growth and development of an economy.

The effect of futures markets on price variability has been the subject of many empirical studies. Most of them tend to show that futures markets reduce price variability, although few (if any) of them distinguish between near-term and distant-term variability.[16]

Futures markets may also help to bring prices in different trading centres of a particular spot market into closer alignment with one another as well as with them. This may occur through the effects that the improved information has on pricing in spot markets. In addition, positions in near-term futures contracts (or in forward contracts, to be discussed) may serve as a substitute for positions in various parts of a spot market. Such substitution (actual or potential) may serve to reduce differences in prices for similar spot transactions at a given point in time that are caused by regulatory barriers. In short, with futures markets, regional differences in price levels are likely to reflect more accurately differences among regions in demand–supply conditions and in transport costs.

Finally, and also of considerable significance, the development of futures markets is likely to increase competition in spot markets. Market power in information about demand–supply conditions may constitute a barrier to effective competition between large entities on one side of a market and small entities on the other. In addition, the likely existence of scale economies in the collection of information may be a barrier to new entrants into an activity as well as to effective competition between large and small entities on the same side of a market.

Easily ascertainable information about near-term futures prices of an asset tends to reduce the cost of securing information about current demand–supply conditions in spot markets. This tends to reduce market power in information of participants on one side of a market, thus serving to equalize the competitive strength of entities on opposite sides of a market; it also tends to reduce scale advantages in the collection of information, thereby helping to remove a barrier to entry and to effective competition between large and small entities on the same side of a market.[17]

In this connection, the futures market for copper apparently helped to dismantle the fix-price (producers') market for spot copper transactions – thereby helping to bring about more competitive copper prices. In June 1978, Kennecott, the largest US copper producer, started a new system of pricing spot copper transactions by tying such prices directly to near-term futures prices. Subsequently, other copper companies adopted similar pricing methods. This new system of spot pricing strengthened a trend that had been under way for some time in the copper industry: producers' control over prices had been rather steadily declining for a few years.

More recently, heating oil futures, which became actively traded in mid-1980, appear to have helped reduce oil companies' market power in information about demand–supply conditions. In so doing, this market appears to have helped equalize the bargaining strength of seller and buyers of oil. Indeed, during the past few months, British Petroleum apparently has adjusted its price almost daily in line with prices in near-term heating oil futures.

The effect of futures markets on competition in spot markets helps illuminate the continual struggle between firms and markets in a free enterprise system. Firms are more or less continually trying to develop and mould markets for their own benefit; however, once established, markets often tend to develop in ways that serve to constrain the market power of firms.

5.2.4 Effects on forward markets

The development of futures markets may also strengthen forward markets. To be sure, many transactions that had been carried out on forward markets will now be done on futures markets. However, futures markets have a complementary relationship as well as a substitutive one with forward markets. Indeed, the pricing mechanism of forward markets is likely to work better because of the new and improved information that futures markets provide. Just as prices in spot markets tend to be tied to near-term futures prices, so prices in forward markets tend to be tied to prices of their counterparts in futures markets. In fact, arbitrage transactions tend to prevent forward prices from getting too far out of line with price developments in futures markets. The improved pricing mechanism of forward markets may encourage forward transactions: firms that previously had not used forward (or futures) markets may now do so, both as a hedge against exposed positions in spot markets and as a substitute for spot transactions.

In addition, the development of futures markets appears to have increased the use of 'to arrive' contracts (that is, forward contracts maturing within 30 days) in relation to that of spot transactions, inasmuch as the 'to arrive' market lies closer to the near-term futures market and thus can benefit more from the latter's development than can spot markets. Indeed, the nature of 'cash market transactions' (that is, spot, forward or futures transactions that result in delivery of an asset) as well as sources of information about such transactions have been changing in response to market forces.

5.2.5 Effects on commercial practices

The development of futures markets also is likely to mould commercial practices in spot and forward markets. Just as futures markets grow out of spot and forward markets and adopt many of their commercial practices (in the terms and conditions of futures contracts), the development of futures markets, in turn, moulds the development of spot and forward markets. For example, in order to realize more fully the benefits from hedging and improved information on expected prices, spot and forward market transactions are likely to take on more and more of the standardized aspects of futures contracts. In fact, some changes in commercial practices in a spot or forward market may be motivated by the expectation that they will induce the formation or improvement of a futures market, and that such development in turn will favour the spot or forward market.

It is interesting to note that the introduction in 1970 of the GNMA-modified pass-through certificates was followed rather quickly by the emergence in 1975 of the GNMA futures market. To be sure, the GNMA certificates were introduced for a different purpose – to bolster the housing industry by stimulating investment in mortgages.[18] In addition to their original purpose, the standardized GNMA certificates allowed first a forward market and then a futures market in GNMAs to develop. This experience may well provide a useful lesson to participants in other spot markets.

5.2.6 Effects of recent innovations

The recently established futures for financial instruments and foreign currencies will probably generate, over time, the most pronounced benefits of futures markets. For these futures, the effects (direct and indirect) are the same as those for other futures. However, their underlying spot markets are more important than other spot markets: Interest rates affect virtually every firm in the country, while exchange rates affect every multinational firm and many domestic firms. It is well to observe that, although they have only recently emerged, Treasury bond futures already have the highest open interest and largest volume of transactions of any futures market.

The recent establishment of futures markets for debt securities will tend to reduce the costs of some lenders and dealers (including mortgage bankers and securities dealers) in the money and capital markets. Similarly, the recent establishment of futures markets for foreign exchange will tend to reduce the cost incurred by some firms in hedging foreign exchange risk. In addition, the development of these futures markets will improve information on expected interest rates and foreign exchange rates, and this should be of value to private firms (as well as government officials). These new futures markets are growing rapidly (in the types and volume of use), and in time may have a significant effect on the overall performance of our national economy.

5.2.7 *Final observation*

The development of futures markets tends to clarify price expectations, not only for transactions and decision-making in the given and related markets (including interpolative maturities), but also for transactions and decision-making in the non-market arena – maturities beyond the most distant-term ones of existing markets, as well as assets that do not at present have markets. The improvement of price expectations about non-market phenomena may, over time, lead to the emergence of new markets. In the meantime, the improvement of such expectations – particularly about distant-term future prices – may still have wide-ranging effects on firms' decision-making, including the negotiation of contracts for future transactions and the improvement of long-term planning. Such effects – especially for debt securities and foreign exchange – may be of some importance to the development of our economy.

Notes

1 Government policy, however, has an important bearing on market development – in terms of both the setting (or environment) in which market development occurs and the various regulatory measures directed at markets. In addition, market development affects government policy (regulatory and non-regulatory). On the interrelationship of futures markets and government policy, see Burns (1979, especially chs 3, 6 and 7).

2 Cf. Hicks (1962).

3 Because market conditions do not remain constant, most assets' underlying value (at any given point in time) can never be known with certainty.

4 An optimal amount of transactions cost is assumed to be incurred so as to realize the maximum expected net price during the period of time considered.

5 Cf. Menger (1981).

6 The optimal level of market efficiency should be considered in a dynamic context. See, e.g., Streit (1982, pp. 16–17).

7 Market regulation, if undertaken at all, should be directed towards improving market operations (trading conditions or market organization) or assuring the operating efficiency of markets. Unless the benefits and costs of changes in a market's operations are understood, regulation may be carried too far or not far enough. Indeed, it is important that the perceived and actual usefulness of regulation be the same.

8 On the ways in which these factors affect a market's efficiency, see Burns (1979, ch. 2). Also, see Marshall (1920, book V, ch. 1).

9 Cf. Marshall (1920, book V; 1927, pp. 256–7).

10 The distinction between commercial firm and speculative investor, although perhaps useful for analytical purposes, is overdrawn. The commercial firm engaging in selective hedging is, in effect, also engaging in selective speculation. The speculative investor engaging in selective speculative investment is, in effect, also engaging in selective hedging.

11 On the reasons for this market power, see Burns (1982, pp. 37–9).

12 This point was made by several industry officials in conversations with me.

13 This point was made by several industry officials in conversations with me. In addition, see Jones and Ferguson (1978, p. 43).

14 Cf. Schumpeter (1942).

15 For a fuller discussion, see Burns (1982, pp. 39–40).

16 The studies that analyse price variability before and after a period of futures trading are probably the most informative. Such comparisons can be made when the government prohibits trading of futures in certain markets – such as onion futures in the United States – after the markets had been in existence. The case of onions is examined in Working (1963). Also, see Goss and Yamey (1976).

17 The customary opposition to new futures markets by large dealers and producers is consistent with this competition-enhancing effect. We have recently witnessed such opposition to new futures markets in zinc, rice, aluminium, nickel, coal and some financial assets and foreign currencies.

18 The certificates enable investors to purchase shares in a pool of FHA/VA-insured mortgages, whose interest payments and repayment of principal are insured by GNMA; this insurance reduces uncertainty about the quality of mortgages and thereby fosters investor demand.

The views expressed are solely those of the author and do not necessarily reflect those of the Antitrust Division, US Department of Justice. The paper is based in large part on material in Burns (1979). The author acknowledges with gratitude the suggestions of Albert Smiley on the present paper.

References

Burns, J. M. (1979), *A Treatise on Markets*, Washington DC.

Burns, J. M. (1982), 'Electronic Trading in Futures Markets', *Financial Analysts Journal*, 38.

Fama, E. (1970), 'Efficient Capital Markets: A Review of Theory and Empirical Evidence', *Journal of Finance*, 25.

Goss, B. A. and Yamey, B. S. (1976), 'Introduction: The Economics of Futures Trading', in B. A. Goss and B. S. Yamey (eds), *The Economics of Futures Trading*, New York.

Hicks, J. R. (1962), 'Liquidity', *Economic Journal*, 72.

Jones, N. H. Jr and Ferguson, A. (1978), *Competition and Efficiency in the Commodity Futures Market*, report prepared for the Commodity Futures Trading Commission, Public Interest Economics Center, Washington DC.

Marshall, A. (1920), *Principles of Economics* (8th ed.), New York.

Marshall, A. (1927), *Industry and Trade* (3rd ed.), London.

Menger, C. (1981), *Principles of Economics* (1871), New York.

Schumpeter, J. A. (1942), *Capitalism, Socialism and Democracy*, New York.

Streit, M. E. (1982), 'Information Processing in Futures Markets – An Essay on the Adequacy of an Abstraction', European University Institute, Working Paper no. 9.

Working, H. (1963), 'Futures Markets under Renewed Attack', *Food Research Institute Studies*, 4.

4

Futures Markets and Risk: A General Equilibrium Approach

JOSEPH E. STIGLITZ

1 Introduction

Futures markets for agricultural commodities provide an important mechanism by which both producers and users of the agricultural products may reduce the risks that they face. Although this has long been recognized, there have been few attempts to analyse in detail the functioning of the futures market in reducing, transferring and spreading risks. That is the object of this paper.

After formulating a general model of a futures market (in section 3), we use the model to address several questions of interest. The central question we ask is, does the futures price provide an unbiased estimate of the future spot price, in an 'efficient' market?

The issue of market bias has attracted almost continuous attention since Keynes first advanced his theory of normal backwardation in 1927. Keynes argued that the futures prices were downward-biased estimates of the final expiration values, the bias representing the risk premium for speculators. Since then, considerable empirical effort has been devoted to trying to find this risk premium, with mixed success (see, for example, the selection of papers in Peck, 1977).

There are a number of problems in testing econometrically the hypothesis of unbiasedness. We approach the question from a theoretical perspective: we ask what conditions would normally lead to 'backwardation'; what conditions are required for unbiasedness? We show that there is some presumption that the market will be biased but no *a priori* basis for ascertaining the direction of the bias. We identify a number of factors determining the direction of the bias, including the extent of participation by users and producers in the futures market and the source of disturbances in the market (i.e., whether the price variability arises out of output variability or out of demand variability).

We also use the model to ask a number of other questions of interest. For instance, we ask, what determines the volatility[1] of futures prices? We show that, although the volatility of the insurance market may be very large, the futures market still may be able to provide effective insurance. For example, if there were no supply risk, the futures market could eliminate all income risk for that particular year. Hedging 'within the year' may be very valuable.

Another related question that we address is an evaluation of the ability of the futures market to reduce the risk faced by producers, in comparison with the risk reduction provided by a commodity price stabilization scheme. We establish conditions under which the futures market leads to a higher level of welfare than even a perfect price stabilization scheme.

A final related question that we address is under what circumstances producers or users will hedge, particularly in an unbiased futures market. We show that there is a strong presumption that the producers will be incompletely hedged if the source of price variability is output risk, but that they will be completely hedged if the source of price variability is from demand shocks. Whether users are more or less than completely hedged turns out to be a more complicated matter.

Section 2 establishes the framework of the analysis, while in section 3 we formulate a simple but general (non-parametric) model of the futures market. In section 4 we consider in detail the supply of futures by producers, and in section 5 we analyse the market equilibrium under the assumption that only producers participate in the futures market. Section 6 analyses the demand for futures by users, while section 7 ascertains the nature of the equilibrium that would emerge in a market dominated by users. Finally, section 8 analyses the nature of market equilibrium where users, producers and speculators are all active.

Section 9 compares the welfare gains associated with commodity price stabilization schemes with those associated with futures markets. The important results of the paper are summarized in section 10.

2 Basic framework of analysis

Futures markets differ from securities (bond, stock) markets in one extremely important way: the income from other sources of a significant number of individuals is correlated with the return on futures contracts. This means that the futures market provides a limited kind of 'income insurance'. The exact extent to which it does this is one of the subjects of investigation here.

For our purposes, it is important to identify three different groups of participants in futures markets.

2.1 Producers

Producers can use futures markets to 'hedge' some of the uncertainty associated with the price at which they can sell their output. Since output and price are inversely correlated, they will not, in general, wish to become perfectly hedged. For instance, if the demand curve for a commodity had unitary elasticity, a representative producer would have no income variability if he did not sell any futures contracts. Thus, if the futures price equalled the expected spot price, the producer would neither sell nor buy futures. There are some cases, in fact, where a producer may want to buy futures rather than sell them, when the futures price equals the expected spot price.

The effect of selling the crop forward on the futures market on income variability may be seen diagrammatically. There are three cases to consider. In the first case output and price are assumed to be positively correlated, so that when output is high, price is high. Then, in the absence of futures markets, at a given level of input, the relationship between output and income is depicted in figure 1(a). Because the price increases with output, income increases rapidly with output. If the individual sells a part of his crop forward, he receives in exchange for a variable income a certain income; thus his lowest income is increased, and his highest income is reduced. If, as assumed, the futures price equalled the expected value of the spot price, then the riskiness of the individual's income would be unambiguously reduced (in the sense of Rothschild and Stiglitz, 1971). Figure 1(b) depicts the distribution function of his income before and after the sale of part of his crop on the futures market.

In the second case, price and output are negatively correlated, but not so negatively correlated that the price variability offsets the output variability. Hence, income variability is less than output variability. By selling some of his crop in the futures market, the individual can increase his income in states in which the price is low, i.e., in which output and income are high, at the expense, of course, of reducing it in states where income and output are low. But because of the diminishing marginal utility, since the marginal utility in the high-income states is lower than in the low-income states, he

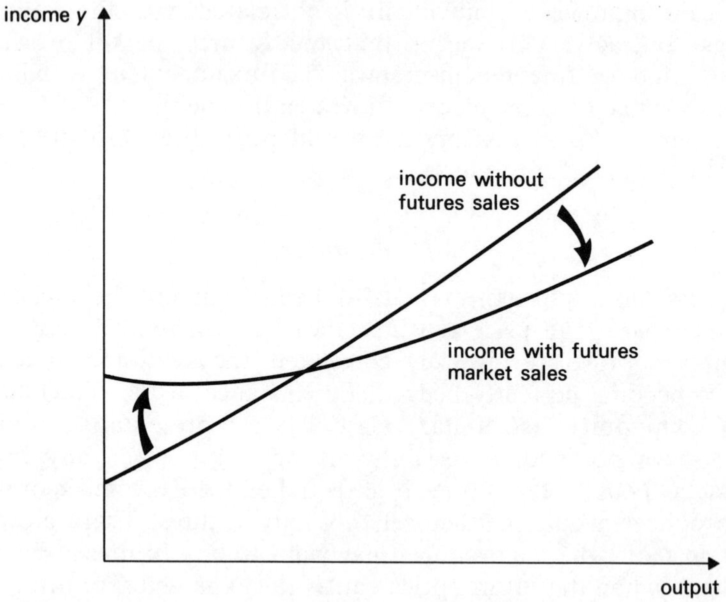

Fig. 1(a) Price and output positively correlated: income as a function of risk

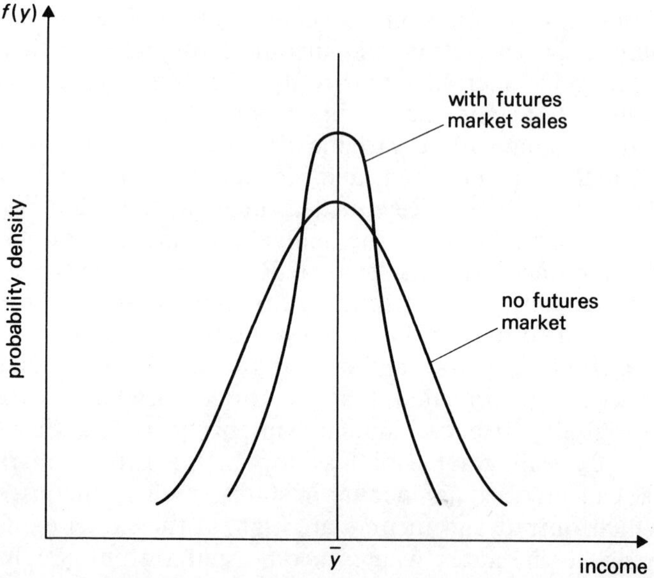

Fig. 1(b) Price and output positively correlated: density function of income

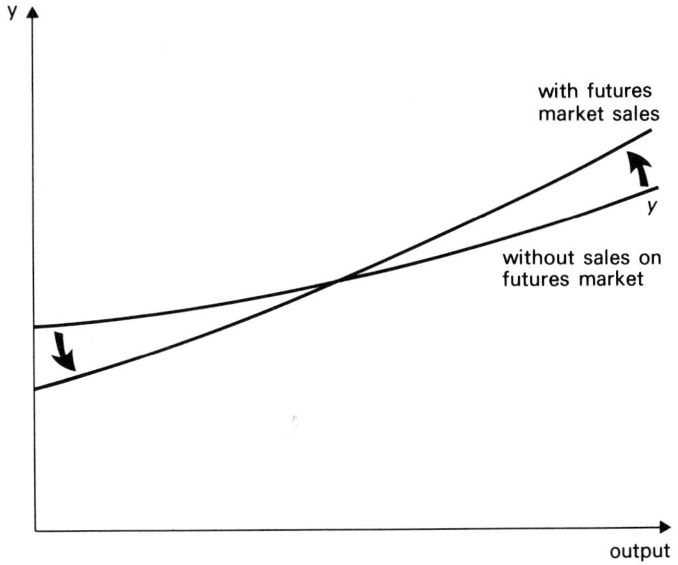

Fig. 2(a) Price and output slightly negatively correlated: with and without sales on futures markets

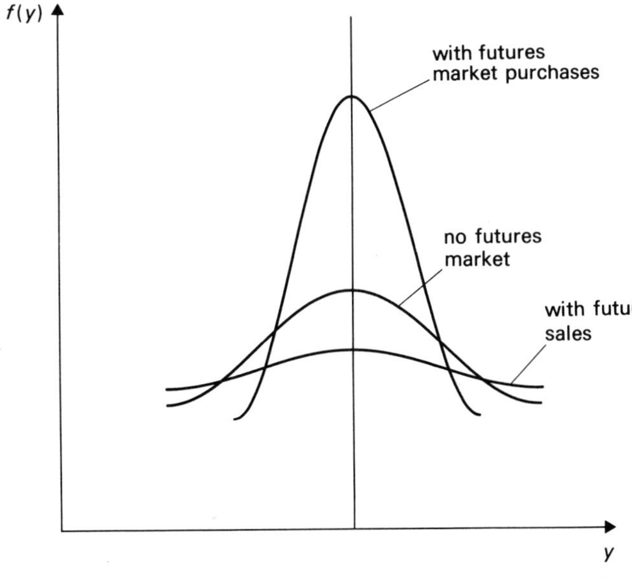

Fig. 2(b) Price and output slightly negatively correlated: with futures market sales and purchases

would not wish to engage in actuarially fair trades and so will not sell any of his crops forward. This is shown in figures 2(a) and 2(b).

The third case is that in which prices and output are very negatively correlated – so negatively correlated that income decreases when output increases, as shown in figure 3(a). This case is an important one in the subsequent analysis. Note that selling the crop on the futures market increases income when price is low, i.e. when output is high but income is low. Thus, in this case he will wish to engage in an actuarially fair trade.

2.2 Users

Firms that purchase the commodity as an input use the futures market to 'hedge' some of the uncertainty associated with the price at which they can buy the good. Since profits will, in general, decline with an increase in the cost of an input, if nothing else changes – i.e. if the price of the user's output and his other inputs remains unchanged – if the futures price were equal to the expected spot price,

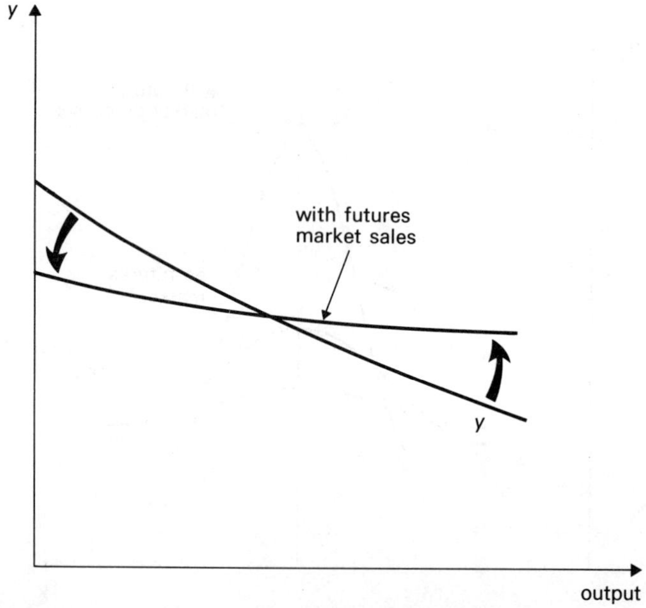

Fig. 3(a) Price and output very negatively correlated: with futures markets sales

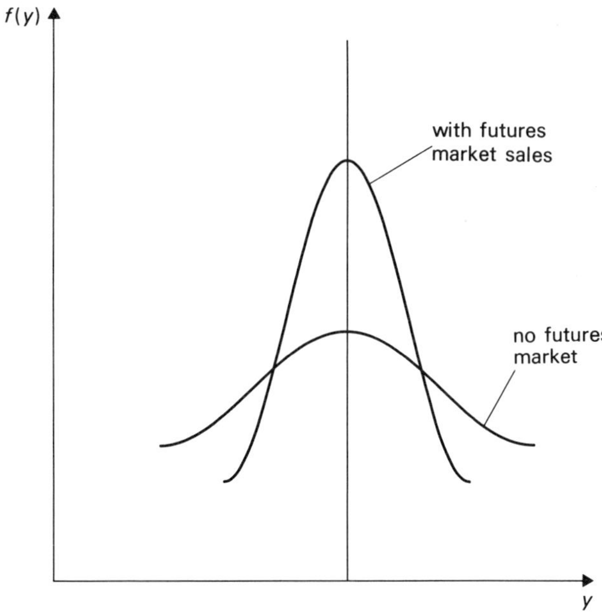

Fig. 3(b) Price and output very negatively correlated: with and without futures market sales

firms could reduce the variability of their income by buying futures. But if the users of the agricultural commodity are, say, firms that process this commodity, and the source of the price variability is, say, from the demand for the user's final output, then states of nature in which the agricultural price is high are states in which profits are high; hence users will wish to sell futures rather than buy them, in an unbiased market.

2.3 Pure speculators

These are defined as individuals (firms) whose income from other sources is uncorrelated with the return on futures contracts. Thus, they are not using the futures market as a hedging device, as a method of obtaining income insurance; rather, they can be thought of as selling insurance to producers and/or consumers. When there is a sufficiently large number of speculators, even if they are risk-averse, competition will result in the expected return on a futures contract being zero; i.e. the futures price will equal the expected spot price. We shall assume that speculators are risk-averse, and that there is only a limited number of them. We shall focus our attention on the producers and consumers, and the exchanges that occur between them. We shall attempt to see how changes in the various parameters that determine the structure of the market, for example the probability distribution of output, the level of profits, etc., affect the equilibrium on the futures market. An important aspect that we shall ignore are asymmetries of information and the role of the futures market in conveying information. We focus here, in other words, on the risk functions of these markets.

3 The model

3.1 Producers

Producers are assumed to be risk-averse. For simplicity, we shall assume that the producer has no source of income other than the production of the commodity in question. The ith producer's output is q_i. In general, q_i is a random variable. Again, in general, the ith farmer's output and the aggregate output, Q_i, are not perfectly correlated.

The spot price is denoted by p_s. The spot price is assumed to be a function of the aggregate output Q and a general demand parameter, θ:

$$p_s = p_s(Q, \theta) \tag{1}$$

where we denote by

$$-\frac{d \ln p_s}{d \ln Q} = \frac{1}{e} \tag{2}$$

the inverse of the price elasticity. Without loss of generality, we let $E\theta = 1$.

To simplify the analysis, we model the futures market in a somewhat idealized way. A futures contract is a gamble on the price of the commodity next period. Typically, money is exchanged at the time the contract is made. We ignore this and assume that all money is exchanged next period. The seller of the futures contract receives

$$p_f - p_s$$

next period, where p_f is the (fixed) futures price and, as before, p_s is the (random) spot price. (If $p_f < p_s$, the seller of the futures contract pays the buyer the amount $p_s - p_f$.) Let x be the number of such contracts he sells. Then his income is

$$y_i = p_s q_i + x(p_f - p_s) \tag{3}$$

with

$$Ey_i = Ep_s(q_i - x) + xp_f \tag{4}$$

and

$$\sigma^2_{y_i} = E(y_i - \bar{y}_i)^2 = E[p_s(q_i - x) - Ep_s(q_i - x)]^2. \tag{5}$$

The first-order condition for the producer is now easily derived. He chooses x to maximize his expected utility:

$$\max EU^i(y_i). \tag{6}$$

The producer is risk-averse; i.e. $U^{i'} > 0$, $U^{i''} < 0$. He sets

$$EU^{i'}(p_f - p_s) = 0. \tag{7}$$

Much of the subsequent analysis consists of interpreting (7) and pursuing its implications under various assumptions. For now, we simply observe that (7) can be solved for x_i, the ith producer's 'supply' of future contracts, as a function of p_f, the futures price, and the probability distributions of spot price and output:

$$x_i = x_i(p_f; \tilde{p}_s, \tilde{q}_i). \tag{8}$$

3.2 *Users*

The purchasers of the commodity are also modelled as being risk-averse. We write the (maximum) level of profits that they can attain as a function of the input price, p_s, the random variable θ and a vector of other prices m, which in turn are affected by our random variables, p_s and θ:

$$\pi = \pi[p_s, \theta, m(p_s, \theta)] \tag{9}$$

where, by standard results,

$$\frac{\partial \pi^j}{\partial p_s} = -q^j \tag{10}$$

where q^j is the jth firm's purchases of the commodity.

As we asserted earlier, users can affect the variability of their income by selling futures contracts. Denoting their total income by z, we have

$$z = \pi(p_s, \theta, m) + x(p_f - p_s). \tag{11}$$

Hence

$$Ez = E\pi(p_s, \theta, m) + x(p_f - \bar{p}_s) \tag{12}$$

and the variance of z

$$\sigma_z^2 \equiv E(z - \bar{z})^2 \equiv E\{\pi(p_s, \theta, m) - E[\pi(p_s, \theta, m)]\}^2 + x^2 E(p_s - \bar{p}_s)^2 - 2xE(p_s - \bar{p}_s)[\pi(p_s, \theta, m) - E\pi(p_s, \theta, m)]. \tag{13}$$

If a firm has an (indirect) utility function $V(z, p)$,

$$V_z > 0, \quad V_{zz} < 0, \tag{14}$$

then x is chosen to

$$\max EV \tag{15}$$

yielding the first-order condition

$$EV_z(p_f - p_s) = 0. \tag{16}$$

Again, we shall devote considerable attention to interpreting (16); for now, we simply note that (16) can be solved for their demand for futures:

$$x^j = x^j(p_f; \tilde{p}_s, \tilde{\theta}). \tag{17}$$

Clearly, their demand will depend not only on the price of futures, p_f, but also on the (joint) probability distribution of the spot price and the random variable θ.

3.3 Speculators

The speculator is assumed to have an income from other sources of Y_s^*, with

$$E(Y_s^* - \bar{Y}_s^*)(p_s - \bar{p}_s) = 0. \tag{18}$$

His income from other sources is uncorrelated with the spot price. If he sells futures contracts, his income is

$$Y_s = Y_s^* + x(p_f - p_s) \tag{19}$$

with

$$EY_s = Y_s^* + x(p_f - Ep_s) \tag{20a}$$

$$\text{var } Y_s = \text{var } Y_s^* + x^2 \text{ var } p_s. \tag{20b}$$

Thus, if $p_f = Ep_s$ (a circumstance that we shall later refer to as one in which the market is unbiased), either buying or selling futures increases the variance of the speculator's income but leaves his mean unchanged. The speculator will thus engage in speculation, if he is even slightly risk-averse, only if the expected return is positive. More formally, the speculator chooses x to maximize his expected utility. If we let W represent his utility function, $W' > 0$, $W'' < 0$ (he is risk-averse), then he will

$$\max EW(Y_s) \tag{21}$$

so we obtain the first-order condition

$$EW'(p_f - p_s) = 0. \tag{22}$$

Again, we can solve the first-order condition for the demand for futures contracts as a function of the random spot price, and the variability of other income:

$$x_s = x_s(p_f; \tilde{p}_s, Y_s^*). \tag{23}$$

3.4 Market equilibrium

Market equilibrium in the futures market is now easy to describe. We simply require that the futures price be such as to make the demand for futures contracts equal the supply, or in our notation,

$$\Sigma x_i = 0 \tag{24}$$

where we have summed up over all the contracts of producers, users and speculators.

In the next section, we shall investigate in detail the structure of producers' demands for futures. We then apply the results obtained to analyse equilibrium in a futures market dominated by producers. The following section investigates in detail the structure of users' demands for futures, and explores the implications of these results for a market equilibrium in an economy in which users dominate the futures market. The final section considers equilibrium in a futures market in which users, producers and speculators are all active traders.

4 The supply of futures by producers

In this section we characterize the demand function for futures by producers, paying particular attention to two special situations.

Futures prices will be said to provide an unbiased estimate of future spot prices if

$$p_f = Ep_s. \tag{25}$$

We shall refer to market equilibrium of this form as exhibiting market risk neutrality.

Individuals will be said to be perfectly hedged if they sell futures equal to their expected output,

$$x = Eq_i.$$

We will say they are partially hedged if

$$0 < x < Eq_i.$$

If $x < 0$, we will say that they are negatively hedged (or that they have taken a speculative position), and if

$$x > Eq_i$$

we will say that they are hedged more than 100 per cent.

This vocabulary may be slightly misleading: as long as q_i is a random variable, the individual cannot eliminate all risk.

We are now prepared to prove two propositions characterizing producers' behaviour in the futures market.

PROPOSITION 1. In an unbiased market, whether a producer is more or less than completely hedged, i.e., whether $x_i \gtrless \bar{q}_i$, depends on (among other things) the correlation between his output and the market price and the level and rate of change of his degree of (absolute) risk aversion, the magnitude of the price variability, and the relationship between the variance of output, conditional on the spot price, and the spot price.

To see this, we take a Taylor series expansion of the first-order condition (7) around $p_s = \bar{p}_s$, $q_i = \bar{q}_i$ and $x = \bar{q}_i$ (ignoring terms of fourth-order or smaller) to obtain[2]

$$\begin{aligned} U'E(p_s - \bar{p}_s) &+ U''[(\bar{q}_i - x_i)\,E(p_s - \bar{p}_s)^2 + \bar{p}_s E(q_i - \bar{q}_i)(p_s - \bar{p}_s)] \\ &+ E(p_s - \bar{p}_s)^2\,(q_i - \bar{q}_i) + U'''[2\bar{p}_s E(p_s - \bar{p}_s)^2\,(q_i - \bar{q}_i) \\ &+ \bar{p}_s^2 E(q_i - \bar{q}_i)^2\,(p_s - \bar{p}_s)] \approx 0. \end{aligned}$$

Hence

$$\begin{aligned} x_i - q_i \approx \{&\bar{p}_s E(q_i - \bar{q}_i)(p_s - \bar{p}_s) + E(p_s - \bar{p}_s)^2\,(q_i - \bar{q}_i) \\ &+ \frac{U''}{U}\,\bar{p}_s[2E(p_s - \bar{p}_s)^2\,(q_i - \bar{q}_i) + \bar{p}_s^2 E(q_i - q_i^2)(p_s - \bar{p}_s)]\}/E(p_s - \bar{p}_s)^2. \end{aligned} \tag{26}$$

This can be rewritten as

$$\frac{x_i - \bar{q}_i}{\bar{q}_i} \approx \frac{\rho_{is} + \dfrac{E(p_s - \bar{p}_s)^2 (q_i - \bar{q}_i)}{\bar{p}_s^2 \bar{q}_i} + \dfrac{U''' \bar{y}_i}{U''}\left[\dfrac{2E(p_s - \bar{p}_s)^2 (q_i - \bar{q}_i)}{\bar{p}_s^2 \bar{q}_i} + \dfrac{E(q_i - \bar{q}_i)^2 (p_s - \bar{p}_s)}{\bar{q}_i^2 \bar{p}_s}\right]}{s_{p_s}^2} \tag{27}$$

where

$$s_{p_s} = \frac{[E(p_s - \bar{p}_s)^2]^{1/2}}{\bar{p}_s}, \tag{28a}$$

the coefficient of variation of p_s, and

$$\rho_{is} = \frac{E(q_i - \bar{q}_i)(p_s - \bar{p}_s)}{\bar{p}_s \bar{q}_i}, \tag{28b}$$

the normalized covariance between the ith farmer's output at the spot price.

This can be further simplified by defining

$$V \equiv \frac{U'''}{U''}\, \bar{y}_i = \frac{A' - A^2}{A} \tag{28c}$$

where

$$A = -\frac{U''}{U'}, \tag{28d}$$

the measure of absolute risk aversion.

Note that, if there is constant relative risk aversion, i.e. if

$$R \equiv \frac{-U''y}{U'} = \text{constant}, \tag{28e}$$

then

$$V = R - 1. \tag{28f}$$

We further approximate

$$E(q_i - \bar{q}_i)^2 (p_s - \bar{p}_s) \approx \frac{d \operatorname{var} q_i | p_s}{dp_s} E(p_s - \bar{p}_s)^2 \tag{29a}$$

$$E(p_s - \bar{p}_s)^2 (q_i - \bar{q}_i) \approx \frac{d \operatorname{var} p_s | q_i}{dq_i} E(q_i - \bar{q}_i)^2. \tag{29b}$$

Substituting into (26), we obtain

$$\frac{x_i - \bar{q}_i}{\bar{q}_i} \approx \frac{\rho_{is} + (1+2V)\dfrac{d \ln \text{var}\, p_s | q_i}{d \ln q_i} s^2_{p_s | q_i}}{s^2_{p_s}} + V \frac{d \ln \text{var}\, q_i p_s - s^2_{q_i | p_s}}{d \ln p_s} \tag{30}$$

where, in the obvious notation, s_{q_i} is the coefficient of variation of q_i; $s_{p_s | q_i}$ is the coefficient of variation of p_s conditional on q_i (evaluated at $\bar{q}_i$); and $s_{q_i | p_s}$ is the coefficient of variation of q_i conditional on p_s (evaluated at $\bar{p}_s$).

This result is important in demonstrating that one simply cannot infer, from the fact that producers are risk-averse, that they will wish to hedge on the futures market. Their behaviour depends on the average relationship between their output and price, which depends, in turn, on the elasticity of demand and the correlation between their output and aggregate output; and it depends on the third derivative of their utility function (which is related to whether risk aversion increases or decreases with wealth), and on how the variance of output changes with price. If, for instance, in situations of drought – when average output is low and price is high – the variability (across farms) is very large, even if the elasticity of demand is such that average income is high, so that, if the marginal utility at the average income is low, the expected marginal utility of income may be high.

Note that the magnitude of the level of hedging or speculation depends on the third and fourth derivatives of the utility function as well as on the relationship between the variance of q_i, conditional on p_s, and on p_s.

This analysis makes clear the special nature of some of the particular parameterizations of utility functions and stochastic structures that have been investigated more extensively in the literature. Many of the results using, for instance, quadratic utility functions (for which $U''' = 0$) are special, and may not generalize. In the next section we treat several special cases.

4.1 Some special cases

4.1.1 Output not variable

If output is not variable, if the producer hedges completely, i.e.

$$x_i = q_i$$

then

$$y_i = p_f q_i$$

and he faces no risk. (This is equivalent to the producer selling his entire crop forward.) Thus

$$EU'(p^s - p^f) = U'E(p^s - p^f) = 0;$$

i.e. the first-order condition is satisfied.

PROPOSITION 1(a). If the producer's output is not variable, he takes a perfectly hedged position in an unbiased futures market; if the futures price exceeds the expected spot price ($p^f > Ep^s$), then the producer speculates on the futures market, regardless of his attitude towards risk aversion. If the futures price is less than the expected spot price ($p^s < Ep^s$), then the producer is imperfectly hedged, regardless of his attitude towards risk aversion.

Risk aversion affects the size of the position ($|x_i - q_i|$) that the producer takes; it is straightforward to establish (using standard techniques of risk aversion) that, the less risk-averse the farmer, the larger the position he taxes.

Proposition 1(a) has an immediate corollary: when the sole source of price variability is demand variability, a commodity price stabilization scheme that perfectly stabilized prices at the mean price is equivalent, in its effect on producers, to a futures market in which producers are perfectly hedged.

A special case where closed form solutions can be obtained is that where the utility function is constant absolute risk aversion, $U = -e^{-Ay}$. Then, if $M(s)$ is the moment generality function associated with the distribution of p_s, i.e.

$$M(s) = Ee^{-sp_s},$$

then $q_i - x_i$ is the solution to

$$E(p_f - p_s)^{-Ay} = (e^{-Axp_f})\{(p_f - \bar{p}_s)\, M[A(q_i - x_i)] + Ee^{-A(q_i - x_i)\,p_s}(p_s - \bar{p}_s)\} = 0.$$

Hence, if p_s is normally distributed, y is normally distributed, and

$$EU = e^{-A\bar{y} + \frac{1}{2}A\sigma_y^2}$$

where σ_y is the variance of y and $\bar{y}$ its mean, and

$$q_i - x_i = \frac{p_f - \bar{p}_s}{A\sigma_{p_s}^2}.$$

4.1.2 Quadratic utility function

In this case,

$$u'_y = c - gy_i.$$

Hence

$$\begin{aligned} EU'_i(p_s - \bar{p}_s) &= -gEy_i(p_s - \bar{p}_s) \\ &= -gEp_s(q_i - x_i)(p_s - \bar{p}_s) \\ &= -g[Ep_s(q_i - \bar{q}_i)(p_s - \bar{p}_s) + (\bar{q}_i - x_i)\,E(p_s - \bar{p}_s)\,p_s] \end{aligned}$$

or

$$q_i - x_i = \frac{\bar{p}_s E(q_i - \bar{q}_i)(p_s - \bar{p}_s) + E(p_s - \bar{p}_s)^2(q_i - \bar{q}_i)}{\text{var}\; p_s}.$$

4.1.3 Constant absolute risk aversion with normal distributions of output; all producers with perfectly correlated risks

The problem with obtaining closed-form solutions for the demand for futures, even with normal distributions of output, is that, in general, price will be a function of output, and hence income that contains a term in the product of price and quantity will not be normally distributed. There is one case in which closed-form solutions can be obtained. If the demand curve is linear,

$$p_s = -aQ + b,$$

then, if there are n identical farmers,

$$\begin{aligned} p_s q_i &= -anq_i^2 + bq_i \\ y_i &= -anq_i^2 + bq_i - anx(\bar{q}_i - q_i), \end{aligned}$$

which is a quadratic form in a normal random variable, and is distributed as a non-central X^2 distribution. Expected utility can be written

$$-Ee^{-Ay_i} = -Ee^{Ana\left(q_i - \frac{b+anx_i}{2an}\right)^2 + Aan\left[\bar{q}_i x_i - \left(\frac{b+anx_i}{2an}\right)^2\right]}$$

$$= -(1-2\,Aan\sigma_q^2)^{-\frac{1}{2}\exp\left\{Aan\left[\bar{q}x_i - \left(\frac{b+anx_i}{2an}\right)^2\right] + Aan\sigma_q^2\left(\frac{b+anx_i}{2an}\right)^2 \Big/ 1-2Aan\sigma_q^2\right\}}$$

Hence x_i is chosen to maximize

$$\bar{q}_i x_i - \left(\frac{b + anx_i}{2an}\right)^2 + \sigma_q^2 \left(\frac{b + ax_i}{2an}\right)^2 \; 1 - 2\, Aan\sigma_q^2;$$

i.e.

$$\bar{q}_i = \frac{b + anx_i}{an}\left(1 - \frac{\sigma_q^2}{1 - 2\, Aan\sigma_q^2}\right)$$

or

$$x_i = \frac{\bar{q}_i - b/an}{1 - \sigma_q^2/1 - 2\, Aan\sigma_q^2}.$$

The individual will, in general, be imperfectly hedged.

4.2 *Do producers even speculate?*

Our analysis makes it clear that it may well be the case that the producer hedges less than completely. Will he ever speculate; i.e. will $x_i < 0$? The answer to this question is provided by

PROPOSITION 2. Producers hedge or speculate (i.e. $x_i \gtrless 0$) in an unbiased market as cov $(p_s q_i, y_i) \gtrless 0$.

To see this, we examine the value of

$$EU'(p_f - p_s)$$

when $x = 0$, and $Ep_s = p_f$. Taking a Taylor series expansion for small variances in q_i and p_s, we obtain

$$EU'(\bar{p}_s - p_s) \approx U''(Ep_s q_i) \operatorname{cov}(p_s q_i, p_s) + \frac{U'''}{2} E(p_s q_i - Ep_s q_i)^2 (\bar{p}_s - p_s).$$

Hence, ignoring terms of the third order and smaller, we see that

$$x \gtrless 0 \qquad \text{as } \operatorname{cov}(p_s q_i, p_s) \gtrless 0.$$

Certain limiting cases can easily be analysed. If the only source of price variability is output variability, and the output of all producers is perfectly correlated, so if there are n producers,

$$Q = nq_i,$$

then

$$\operatorname{cov}(p_s q_i, p_s) \lesseqgtr 0$$

as the elasticity of demand is greater or less than unity.

If the only source of price variability is demand variability (aggregate output is constant, with high yields on one farm being exactly offset by low yields on another), then the covariance between income and price will be positive, implying that the producer will in fact hedge to some extent.

If the demand function is linear, so

$$p = -aQ + b\theta,$$

and if production on the ith farm is described by

$$q_i = \beta_i M + \epsilon_i, \qquad \Sigma\beta_i = 1, \qquad E\epsilon_i = E\epsilon_i M = E\epsilon_i \epsilon_j = 0,$$

i.e. output on each farm is affected by a common factor, M, and by a set of idiosyncratic shocks, represented by ϵ, then if the demand and supply shocks are independent,[3] the sign of cov $(p_s q_i, p_s)$ depends on

$$a^2\beta_i[\bar{M}\sigma_M^2 + E(M - \bar{M})^3] + \beta_i^2 E\epsilon_i^3.$$

Thus, if ϵ_i and M are symmetrically distributed, whether the covariance is positive or negative depends simply on whether $\beta_i \gtrless 0$; i.e. the covariance between price and income depends simply on the covariance between the farmer's output and aggregate output.

5 Market equilibrium with only producers

As a preliminary to the more general analysis to follow in section 8, we ask here what the market equilibrium would look like in an economy in which there are only producers and all producers are identical. Although no trade would occur in a futures market in such a situation, we can still talk about what price would clear (at zero trade) the futures market.

5.1 Relation between the futures price and the expected spot price

Since, at $x = 0$, the first-order condition must be satisfied, we have

$$p_f = \frac{EU'(p_s q)\, p_s}{EU'}.$$

The futures price is a weighted average of spot prices with weights depending on marginal utilities. An immediate implication of Proposition 2 is

PROPOSITION 3. The futures price may either exceed or be less than the expected spot price. If farmers are risk-averse, and there is no output variability, then the futures price is less than the expected spot price.

5.2 *Risk aversion at the futures price*

A question of some interest is how changes in the various parameters affect the futures price. For instance, it is easy to see that an increase in farmers' risk aversion increases the discrepancy between p_f and Ep_s; in the limit, with risk-neutral farmers, $p_f = Ep_s$.

5.3 *Volatility of the futures price*

Is it possible for p_f to be more volatile than p_s? Assume there were a variety of kinds of information available in the beginning of each period, generating a probability distribution of the spot price at the end of the period. If the environment were the same period after period, the futures price at the beginning of the period would always be the same. But it changes, and hence p_f changes. Consider, for instance, the case of multiplicative shifts in the demand function. We write

$$p_s = p_s(\theta, Q)\,\gamma.$$

γ is observed at the beginning of the period (before the futures market opens).

Assume that Q is not variable and $\operatorname{cov}[p_s(\theta, Q), \gamma] = 0$. Then

$$\operatorname{var} \ln p_s = \operatorname{var} \ln \gamma + \operatorname{var} \ln p_s(\theta, Q)$$

while

$$\operatorname{var} \ln p_f \approx \frac{d \ln p_f}{d \ln \bar{p}_s} \operatorname{var} \ln \gamma.$$

The variability in the futures price may well exceed the variability in the spot price, if $d \ln p_f / d \ln p_s$ exceeds unity (the conditions for this are derived in the Appendix).

Not too much importance should be attached to this result, since it is a consequence of the particular measure of volatility (the variance of the logarithm of price) that we have employed. If we had used an alternative measure – the range of the distribution – we would not have obtained the result. The range of the spot price has to be greater than the range of the futures price, provided that there is uncertainty; consider, for instance, the highest value of the futures price. Since there is some probability that the spot price will be less than the futures price, there must be some probability that the spot price will be greater than the futures price. Hence the highest spot price must be greater than the highest futures price; and conversely, the lowest spot price must be lower than the lowest futures price. On the other hand, our analysis does alert us to the fact that the futures price may indeed be very volatile. Consider, for instance, a situation (different from that considered above) where, at the beginning of the period, producers learn that the spot price is going to be strongly correlated with their income either very positively or very negatively. This information will lead to large variations in the futures price; in one case the futures price will be low and in the other high, even though the mean spot price in the two situations is the same. The relationship between the variability in the futures market and the variability in the spot market is complex.

It is still the case that the futures market is providing an important service in transferring risk even though the variability in the futures price may be quite high.

6 The demand for futures by users

While an increase in the price of the commodity makes producers better off, it makes users worse off. It is this asymmetry in the effect of price changes that provides the natural motivation for producers and users to trade in the futures market.

In this section we analyse the demand for futures by users, using the results obtained in the next section to analyse the structure of equilibrium in a futures market dominated by users.

We again will focus our attention on hedging behaviour, this time of users. A user will be said to be perfectly hedged if he buys futures to cover his mean level of purchases, i.e. if $x+q^j=0$, where q^j are his purchases of the commodity. To ascertain whether $x+q^j \gtrless 0$, we take a Taylor series expansion of the first-order condition (16) around $\bar{p}_s$ and $x=-\bar{q}^j$, the mean level of purchases of the commodity by the jth user. For simplicity, we focus on the case where

$p_f = Ep_s$, and postulate that m (prices of output and other inputs) is a function of θ and p_s. Then

$$EV_z(p_s - \bar{p}_s) \approx V_{zp}E(p_s - \bar{p}_s)^2 + V_{zz}\left[\left(\pi_\theta + \pi_m \frac{dm}{d\theta}\right)E(\theta - \bar{\theta})(p_s - \bar{p}_s) + \pi_m \frac{dm}{dp_s}E(p_s - \bar{p}_s)^2 - (x+q)\,E(p_s - \bar{p}_s)^2\right];$$

i.e.

$$x^j + q^j \approx \left(\pi_\theta + \pi_m \frac{dm}{d\theta}\right)\frac{E(\theta - \bar{\theta})(p_s - \bar{p}_s)}{\operatorname{var} p_s} + \pi_m \frac{dm}{dp_s} + V_{zp}.$$

Some special cases immediately emerge.

(a) If the output price and other input prices are constant and there is no demand variability, then users will take a perfectly hedged position (with an unbiased market) if their marginal utility of income is independent of the relative price of the commodity ($V_{zp} = 0$). If their marginal utility of income is increased by an increase in the price of the commodity, then $x^j + q^j \leqslant 0$; if the marginal utility of income is decreased by an increase in the price of the commodity, $x^j + q^j \geqslant 0$. In any case, so long as the user spends relatively little of his income on purchases of the commodity (in his role as consumer), V_{zp} will be small (see Newbery and Stiglitz, 1981). Hence, under these conditions, as a first approximation, users will be perfectly hedged.

(b) On the other hand, it is reasonable to assume that output prices and input prices will be correlated. Thus, if some of the increased costs of users are passed on to final consumers in the form of higher prices,

$$\frac{dm}{dp_s} > \theta \quad \text{and} \quad \pi_m > 0,$$

then $x^j + q^j > 0$. Producers are imperfectly hedged.

(c) If the only source of variability in price is from demand, then $E(\theta - \bar{\theta})(p_s - \bar{p}_s) > 0$. If the demand shock leaves other prices unchanged, then

$$x^j + q^j \gtrless 0 \quad \text{as} \quad \pi_\theta \gtrless 0.$$

Assume all users face perfectly correlated shocks; since

$$q^j = -\pi^j_{p_s}$$

and

$$\frac{dq^j}{d\theta} = -\pi^j_{p_s\theta} > 0.$$

It is clearly possible for this to be true and for π_θ to be of either sign.

(d) A limiting case is that of a final consumer, for whom $\pi \equiv 0$. Then, to the first order of approximation, whether an individual is more or less than perfectly hedged depends on the sign of V_{pz}.

7 Equilibrium in a futures market with only users

We can use the results of the previous section to analyse market equilibrium under the assumption that the only traders in the futures market are the users of the commodity. We assume all users are identical. Then the equilibrium price in the futures market (at which no trade occurs) is given by

$$p_f = \frac{EV_{zp_s}}{EV_z}.$$

Again, we ask, at $x = 0$, is

$$\frac{EV_{zp_s}}{EV_z} \gtrless Ep_{s_j};$$

i.e. is

$$E(V_z - \bar{V}_z)(p_s - \bar{p}_s) \gtrless 0?$$

A sufficient condition for $p_f \gtrless \bar{p}_s$ is that

$$\frac{dV_z}{dp_s} = V_{zp} + V_{zz}\frac{d\pi^j}{dp_s} \gtrless 0.$$

The normal presumption is that the futures price exceeds the expected spot price. This will be the case if (a) $V_{zp} \geqslant 0$ or V_{zp} is small (as we argued would normally be the case); and (b) the only source of price variability is output, and the increased costs (p_s) are not completely shifted on to consumers; i.e.

$$\frac{d\pi}{dp_s} = \frac{\partial \pi}{\partial p_s} + \frac{\partial \pi}{\partial m}\frac{\partial m}{\partial p_s} = -q^j + \frac{\partial \pi}{\partial m}\frac{\partial m}{\partial p_s} < 0;$$

or else there is demand variability, but

$$\frac{\partial \pi^j}{\partial \theta} - q^j \frac{\partial p^s}{\partial \theta} + \frac{\partial \pi}{\partial m}\frac{\partial m}{\partial \theta} < 0.$$

For example, the increase in profitability from the increased demand for the user's products is less than the decrease in profitability from the corresponding increase in the price of the inputs resulting from the shift in the derived demand curve.

It should be clear that, when there is a demand-induced variability in the price, the futures price can well be less than the expected spot price.

8 Futures markets with producers and consumers

We now assume that both producers and users wish to hedge on the futures market. We wish to know whether there is any *a priori* presumption concerning the relative magnitude of the futures price and the expected spot price.

For simplicity, we assume that all producers are identical and all consumers are identical. Then equilibrium is described by the pair of equations

$$V_z[\pi(p_s) - x(p_f - p_s)](p_f - p_s) = 0$$

$$EU'[p_s q + x(p_f - p_s)](p_f - p_s) = 0.$$

Assume

$$p_f = Ep_s.$$

The analysis of sections 3–7 provides us with a framework within which we can ascertain whether producers' demand for futures will be greater or less than the users' supply of futures.

PROPOSITION 4. If there is only supply variability, then whether $p_f \gtreqless Ep_s$ *depends simply on whether*

$$x^j + q^j \lesseqgtr 0.$$

This result follows immediately from proposition 1, in which we established that the total demand for futures was equal to the aggregate supply, when there was no output variability and when the futures price was equal to the expected spot price.

Note from our discussion of section 6 that, under quite plausible conditions, $x^j + q^j$ may be either greater or less than zero. The futures price may be greater or less than the spot price. We suspect that the normal presumption in these circumstances is where, say, the agricultural output is an intermediate good (so its demand is a derived demand); those states in which final demand is very high will correspond to states with high profitability and high prices for the agricultural good. Then

$$x^j + q^j > 0.$$

Hence, in spite of the risk aversion of users, we would expect the futures price to be less than the expected spot price.

PROPOSITION 5. If there is only supply variability, if the magnitude of its variability is small, and if output variance, conditional on the spot price, is independent of the spot price, then, provided users' marginal utility of income is independent of price, and provided that other prices faced by users are constant, the futures price will be greater than the expected spot price.

This result follows again from proposition 1 (which establishes that, under these conditions for producers, $x_i < q_i$); while the analysis of section 6 established, that under these circumstances, for producers, $x^j + q^j \approx 0$. Thus there is an excess demand for futures when $p_f = Ep_s$.

Similar results obtain provided $V_{pz} < 0$; and $\pi_\theta < 0$, again, provided that other prices faced by the user remain constant. On the other hand, in the more general case, we normally expect that prices of output be correlated with the price of p_s, and as a result it is possible that, for the representative user, $x^j > -q^j$ when the futures price is equal to the expected spot price. Then, whether in equilibrium futures prices are greater or less than the expected spot price depends on a detailed analysis of the degree of risk aversion of users and producers, the correlations between the spot price and output of the producer, and the spot price and other factors affecting the profitability of the user.

8.1 Speculators

So far, in our analysis, we have ignored the role of what we defined as pure speculators in section 3. These do not have any effect on the direction of bias of the market, i.e., on the relationship between the expected price and the futures price. What they affect is the magnitude of the bias. It will, in general, be smaller than it would have been in the absence of speculators. However, so long as they are not risk-neutral, they will only take a speculative position provided that $|p_f - Ep_s| > 0$.

9 Comparison between futures markets and commodity price stabilization schemes

The framework we have already established enables us to make quick comparisons between commodity price stabilization schemes and the futures market. We are interested in the relative effectiveness of these two in reducing the risk borne by producers. (Similar calculations may be made for consumers.) To keep the comparisons as simple as possible, we need to abstract from what Newbery and Stiglitz (1981) have referred to as the 'transfer effect' the fact that, in establishing either scheme, the mean income of producers may change. If we assume that the demand function is (approximately) linear, and stochastic disturbances to the demand function are additive,

$$p_s = a - bQ + \theta.$$

Then stabilizing the price will leave mean price unchanged. Then, expected income is

$$Ep_s q = \bar{p}_s \bar{q} + E(p_s - \bar{p}_s)(q - \bar{q}).$$

Expected income is raised or lowered by a commodity price stabilization scheme depending on the correlation between price and output.

With a commodity price stabilization scheme, producers still face variability in their income. The loss in welfare is given by

$$-\frac{1}{2}\frac{U''}{U'} p_s^2 \operatorname{var} q.$$

Contrast this with a futures market, which we assume for simplicity is unbiased. Then the individual's expected utility can be approximated by

$$U(\bar{p}_s \bar{q}) + \tfrac{1}{2} U''[p_s^2 \operatorname{var} q + (\bar{q} - x)^2 \operatorname{var} p_s + 2\bar{p}_s(\bar{q} - x) \operatorname{cov}(p_s, q)]. \tag{31}$$

But x is chosen optimally (as in our earlier discussion). When the optimal value of x is substituted into (31), we obtain that the loss in welfare from the remaining risk to farmers is just

$$-\frac{1}{2}\frac{U''p_s^2}{U'}\left[\text{var } q-\frac{\text{cov }(p_s, q)}{\text{var } p_s}\right].$$

When farmers have output variability, neither futures markets nor commodity price stabilization programmes completely eliminate the risks they face. On *a priori* grounds, it is not obvious that one system should be unambiguously superior to the other, since they provide different kinds of 'insurance'. Effectively, the commodity price stabilization scheme allows the individual to hedge (sell forward) whatever amount he produces; in futures markets, the individual must sell a fixed amount; he hedges before he knows what his output is (for sure). On the other hand, the futures market allows the individual to hedge whatever amount he wishes – it provides him an extra element of discretion. This latter effect dominates the former effect provided $\text{cov }(p_s, q) > 0$. If $\text{cov }(p, q) < 0$, the commodity price stabilization scheme is preferable. In general it is desirable to have both.

10 Concluding comments

This paper has been concerned with the analysis of equilibrium in futures markets. Since futures are, in many respects, like investments in any other asset, a natural question that arises is, why can we not simply borrow the well developed theory of equilibrium in asset markets (e.g., the capital asset pricing model) and apply it to the analysis of futures markets? If the output of some crop is distributed independently of 'the market' (the business cycle and the weather are not highly correlated), then if the only source of variability in price were supply variability arising from, say, variability in weather, price on the futures market should be equal to the expected spot price. If there is also demand variability, and the demand for the crop is cyclical, and farmers do not perfectly anticipate the cycle (so do not adjust their plantings accordingly), then price will be positively correlated with the cycle. Hence, if the capital asset pricing model (or any of a number of similar analyses) were directly applicable, the futures price should be less than the expected spot price.

We have suggested, however, that there is an important difference between the stock market and futures markets: a significant fraction of the participants in the futures markets have income that is not directly insurable; there are only limited markets for crop insurance; and most farmers cannot diversify out of their own risk by selling shares in their farms. The firms that use the agricultural commodities as inputs should, in principle, be able to diversify out of the risks that they face; on theoretical grounds, we should therefore expect them to act in a risk-neutral manner. Moreover, if the perfect capital market hypothesis were correct, there would be no need for them to engage in hedging operations. Stiglitz's generalization of the Modigliani–Miller theorem shows that all financial transactions are (in such a world) irrelevant to the value of the firm. Yet, these firms do engage in hedging operations; whether they behave in a risk-neutral or risk-averse manner is a moot question. For reasons discussed elsewhere (Stiglitz, 1982a), we suspect that it is more plausible that the managers act in a risk-averse manner, and it is this hypothesis that we have explored in detail here.

Thus the objective of this paper has been to construct a general equilibrium model of risk-averse producers and users (consumers), in which the futures market can play an important role in transferring risks. Moreover, we have attempted to construct a model that is simple enough that interesting comparative statics propositions can be derived within it. At the same time, we have attempted to avoid the unnecessarily restrictive assumptions that have been employed in earlier studies (e.g., constant absolute risk aversion), which, we have noted, lead those models to have very special properties. The models employing these assumptions do not appear, on the basis of the analysis contained here, to be very robust.

Among the most notable results we have derived are the following.

(a) A primary determinant of the extent of hedging activity of producers in an unbiased market is the correlation of the spot price with their income (or with their output). If there is zero correlation – as there would be if producers faced no output variability – then they hedge completely; i.e. they sell a quantity of futures equal to their expected output. Although for most agricultural commodities there is a presumption that, on average, the correlation is positive (since the demand elasticity is less than unity, so that high prices correspond to low yields, but high incomes), this need not be the case; under this 'normal' presumption, producers are incompletely hedged; i.e. they sell a quantity of futures that is less than their expected output. (It is possible, in fact, for producers to buy futures rather than sell their crop forward.) Three primary determinants of the correlation between a 'representative' farmer's output and the price are: (i) the source of price variability, i.e. whether price variations arise from demand or supply; (ii) the correlation between the output of different farmers; and (iii) the demand elasticity. Although the correlation between a representative farmer's output and the spot price was the primary determinant of the extent of hedging in an unbiased market, we have identified a number of other parameters that may play an important role as well.

A primary determinant of whether users become perfectly hedged, i.e. whether they buy a quantity of futures equal to their expected purchases, is whether the source of price variability is demand shocks or supply shocks. With supply shocks, though it is possible that users are more or less than completely hedged, there is some presumption that they will, at most, take a small position. With demand shocks, however, this presumption is no longer valid. If the source of the variability in the price of the given agricultural commodity is variability in the demand for the output of the user, then there is some presumption that the user in an unbiased futures market will sell futures, taking the opposite position that one would normally expect. He is like a farmer, with high profits and a low marginal utility of income in those states where the price is high. On the other hand, if the source of the demand variability is the increase in the price of another input, the user may more than cover his position.

(b) As a result of these properties of the demands and supply of futures by users and producers, in situations in which all have easy access to the futures market and participate in it, whether the futures price will exceed or be less than the expected spot price depends, among other things, on whether the source of uncertainty is supply shocks or demand shocks, and if demand shocks, whether the source of the disturbance is from the price of another input employed by the user, or from the demand for the user's output.

Differential rates of participation in the market by producers and users may play an equally or more important role in determining the direction of bias in the futures market.

Our general analysis has established that there is no *a priori* basis for expecting the futures price to be greater or less than the expected spot price.

So long as there is a limited number of risk-averse speculators, speculators will reduce the magnitude of the bias in the market, but will not eliminate it.

(c) Changes in information and beliefs about the probability distribution of the spot price, and changes in the probability distribution of outputs, which may give rise to changes in the probability distribution of spot prices, will in general give rise to changes in the futures price. The variability in these parameters will thus give rise to variability in futures prices. The fact that the variability in the futures price could be larger does not vitiate the important role of the futures market in transferring risks.

(d) We compared the performance of the futures market in reducing the risk faced by producers with that of an idealized buffer stock scheme which perfectly stabilized the price facing producers (no buffer stock scheme, with finite stocks, could actually do this). Neither programme completely eliminated the risks faced by producers, but we established that whether the loss in welfare from the remaining risk faced by producers was greater or smaller under the price stabilization scheme than with a futures market depended on the covariance between spot price and output.

This paper has focused on the role of the futures market in the sharing and transferring of risks (in any economy with an incomplete set of risk markets). We have focused on characterizing the equilibrium, with describing its properties, rather than evaluating the efficiency with which it transfers and exchanges risks. Using the techniques of analysis developed in Greenwald and Stiglitz (1982), Stiglitz (1982b) and Newbery and Stiglitz (1981), we can show that in fact the futures market does not attain a constrained Pareto optimum; that is, in general, there exists a set of taxes/subsidies on the trading of futures that will lead to a Pareto improvement.[4]

We have assumed throughout that all traders have identical beliefs about the probability distribution of prices and that these beliefs corresponded to the actually observed distributions. (It was thus meaningful for us to speak of the 'expected spot price'.) If individual beliefs differ, it is, of course, the individual's subjective expectations that are relevant for determining his demand for or supply of futures.

Our analysis thus models only one of the important functions served by futures markets and focuses on only one of the important reasons that individuals trade in futures markets. Just as differences in beliefs are what make a horse race, so too do differences in beliefs about prices give rise to trading on the futures market. The extent to which those differences in beliefs, by themselves, can account for rational trading in futures is a moot question.

Elsewhere (Stiglitz, 1982a), we have argued that, even with asymmetries of information (differences in beliefs), it is not rational for risk-averse individuals to trade risks with each other simply because of those differences in beliefs; that is, if individuals are trading risks because of differences in risk aversion or in their economic circumstances (as in our model of the futures model, where there are clear motives for users and producers to trade even with identical beliefs), then differences in beliefs will affect the extent of trading. But in the absence of some motive, such as sharing or transferring risks, it is not rational for risk-averse individuals to trade in such a market. Still, individuals bet on horse races, even though it is not rational for them to do so. One view of the stock market and futures markets is that they are the rich man's gambling casino. Our analysis has ignored this interpretation of futures markets.[5]

When individuals do have different information, and when the futures market is performing an important role in transferring and sharing risks, then the futures market serves, at the same time, an additional function: it aggregates the disperse information of the various participants in the market. Under certain circumstances the price on the futures market summarizes all the relevant available information for forecasting the spot price (see Bray, 1981; Grossman, 1977; and Grossman and Stiglitz, 1980). In a sequel, we show that the conditions under which the futures price is fully revealing are indeed very restrictive.

A more complete analysis of equilibrium in futures markets, when they simultaneously transfer risks and convey information, and when the information enhancement and risk reduction possibilities provided by the futures market affect the production and consumption decisions of producers and users, must await another occasion.

Appendix

Effect of multiplicative shift in the distribution of the spot price on the futures price, in a futures market with identical producers[6]

Assume that

$$p_s = p_s(\theta, Q, \gamma) = \gamma \hat{p}_s(\theta, Q).$$

Recall that

$$p_f = \frac{EU'p_s}{EU'}$$

$$= \gamma \frac{EU'\hat{p}_s}{EU'}.$$

$$\frac{d \ln p_f}{d \ln \gamma} = 1 + \frac{d \ln EU'\hat{p}_s/EU'}{d\gamma}.$$

With constant relative risk aversion,

$$\frac{EU'(\gamma\hat{p}_s q)\,\hat{p}_s}{EU'(\gamma\hat{p}_s q)} = \frac{EU'(\hat{p}_s q)\,\hat{p}_s}{EU'\hat{p}_s q}$$

independent of γ. More generally,

$$\frac{d \ln EU'\hat{p}_s}{d \ln \gamma} = \frac{EU''y\hat{p}_s}{EU'\hat{p}_s} = -\frac{ERU'\hat{p}_s}{EU'\hat{p}_s} \approx -R(\bar{y}) - R'\bar{y}\left[\frac{\text{cov}\,(p_s, y)}{\bar{p}_s\bar{y}} - Rs_y^2\right]$$

$$\frac{d \ln EU'}{d \ln \gamma} = \frac{EU''y}{EU'} = -\frac{ERU'}{EU'} \approx -R(\bar{y}) - \frac{R'}{U'}\,\text{cov}\,(y, U')$$

$$\approx -R(\bar{y}) - R'yRs_y^2$$

where $s_y^2 = \sigma_y^2/\bar{y}^2$, the coefficient of variation. Hence

$$\frac{d \ln p_f}{d \ln \gamma} \gtreqless 1 \quad \text{as} \quad -R'\,\text{cov}\,(p_s, y) \gtreqless 0.$$

The effects of other changes in the distribution of the spot price may be analysed in a similar manner.

Notes

1 We focus our attention throughout on a non-storable good. This enables us to avoid some important but difficult issues of intertemporal arbitrage.

2 Somewhat more generally, to determine whether $x_i \gtreqless Eq_i$, we can ask, at $x_i = Eq_i$, what the sign of $EU'(p_s - \bar{p}_s)$ is.

$$x \gtreqless Eq_i \quad \text{as} \quad \left.\frac{dEU'(y_i)\,|\,p_s}{dp_s}\right|_{x=Eq_i} \lesseqgtr 0.$$

3 More precisely, we require

$$E(\theta - 1)(M - \bar{M}) = E\epsilon_i(M - \bar{M}) = E\epsilon_i\epsilon_j M = E\epsilon_i^2 M = E\epsilon_i(M - \bar{M})\,\theta = E\epsilon_i^2\epsilon_j$$
$$= E(M - \bar{M})^2(\theta - \bar{\theta}) = 0.$$

4 The term 'constrained' Pareto optimality is employed to remind us that there is an incomplete set of markets. Government intervention is restricted; the government is not allowed to create additional markets.

5 A quite different motive for trading in futures markets, at least prior to 1981, is that it provides a convenient way of tax avoidance. We have not investigated the implications of tax considerations for equilibrium in the futures market. Tax considerations may, however, be of critical importance.

6 And in which users do not participate.

Parts of this paper represent extensions and developments of arguments originally put forth in Newbery and Stiglitz (1981, chapter 12). Research support from the Center for the Study of Futures Markets, Columbia University, and the National Science Foundation, is gratefully acknowledged. I am indebted to Robin Lindsey, David Newbery, Manfred Streit and the other participants of the seminar at Florence for their helpful comments.

References

Bray, M. (1981), 'Futures Trading, Rational Expectations, and the Efficient Markets Hypothesis', *Econometrica*, 49.

Green, J. (1978), 'Information, Efficiency, and Equilibrium', Research Paper 284, Harvard Institute of Farmer Research, Cambridge, Mass.

Greenwald, B. and Stiglitz, J. E. (1982), 'Pecuniary Externalities', Murray Hill (mimeo).

Grossman, S. (1977), 'The Existence of Futures Markets, Noisy Rational Expectations and Informational Externalities', *Review of Economic Studies*, 64.

Grossman, S. and Stiglitz, J. E. (1980), 'On the Impossibility of Informationally Efficient Markets', *American Economic Review*, 70.

McKinnon, R. I. (1967), 'Futures Markets, Buffer Stocks, and Income Instability for Primary Producers', *Journal of Political Economy*, 75.

Newbery, D. M. G. and Stiglitz, J. E. (1981), *The Theory of Commodity Price Stabilization*, Oxford.

Peck, A. E. (ed.) (1977), *Selected Writings on Futures Markets*, vol. II, Chicago.

Rothschild, M. and Stiglitz, J. E. (1971), 'Increasing Risk II: Its Economic Consequences', *Journal of Economic Theory*, 3.

Stiglitz, J. E. (1974), 'On the Irrelevance of Corporate Financial Policy', *American Economic Review*, 64.

Stiglitz, J. E. (1982a), 'Information and Capital Markets', in C. Cootner and W. Sharpe (eds), *Financial Economics: Essays in Honor of Paul Cootner*, Englewood Cliffs, New Jersey.

Stiglitz, J. E. (1982b), 'The Inefficiency of the Stock Market Equilibrium', *Review of Economic Studies*, 49.

5

Interest Rate Futures Markets, Interest Rate Variability and the Demand for Investment

DAVID LEVHARI and MICHAEL ROTHSCHILD

1 Introduction

Many economic theorists would, if asked, state that one of the important functions of futures markets is to complete markets, to make them approach more closely the Arrow–Debreu ideal model in which insurance markets work perfectly and costlessly. This belief rests on two observations: first, what is required for markets to attain Arrow–Debreu perfection is lots of securities; second, futures markets create new securities. Thus, it seems natural to argue that futures markets bring economies closer to completion. This argument was made formally by Robert Townsend (1978), who proved, in the context of a one-period model, that, if there were as many goods as there were states of nature, then a market regime in which unconditional claims to goods (futures) were traded before uncertainty was resolved and a spot market opened after uncertainty was resolved could achieve any Pareto-optimal allocation that a market with complete contingent commodities could achieve.

This view of futures markets is, at least as applied to interest rate futures, at best a half truth. A genuinely dynamic economy – one in which markets continually open and reopen – which does not have complete markets functions very differently from an Arrow–Debreu economy. This is because, in Arrow–Debreu economies, there is, in a sense, no price uncertainty and thus no opportunities (or need) for price speculation. However, in any dynamic models that do not meet the rigorous demands of this theory there is an opportunity for speculation. (See Radner, 1978, 1982, for a discussion of this point.) While adding futures markets may make markets more complete, we doubt that, in any realistic case, future markets make markets so complete that there is no opportunity for speculation.

The second reason why interest rate futures markets do not bring about complete markets is that they add very little to the set of securities that are traded. Forward markets in bonds allow traders to do nothing that they could not do by buying (and selling short) bonds of different maturities. Thus, a market with forward contracts in bonds has no more securities than a market with a term structure in which the usual perfect capital markets assumptions are satisfied. However, interest rate futures markets do complete markets in two senses. First, the perfect capital markets assumptions are not satisfied for markets with bonds of various maturities. It is difficult and costly for small investors to sell bonds short. Futures markets provide a cheap way for small investors to make almost the same transactions they could make on a perfect capital market with a term structure. Thus, even if they do not create new securities, interest rate futures make the markets for extant securities function better. For many traders interest rate futures do in effect add markets. Second, and less important, futures markets, with their 'mark-to-market' feature, do create some securities not present when traders can trade only bonds of different maturities. However, the additional securities that futures markets create fall short of providing complete Arrow–Debreu securities. These arguments are made in section 2 below.

Interest rate futures markets do not complete markets to such an extent that traders have no desire to speculate or hedge; instead, they make the markets on which traders can speculate and hedge much more liquid. In section 3 we attempt to analyse the effect of this on the operation of stabilization policy. Our approach is partial and indirect. The main effects of interest rate futures markets on stabilization policy will necessarily work through the enhanced speculation and hedging opportunities that these markets bring about. We find it difficult to conjecture on the likely direct effect on stabilization policy; that is, we have nothing to say about the effect of interest rate futures markets on the demand for money or other such aggregate economic relationships. However, there is an important indirect effect about which we do have something to say. Economists have long thought that the existence of opportunities to speculate and hedge will change the variability of the underlying spot market. Unfortunately, they have not agreed about the direction of the change. Most economists argue that speculation is stabilizing, but a sizeable minority have argued that the opposite is true. We do not take sides in this debate; however, we believe we can add another reason for wanting to know the answer. In section 3 we present an argument that suggests that the aggregate supply of investment is affected by the variability or stability of the underlying spot market, which in this case is the short-run interest rate. Thus we think that interest rate futures markets affect the investment supply schedule through their effect on the variability of the short-run interest rate.

Our theoretical argument is quite simple. An investor who completes the first stage of a multi-stage investment project is in the same position as the owner of a portfolio of options on securities whose values are determined by future interest rates. As is well known, options become more valuable when the security on which they are written becomes more variable. Variability of interest rates increases the value of multi-period investment projects and leaves unchanged the value of investment projects that do not have this option feature. Thus, as interest rates become more variable, investment increases. And as interest rates become more variable, the composition of investment changes. Projects with an option value become relatively more valuable. We show through the analysis of an extended example that this may have the effect of making the investment supply schedule less interest-elastic. Although the example we present is very special, the result seems sensible. As interest rates become more uncertain, economic actors in effect purchase insurance against this variability. Thus they need to react less to any particular change in the interest rate. An immediate implication is that stabilization policy, at least in so far as it operates through the interest elasticity of investment, is less effective in an economy in which interest rates are relatively variable than in an economy in which they are relatively predictable.

2 Additional securities created by futures markets

In this section we show, first, that interest rate futures do not significantly increase the number of securities available to investors; we then argue that interest rate futures do make the markets on which bonds are traded approach more closely the economist's concept of perfect capital markets with low transactions costs and no restrictions on short sales.

Our argument in brief is as follows. There are two different approaches to the question of whether interest rate futures complete markets. The first, which is strictly algebraic, follows from the Arrow–Debreu tradition of counting securities and states of natures. This approach ignores transactions costs, questions of thickness or thinness of markets and all other institutional details; instead, it simply lists the number and kind of transactions that market institutions permit. It is not possible, following this approach, to differentiate among markets; whether a market exists is a simple 'yes' or 'no' question. If we take this approach to the question of whether interest rate futures markets increase the trading opportunities available to market participants we find two things. First, forward markets in bonds do not add to the set of markets available to traders in an economy in which bonds of every maturity are traded. Second, because they are marked to market, interest rate futures contracts have slightly different algebraic properties than do forward contracts. Thus they do create markets that are not implicit in the term structure of interest rates. We doubt that the additional securities that futures markets create are of any practical significance.

There is another, less theoretical, approach to the question of whether interest rate futures markets add to the trading opportunities available to the participants in an economy. In this approach one asks how easy it is to make transactions. Instead of counting equations and unknowns, one counts potential market participants, and measures transactions costs. From this more practical point of view, interest rate futures contracts are superior to forward markets because they encourage participation of more traders. They have lower transactions costs and can more easily accommodate trades between strangers. Thus the development of interest rate futures has made the markets on which traders can speculate on and hedge against short-run movements in the interest rate more nearly perfect markets. In this sense, interest rate futures contracts have created or completed markets.

Let $P(t, T)$ be the price at time t of a pure discount bond paying \$1 at time T. Then, as T varies, $P(t, T)$ traces out the term structure of interest rates prevailing at time t. We focus on pure discount bonds because a coupon bond is a portfolio of discount bonds and almost everything we have to say about individual bonds generalizes to portfolios of bonds. A forward transaction is an agreement to deliver a commodity on a specified date (the execution date) at an agreed-upon price. While all the particulars of the transaction may be spelled out prior to the execution date, nothing – neither money nor goods – actually changes hands until the execution date. Forward contracts in bonds involve the delivery of (portfolios of) discount bonds. Thus the only important forward prices are $P(s, T; t)$, which are the price (agreed to at time t) at which a discount bond paying $1 at time T will be sold at time s. For this definition to make sense, we must have $t \leqslant s \leqslant T$. It is easy to show that forward prices are completely determined by the term structure, or that

$$P(t, T) = P(t, s)\, P(s, T; t) \qquad (1)$$

so that

$$P(s, T; t) = P(t, T)/P(t, s).$$

To see that (1) must hold, simply note that the left-hand side of (1) is the cost at time t of a discount bond paying $1 at time T. The right-hand side of (1) is also the cost of $1 at time T. If one makes a forward contract to buy discount bonds paying off at time T for the price $P(s, T; t)$ one will need to have $\$P(s, T; t)$ at time s. But, the cost at time t of $\$P(s, T; t)$ is just $\$P(t, s)\, P(s, T; t)$. Thus, forward market prices are completely determined by the term structure; forward transactions create no securities that are not present when bonds of all maturities are traded.

Futures markets, because of their 'mark-to-market' feature, do create securities that are not available to traders who deal only in bonds of varying maturities. We illustrate this with a simple example (which will also explain how futures contracts are marked to market). The example further illustrates that, while futures markets add securities, they do not create complete markets.

Consider an economy that lasts four periods, denoted 0, 1, 2 and 3. Markets in this economy are open at dates 0, 1 and 2. There is a single good which can be consumed only at date 3. Units of the good grow between market dates. A unit stored in period 0 produces $\mathbf{a}$ units in period 1. The growth factor between periods 1 and 2 and between periods 2 and 3 is random. A unit of the good invested in period 1 will produce $\mathbf{b}_i$ units of output in period 2, and a unit invested in period 2 will produce $\mathbf{c}_i$ units of output in period 3 (which are then consumed). Since there is no consumption until period 3, each unit of period 0 goods will produce $\mathbf{a}\mathbf{b}_i\mathbf{c}_i$ units of period 3 consumption. We suppose that the value of the random variable i is revealed to all market participants after the market in period 0 has closed and before the market in period 1 has opened. The random variable i can take on I distinct values, where I is a large integer. Consider first how this market operates when there are forward markets or, equivalently, when bonds of all maturities are marketed. In period 0 individuals buy and sell rights to the (uncontingent) delivery of securities in periods 1, 2 and 3. Thus a trader in period 1 will have a portfolio of W_{11} units of period 1 output, W_{12} units of period 2 output and W_{13} units of period 3 output. Since uncertainty is resolved by the time period 1's market meets, there is no point in any further trading. This portfolio will yield

$$W_{11}\mathbf{b}_i\mathbf{c}_i + W_{12}\mathbf{c}_i + W_{13}$$

units of consumption in period 3. When purchased in period 0, this portfolio entitles its owner to a random variable which we denote

$$W_{11}\mathbf{bc} + W_{12}\mathbf{c} + W_{13}\mathbf{e} \tag{2}$$

where $\mathbf{bc}$ is a vector whose ith component is $\mathbf{b}_i\mathbf{c}_i$, and $\mathbf{e}$ is a vector of ones. Of course, the ith component of a vector denotes consumption in state i. If $P(0, 1)$, $P(0, 2)$ and $P(0, 3)$ are prices of discount bonds of varying maturity, then the investor can choose for his consumption any vector of the form (2), where W_{11}, W_{12} and W_{13} satisfy the budget constraint

$$W_0 = W_{11}P(0, 1) + W_{12}P(0, 2) + W_{13}P(0, 3). \tag{3}$$

Thus the consumption set available to an investor is (a translate of) a low-dimensional subspace of R^I.[1] If $\mathbf{bc}$, $\mathbf{c}$ and $\mathbf{e}$ are linearly independent, then it is of dimension 3. If I is large, forward markets do not provide complete contingent claims.

For our analysis of futures markets it is useful to note that, once the random variable i is revealed, the prices of all discount bonds issued in period 1 are established. A unit of period 1 output will produce $\mathbf{b}_i\mathbf{c}_i$ units of period 3 output. Thus, a discount bond paying off one unit in period 3 can be had for $(\mathbf{b}_i\mathbf{c}_i)^{-1}$ units of period 1 output, or

$$P_i(1, 3) = \mathbf{b}_i\mathbf{c}_i{}^{-1}. \tag{4}$$

Similarly, in period 2, a unit of input will produce $\mathbf{c}_i$ units of period 3 consumption, so that

$$P_i(2, 3) = (\mathbf{c}_i)^{-1}. \tag{5}$$

An arbitrage argument shows that

$$P_i(1, 3) = P_i(1, 2)\, P_i(2, 3)$$

so

$$P_i(1, 2) = P_i(1, 3)/P_i(2, 3)$$

or

$$P_i(1, 2) = \mathrm{b_i}^{-1}. \tag{6}$$

We now consider how this economy operates with a futures market. In this economy, the only possible futures market can be for one-period discount bonds issued in period 2. A trader participates in the futures market by agreeing to buy in time 2 a fixed number, N, of one-period bonds at a fixed price, F_0. At period 1 the contract is marked to market, which means that, if the market price in period 1 for one-period bonds delivered in period 2 is F_1, then the buyer of bonds pays to (or collects from) the futures market the amount he has made or lost on his future contracts. If the price has risen ($F_1 > F_0$), he collects $F_1 - F_0$ for each bond he has purchased. If the price has fallen ($F_0 > F_1$), he pays $F_0 - F_1$ to the market for each bond he has purchased. In our example, the price of period 3 bonds in period 2 will be known at the end of period 1; it will be (as observed in (5) above)

$$P_i(2, 3) = \mathrm{c_i}^{-1}.$$

Furthermore, in our example the marking to market that occurs in period 1 is the only consequence of buying a futures contract. For when period 2 arrives the trader has the right (and the duty) to buy N units of period 3 consumption at F_1. However, since $F_1 = p_i(2, 3)$, the present market price, this contract is worth precisely nothing. Thus the only effect of entering into futures contract in period 0 is to increase one's holdings of period 1 output in period 1 from W_{11} to $W_{11} + N(F_1 - F_0)$. Thus the person who buys W_{11}, W_{12} and W_{13} units of consumption in periods 1, 2 and 3 and sells N futures contracts at price F_0 will have a portfolio of

$$[W_{11} + N(F_1 - F_0)]\,\mathbf{bc} + W_{12}\mathbf{c} + W_{13}\mathbf{e} = (W_{11} - NF_0)\,\mathbf{bc} + W_{12}\mathbf{c} + W_{13}\mathbf{e} + N\mathbf{b}. \tag{7}$$

The values W_{11}, W_{12} and W_{13} are restricted by the budget constraint (3), while N is unconstrained. We see that, in contrast to (2), (7) is (a translate of) a four-dimensional subspace of R^I. Thus, futures markets, in contrast to forward markets, create new securities; traders in an economy with interest rate futures have opportunities not available to traders who can deal only in bonds of different maturities.

However, this difference between futures and forward markets should not be overstressed. Markets with futures are still incomplete.

In our example, futures markets add but a single security when many are needed to complete markets. Although this example is quite special, we believe that the conclusion holds generally. Cornell and Reinganum (1981) have presented evidence that suggests that futures and forward prices are very similar; it seems unlikely that futures and forward contracts could create vastly different hedging opportunities if their prices were so similar. Thus it seems reasonable, at least as a first approximation, to treat markets in interest rate futures as if they were forward markets; in the next section we analyse interest rate futures markets as if they were simply markets for bonds of various maturities.

While markets in interest rate futures do not, at least to any important extent, create trading opportunities not available to those who trade in bonds of various maturities, the futures market much more closely approximates the economist's concept of a perfect market than does either the spot market in bonds of various maturities or the forward market.[2] Consider first how a trader would use the spot market to arrange to sell a discount bond paying $1 in period s at price

$$P(s, T; t) = P(t, T)/P(t, s).$$

First, the trader would sell a T-period discount bond for price $P(t, T)$ and use the proceeds to buy $P(t, T)/P(t, s)$ s-period discount bonds. In period s he would have $P(t, T)/P(t, s) = P(s, T; t)$ in cash. To close out his position he would have to buy a T-period bond at the current price, $P(s, T)$. His net gain or loss from these transactions would be

$$P(t, s) - P(s, T; t),$$

just as if he had sold a T-period bond in t for delivery in s at price $P(s, T; t)$.

Using the spot market in this way to mimic the forward market is difficult. Three spot transactions are required where one forward transaction will do. Furthermore, to complete the spot transaction the trader must either issue his own T-period discount bond or have one on hand before he initiates the transaction. Thus he must either have a particular asset position prior to beginning the trade or find someone to trust him. Either requirement considerably limits participation in the market.

Using forward markets rather than spot markets lowers transactions costs (as one rather than three trades are required). However, the difficulties of credit and trust remain. The forward market in bonds is primarily a market for private placements. If I wish to buy or sell bonds forward, I have to find someone who wants to take the other side of the transaction. Furthermore, we have to trust each other to carry out the transaction we have agreed to. This means we have to know something about each other's character and about each other's liquidity.

Organized futures markets avoid these problems by interposing the market on one side of every transaction, by imposing margin requirements, and by marking contracts to market. (These last two procedures guarantee that a trader will always be able to fulfil the terms of the contract he has made; if his margin account is insufficient, the exchange will close his contract out.) Anyone who can put up the necessary margin can participate in the futures market. Furthermore, transactions costs on organized futures markets are generally quite low (relative to the transactions costs on the corresponding spot markets).[3] These advantages come at cost. While thousands of different bonds are traded on organized exchanges, futures markets exist for only a few interest rate instruments. However, active futures markets are more liquid and more perfect markets than are the spot or forward markets in bonds.

3 Effects of interest rate uncertainty on the investment supply schedule

In this section we analyse the effect of interest rate uncertainty on the investment supply schedule. We build a simple model in which investment increases as interest rates become more uncertain. We also present an example where, as interest rates become more uncertain, the interest elasticity of investment may decrease.

Consider a one-commodity economy which has available to it a number of investment projects. In such an economy an investment project is nothing more than a sequence of inputs and outputs. In a certain world with perfect capital markets an investment project will be undertaken if, and only if, its discounted present value (using the market rates of interest) is positive. That is, an investment project available at time t can be described by a vector

$$\mathbf{Y} = [Y(t), Y(t+1), \ldots, Y(T)]$$

where $Y(s) > 0$ is an output and $Y(s) < 0$ is an input. The project $\mathbf{Y}$ will be undertaken if and only if

$$\sum_{s=t}^{T} Y(s)\, P(t, s) > 0$$

where, again, $P(t, s)$ is the price in time t of a discount bond paying \$1 in period s (or the present value of a dollar at time s). Interest rates, $P(t, s)$, determine which projects will be carried out. As $P(t, s)$ rises, a project with a net payout in period s becomes more profitable while a project that requires an input in period s becomes less profitable.

We want to examine the effect on investment of variability of interest rates. To do this it is useful to simplify our model and suppose that investment projects involve at most a two-period horizon. Thus we analyse only investment projects described by vectors $\mathbf{Y} \in R^3$. Potential investments require an initial investment of $Y(0) < 0$, and yield a payoff of $Y(2) \geqslant 0$ two periods later. The intermediate period may either require further investment ($Y(1) < 0$) or return a payoff ($Y(1) \geqslant 0$).

At time 0, when the initial investment is made, the first-period interest rate (determined by $P(0, 1)$) is known; the second-period short rate $P(1, 2)$ is a random variable. At first blush it would appear that interest rate uncertainty should have no effect on the adoption of an investment project. Since perfect markets for bonds of all maturities exist, a prospective investor can still apply the present value rule and undertake an investment project only if its present discounted value,

$$Y(0) + Y(1)\,P(0, 1) + Y(2)\,P(0, 2), \tag{8}$$

is positive. Thus unless uncertainty about future interest rates changes the level of current interest rates, uncertainty *per se* cannot alter the value of an investment project. This is, of course, an oversimplification. Uncertainty about future interest rates can alter the present value of discount bonds. We have neglected this effect.

While this reasoning is correct, it is incomplete, because it neglects an important aspect of sequential investment projects. They can at any time be discontinued. An investor may decide to discontinue a project that requires a positive investment in period 1 if it turns out that the short rate in period 1 is sufficiently high that completing the investment is unprofitable. That is, when time 1 arrives, the investor who has made an investment at time 0 has the right to invest $Y(1)$ and receive $Y(2)$ in period 2. This will be profitable if $Y(1) < Y(2)\,P(1, 2)$. However, if the short rate is sufficiently high, $P(1, 2) < Y(1)/Y(2)$, there is no point in completing the project. It is more profitable to invest in short-term bonds than to invest $Y(1)$ now to get $Y(2)$ next period. The investor who puts up $Y(0)$ in period 0 not only gets an investment project with a present value given by (8) (which he can realize immediately by using the bond market), but he also has a put option on future short-term bonds. In period 0, the investor buys $Y(0)$ units of current output and $Y(1)$ units of period 1 output, and sells $Y(2)$ units of period 2 output. When period 1 occurs he makes arrangements to deliver period 2 output by either investing $Y(1)$ in the production process or investing $Y(2)\,P(1,\,2)$ in short-period bonds, whichever is cheaper. If $Y(1) < Y(2)\,P(1,\,2)$, then he will keep the excess as a profit (for he has already arranged to have $Y(1)$ delivered in period 2). Thus his period 1 profits are

$$\max\,[Y(1)-Y(2)\,P(1,\,2),\,0] = Y(2)\max\,[Y(1)/Y(2)-P(1,\,2),\,0],$$

which is the value of a put option, the right to sell $Y(2)$ one-period discount bonds at price $Y(1)/Y(2)$. The value of the investment to a risk-neutral investor at time 0 is its expected present discounted value,

$$P(0,\,1)\,Y(2)\,E_0\max\{[Y(1)/Y(2)]-P(1,\,2),\,0\}.$$

The quantity $E_t z$ is the expectation of the random variable z where the expectation is made on the basis of information available at time t. Since $\max\,[Y(1)/Y(2)-P(1,\,2),\,0]$ is a convex function of the random variable $P(1,\,2)$, increased interest rate uncertainty increases the value of the investment.

We now present an extended example which will allow us to analyse the effect of increased interest rate uncertainty on the supply of investment. The example makes the point that increased uncertainty is likely to make the investor supply schedule less interest-elastic.

Before we begin the analysis, we must introduce some notation and some concepts. Let

z = spot one-period discount factor,
$Q(z)$ = spot two-period discount factor, and
$F(s;z)$ = probability that next period's one-period discount factor is less than or equal to s, given this period's discount factor is equal to z.

In terms of our old notation, $z = P(0,\,1)$, $Q(z) = P(0,\,2)$ and

$$\int s\,dF(s;z) = E_0[P(1,\,2)].$$

We have implicitly assumed that the discount factor follows a Markov process.

We now consider two interesting special cases. If

$$Q(z) = z^2, \tag{9}$$

then the term structure is flat. If, in addition, the local expectations hypothesis (Cox *et al.*, 1981a) holds, $P(0, 2) = P(0, 1)\,E_0[P(1, 2)]$, so that

$$E_0[P(1, 2)] = z \tag{10}$$

and the discount factor is a martingale.[4] If the one-period discount factor is an identically and independently distributed random variable with mean μ, and the local expectations hypothesis holds, then

$$Q(z) = z\mu \tag{11}$$

and

$$F(s; z) = F(s). \tag{12}$$

We will assume that increases in this period's discount factor make increases in next period's discount factor more likely, in the sense that $z > z'$ implies $F(s; z')$ stochastically dominates $F(s; z)$. That is, if $u(\ )$ is an increasing function, then

$$\int_0^\infty u(s)\,dF(s; z) \geqslant \int_0^\infty u(s)\,dF(s; z'). \tag{13}$$

An investment project is defined by its input and output requirements. All investment projects are assumed to produce 1 unit of output in period 2. Given this normalization we can describe an investment project that has no option value by two numbers x and b. An (x, b) investment project requires an investment of x in period 1 and returns bx in period 1 and 1 in period 2. In the sequel we will in general fix the coefficient b and vary x. We call all investment projects with b fixed, type b investments. The present value of such a project is

$$G(x, z; b) = -x + zbx + Q(z). \tag{14}$$

We will assume that $bz < 1$ so that $G_x < 0$. Thus the value of type b investment projects decreases as x increases. We complete our specification of the technology by writing for each b a schedule:

$J(X; b)$ = the number of investment projects of type b for which the first period input x is less than or equal to X. (15)

The assumptions we have made imply that, when the discount factor is z, the amount of investment in type b projects will be $J[x^*(z), b]$ where $x^*(z)$ is the marginally profitable project of type b. That is, $x^*(z)$ satisfies

$$G[x^*(z), z] = 0. \tag{16}$$

Assuming for the moment that there is only one kind of investment project, the responsiveness of investments to changes in the discount factor is given in elasticity form by

$$\eta_b = \eta_J \cdot \eta_{x^*_b}, \tag{17}$$

where η_b is the elasticity of type b investment with respect to changes in z;

$$\eta_J = J_x[x^*(z); b]\, x^*(z)/J[y^*(z); a],$$

is the elasticity of the supply of investment projects; and

$$\eta_{x^*_b} = \frac{dx^*(z)}{dz} \frac{z}{x^*(z)}$$

is the elasticity of the marginal investment project (of type b) with respect to the interest rate. It is easy to calculate that

$$\eta_{x^*_b} = \frac{zby}{Q(z)} + \frac{Q'(z)z}{Q(z)}. \tag{18}$$

For investments with an option value, the elasticity is a bit more complicated to calculate. Again, an investment can be described by two numbers, y and a. A typical investment requires inputs of y and ay in periods 0 and 1 and returns 1 unit of output in period 2. The input in the second period, ay, is optional. It will not be made if interest rates are too high. The value of such an investment is

$$M(y, z; a) = -y - zay + Q(z) + z\int_0^{ay} (ay - s)\, dF(s; z). \tag{19}$$

The last term reflects the option value of the investment.

Clearly, in this case, as y increases, the value of a project decreases. Thus, if

$$K(Y; a) = \text{the number of investment projects of type } a \text{ for which the first period input } y \text{ is less than or equal to } Y, \tag{20}$$

then the number of investment projects of type a that will be made when the discount factor is z is $K[y^*(z), a]$ where $y^*(a)$ is the solution to

$$M[y^*(z), z; a] = 0. \tag{21}$$

The elasticity of investment projects of type a with respect to the discount factor is then

$$\eta_a = \eta_K \cdot \eta_{y^*_a} \tag{22}$$

where

$$\eta_K = K_y [y^*(z), a]\, y^*(z)/K[y^*(z), a]$$

and

$$\eta_{y^*_a} = \frac{dy^*(z)}{dz} \frac{z}{y^*(z)}.$$

It is straightforward to calculate that

$$\eta_{y^*_a} = \left[Q'(z) - \int_0^{ay} s\, dF(s;z) - ay \int_{ay}^{\infty} dF(s;z) + z \frac{\int_0^{ay} (ay-s)\, dF(s;z)}{\partial z} \right] \div \left\{ [Q(z)/z] - \int_0^{ay} s\, dF(s;z) \right\}. \tag{23}$$

Since the last term in the numerator of (23) can be written

$$z \frac{\left[\partial \int_0^{\infty} \max(ay - s, 0)\, dF(s;z)\right]}{\partial z},$$

it is negative by (13). Thus

$$\eta_{y^*_a} \leqslant \frac{Q'(z) - \int_0^{ay} s\, dF(s;z) - ay \int_{ay}^{\infty} dF(s;z)}{[Q(z)/z] - \int_0^{ay} s\, dF(s;z)}.$$

It is tedious but straightforward to calculate that, if

$$F(ay^*; z) \leqslant Q(z)/Q'(z)\, z, \tag{24}$$

then

$$\eta_{y^*_a} \leqslant Q'(z)\,z/Q(z). \tag{25}$$

The condition (24) is not a very stringent one. $F(ay)$ is the probability that the marginal investment project of type a will be cancelled. If the term structure is flat, $Q(z)=z^2$ and $Q(z)/Q'(z)z=\frac{1}{2}$. If the discount factor is an independently and identically distributed random variable and the local expectations hypothesis holds, then $Q(z)=z\mu$ and $Q(z)/Q'(z)z=1$. We suspect most reasonable cases will put $Q(z)/Q'(z)z$ between $\frac{1}{2}$ and 1. We note for future reference that, if $\frac{1}{2}\leqslant Q(z)/Q'(z)z\leqslant 1$, then

$$2\geqslant Q'(z)\,z/Q(z)\geqslant 1 \tag{26}$$

so that (18) implies that $\eta_{x^*_b}\geqslant 1$.

We have analysed the elasticity of new investments with and without option value. The other kind of investment is completion investment. If last period the marginal investment of type a was $\hat{y}$, and this period's discount factor is z, then this investment will be completed if any $ay\geqslant z$. Thus completion investment of type a is

$$aK[\min\,(z/a,\hat{y}),a]$$

and the elasticity of completion investment of type a is

$$\eta_a^c=\begin{cases}\eta_K & \text{if } z<\hat{y}/a\\ 0 & \text{if } z\geqslant\hat{y}/a.\end{cases} \tag{27}$$

We can now use these calculations of elasticities to calculate the effect of increases in interest rate variability on the investment supply schedule. Net investment in a period has three components: new investment in projects with no option value; new investments in projects with an option value; and completion of investment projects with an option value that were started last period. The elasticity of the entire investment supply schedule is a weighted average of the elasticities of each of these schedules. We saw in equation (17) that the elasticity of new investment projects without option value was the product of a term η_J, reflecting the availability of investment projects and a term, $\eta_{x^*_b}$, reflecting the sensitivity of the marginal investment project to changes in the discount factor. Similarly, (22) shows that elasticity of new investment projects with option value is the product of a term reflecting the availability of investment projects, η_K, and a term $\eta_{y^*_a}$ reflecting the sensitivity of the marginal investment project to changes in the discount factor. We also saw from (18) and (25) that, under weak assumptions,

$$\eta_{x^*_b} \geqslant \eta_{y^*_a}. \tag{28}$$

Furthermore, (27) shows that the elasticity of completion investment is just η_K times 0 or 1. We have argued that $\eta_{x^*_b} \geqslant zQ'(z)/Q(z)$ and that $zQ'(z)/Q(z)$ is probably between 1 and 2. Thus, unless the availability of investment projects with option value is very different from the availability of investment projects without option value, the supply of projects without option value is likely to be more elastic than the supply of projects with option value, and more elastic than the supply of completion investment. For the special case, $\eta_J = \eta_K = \gamma$, a constant for all values of a and b, this conclusion clearly follows.

We argued in the first part of this section that increases in interest rate variability will increase the supply of investment with an option value relative to the supply of investment without an option value. Since both completion investment and new investment with an option value are less elastic than new investment without an option value, the result will probably be that increases in the variability of interest rates will make the aggregate investment schedule less interest-elastic.

This example is meant to be suggestive rather than compelling. It is quite special, and other parameterizations could lead to the opposite conclusion.[5] Still, we believe the result is sensible. As interest rates become more variable and changes in interest rates become more likely, investors purchase insurance that makes them less responsive to particular changes in interest rates.

Notes

1 Here and in the sequel we ignore non-negativity restrictions, which add nothing to the argument.

2 We are grateful to Dwight Jaffee for pointing out to us that there is more to market efficiency than is dreamt of in textbooks of linear algebra.

3 See Arak and McCuroy (1979/80) for a discussion of transaction costs and margin requirements on futures markets and for a comparison of organized futures markets with more personalized and idiosyncratic forward markets.

4 Since the discount factor is bounded below, the Martingale convergence theorem implies these two assumptions cannot continue to hold: if they did, the discount factor would converge or grow without limit.

5 One particularly strong assumption we have made is that all investments that require inputs in period 2 may be discontinued. If instead we permit *b* to be negative – which amounts to recognizing that some investments cannot be cancelled – then the conclusion that increases in interest rate variability decrease the elasticity of the investment demand schedule requires much stronger assumptions.

We are grateful to Dwight Jaffee and Steve Ross for helpful discussion and to the National Science Foundation for research support. This paper was written while Rothschild held the Oskar Morgenstern Distinguished Fellowship at Mathematica, Inc.

References

Arak, M. and McCuroy, C. J. (1979/80), 'Interest Rate Futures', *Federal Reserve Bank of New York, Quarterly Review*, winter.

Bernake, B. S. (1983), 'Irreversibility, Uncertainty, and Cyclical Investment', *Quarterly Journal of Economics*, 97

Cornell, B. and Reinganum, M. (1981), 'Forward and Future Prices: Evidence from the Foreign Exchange Markets', *Journal of Finance*, 36.

Cox, J. C., Ingersoll, J. E. Jr and Ross, S. A. (1981a), 'A Re-examination of Traditional Hypotheses About the Term Structure of Interest Rates', *Journal of Finance*, 36.

Cox, J. C., Ingersoll, J. E. Jr and Ross, S. A. (1981b), 'The Relation between Forward Prices and Future Prices', Working Paper Series, *Journal of Financial Economics*, 9.

Radner, R. (1978), Competitive Equilibrium under Uncertainty', *Econometrica*, 36.

Radner, R. (1982), 'Equilibrium Under Uncertainty', in K. F. Arrow and M. D. Intriligator (eds), *Handbook of Mathematical Economics*, vol. II, Amsterdam.

Townsend, R. A. (1978), 'On the Optimality of Forward Markets', *American Economic Review*, 68.

6

The Informational Role of Futures Markets: Some Experimental Evidence

DANIEL FRIEDMAN, GLENN W. HARRISON and
JON W. SALMON

1 Introduction

We have recently undertaken a series of experiments that examine the behaviour of futures markets. We are particularly concerned with the informational role of futures prices in allowing traders to achieve efficient outcomes, and with the implicit learning process that takes place in such markets. In the present paper we lay out our basic approach and present the results of our first set of experiments.

Generally speaking, our experiments so far confirm the belief that the existence of active futures markets promotes a more efficient operation of spot markets. We find that prices tend to converge to more informationally efficient equilibria when futures markets operate and when traders are experienced (hypotheses H1–H7 of section 4). We also find that spot prices tend to be less volatile under these circumstances (H9, H10 and H12). The significance of learning behaviour, both within and across market experiments, is evident in our results (H11). The informational content of futures prices appears to have a systematic effect in shifting spot prices (H8). On the other hand, our results do not confirm the value of futures markets in helping traders to achieve more efficient allocations of assets (H13 and H14). The observed combination of price efficiency and allocational inefficiency points up the inadequacy of traditional theoretical ('Walrasian') approaches to equilibrium (see discussions in section 3 and at the end of section 4).

The paper is organized as follows. In the next section we review the salient features of experimental methodology in economics as it has emerged in recent years. We then describe the design of our current experiments.

In section 3 we extract a few basic concepts from the theoretical literature on asset markets, and provide a detailed numerical example to familiarize the reader with the operation of our experimental markets. We then derive theoretically the equilibrium properties of our experimental markets. From the theory presented we isolate a number of testable hypotheses.

In section 4 we present our experimental data descriptively and then test our hypotheses. In the final section we describe our agenda for further work in experimental futures markets.

2 Experimental design

2.1 Established experimental methodology

Experimental auction markets involve recruited subjects who are induced (by means of controlled market trading schedules and standard incentive structures) to display real-time market behaviour. Experimental control of market conditions (the 'treatment variables') allows one to design groups of such experiments to gauge the effects of those variables on observed behaviour (e.g., the strength of equilibrium tendencies, the efficiency of market outcomes and the variability of price movements). Each of the hypotheses to be studied involves the specification of well-defined, and hence replicable, sets of trading rules, informational imperfections and other institutional features.

The first methodological point to note is that the experimental method does provide evidence on 'real-world' markets. The fact that these experiments typically involve small numbers of traders, that we deal with homogeneous commodities, and that the experimenter can control the notional trading schedules does not render these markets irrelevant. They are indeed special, but so are the institutional realities of most organized exchanges. The main point, however, is the purpose for which our markets have been conducted: to provide evidence on general theories. If a theory or economic principle is general it should cover special cases.

The second methodological point follows from the first: if we cannot confirm or reject general theories in the context of controlled environments designed for the purpose of testing the theory, then the theory cannot be regarded as operational in any useful respect. Moreover, it is often difficult to 'control' for all conceivably relevant influences on market behaviour with econometric methods and actual market data; see Leamer (1978) for a comprehensive statement of the methodological weaknesses of standard econometric method here.

A final methodological point relates more particularly to our use of the experimental technique to analyse the role of information in market behaviour. One common difficulty in analytic models of the informational aspects of markets is the precise definition of 'the information sets' of traders. Our experiments allow very detailed knowledge of that set – for instance, the ability to control which traders know what information.[1]

Since the pioneering work of Vernon Smith (1962), applications of experimental methodology have grown quite rapidly, but such studies of asset markets have emerged only recently and can be quickly enumerated. In the tradition of Samuelson's (1957) intertemporal pricing model, Miller, Plott and Smith (1977), using a two-period stock–flow market model, experimentally examined the effect of carry-over decisions on equilibrium inter-temporal price determination. The implied operational definition of speculation was limited to agents' potential inventory responses to perceived and repetitively stationary 'seasonal' differences in market supply and demand conditions. In the absence of 'event' risk – risk arising from uncertainty as to which state of supply/demand will occur next period – the type of speculative behaviour analysed by Miller, Plott and Smith might be called non-informative speculation.[2] The only datum that the agents are required to learn about is the future period market-clearing price that affects current and future excess demand decisions. Williams (1979) and Plott and Uhl (1981) essentially replicate this experimental design. Plott and Agha (1982) extend this institutional arrangement to consider random variations in future demand valuations according to some probabilistic rule about which agents had some prior knowledge.

The study that most closely resembles our own is Forsythe, Palfrey and Plott (1982a; hereafter FPP(a)). FPP(a) are concerned with inventory decisions and equilibrium price search. In particular, they address the following questions:

(a) Do asset prices and inventories exhibit systematic temporal characteristics relative to the underlying market parameters?
(b) Which of several competing hypotheses concerning the nature of

asset price determination does the experimental data evidence favour?

FPP(a) are particularly concerned with the extent to which the formation of market-clearing prices aggregates agents' diverse stock demand preferences. Although FPP(a) is the first experimental study to model trading rules and induced stock demand valuations that reflect some of the salient aspects of organized futures markets, their futures market design was an incidental feature of their paper – an 'institutional perturbation' designed to check on the robustness of the striking results generated by their spot market experiments.

Forsythe, Palfrey and Plott (1982b; hereafter FPP(b)) extended their earlier study in two respects. They adopted a pay-out structure that was 'time-interdependent', in the sense that agents could not simply add their earnings from each trading period together to compute their earnings for the entire market experiment.[3] The other extension was to study the informational role of futures markets in sequential asset markets more systematically than was done in FPP(a). Nine experiments were conducted: five included a futures market and four did not. FPP(b) are primarily concerned with the joint variable of the 'experience and the presence of an active futures market'. Their control or benchmark experiments (nos. 1, 3, 6 and 8) employed inexperienced subjects in a sequential spot market coupled with an active futures market. Their comparison experiments (nos. 2, 4, 7 and 9) employed experienced subjects in a sequential spot market without the presence of a futures market.[4] FPP(b) intentionally designed their treatment variable in this manner in order to provide a strong test of the proposition that sequential spot markets converge more rapidly to an informationally efficient equilibrium when futures markets are present.[5] We are particularly concerned in the present study to isolate the separate roles of 'experience' and 'futures markets'.

Thus a primary purpose of our paper is to generalize the FPP(a, b) experimental design of futures markets. In doing this we are able to:

(a) check the robustness of the FPP(a, b) futures market experiments;
(b) provide additional evidence on market-clearing prices as aggregators of privately held information;[6]
(c) provide a more refined characterization of possible price/information equilibria; and
(d) lay the foundation for further experiments designed to analyse

the impact of event uncertainty and informational asymmetries on futures market trading performance.

2.2 Design of current experiments

The participants in our market experiments (referrred to as 'traders') were recruited primarily from MBA (Master in Business Administration) classes at the UCLA Graduate School of Management – as likely a habitat for '*Homo economous*' as we could think of. After distributing and reviewing the instruction sheets,[7] we conducted double oral auction markets. Our traders could announce bid and offer prices and accept the bids or offers of others (provided they did not violate any budget constraint, as discussed below). Transacted prices were publicly recorded. The assets traded were called 'certificates'; they yielded cash returns, called 'dividends', to traders who possessed them at the end of each trading period.

Each experiment consisted of a series of 'market years', which can be thought of as Hicksian weeks. Within each market year there were three trading periods, referred to as periods A, B and C. Each trading period lasted for five minutes (real time) and each trader could buy or sell one certificate at a time. Lot sales and short sales were prohibited and cash balances were required to be non-negative. At the beginning of each market year each trader was endowed with two certificates and a loan of $20 cash on hand, sufficiently large that the implied liquidity constraint was never an impediment to trade.

Incentives for exchange among traders were provided by varying the per certificate dividends across individuals as well as across periods. There were three trader types, with individuals randomly assigned to each group; table 1 provides details of the parameterizations for each experiment. The underlying period-specific certificate returns were identical across market years – identical in the aggregate and for each individual.[8] Thus the markets were repetitively stationary from year to year. Note that traders were not informed of this stationarity: they had to learn about it in 'real time'. Each individual was carefully monitored so that his/her private dividend profile was not observed by any other trader. Possibilities for explicit or implicit collusion were effectively nil.

To motivate the experimental setup, one can think of the traders as grain merchants trading in warehouse certificates that have a par value of zero but provide each trader with a finite time profile of convenience yields. Of course, in our experiments traders actually

Table 1 Induced experimental market parameters*

Experiment	Market institution	Agents Type	Agents ID no.	Dividend profile A	Dividend profile B	Dividend profile C
				$	$	$
1	Pure stock	I	2, 4, 9	0.40	0.15	0.25
	No futures	II	3, 6, 8	0.30	0.45	0.40
	Inexperienced	III	1, 5, 7	0.10	0.30	0.60
2	Pure stock	I	1, 3, 6	0.40	0.25	0.15
	Futures	II	4, 7, 9	0.25	0.30	0.60
	Inexperienced	III	2, 5, 8	0.10	0.45	0.40
3	Pure stock	I	1, 3, 6	0.45	0.45	0.45
	No futures	II	4, 7, 9	0.70	0.30	0.10
	Experienced	III	2, 5, 8	0.10	0.30	0.70
4	Pure stock	I	5, 7, 9	0.75	0.20	0.10
	Futures	II	1, 3, 6	0.40	0.45	0.45
	Experienced	III	2, 4, 8	0.15	0.30	0.80

* In year 5 of experiment 4 a random re-assignment of agents to trader type occurred; investor type I consisted of agents 1, 3 and 5; type II of agents 4, 6 and 8; and type III of agents 2, 7 and 9. The parameters shown here pertain to all other market years.

received a cash 'dividend' for each certificate held at the end of each trading period, and the certificates expired after the market year ended.

In experiments 1 and 3 trading consisted of an immediate exchange of cash for certificates at accepted bid or offer prices (i.e. spot transactions only). In experiments 2 and 4 we permitted futures transactions as well. The futures contract consisted of the delivery of a certificate in period C, and futures contracts as well as spot contracts could be written in both period A and period B. In periods A and B dividends were paid as usual for each certificate held at the end of that period. No transactions were allowed in period C in experiments 2 and 4, but deliveries previously contracted for were performed. An individual with a net long (short) futures position was required to take (make) delivery of the certificates, and then period C dividends were distributed. A natural interpretation of period C is that it corresponds to the day after the last trading day in the delivery month of a futures contract. Note that an agent had ample opportunity to offset futures positions during periods A and B, so offset procedures were fully operational in our design. However, because of the restriction on short sales, agents' short positions were limited to the quantity of inventoried spot certificates at any point in time. For a given net short position an agent's spot sales were also constrained. Subject to this limitation, discretionary hedging positions were allowed.

In all experiments traders were given a small trading commission of 1 cent per transaction. Such commissions are a standard feature of most experimental market studies; the usual rationale for their inclusion is to overcome subjective transaction costs, which might be especially relevant when transacted prices are very close to a market-clearing price. At the end of each experiment we paid our traders in cash for all profiles accrued from dividends and trading.

Our experimental design differs from FPP(a) in four respects. First, they had only two trading periods per market year. We included a third period, largely to create richer strategic opportunities and to provide greater flexibility in designing later experiments. Second, we employed trader experience as a treatment variable as part of our concern with learning behaviour; FPP(a) did not do so.[9] Third, FPP(a) expressed their dividend schedules in terms of an arbitrary unit of account ('francs'); we used dollars and thus avoided what seems to us the needless complication (for traders) of converting francs to dollars. Finally, we followed the standard practice of employing small transactions commissions; FPP(a) did not. Overall, then, our designs are quite similar.

3 Information, equilibrium and futures markets

3.1 Previous literature: learning and information

In a real-time trading process such as that of our experiments, equilibrium can be achieved only as agents learn about their opportunities for gain through trade. In our experiments this learning can take place within each period as traders observe bids, offers and transactions (intra-period learning) – across periods and market years as traders observe trends in prices and the outcomes of their activities (inter-period learning), and across experiments as traders gain a better idea of what information is relevant and refine their strategies (experience). Traders presumably base their bids, offers and acceptances on some sort of reservation prices that they modify as they learn. We will not attempt to model this process formally here, despite its great theoretical and practical importance.[10] Instead, we will content ourselves with a brief review with comments on discussions of (mostly inter-period) learning in the experimental markets literature.

A crucial experimental design feature introduced in the classic paper by Smith (1962) – sequential replication – is fundamental to inter-period learning across market years. Discussing an early experimental market[11] that was closed after only one trading period, Smith (1962, p. 114) notes that:

There is therefore less opportunity for traders to gain experience and to modify their subsequent behaviour in the light of such experience. It is only through some learning mechanism of this kind that I can imagine the possibility of equilibrium being approached in any real market.

In the context of experimental asset markets similar to ours, FPP(a) examine Grossman's (1978) suggestion that sequential replication is necessary for convergence to a perfect foresight (or rational expectations) equilibrium. They note that:

In these markets investors enter in year one with no idea (or perhaps only a vague idea in the case of 'experienced' investors) of the market price and they learn more about it in each subsequent year. Specifically, in year one investors bring only their own private information to the market place. However, the perfect foresight equilibrium implicitly requires agents to possess information which they will normally receive by observing prices. Once prices are observed, the lack of information which previously impeded attainment of a perfect foresight equilibrium no longer exists. Due to this, one would expect the trading to begin at the naive equilibrium price and monotonically converge to the perfect foresight equilibrium price as trading publicizes information that originally was private. In the absence of a period B [in our case, period C – FHS], investors will be unable to incorporate period B price information in their period A decisions until after the first year of trading. [FPP(a), pp. 546–7]

FPP(a) call this their 'swingback' hypothesis. In our three-period asset market, information about period C must swing back to period B before in turn influencing period A prices. In short, there must be two such 'swingbacks' for period A prices to reflect the relevant private information pertaining to periods B and C.

Harrison *et al.* (1982) formally model the Bayesian learning behaviour of traders in a sequentially stationary and non-stationary double oral auction for a perishable commodity. Traders begin in period A with appropriately diffuse priors about market price, and choose in each succeeding period how much weight to attach to the belief that the market equilibrium has shifted 'fundamentally'. If traders behave as if searching and bidding for 'good' prices[12] from a fixed distribution in each period, then convergence in observed bids and offers follows a common public perception of the equilibrium price based on such learning behaviour.[13] The key to explaining convergence, then, is the increasing precision of this public (common) perception. In the present case of asset markets, this argument implies that the extent of any 'swingback' depends as much on the attainment of equilibrium prices (in period C), in the sense of absence of bias, as on the precision of that perceived equilibrium.

Our present focus, however, is more on information than on learning *per se*. In recent years, theorists have become increasingly interested in the informational rôle of prices in general and futures prices in particular (see, for instance, Grossman, 1977a, 1977b, 1978; Bray, 1981; and Grossman and Stiglitz, 1976, 1980).[14] The models employed in this literature are stochastic, and information typically takes the form of samples drawn from some normal distribution whose parameters affect the outcomes of agents' decisions. The models all employ a 'large' number of price-taking agents (or even a continuum of agents – in Hellwig, 1980). Hence one cannot directly apply the conclusions reached in this literature to our market experiments, in which the agents are permitted to set prices and are few in number, and in which (at least in the current round of experiments) the markets have no (exogenous) stochastic features. Nevertheless, our experiments involve dispersed personal information in the form of divided schedules, and prices do provide useful, perhaps even perfectly revealing, information to our agents. Therefore, the literature is suggestive and instructive as we proceed in the next few sections to frame appropriate concepts of equilibrium and to extract testable hypotheses.

3.2 An example

Before presenting a theoretical analysis of our experimental markets, an informal discussion of agents' behaviour, including numerical examples, may be in order. Consider the hypothetical divided profile and agent assignment shown in table 2. Consider the strategic opportunities available to (say) agent 9 in period C – the last trading period of a market year with spot trading only. Since he has a divided profile of type III, he will receive \$0.70 for each certificate he owns at the end of the period's trading, and the certificates have no further value to him or anyone else. Hence, \$0.70 represents his 'reservation price': he will profit by any purchases he can make at a lower price and sales at any higher price. Agent 9 has no direct knowledge of the reservation prices of other agents. He will soon discover, however,

Table 2 Hypothetical experimental market parameters

Experiment	*Market institution*	*Agents*		*Dividend profile*		
		Type	*ID no.*	*A*	*B*	*C*
				$	$	$
		I	1, 2, 3	0.45	0.45	0.45
Hypothetical		II	4, 5, 6	0.70	0.30	0.10
		III	7, 8, 9	0.10	0.30	0.70

that nobody can afford to outbid him, while he can't undersell anyone. Hence, he may find that, if he actively bids and aggressively accepts offers, he will acquire certificates at prices below his reservation price – but probably not much below and not for long. Agents 7 and 8 also have a reservation price of $0.70, so if either one of them notices that agent 9 is snapping up certificates at (say) $0.60, one or both are likely to begin to bid, say, $0.62 or $0.65, in an attempt to acquire the certificates. This process may be expected to raise the transacted price to $0.70 in fairly short order (recall the trading commission), as long as at least two of the type III traders actively attempt to buy up 'cheap' certificates. Evidently $0.70, the highest reservation price,[15] is the equilibrium price for period C, and the corresponding allocation involves all certificates being held by the type III agents. Presumably the most aggressive bidder among them gets the lion's share.

Let us now consider trading in the prior period B. At this point, agent 9 knows a certificate will yield him at least $0.30 (current dividend) + $0.70 (period C dividend) = $1.00, and possibly more if he were able to resell in the current period at a price above $1.00 or in period C at a price above $0.70. We are unable to determine his reservation price in this period without knowing his attitude to risk and the probabilities he assigns to these resale possibilities, but we do know that it is bounded below by his 'security level' of $1.00. Agent 1 is in a more interesting position: he has a lower security level ($0.45 + $0.45 = $0.90), but if he has seen this market operate for several market years he may become quite confident of his ability to resell in period C at $0.70. In this case his reservation price will be approximately $0.45 (current dividend) + $0.70 (resale value in period C) = $1.15, so he is likely, at least in later market years, to outbid agent 9 and the other type III agents. Once again, the price should be bid up to the highest reservation price among the agents of type I if the others (agents 2 and 3) also come to realize (either independently or through noticing agent 1's 'windfall profits') that certificates might be worth more than \$1.00 to them in period B. Consequently, the period B price should settle somewhere between \$1.00 (the highest security level) and \$1.15 (highest 'rational' reservation price), with the price rising towards the higher value as agents accumulate experience over the years. For closing prices in excess of \$1.00, all certificates should be held by type I traders.

Similar considerations apply to period A trading. The highest security level belongs to type I traders ($\$0.45 + \$0.45 + \$0.45 = \$1.35$), but if type II traders begin to anticipate the ability to resell in period B at a price approaching \$1.15, their reservation price would be near $\$0.70 + \$1.15 = \$1.85$, and, over the years, learning may allow the closing period A price to rise from \$1.35 to nearly this value.

Suppose now that the data in table 2 refer to an experiment in which futures trading *is* permitted, and consider the strategic possibilities available to agent 1 in period B. He personally would be willing to bid at most \$0.45 for futures contracts (i.e. period C delivery of certificates), but for reasons discussed above it seems likely that agents of type III will bid up the price of this contract to \$0.70. With a currently quoted futures price of \$0.70, agent 1 now has a security level for spot transactions of \$1.15, not \$0.90 as before: for each certificate he acquires he can still earn his current period dividend of \$0.45, while 'locking in' an additional \$0.70 return by selling a futures contract; he need not speculate, as was the case in the spot-only market, as to its future resale value. Hence a period B spot price of \$1.15 and a futures price of \$0.70 can arise from information directly available to the agents. Note that spot trading in period C would be redundant, given the operation of the futures market in prior periods.

The strategic opportunities in period A are quite rich. The opportunities discussed above still obtain, but the futures price provides additional information. Thus, if the futures price for period C delivery of certificates converges to \$0.70 in period A, then agents of type II will have a security level of \$1.70 ($\$0.70$ current dividends $+$ $\$0.30$ period B dividends $+$ $\$0.70$ proceeds from the futures transaction). Hence we may anticipate that these agents (together with type I agents) will more quickly bid up spot prices when the futures market is active.

3.3 *Equilibrium concepts*

We now proceed to formalize our experimental market model. For purposes of equilibrium analysis,[16] we may take time as discrete:

$t = 0, 1, 2, 3$, where 0 refers to the beginning of period A and 1, 2, 3 refer to the end of periods A, B and C respectively. The economy consists of agents $i = 1, \ldots, 9$, each characterized by his dividend schedule $D(i, t)$, $t = 1, 2, 3$, and by his initial endowment of certificates and money: $w(i) = [c(i, 0), m(i, 0)] = (2, \$20.00)$. We assume that i's preferences depend positively on year-end wealth $m(i, 3)$ and are independent of other variables.[17]

We define agent i's private information reservation price in period t as

$$R(i, t \mid PI) = \sum_{s=t}^{3} D(i, s),$$

the sum of his remaining per certificate dividend yields. Then the private information price is given by

$$P(t \mid PI) = \max_{i} R(i, t \mid PI).$$

This price never exceeds the perfect foresight price, given by

$$P(t \mid PF) = \sum_{s=t}^{3} \max_{i} D(i, s).$$

In the above numerical example and in experiment 3, $P(\,.\mid PI) = (\$1.35, \$1.00, \$0.70)$ while $P(\,.\mid PF) = (\$1.85, \$1.15, \$0.70)$. FPP(a), following Grossman (1978), refer to $P(t \mid PI)$ as the 'naive equilibrium price' and $P(t \mid PF)$ as the 'rational expectations equilibrium price'.

Note that there are really four 'goods' in this economy: certificates held at $t = 1$, 2 and 3, and money. Consider the case of complete markets (i.e. simultaneous trade in all three dated goods against money), which may be envisioned as a single round of trading in period A in spot and two futures contracts: a fictitious one for delivery in period B, as well as the period C contract we actually employed in some experiments. Consideration of this economy is suggested by the fictitious economy of full information mentioned in note 14 above. It provides a benchmark for efficiency considerations; although competitive equilibrium in virtually any economy is *ex ante* Pareto-efficient given informational constraints, these equilibria *ex post* will generally be less efficient than that of our complete markets economy, in the sense that further gains from trade would have been possible if agents had access to all information.

It is not hard to verify for our complete-markets economy that $P(\,.\mid PF)$ are the unique 'competitive equilibrium' (CE) prices, and that, in any corresponding allocation, $c(.,.)$, we have $c(j, t)=0$ unless $D(j, t)=\max D(i, t)$; i.e. in each period certificates are all held by traders of the type receiving the highest dividends in that period.

Another way of formalizing our market experiments, perhaps more appropriate in view of traders' ability to set prices ('price-searchers'), is as a game in either extensive or normal form. The complete-markets version in normal form may be regarded as a case of the market game in Dubey (1982), wherein agents' strategies consist of price–quantity pairs of both bids and offers. It appears that his theorem 1 applies, so we may conclude that the competitive equilibria in the previous paragraph coincide with 'active Nash equilibria' (ANE) of our fictitious complete-markets game. 'Active' for our purposes means that at least two agents of each type participate in exchange.[18]

However, our actual experiments do not employ complete markets. In the experiments without futures markets, agents must (at least implicitly) make forecasts of prices that will obtain in later periods. Let $R(i, t \mid f(i))$ be agent i's reservation price given his forecasts $f(i)$ of these prices and his risk preferences. A simple argument, illustrated in the previous subsection, shows that

$$P^*(t) = \max_i R(i, t \mid f(i))$$

where $P^*(.)$ are equilibrium prices, if agents of the same type have the same reservation prices, and that in any case

$$P^*(t) \geqslant P(t \mid PI).$$

If agents are so risk-averse and uncertain as to employ maximum strategies, then

$$P^*(t) = P(t \mid PI).$$

We refer to this case as the 'private information equilibrium'. Of course, no uncertainty remains in the last period, so things are more clear-cut:

$$P^*(3) = P(3 \mid PI) = P(3 \mid PF).$$

The corresponding allocations $c(.,.)$ should still satisfy $c(i, t) = 0$ if $R(i, t \mid f(i)) < P(t)$ in every case.

Without restrictions on agents' probabilistic beliefs or risk preferences, little more can be said about period 1 and 2 equilibrium prices and allocations. Under the extreme assumption of rational expectations, however, only the equilibria of the complete-markets economy remain; we refer to this case as the 'perfect foresight equilibrium'.

In our experiments with (period C) futures trading we can make somewhat sharper statements. Equilibrium (CE or ANE) prices are now determinate at $t=2$ (period B) as well as at $t=3$ (period C). The argument again was suggested in the numerical example, and we now make it explicit. Let $P(3, t)$ be the futures price, and define

$$R(i, t \mid MI) = \sum_{s=t}^{2} D(i, s) + P(3, t)$$

as the market information reservation price, and define the market information price as

$$P(t \mid MI) = \max_i R(i, t \mid MI) \geqslant P(t \mid PI).$$

The last inequality will usually be strict; it is a consequence of the additional information provided by the futures market. In the numerical example,

$$P(\,.\mid MI) = (1.70, 1.15, 0.70) \quad \text{for } P(3, t) = P^*(3) = \$0.70.$$

Note that, in an equilibrium,

$$P(3, t) = P^*(3) = \max_i D(i, 3)$$

for each $t(=1, 2)$. In this case,

$$P(2 \mid MI) = \max_i R(i, 2 \mid MI) = P(2 \mid PF) = P^*(2).$$

where $P^*(2)$ denotes the equilibrium period B price.

Thus equilibrium prices are indeed determinate at $t=2$. Equilibrium prices are not determinate at $t=1$, but as long as agents incorporate the information in the futures price and it reaches its equilibrium level, we can raise the lower bound on $P^*(1)$ to $P(1 \mid MI)$. The usual statements about equilibrium allocations still apply.

3.4 Testable hypotheses

We now list the empirical hypotheses suggested by our discussion in the last two subsections of learning and equilibrium in stationary non-stochastic asset markets. All hypotheses will be presented as null hypotheses with the understanding that the implicit alternative hypothesis in each case is a two-tail, compound hypothesis; i.e. if *a* and b represent two parameters of interest, then the null is of the form $a = b$ and the alternative is $a \langle\rangle b$. In this section we will use the convention that upper-case variables represent *a priori* values given by theory and market parameters, while lower-case symbols represent the mean value (arithmetic average) of observed variables over the relevant time period.

In section 3.3 we showed that several ways of deriving period C equilibrium all led to the same result, depicted in figure 1. An implication of the discussion of learning is that equilibrium is not likely to be attained immediately; therefore hypotheses concerning prices will be defined in terms of the mean transacted price for each year. We will also test the hypotheses using closing price data. The first three hypotheses, then, concern period C

H1: for experiments 1 and 3,

$$P(C) = \max_i D(i, C) = P^*(C).$$

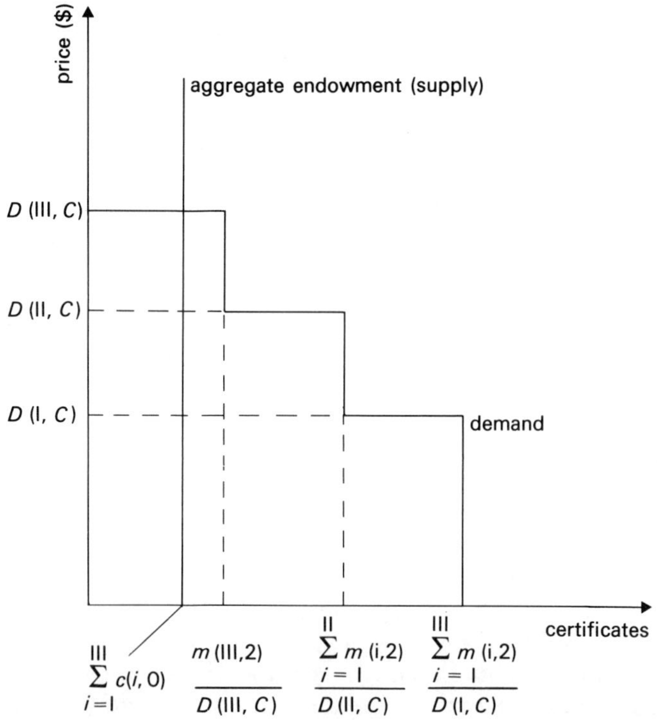

Fig. 1 Theoretical period C market demand and supply schedules

In words, the mean transacted period C spot price will equal the theoretical equilibrium price. Given our model parameters, the predicted prices are \$0.60 and \$0.70 for experiments 1 and 3 respectively. For a complete summary of all price predictions see table 1; hereafter only the hypotheses and not the specific parameter values will be listed.

We may also apply H1 to the periods A and B futures price data (period C delivery) since the theoretical argument is the same. Therefore, for period A,

H2: for experiments 2 and 4,

$$p(C, A) = \max_i D(i, C) = P^*(C)$$

and for the period C futures price transacted in period B,

H3: for experiments 2 and 4,

$$p(C, B) = \max_i D(i, C) = P^*(C).$$

The mean transacted futures price in periods A and B will converge to the notional Walrasian equilibrium price. By 'converge' we mean that the average (or closing) price will be insignificantly different from the predicted price.

Private information price predictions for period B spot prices are captured by the following hypothesis:

H4: for experiments 1, 2, 3 and 4,

$$p(B) = P(B \mid PI) = \max_i \,[D(i, B) + D(i, C)].$$

The mean transacted period B spot price will converge to the private information equilibrium price. The competing hypothesis to H4 is the perfect foresight hypothesis, given by

H5: for experiments 1, 2, 3 and 4,

$$\begin{aligned} p(B) = P(B \mid PF) &= \max_i D(i, B) + \max_i D(i, C) \\ &= \max_i D(i, B) + P^*(C). \end{aligned}$$

The mean transacted period B spot price will converge to the perfect foresight equilibrium price.

Similarly, for period A spot prices,

H6: for experiments 1, 2, 3 and 4,

$$p(A) = P(A\,|PI) = \max_i\,[D(i, A) + D(i, B) + D(i, C)].$$

H7: for experiments 1, 2, 3 and 4,

$$p(A) = P(A\,|PF) = \max_i D(i, A) + \max_i D(i, B) + \max_i D(i, C).$$

The relevance of our market information reservation price concept and the role of futures markets in conveying equilibrium price information is examined in our next hypothesis. Recall from the discussion in section 3.3 that information incorporated in futures prices raises the reservation spot prices and the lower bound on the equilibrium prices. Taking $I = [P(\,.\,|MI) - P(\,.\,|PI)]$ as a proxy for this information, we hypothesize the following regression relationship:

$$[p(\,.\,|\text{futures}) - p(\,.\,|\text{spot})]_t = a + b(I)_t$$

where $p(\,.\,|\text{futures})$ represents the transacted period A and B spot prices given an operating futures market (experiments 2 and 4); and $p(\,.\,|\text{spot})$ represents the transacted period A and B spot prices when only spot markets are operating (experiments 1 and 3). Given our model parameters, we would expect transacted spot prices to be higher when futures markets are active relative to when they are not. We have no sharp prior for the intercept term if the relationship is not linear; however, assuming that it is, our specific hypothesis becomes:

H8: comparing experiments 1 and 2, or 3 and 4,

$$a = 0 \quad \text{and} \quad b > 0.$$

Other hypotheses regarding the informational role of futures markets implicit in our earlier discussion may now be formulated explicitly:

H9: period A spot prices will converge to an equilibrium in fewer market years in experiments with futures trading than in corresponding experiments without futures trading.

H10: period B spot prices will converge to an equilibrium in fewer market years in experiments with futures trading than in corresponding experiments without futures trading.

The FPP(a) 'swingback' hypothesis is represented by:

H11: for experiments 1 and 3 and for each market year, convergence in period A occurs after convergence in period B, which in turn follows convergence in period C.

The impact of futures market trading on agents' ability to learn about market-clearing prices can be operationalized by examining the standard deviation (or coefficient of variation) of transacted prices. The conjecture is that the standard deviation of transacted prices is a proxy for (the reciprocal) of an agent's precision concerning the underlying market clearing price. Therefore, the hypothesis is:

H12: the coefficient of variation of transacted spot prices will be smaller when futures trading opportunities exist.

We shall employ the coefficient of variation of transacted spot prices when testing this hypothesis, since the perfect foresight equilibrium prices vary from experiment to experiment.

Finally, we will examine two hypotheses stemming from the discussion in section 3.3 about the final allocation of certificate holdings at the end of each trading period. These are:

H13: the allocation of certificate holdings will be that of the private information equilibrium.

H14: The allocation of certificate holdings will be that of the perfect foresight equilibrium.

In other words, all certificates will be held by agents of the type that has the highest reservation price, under the various assumptions of how these prices are formed.

4 Experimental evidence

We discuss the results of our four experiments in two subsections. The first provides a descriptive account of the results, providing the reader with our application of Savage's renowned 'Interocular Trauma Test'; the second section takes up the testable hypotheses introduced above in a somewhat more formal statistical manner.

4.1 The experimental results

The complete set of experiments, again, is:

1 a pure stock market with three period-specific spot certificates, and with inexperienced subjects;
2 a pure stock market with two period-specific spot certificates and a third-period futures certificate tradable simultaneously with the spot contracts. This experiment also uses inexperienced subjects;
3 the same institution as experiment 1, but with experienced subjects;
4 the same institution as experiment 2, but with experienced subjects.

It is convenient to consider experiments 1 and 2 as a pair, and likewise experiments 3 and 4.

4.1.1 Results with inexperienced subjects

Tables 3 and 4 summarize the observed price behaviour in our four experiments. For ease of comparison, we first list the numerical values of the theoretical spot equilibria introduced in section 3.3 for each experiment, based on the parameters in table 1. For each market year and trading period we then show the closing transaction price (spot only for experiments 1 and 3; spot and futures for experiments 2 and 4), the mean (and standard deviation in parentheses) of the transacted prices, and the same statistics for non-transacted prices.[19] Figures 2 and 3 graphically display the time series data on transacted prices; 'X' refers to spot prices and '0' to futures prices.

Consider first the period C prices over the lives of the first two experiments. By year 2 the mean price in experiment 1 was only 1 cent short of the equilibrium level of $0.60, with a standard error of only 4 cents. In experiment 2 the futures market in period C certificates does not settle down to the equilibrium level of $0.60 until period B of year 3; note that, with a standard deviation of only 1 cent or less, it thereafter provides a very clear signal as to the value of a period C certificate. Our period C results with inexperienced subjects are therefore mixed – although the price of futures contract settles down more quickly than that of the spot period C contract, its bias in year 1 is much greater.[20]

Period B spot prices in both experiments eventually converge on the private information (PI) equilibrium and do not converge to the perfect foresight (PF) equilibrium. Convergence to the PI equilibrium in period B is rapid in experiment 1; again, in experiment 2 we find the comparable price converging more closely but with a greater initial bias. We observe more rapid convergence to the period A PI equilibrium in experiment 2 (year 2) that in experiment 1 (year 3). This is true with respect to both bias and precision.

We attribute the failure to converge to a perfect foresight equilibrium or a market information equilibrium to the inability of inexperienced traders to employ more profitable strategies. Quite simply, they did not use the market signals available.

4.1.2 Results with experienced agents

Experiments 3 and 4 repeat the institutional design of experiments 1 and 2, respectively, but with experienced subjects. Eight out of nine of our traders had previous experience with the experimental design in experiment 4, and all nine had such experience in experiment 3. The results are shown in tables 3 and 4, and figures 4 and 5.

Period C prices[21] in experiment 3 do not converge to the equilibrium value of \$0.70 (using closing transacted prices) until year 3, so it is not surprising that period A and B mean prices are at the PI equilibrium in year 1. Only when period C prices show repeated signs of converging (by year 4, given the initial convergence in year 3) do period A and B prices significantly tend towards the PF equilibrium. This trend is not completed for period A prices by year 5, but period A prices are strongly tending towards the PF equilibrium value.

Experiment 4 strikingly demonstrates the role of futures market for experienced traders who have become aware of the informational value of futures prices. The equilibrium value of a period C futures certificate in this case is \$0.80. By year 2 the average price of the futures certificate reflects this value; moreover, periods A and B of that year provide a clear repeated signal to this effect. By year 3 period B spot prices have converged on the market information (MI) or PF equilibria (which are identical here), and remain significantly above the PI equilibrium values. Similarly, mean period A spot prices in year 3 (\$1.85) are roughly midway between the MI equilibrium (\$1.75) and the PF equilibrium (\$2.00). By year 4 all spot prices have converged to the PF equilibrium.

In year 5 of experiment 4 we randomly re-assigned agents to different dividend profiles, without altering the aggregate market parameters. The issue here is the ability of agents to distinguish the market signal from their private signal (viz., their own dividend

Table 3 Observed and predicted prices in experiments 1 and 3

Experiment	Year	Period	Theoretical spot equilibrium prices Private	Theoretical spot equilibrium prices Perfect	Closing transacted prices Spot	Mean transacted price (and standard deviation) Spot	Mean non-transacted price (and standard deviation) Spot
			$	$	$	$	$
1	1	A	1.15	1.45	1.00	0.93 (0.18)	0.85 (0.15)
		B	0.90	1.05	0.90	0.91 (0.04)	0.87 (0.12)
		C	0.60	0.60	0.60	0.63 (0.10)	0.61 (0.17)
	2	A	1.15	1.45	1.10	1.02 (0.08)	1.01 (0.10)
		B	0.90	1.05	0.85	0.89 (0.02)	0.89 (0.07)
		C	0.60	0.60	0.58	0.59 (0.04)	0.59 (0.08)
	3	A	1.15	1.45	1.16	1.07 (0.08)	1.08 (0.09)
		B	0.90	1.05	0.90	0.90 (0.02)	0.90 (0.07)
		C	0.60	0.60	0.60	0.59 (0.02)	0.54 (0.13)

3	1	A	1.35	1.85	1.46	1.36 (0.09)	1.33 (0.15)
		B	1.00	1.15	1.00	0.99 (0.06)	1.00 (0.09)
		C	0.70	0.70	0.60	0.57 (0.10)	0.65 (0.12)
	2	A	1.35	1.85	1.50	1.44 (0.06)	1.50 (0.14)
		B	1.00	1.15	1.01	1.02 (0.02)	1.01 (0.03)
		C	0.70	0.70	0.68	0.62 (0.03)	0.67 (0.12)
	3	A	1.35	1.85	1.70	1.61 (0.05)	1.59 (0.12)
		B	1.00	1.15	1.05	1.03 (0.01)	1.03 (0.08)
		C	0.70	0.70	0.70	0.67 (0.02)	0.65 (0.12)
	4	A	1.35	1.85	1.72	1.70 (0.03)	1.67 (0.13)
		B	1.00	1.15	1.11	1.09 (0.03)	1.08 (0.04)
		C	0.70	0.70	0.70	0.68 (0.01)	0.70 (0.07)
	5	A	1.35	1.85	1.83	1.77 (0.04)	1.78 (0.04)
		B	1.00	1.15	1.14	1.15 (0.004)	1.11 (0.08)
		C	0.70	0.70	0.70	0.69 (0.003)	0.71 (0.05)

Table 4 Observed and predicted prices in experiments 2 and 4

			Theoretical spot equilibrium prices			*Closing transacted prices*		*Mean transacted price (and standard deviation)*		*Mean non-transacted price (and standard deviation)*	
Experiment	*Year*	*Period*	*Private*	*Market*	*Perfect*	*Spot*	*Futures*	*Spot*	*Futures*	*Spot*	*Futures*
			$	$	$	$	$	$	$	$	$
2	1	A	1.15	1.25	1.45	1.15	0.70	1.01 (0.11)	0.64 (0.07)	1.03 (0.11)	0.65 (0.13)
		B	0.90	1.05	1.05	0.97	0.75	1.02 (0.05)	0.77 (0.04)	1.00 (0.12)	0.78 (0.08)
	2	A	1.15	1.25	1.45	1.10	0.70	1.12 (0.06)	0.70 (0.03)	1.12 (0.07)	0.71 (0.07)
		B	0.90	1.05	1.05	1.00	0.56	1.00 (0.001)	0.57 (0.03)	0.91 (0.10)	0.67 (0.06)
	3	A	1.15	1.25	1.45	1.16	0.62	1.15 (0.02)	0.65 (0.02)	1.12 (0.15)	0.66 (0.06)
		B	0.90	1.05	1.05	0.90	0.62	0.89 (0.02)	0.60 (0.01)	0.84 (0.14)	0.60 (0.03)
	4	A	1.15	1.25	1.45	1.17	0.61	1.17 (0.004)	0.60 (0.01)	1.08 (0.18)	0.60 (0.04)
		B	0.90	1.05	1.05	0.90	0.60	0.90 (0.003)	0.60 (0.003)	0.92 (0.21)	0.61 (0.02)
	5	A	1.15	1.25	1.45	1.18	0.59	1.17 (0.003)	0.59 (0.001)	1.18 (0.11)	0.59 (0.001)
		B	0.90	1.05	1.05	0.89	0.59	0.90 (0.003)	0.60 (0.003)	0.90 (0.04)	0.59 (0.03)

4	1	A	1.30	1.75	2.00	1.60	0.75	1.49 (0.14)	0.75 (0.001)	1.34 (0.24)	0.69 (0.06)
		B	1.10	1.25	1.25	1.09	0.76	1.07 (0.10)	0.72 (0.09)	1.06 (0.09)	0.64 (0.12)
	2	A	1.30	1.75	2.00	1.72	0.77	1.67 (0.06)	0.76 (0.01)	1.67 (0.09)	0.75 (0.03)
		B	1.10	1.25	1.25	1.21	0.79	1.17 (0.02)	0.78 (0.01)	1.17 (0.06)	0.79 (0.02)
	3	A	1.30	1.75	2.00	1.95	0.75	1.85 (0.08)	0.75 (0.001)	1.83 (0.09)	0.75 (0.02)
		B	1.10	1.25	1.25	1.25	0.79	1.24 (0.01)	0.79 (0.004)	1.21 (0.04)	0.79 (0.02)
	4	A	1.30	1.75	2.00	1.99	0.79	1.98 (0.01)	0.78 (0.01)	1.96 (0.06)	0.76 (0.04)
		B	1.10	1.25	1.25	1.25	0.80	1.25 (0.001)	0.80 (0.003)	1.25 (0.01)	0.80 (0.005)
	5	A	1.30	1.75	2.00	2.05	0.80	2.02 (0.03)	0.80 (0.01)	2.01 (0.05)	0.79 (0.01)
		B	1.10	1.25	1.25	1.24	0.80	1.23 (0.02)	0.81 (0.01)	1.20 (0.06)	0.81 (0.01)

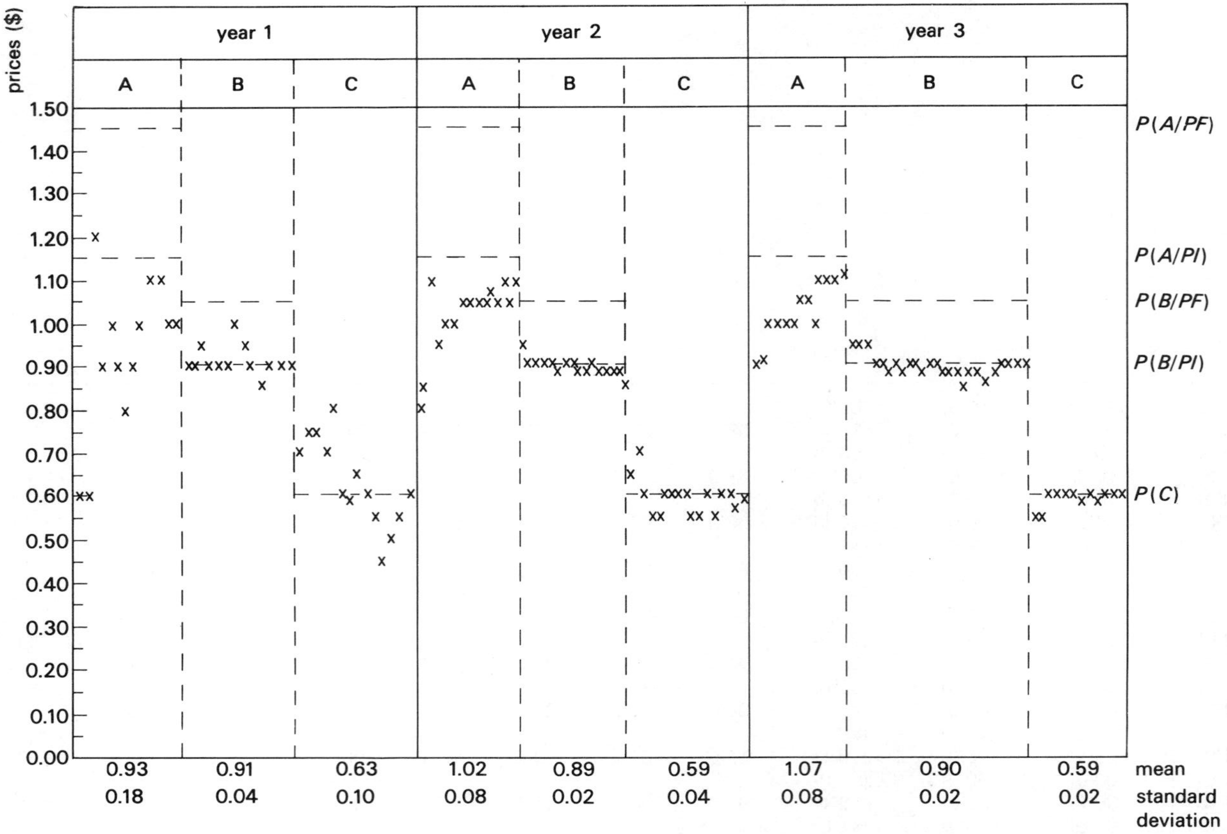

Fig. 2 Observed price behaviour – experiment 1 (inexperienced subjects)

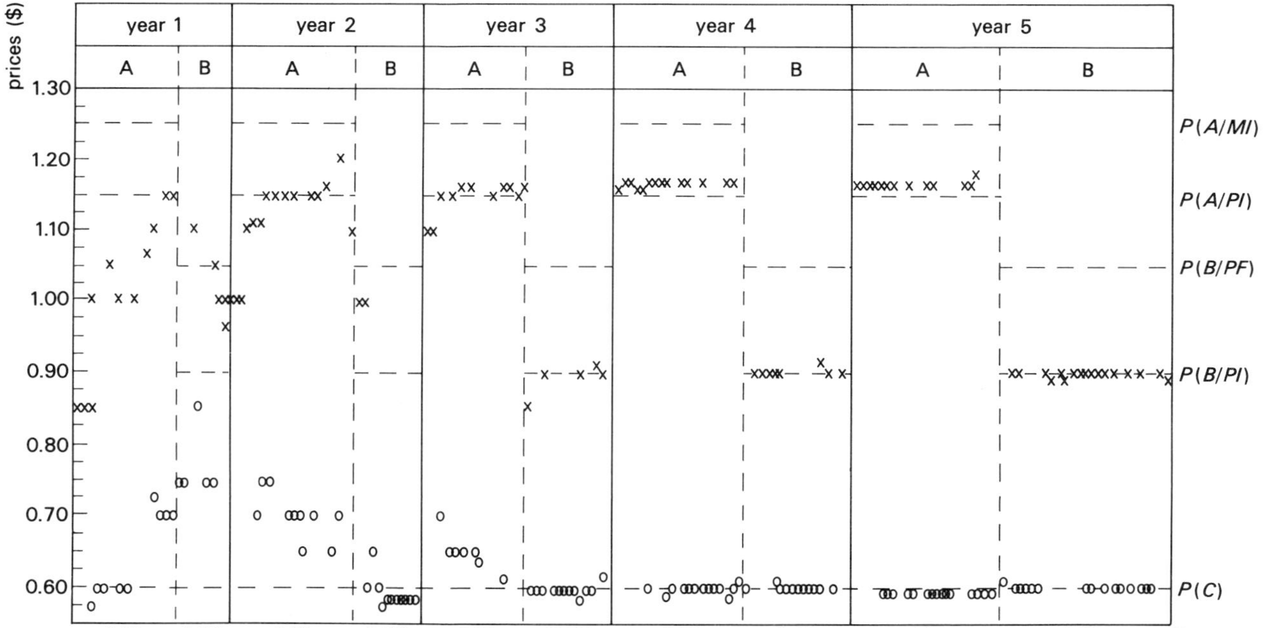

	Year 1 A	Year 1 B	Year 2 A	Year 2 B	Year 3 A	Year 3 B	Year 4 A	Year 4 B	Year 5 A	Year 5 B
Spot mean	1.01	1.02	1.12	1.00	1.15	0.89	1.17	0.90	1.17	0.90
standard deviation	0.11	0.05	0.06	0.001	0.02	0.02	0.004	0.003	0.003	0.003
Futures mean	0.64	0.77	0.70	0.57	0.65	0.60	0.60	0.60	0.59	0.60
standard deviation	0.07	0.04	0.03	0.03	0.02	0.01	0.01	0.003	0.001	0.003

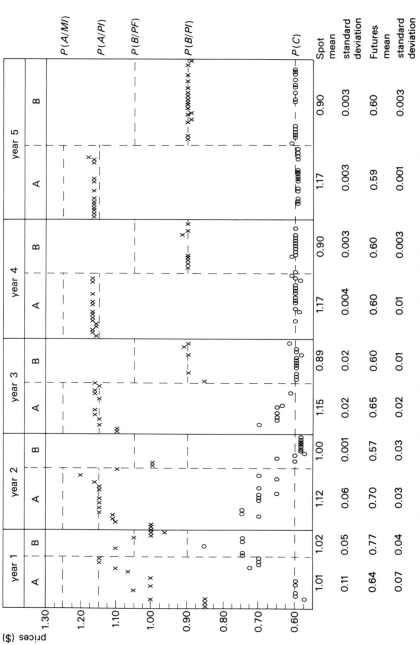

Fig. 3 Observed price behaviour – experiment 2 (inexperienced subjects)

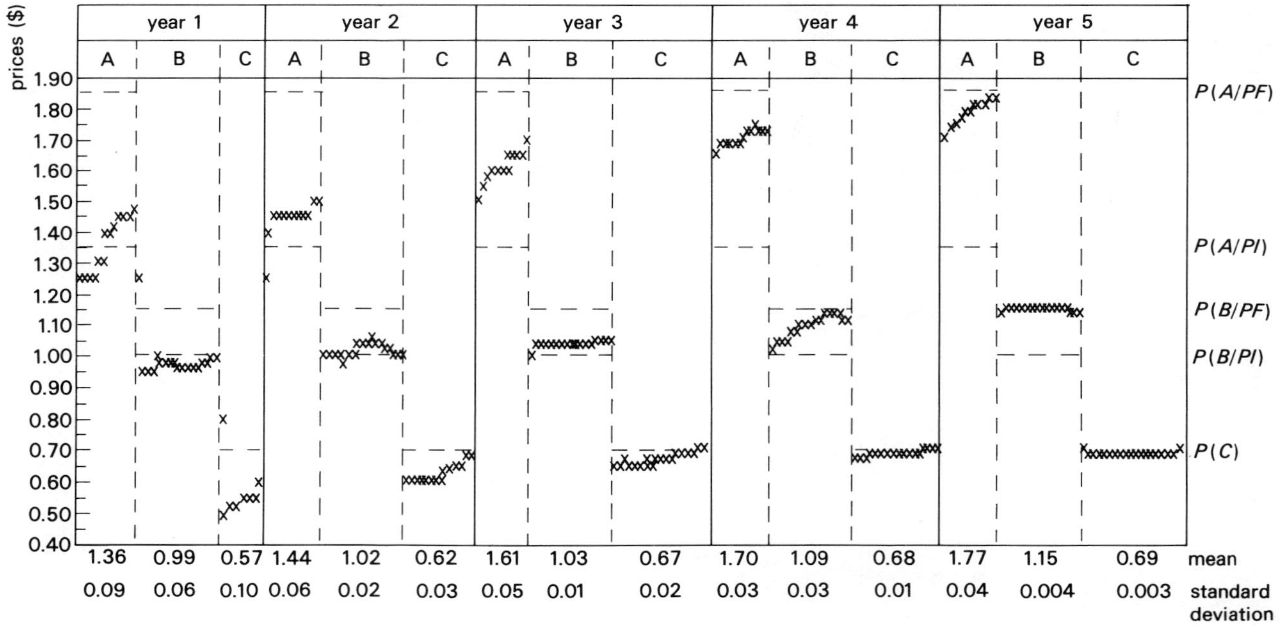

Fig. 4 Observed price behaviour – experiment 3 (experienced subjects)

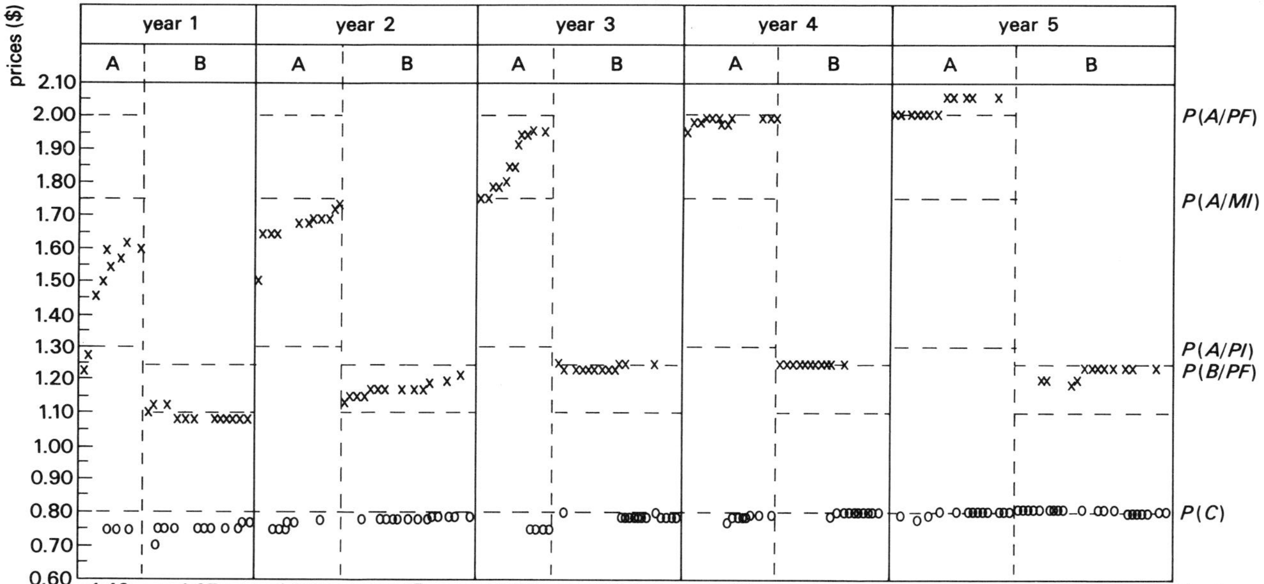

1.49	1.07	1.67	1.17	1.85	1.24	1.98	1.25	2.02	1.23	Spot mean
0.14	0.10	0.06	0.02	0.08	0.01	0.01	0.001	0.03	0.02	standard deviation
0.75	0.72	0.76	0.78	0.75	0.79	0.78	0.80	0.80	0.81	Futures mean
0.001	0.09	0.01	0.01	0.001	0.004	0.01	0.003	0.01	0.01	standard deviation

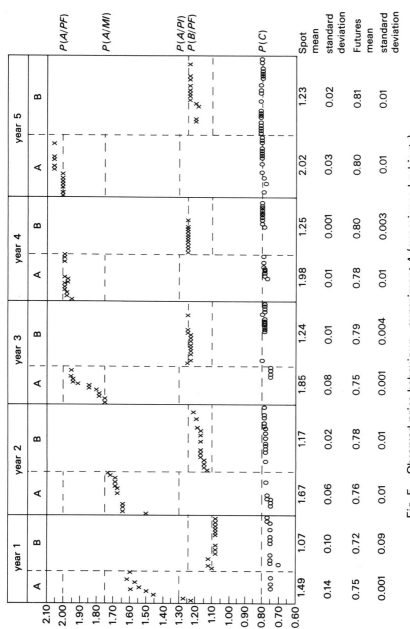

Fig. 5 Observed price behaviour – experiment 4 (experienced subjects)

profile) – the essence of our competing equilibrium notions. Despite a 'technical reaction' of sorts, the results essentially repeat the behaviour of year 4. The fact that we observe convergence to the PF price in year 4 indeed tells us that agents had made the distinction in forming their trading strategies between private and market signals; our year 5 results confirm this conclusion.

The closing transacted prices shown for each experiment also reveal the presence of significant intra-period learning behaviour. They are typically higher than the corresponding average transacted prices, and closer to the average price behaviour in the succeeding comparable trading period.

4.2 Evaluating the testable hypotheses

4.2.1 Price convergence hypotheses

Table 5 presents the results for hypotheses H1–H7 using 95 per cent confidence intervals for the mean transacted price in the final market year. When examining these results the reader should keep in mind the following comments and qualifications. That H1 is accepted for experiment 1 and rejected for experiment 3 can be explained by noting that experiments using inexperienced subjects (experiments 1 and 2) displayed period C price convergence from above and that the dispersion of transacted prices within a market year (from which confidence intervals were computed) was consistently larger for inexperienced than for experienced traders.[22] The fact that the coefficient of variation was consistently smaller for experienced traders suggests that the inexperienced/experienced distinction is an important one. As noted previously, one can characterize agents' reservation price behaviour by their subjective probability distribution. A smaller coefficient of variation, then, suggests that experienced traders behave as if they hold their probability beliefs with greater precision than inexperienced traders. Thus they will not accept bids or offers 'too far away' from the expected value of the market-clearing price. If we were to use closing transacted prices as the location parameter estimate for the 95 per cent confidence interval, we would accept H1 for experiment 3.

Although H2 is rejected for year 5 of experiment 2, we cannot reject it for year 4. The standard deviation in year 5 was so small (effectively zero in this case) that being only 1 cent off the equilibrium price causes one formally to reject the null hypothesis. Given the above caveats, we conclude that H1–H3 are favoured by the experimental data; that is, all market experiments displayed fairly

Table 5 Summary of confidence intervals for H1–H7
(Intervals refer to final market year)

Experiment	*Period (actual delivery)*	*95% confidence interval on mean transaction price*	*Accept or reject hypotheses*
1	C	0.58 < 0.59 < 0.60	Accept H1
3	C	0.688 < 0.69 < 0.692	Reject H1
2	A (C)	0.59	Reject H2
4	A (C)	0.796 < 0.80 < 0.804	Accept H2
2	B (C)	0.598 < 0.60 < 0.602	Accept H3
4	B (C)	0.795 < 0.80 < 0.805	Accept H3
1	B	0.893 < 0.90 < 0.907	Accept H4 (PI) Reject H5 (PF)
2	B	0.898 < 0.90 < 0.902	Accept H4 (PI) Reject H5 (PF)
3	B	1.148 < 1.15 < 1.152	Reject H4 (PI) Accept H5 (PF)
4	B	1.25	Reject H4 (PI) Accept H5 (PF)
1	A	1.03 < 1.07 < 1.11	Reject H6 (PI) Reject H7 (PF)
2	A	1.168 < 1.17 < 1.172	Reject H6 (PI) Reject H7 (PF)
3	A	1.760 < 1.78 < 1.80	Reject H6 (PI) Reject H7 (PF)
4	A	2.00 < 2.02 < 2.04	Reject H6 (PI) Accept H7 (PF)

rapid convergence to the period C equilibrium price. However, the convergence-from-above phenomena for inexperienced traders remains to be explained.

The distinction between experienced and inexperienced traders also makes a difference when comparing H4 and H5 – the private information and perfect foresight price equilibria hypotheses. We firmly reject H5 for inexperienced traders (experiments 1 and 2), but just as firmly accept H5 for experienced traders (experiments 3 and 4). Experience in market trading, then, significantly affects transacted prices.

The reason we must reject H6 and H7 for experiment 2 is that by the final market year the transacted prices had already passed PI (we cannot reject H6 for market years 2, 3 and 4) and were slowly approaching the PF equilibrium (see figure 3). This is indirect evidence that the market information reservation price strategies were in operation (albeit imperfectly) and that some traders were using futures prices as signals for enlarged future period profit opportunities.

In experiment 3, period A transacted prices began in year 1 at the PI equilibrium price (we cannot reject H6 for year 1) and then moved up towards the PF equilibrium price. If we use the year 5 closing price, we cannot reject H7.

Turning now to H11, the 'swingback' hypothesis, we find that a comparison of the sequence of period-specific price convergence statistics for experiments 1 and 3 indicates that H11 is weakly supported (see table 3). In experiment 1, period C transacted prices converged by year 1; period B prices converged to the PI equilibrium by year 3 and period A prices did not converge. Note that experiment 1 lasted for only three market years. In experiment 3 period C prices converged by year 3 (using the closing transacted price as the criterion); period B prices converged to the PF equilibrium price by year 5, and the period A prices, although clearly moving towards PF, did not quite converge. Given the extra trading period and fewer market years relative to the FPP(a) study, it is not too surprising that our results for H11 are not as strong as those presented by FPP(a). We may none the less conclude that our results provide evidence in favour of a swingback effect for repetitive, stationary markets.

We now evaluate H8. Table 6 presents our regression tests concerning the possible relevance of market information reservation price strategies. The form of the regression equation, again, is as follows:

$$Y_t = a + b(I_t) + e_t$$

where Y is defined as the difference between the average transacted spot price (t refers to periods A and B) with futures trading and the

Table 6 Regression results for H8: market information price behaviour

Experiment number	*a*	*b*	*d*	R^2	*t (0.05 level)*
1 and 2	0.06 (0.89)	0.05 (0.09)	1.08	0.002	2.57
1 and 2	0	0.57 (3.26)	0.90	0.68	2.78
3 and 4	0.02 (0.41)	0.15 (0.71)	0.87	0.06	2.30
3 and 4	0	0.24 (4.00)	0.95	0.65	2.26

average transacted spot price with spot trading only – normalized to reflect differing levels of prices in the two experiments; I is the difference between the equilibrium MI and PI prices (this difference equals \$0.10 in period A and \$0.15 in period B); and e is the error disturbance term. When implementing our test of H8 we use average price data, since the individual data points are not comparable across experiments. The regression equation was run twice for each experiment pair: once using unconstrained OLS, and then constraining the intercept to zero. The intercept constraint was used to check whether the estimated coefficients were orthogonal; clearly they are not. We also report the Durbin–Watson d statistic, critical 95 per cent values of the student's t distribution, and R-squared.

The results in table 6 must be interpreted with some caution. An inspection of the relevant upper and lower cut-off points for the d distribution reveals that one cannot reject the hypothesis of positive first-order correlation for the unconstrained OLS estimates concerning all experiments. Hence, the t statistics for this case are biased upwards. This does no harm in rejecting the hypothesis that the intercept term is significantly different from zero. However, the significance of the slope coefficient is somewhat suspect. The fact that the sign of the slope coefficient is positive and that the constrained estimate is positive, large and significantly different from zero leads us to conclude that the experimental data do tentatively support H8. However, the estimates are based on a very small sample, and so the tests reported are not particularly powerful. Although our results are tentative on this issue, they are suggestive that market information price-strategic behaviour was in evidence. Indirect evidence in favour of H8 is indicated by the fact that in experiment 4 the PI equilibrium was surpassed in the very first market year.

Hypotheses H9 and H10 concern the possible role that futures markets may have in speeding spot price convergence to an equilibrium value. When evaluating these conjectures, we examine both PI and PF equilibrium predictions. For the sake of H9 and H10 we consider convergence to be completed when either the average transacted price or the closing price is insignificantly different from the relevant equilibrium price. Consider the evidence pertaining to period A spot price convergence. Experiment 1 converged to the PI equilibrium by year 3 and did not converge to the PF price. Experiment 2 converged to PI by year 2 and also did not converge to the PF price. This comparison suggests that the presence of futures transacted prices did aid in convergence, but to an inefficient equilibrium. The evidence from experiments 3 and 4 is more forceful.

Table 7 Coefficient of variation comparison: H12

Year	*Period*	*Coefficient of variation of experiment no.* 1	2	3	4
1	A	0.193	0.113	0.065	0.096
	B	0.040	0.050	0.064	0.009
2	A	0.087	0.050	0.043	0.035
	B	0.023	0.0	0.017	0.017
3	A	0.079	0.020	0.033	0.042
	B	0.025	0.026	0.012	0.005
4	A	N/A	0.003	0.016	0.006
	B	N/A	0.004	0.028	0.0
5	A	N/A	0.003	0.020	0.012
	B	N/A	0.004	0.003	0.017

In experiment 3 prices converged to the PF price by year 5, but in experiment 4 prices converged by year 4. Thus we accept H9.

The convergence price patterns for period B spot prices are very similar and imply an even stronger 'speed-up' effect of futures markets on spot price convergence. We claim that the data very strongly support H10.

Finally, we consider the evidence on H12 – the conjecture that the information content of futures prices is reflected in lower standard deviations of transacted prices when futures markets are active. Table 7 shows the coefficient of variation (calculated relative to the average transacted price) by year and period for each of the four experiments. For experiments 1 and 2 we see that, in five out of six instances, spot prices displayed less (or equal) variability when futures markets were active. For experiments 3 and 4, the same comparison indicates less (or equal) variability in seven out of ten instances. This supports the hypothesis that the standard deviations of transacted prices were different between the two market regimes for both experienced and inexperienced traders. This difference favoured a smaller standard deviation of transacted prices when futures markets were in operation. Thus we accept H12.

4.2.2 Allocation hypotheses

The PI and PF equilibrium concepts generally differ in their predictions of final certificate allocations at the end of trading in periods A and B of each market year. They do not differ in their respective predictions for period C. Table 8 shows the alternative predicted allocations by trader type for each experiment. It also shows the deviation of observed holdings (at the end of each period) from the respective predictions. Zero deviations represent correctly predicted allocations. Note that these deviations must sum to zero across agents for each period.[23]

The observed results for experiments 1 and 2 do not agree with either predicted allocation. Allocations observed in experiment 2 generally came closer to the PF than the PI allocation after year 3, but we are unable to discriminate between the two alternative predictions for experiment 1. This is really not too surprising, given that our inexperienced traders evidently had not yet learned effective strategies.

The allocations in experiments 3 and 4 on the whole converge reasonably quickly on the PF prediction. We are able to accept that prediction, as against the PI alternative, with little difficulty. However, the existence of futures markets did not appear to help much. Although deviations from PF allocations were less in year 1 in experiment 3 than in experiment 4, and roughly the same magnitude in years 2 and 3, the deviations in subsequent years were substantial in experiment 4 while the efficient allocation was obtained precisely in experiment 3.

An examination of realized aggregate profits sheds some light on the issues of allocational inefficiencies. In table 9 we list the aggregate profits actually received from the purchase, sale and redemption of certificates within each market year as a percentage of 'maximum' profits.[24] Note that it is possible for a trader to earn profits in excess of the 'maximum' if he transacts at a price more favourable to him than the PF equilibrium price, but such profits come at the expense of the counter-party to the transaction. Trading is a positive-sum game for our traders if they move towards the efficient PF allocation, but excess trading profits due to trade at non-equilibrium prices are zero-sum. Hence the maximum profit is 100 per cent in the aggregate, and the actual aggregate profits are a measure of allocational efficiency (but not price efficiency).

The data in table 9 very clearly suggest that traders' experience promotes allocational efficiency. Aggregate profits earned in experiments 3 and 4 by experienced traders are all higher than the corresponding profits in experiments 1 and 2 of inexperienced traders. Also, in each experiment profits are generally higher in later market years. The major exception to this pattern – in year 4 of experiment 4 – seems attributable to a single trader (of type I) who enthusiastically followed the very unprofitable strategy of buying up contracts in period B. The informational noise created by this

Table 8 Observed and predicted certificate allocations

			Private information equilibrium						Perfect information equilibrium					
			Theoretical			(Actual–Theoretical)			Theoretical			(Actual–Theoretical)		
Experiment	*Year*	*Period*	*I*	*II*	*III*	*I*	*II*	*III*	*I*	*II*	*III*	*I*	*II*	*III*
1	1	A	0	18	0	4	−11	7	18	0	0	−14	7	7
		B	0	0	18	5	5	−10	0	18	0	5	−13	8
		C	0	0	18	4	0	−4	0	0	18	4	0	−4
	2	A	0	18	0	7	−8	1	18	0	0	−11	10	1
		B	0	0	18	4	4	−8	0	18	0	4	−14	10
		C	0	0	18	0	1	−1	0	0	18	0	1	−1
	3	A	0	18	0	12	−12	0	18	0	0	−6	6	0
		B	0	0	18	0	6	−6	0	18	0	0	−12	12
		C	0	0	18	0	1	−1	0	0	18	0	1	−1
2	1	A	0	18	0	9	−9	0	18	0	0	−9	9	0
		B	0	18	0	11	−12	1	0	0	18	14	6	−17
		C	0	18	0	8	−12	4	0	18	0	8	−12	4
	2	A	0	18	0	12	−12	0	18	0	0	−6	6	0
		B	0	18	0	12	−13	1	0	0	18	12	5	−17
		C	0	18	0	2	−5	3	0	18	0	2	−5	3
	3	A	0	18	0	11	−11	0	18	0	0	−7	7	0
		B	0	18	0	8	−8	0	0	0	18	8	10	−18
		C	0	18	0	1	−4	3	0	18	0	1	−4	3
	4	A	0	18	0	17	−17	0	18	0	0	−1	1	0
		B	0	18	0	14	−14	0	0	0	18	14	4	−18
		C	0	18	0	1	−3	2	0	18	0	1	−3	2
	5	A	0	18	0	18	−18	0	18	0	0	0	0	0
		B	0	18	0	11	−11	0	0	0	18	11	7	−18
		C	0	18	0	4	−6	2	0	18	0	4	−6	2

3	1	A	18	0	0	—14	14	0	0	18	0	4	—4	0
		B	0	0	18	3	1	—4	18	0	0	—15	1	14
		C	0	0	18	4	0	—4	0	0	18	4	0	—4
	2	A	18	0	0	—18	18	0	0	18	0	0	0	0
		B	0	0	18	5	2	—17	18	0	0	—3	2	1
		C	0	0	18	0	0	0	0	0	18	0	0	0
	3	A	18	0	0	—18	18	0	0	18	0	0	0	0
		B	0	0	18	16	2	—18	18	0	0	—2	2	0
		C	0	0	18	0	2	—2	0	0	18	0	2	—2
	4	A	18	0	0	—18	18	0	0	18	0	0	0	0
		B	0	0	18	18	0	—18	18	0	0	0	0	0
		C	0	0	18	0	0	0	0	0	18	0	0	0
	5	A	18	0	0	—18	18	0	0	18	0	0	0	0
		B	0	0	18	18	0	—18	0	0	18	0	0	0
		C	0	0	18	0	0	0	0	0	18	0	0	0
4	1	A	0	18	0	13	—14	1	18	0	0	—5	4	1
		B	0	0	18	1	13	—14	0	18	0	1	—5	4
		C	0	0	18	0	0	0	0	0	18	0	0	0
	2	A	0	18	0	13	—13	0	18	0	0	—5	5	0
		B	0	0	18	0	18	—18	0	18	0	0	0	0
		C	0	0	18	0	0	0	0	0	18	0	0	0
	3	A	0	18	0	13	—13	0	18	0	0	—5	5	0
		B	0	0	18	0	18	—18	0	18	0	0	0	0
		C	0	0	18	0	0	0	0	0	18	0	0	0
	4	A	0	18	0	18	—18	0	18	0	0	0	0	0
		B	0	0	18	7	11	—18	0	18	0	7	—7	0
		C	0	0	18	5	0	—5	0	0	18	5	0	—5
	5	A	0	18	0	14	—14	0	18	0	0	—4	4	0
		B	0	0	18	2	16	—18	0	18	0	2	—2	0
		C	0	0	18	2	1	—3	0	0	18	2	1	—3

Table 9 Aggregate profits as a percentage of maximum

	Experiment no.			
Year	*1*	*2*	*3*	*4*
	%	%	%	%
1	17.9	−1.7	64.6	80.2
2	50.0	36.2	96.3	87.9
3	69.1	40.2	87.5	87.9
4	N/A	49.4	100.0	63.5
5	N/A	37.4	100.0	74.7

aberrant behaviour (together with the noise deliberately introduced by shuffling dividend profiles) may have reduced the allocational efficiency and trading profits in the following market year. In any case, the existence of futures markets in experiment 4 evidently was not sufficient to restore the perfect allocational efficiency observed in the last two market years of experiment 3.

It is particularly interesting to observe that these deviations from PF equilibrium allocations occurred despite the rapid convergence of prices to their PF values. Indeed, the price convergence was more rapid with futures markets – compare figures 4 and 5. This result is clearly inconsistent with the 'Walrasian auctioneer' conception of the market adjustment process, but seems quite reasonable in light of our discussion in section 3, which suggested that the price adjustment process is robust to deviant behaviour by a few individual traders.

5 Implications for further work

Our experimental results generally support the conclusion that active futures markets tend to be associated with spot prices that reflect more informationally efficient equilibria. The role of experience in the formulation of trading strategies is clearly demonstrated in our results. Similarly, the role of sequential replication in aiding convergence to such equilibria is evident. Finally, an experimental design for the study of futures market behaviour is established and evaluated.

Much interesting work remains, and we intend to explore several variants of our experimental asset markets. 'Event uncertainty' can be introduced by allowing traders' period-specific certificate returns to be determined by a state of nature (an event) whose realization is a random variable. We can also introduce informational asymmetries by providing certain traders ('insiders') with superior knowledge of the prevailing state of nature. 'Quantity risk' can be incorporated by providing traders with initial endowments that are also event-contingent. Among the many theoretical and practical issues that may be addressed with our extended experimental framework are: the nature and function of informative speculation; the interdependence of 'price risk' and 'quantity risk' in asset pricing behaviour; the informational efficiency of asset markets as aggregators of public and private (inside) information, and the role of active futures markets in modifying our findings on the above issues.

We believe that these experiments, taken as a whole, will provide an important and independent source of evidence upon which to evaluate policy rules that affect the functioning of organized futures markets. The experimental evidence so far generally confirms that the information provided by futures trading activity promotes efficient price determination.

Notes

1 See Smith (1980, 1982) and Wilde (1980) for further discussion of the methodological contribution of experimental techniques.

2 We are indebted to Jack Hirschleifer for bringing this point to our attention.

3 Thus each agent's monetary returns from holding assets in a given time period or 'market year' were a non-additive (indeed, non-linear) function of the number of the assets held in each trading period. The main implication of this design feature is that an agent's return from holding assets in the final trading period of each market year depends on that agent's history of inventory holdings.

4 The definition of 'experience' used in FPP(b) is that the subject pool had previously participated in the respective control experiment.

5 FPP(b) themselves point out that their 'experimental design is intentionally biased against this hypothesis because individuals participating in experiments with futures markets had no previous experience in laboratory asset markets. Individuals who had participated in sequential markets all had previous experience. As indicated by previous experimental work, markets in which the traders have experience tend to equilibrate more quickly. Thus, these markets are designed to provide a strong test of the proposition' (p. 18).

6 Plott and Sunder (1982) present evidence on this issue using a one-period asset market (no carry-over allowed between periods) with asymmetric private information sets experimentally induced (i.e. some traders were 'insiders').

7 Copies are available from the authors on request. They are adapted from those used by FPP(a).

8 A minor exception in year 5 of experiment 4 is noted in table 1.

9 Although FPP(b) did systematically vary the role of subject experience, as discussed earlier, they did not separate out the roles of experience and futures markets. Moreover, their treatment of dividends differs from that employed here and in FPP(a).

10 See Easley and Ledyard (1981), Harrison *et al.* (1982), and Friedman (1982) for recent efforts that concentrate on intra-period learning behaviour.

11 Presented in Chamberlin (1948).

12 Defined quite simply for sellers as those prices greater than the currently perceived equilibrium price, and conversely for buyers as those prices perceived to be below the current period equilibrium.

13 Moreover, there is strong experimental evidence that a competitive equilibrium solution in a double-oral auction constitutes a static Nash equilibrium – see Smith *et al.* (1982). Thus such equilibria, once attained, will be self-reinforcing.

14 These theorists study a world in which information relevant to agents' inter-temporal choices is dispersed throughout the economy. Under some conditions, they find that competitive equilibrium prices will reveal everything that rational agents need to know to make choices that result in an 'efficient' allocation. That is, the economy may achieve an allocation that is the same as that which would arise in a fictitious but otherwise similar economy in which each agent has access not only to his own personal information, but also to the personal information of each other agent. In this case, prices are said to be perfectly revealing or perfect aggregators of information. For example, Grossman (1977b) models a case in which spot prices alone do not perfectly aggregate information, but spot prices together with futures prices do. He argues that such information aggregation is a major function of futures markets (although the aggregation will be less than perfect if information is costly).

15 More specifically, the second highest reservation price among the nine traders, which in the current instance happens to equal the first and third highest, since there are three agents of type III. See Vickrey (1961) for an explanation of the familiar pricing result that the winning bid is the second highest reservation price.

16 See Friedman (1982) for a more complete analysis of real time convergence to equilibrium.

17 Year-end wealth is expressed solely in terms of money, since certificates expire at the end of the market year.

18 See Smith *et al.* (1982, pp. 65–6) for an explanation of 'Nash equilibria' in this context.

19 The term 'transacted prices' refers to those prices at which a transaction occurred, as distinct from unaccepted bids or offers.

20 Root mean squared deviation (RMSD) from the equilibrium value (not the sample average) provides a statistic that allows for both bias and variance. In periods A and B the futures price RMSD is 0.076 and 0.175, respectively; by comparison, the period C spot price RMSD is 0.099.

21 Unless otherwise stated, references to 'prices' are to transaction prices.

22 Convergence-from-above and the larger standard deviation of transacted prices implied wider 95 per cent confidence intervals for experiment 1 than for experiment 3. Hence, there was a greater likelihood of accepting the null

hypothesis (H1) for the market years in experiment 1. Since experienced traders typically displayed a smaller standard deviation of transacted prices, being very close to the equilibrium price (only 1 cent off, for example) makes it difficult to formally accept the null hypothesis. This is the reason that *t* statistics are not reported in our analysis. For experiment 1, period C, the coefficient of variation (relative to the equilibrium price) ranged from 0.167 in the first year to 0.033 in the final year. For experiment 2, the range was 0.14–0.004.

23 Considerable care was taken to ensure that the transactions data did not violate any individual's budget constraints (e.g., no net short sales in experiments 2 and 4). A small number of such errors were discovered *ex post* the corresponding experiment, and the relevant transactions judiciously deleted. Full details of the data, and the nature of these corrections, are available from the authors on request.

24 Maximum profits are those that would be earned in PF equilibrium trade. Trading commissions and profits that would be earned without trade are excluded.

The Center for the Study of Futures Markets, Columbia University, has financially supported this research. We are indebted to the UCLA Department of Economics and the Foundation for Research in Economics and Education for additional research support, and to Len-Kuo Hu for research assistance. We are also grateful to Meyer Burstein, Jack Hirshleifer, Michael Rothschild and Joseph Stiglitz for helpful comments.

References

Bray, M. (1981), 'Futures Trading, Rational Expectations, and the Efficient Markets Hypothesis', *Econometrica*, 49.

Chamberlin, E. H. (1948), 'An Experimental Imperfect Market', *Journal of Political Economy*, 56.

Dubey, P. (1982), 'Price–Quantity Strategic Market Games', *Econometrica*, 50.

Easley, D. and Ledyard, J. (1981), 'A Theory of Price Formation and Exchange in Oral Auctions', Discussion Paper no. 461, Center for Mathematical Studies in Economics and Management Science, Northwestern University.

Forsythe, R., Palfrey, T. R. and Plott, C. R. (1982a), 'Asset Valuation in an Experimental Market', *Econometrica*, 50.

Forsythe, R., Palfrey, T. R. and Plott, C. R. (1982b), 'Futures Markets and Informational Efficiency: A Laboratory Examination', Working Paper no. 11-82-83, Graduate School of Industrial Administration, Carnegie-Mellon University.

Friedman, D. (1982), 'Continuous Double Auctions and Price Formation in Asset Markets', Working Paper, Department of Economics, UCLA.

Friedman, D., Harrison, G. W. and Salmon, J. W. (1982), 'The Informational Efficiency of Experimental Spot and Futures Markets', Working Paper, Department of Economics, UCLA.

Grossman, S. J. (1977a), 'On the Efficiency of Competitive Stock Markets Where Traders Have Diverse Information', *Journal of Finance*, 31.

Grossman, S. J. (1977b), 'The Existence of Futures Markets, Noisy Rational Expectations, and Informational Externalities', *Review of Economic Studies*, 44.

Grossman, S. J. (1978), 'Further Results on the Informational Efficiency of Competitive Stock Markets', *Journal of Economic Theory*, 19.

Grossman, S. J. and Stiglitz, J. E. (1976), 'Information and Competitive Price Systems', *American Economic Review*, Papers & Proceedings, 66.

Grossman, S. J. and Stiglitz, J. E. (1980), 'On the Impossibility of Informationally Efficient Markets', *American Economic Review*, 70.

Harrison, G. W., Smith, V. L. and Williams, A. W. (1982), 'Learning Behaviour in Experimental Auction Markets', Working Paper, Department of Economics, University of Western Australia.

Hellwig, M. F. (1980), 'On the Aggregation of Information in Competitive Markets', *Journal of Economic Theory*, 22.

Hess, A. C. (1972), 'Empirical Evidence on Price Formation in Competitive Markets', *Journal of Political Economy*, 80.

Hirshleifer, J. (1975), 'Speculation and Equilibrium: Information, Risk and Markets', *Quarterly Journal of Economics*, 89.

Leamer, E. E. (1978), *Specification Searches*, New York.

Miller, R. M., Plott, C. R. and Smith, V. L. (1977), 'Intertemporal Competitive Equilibrium: An Empirical Study of Speculation', *Quarterly Journal of Economics*, 91.

Plott, C. R. and Agha, G. (1982), 'Intertemporal Speculation with a Random Demand in an Experimental Market', Invited Paper, Third Conference on Experimental Economics, September 1982, Germany; forthcoming in *Contributions to Experimental Economics* (Mohr, Tübingen), vol. 9.

Plott, C. R. and Sunder, S. (1982), 'Efficiency of Experimental Security Markets with Insider Information: An Application of Rational Expectations Models', *Journal of Political Economy*, 90.

Plott, C. R. and Uhl, J. T. (1981), 'Competitive Equilibrium with Middlemen: An Experimental Study', *Southern Economic Journal*, 47.

Samuelson, P. A. (1957), 'Intertemporal Price Equilibrium: A Prologue to the Theory of Speculation', *Weltwirtschaftliches Archiv*, 79.

Smith, V. L. (1962), 'An Experimental Study of Competitive Market Behaviour', *Journal of Political Economy*, 70.

Smith, V. L. (1976), 'Experimental Economics: Induced Value Theory', *American Economic Review*, Papers & Proceedings, 66.

Smith, V. L. (1980), 'Relevance of Laboratory Experiments to Testing Resource Allocation Theory', in J. Kmenta and J. Ramsay (eds), *Evaluation of Econometric Models*, New York.

Smith, V. L. (1982), 'Microeconomic Systems as an Experimental Science', Working Paper 81-32, University of Arizona, Tucson; also in *American Economic Review*, 72.

Smith, V. L., Williams, A. W., Bratton, W. K. and Vannoni, M. G. (1982), 'Competitive Market Institutions: Double Auctions Versus Sealed Bid-Offer Auctions', *American Economic Review*, 72.

Vickrey, W. (1961), 'Counterspeculation, Auctions, and Competitive Sealed Tenders', *Journal of Finance*, 16.

Wilde, L. L. (1980), 'On the Use of Laboratory Experiments in Economics', In J. Pitt (ed.), *The Philosophy of Economics*, Ontario.

Williams, A. W. (1979), 'Intertemporal Competitive Equilibrium: On Further Experimental Results', in V. L. Smith (ed.), *Research in Experimental Economics*, vol. 1, Greenwich, Conn.

7

Trading Rules for Investors in Apparently Inefficient Futures Markets

STEPHEN J. TAYLOR

1 Introduction

Futures contracts are traded at international markets characterized by high turnover and several price changes every day. Information about assets offered for future delivery is generally cheap and can usually be obtained quickly. Consequently, if all people use the commonly available information, and use it rationally, then it is unlikely that any particular person can persistently achieve better results than average. Some financial economists call a market 'efficient' if the interested parties process all information in a manner that prevents systematic better-than-average results.

Several definitions of an efficient market have been published. Here a market for an asset is called 'efficient', with respect to a sequence of information sets, if the results obtained by using the information to trade are not better than the results obtained by merely using the information to decide optimally the quantity (if any) of the asset held in a static portfolio (cf. Jensen, 1978, p. 96). Trading refers to repeated purchases and sales of the same asset; an investor's results are measured by the risk-adjusted return net of all costs; costs include commission, taxes and any payments for acquiring information; risk adjustments are necessary to ensure that trading strategies are compared with equally risky alternative strategies. The information sets considered here are the sets of present and past prices, recorded daily, although many other sets have been studied (Fama, 1970).

A market will be called 'perfectly efficient' if the prices fully reflect available information, so that prices adjust fully and instantaneously when new information becomes available (Fama, 1976,

p. 140). It is possible for a market to be efficient but not perfectly so. Also, markets can be efficient for one person but inefficient for someone else, depending on individual resources, tax arrangements and attitudes towards risk. The efficiency of futures markets has often been discussed before, some of the more important contributions being Leuthold (1972), Cargill and Rausser (1975) and Praetz (1975, 1976).

Trading rules are developed and tested in this article for six markets, to find out if sophisticated traders can exploit small departures from perfectly efficient pricing in futures markets. These small departures could occur because some traders are not always rational or are not capable of correctly interpreting publicly available information. Section 2 describes the six futures markets studied: cocoa, coffee and sugar traded at London and three currencies traded at Chicago.

Statistical models are summarized in sections 3, 4 and 7.1. These include terms describing price trends consistent with empirical results reported in three recent papers (Taylor, 1980, 1982a, 1982b). All the futures prices display some behaviour that can be modelled by trends. The published, statistical arguments are not repeated here; rather, the economic implications of the statistical results are sought for investors.

Section 5 is a mathematical analysis of the relationship between autocorrelation and inefficient pricing, using simple trading rules and several optimistic assumptions. Section 6 describes better trading rules and defines realistic assumptions for practical evaluations of the rules upon simulated and real prices. The rules have two parameters, which are optimized on simulated prices in section 7. Section 8 then assesses the economic value of the trading rules upon further prices, not used in the process of constructing the rules and choosing their parameters. Currency futures markets appear to have been efficient, at least since 1979. However, some commodity futures markets are apparently inefficient. These and other conclusions are summarized in section 9. Figure 1 summarizes the methodology used.

2 Six futures markets

2.1 Agricultural markets at London

Empirical results have been calculated from daily closing prices recorded at three commodity futures markets in London and at three

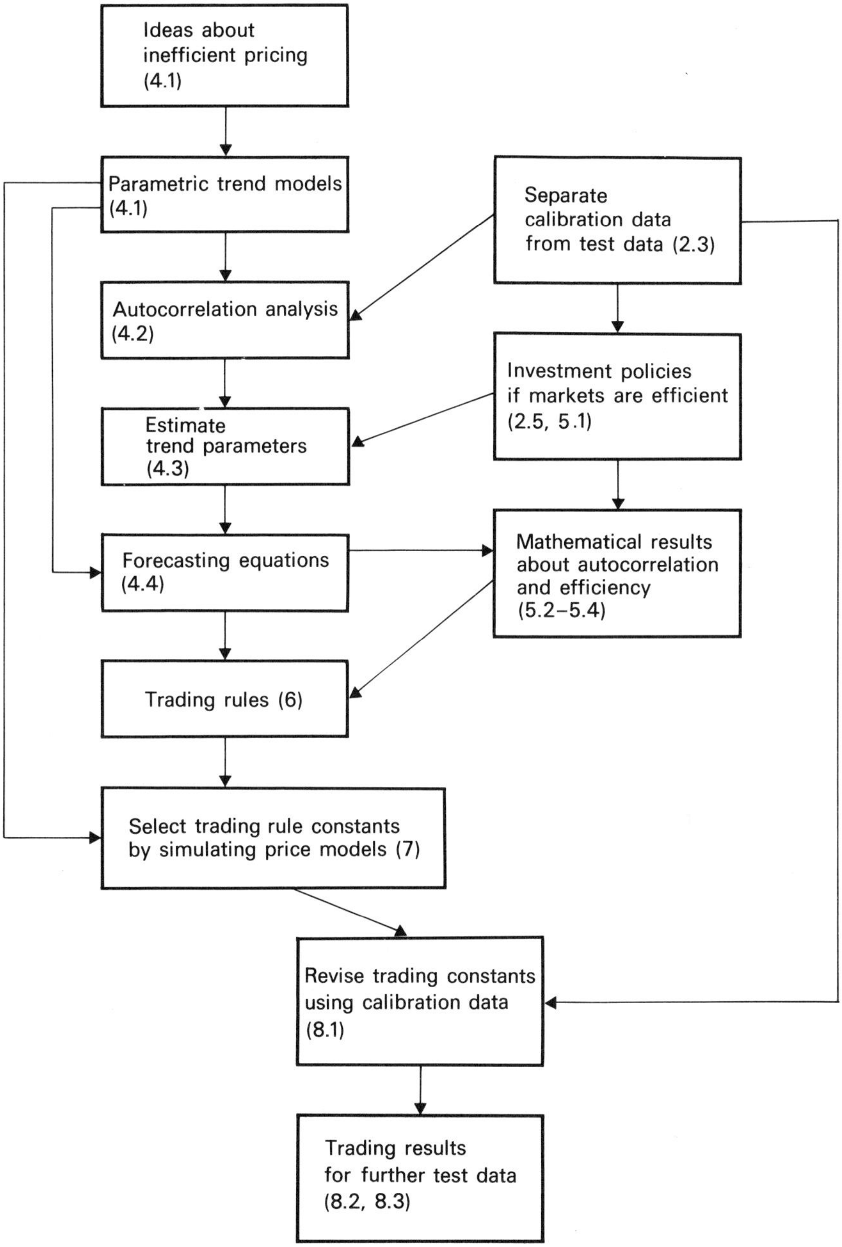

Fig. 1 A summary of the methodology

(Numbers in brackets refer to sections in the text)

Table 1 The most important agricultural futures markets in London, 1980

	Contracts (daily)	*Size (tonnes)*	*Value (£m)*	*Recent price (Feb. 1982) (£)*
Cocoa	2,567	10	25	1,200
Coffee	4,381	5	20	1,280
Sugar	10,067	50	150	180

currency futures markets in Chicago. Cocoa, coffee and sugar are the most important commodities traded at agricultural futures markets in London. Table 1 shows their substantial average daily trading volumes for all futures contracts, the quantities traded in one contract in metric tonnes, and the approximate value of the merchandise traded on an average day in millions of pounds sterling. Official figures for 1980 are quoted. The table also shows prices per tonne in February 1982. Trading costs per contract, defined as the sum of a broker's commission (about £40) plus the difference in bid and ask prices, are between 0.5 and 1 per cent of the contract's value. Brokers usually require an initial margin deposit of about 10 per cent, in cash, to guarantee payment of any losses.

Cocoa and coffee prices from 1971 to 1980 and sugar prices from 1961 to 1980 have been stored in computer files at Lancaster. In this paper September futures are investigated for cocoa and November futures for coffee. December sugar futures are studied from 1961 to 1979, followed by the January 1981 contract from December 1979 to December 1980 because of recent, minor changes in the organization of sugar trading. The prices of each futures contract are usually considered for 13 months, commencing 14 months before the delivery date. Prices recorded in the first month are used only to calculate initial values for statistical and forecasting methods. Thereafter, prices for one year are available for statistical tests and trading evaluations, starting 13 months before the delivery date and finishing 1 month before it. Thus only one price a day is used in the major analyses.

It is assumed that prices recorded several months before a delivery date are reliable. In particular, it is assumed that trading volume is sufficient to permit trades at the prices used. Further research will assess the relationship between the time to delivery and trading results.

2.2 *Currency markets at Chicago*

Sterling, the deutschmark and the Swiss franc are the European currencies traded in large quantities by futures contracts at the International Monetary Market (IMM) in Chicago. These three currencies are studied. The IMM trades comparable quantities of Canadian dollars and Japanese yen but only insignificant amounts of French francs and Dutch guilders.

After the IMM opened in May 1972, trading volumes for the studied currencies rose quickly, particularly from 1977 to 1980. Table 2 gives the 1980 figures for average daily volume in trading units, the quantity of currency in one unit and the approximate value of daily business at the IMM in millions of US dollars. Also given are some recent (February 1982) prices.

Daily trading values for the currencies at the IMM and for sugar in London are similar and far exceed those for cocoa and coffee. IMM trading costs depend on the broker employed but are usually about $50 per unit or 0.2 per cent of the value traded. The minimum, permitted, initial margin deposits vary from $1,500 to $2,000, which are about 3 per cent of one unit's value. Treasury bills can sometimes be used as deposits to increase an investor's expected income. IMM clients thus have favourable trading costs and margins compared with clients of the London markets.

Daily settlement prices have been transcribed from the yearbooks of the IMM, for June and December futures from January 1974 to November 1980. As these prices are the average price over the final minute of trading, they are effectively closing prices.

The IMM published the trading volume of each futures contract near the settlement price. Volumes are always relatively low when the delivery date is more than six months away. Consequently, the June contract is usually studied from 1 December until the following

Table 2 Trading of selected currency futures at the International Monetary Market, Chicago, 1980

	Units (daily)	*Size (1 unit)*	*Value ($m)*	*Recent price (Feb. 1982)*
Sterling	5,025	25,000 £	290	1,88 $/£
Deutschmark	3,668	125,000 DM	250	0.43 $/DM
Swiss franc	3,292	125,000 SF	250	0.54 $/SF

31 May and the December contract from 1 June until 30 November; the single exception is the commencement of the June 1974 records on 2 January. A further month of prices per contract are used to obtain various initial values, as already described for the agricultural futures.

It is possible to identify all the days when there was no trading in a contract, from the information about volumes. For sterling these occurred for 12 per cent of market days before June 1976 and the percentages are smaller for the other currencies. After June 1976, the percentages decreased rapidly because the trading volume accelerated upwards. When the volume was zero but the IMM announced a settlement price it was used; otherwise the preceding day's price was used. Thus one price a day was obtained for the subsequent analyses. Prices for 1,739 days are considered, covering seven years and 14 contracts for each currency.

On a few days trading was stopped because the change in price since the previous settlement equalled the IMM's daily limit. The normal limit is about 2 per cent of the settlement price.

2.3 Subsets of the prices

A rigorous study of trading rules requires a partition of the available prices into two subsets. Only the information present in the first subset should be used to invent a rule and choose the values of its parameters. Subsequently, the rule can be evaluated on the second subset, but without changing parameter values, and only these results can be used for correct tests of the efficient market hypothesis. The terms 'complete data', 'calibration data' and 'test data' for a commodity or currency will refer, as appropriate, to all the data and the two subsets. The choice of the time used to split a series into two subsets can be difficult and can influence the final conclusions. This is an interesting subject for further research.

Some of the London prices have already been shown to refute the random walk hypothesis (Taylor, 1980, 1982b). They are now used as calibration data, for cocoa and coffee from 1971 to 1976 and for sugar from 1961 to 1973. This leaves four years of cocoa and coffee prices and seven years of sugar prices for test data.

I had not studied IMM prices before this study of efficiency. Prices from 1974 to 1978 were chosen to be calibration data, because experience shows that helpful random walk tests and price-trend estimates require at least 1,000 prices. Tests and estimates follow in section 4. The IMM test data cover the other two years, 1979 and 1980.

2.4 Summary statistics

Denoting the observed closing price of an asset on day t by z_t, the return obtained by possessing it from day $t-1$ to day t is defined to be $x_t = \log(z_t) - \log(z_{t-1})$. Lower-case letters will denote observed data (z_t, x_t), which are interpreted as realizations of random variables denoted by the corresponding upper-case letters (Z_t, X_t).

Table 3 presents the sample means, standard deviations and kurtoses for the daily returns, separately for the complete, calibration and test datasets. For n returns these statistics are calculated as

$$\bar{x} = \Sigma x_t/n, \quad s = \sqrt{\{(n-1)^{-1}\Sigma(x_t-\bar{x})^2\}},$$
$$\text{and } k = (n-1)^{-1}\Sigma(x_t-\bar{x})^4/s^4.$$

It can be seen from table 3 that the means and standard deviations of the commodity returns far exceed those for the currency returns. These differences are later shown to have important implications for investigations into market efficiency. The standard deviation of returns determines the speed of changes in prices. Thus the commodity prices, with a typical deviation of 0.02, change much faster than the currency prices, whose deviations are only about 0.006. For comparison, returns on individual US stocks have daily standard deviations whose average is around 0.02 (Brown and Warner, 1980, p. 211; Oldfield and Rogalski, 1980, p. 734) and the figure for Standard and Poor's US stock index is about 0.007 (French, 1980, p. 58). Investments in commodity futures and individual stocks thus have comparable risks, if the daily standard deviation is used as a risk measure. Normal distributions have kurtosis equal to 3, so table 3 shows that all the returns studied here are leptokurtic and fat-tailed.

2.5 Risk premia

Dusak (1973) did not find any premium for US wheat, corn and soyabeans futures between 1952 and 1967. Bodie and Rosansky (1980), in contrast, estimated the annual return from long positions in US commodity futures to be 14 per cent between 1950 and 1976, after including some interest from Treasury bills but excluding commission costs. Bills alone returned about 4 per cent so the implied premium appears to be 10 per cent per annum. Uncertainty about the existence of risk premia is due partially to the difficult problem of accurately estimating expected returns from samples (Merton, 1980). This applies even to the large datasets investigated here.

Table 3 Summary statistics

	From	*To*	*Returns*	*Mean* $\times 10^4$	*St. dev.* $\times 10^2$	*Kurtosis*
Complete data						
Cocoa	4/1/71	29/8/80	2,432	7.81	1.93	9.58
Coffee	4/1/71	31/10/80	2,477	5,86	2.16	17.25
Sugar	3/1/61	30/12/80	5,049	3.31	2.33	8.62
Sterling	2/1/74	28/11/80	1,738	1.86	0.55	6.71
Deutschmark	2/1/74	28/11/80	1,738	0.88	0.55	5.40
Swiss franc	2/1/74	28/11/80	1,738	1.93	0.69	4.59
Calibration data						
Cocoa	4/1/71	31/8/76	1,427	14.19	1.87	5.03
Coffee	4/1/71	29/10/76	1,470	11.42	1.62	54.47
Sugar	3/1/61	28/11/73	3,270	3.01	1.95	8.11
Sterling	2/1/74	30/11/78	1,236	0.66	0.53	8.60
Deutschmark	2/1/74	30/11/78	1,236	1.99	0.54	5.58
Swiss franc	2/1/74	30/11/78	1,236	4.09	0.66	4.51
Test data						
Cocoa	1/9/76	29/8/80	1,005	−1.25	1.99	14.42
Coffee	1/11/76	31/10/80	1,007	−2.27	2.76	6.40
Sugar	29/11/73	30/12/80	1,779	3.88	2.90	7.13
Sterling	1/12/78	28/11/80	502	4.83	0.60	3.56
Deutschmark	1/12/78	28/11/80	502	−1.87	0.55	5.12
Swiss franc	1/12/78	28/11/80	502	3.39	0.76	4.68

Although there appear to be risk premia available at the London markets, their existence cannot be proved rigorously.

Suppose a UK investor buys London contracts, sends all requested margin deposits to a broker and invests the remainder of the initial value of the contracts in a fast withdrawal bank account. The annual returns r_i from the 40 London contracts are defined by the difference between the final and initial prices divided by the initial price. Ignoring taxes, commission and bank interest, sugar averaged 37 per cent per annum, cocoa 36 per cent and coffee 26 per cent with an overall average of 34 per cent. If the investor could have bought the 40 contracts at yearly intervals, always investing the wealth at the end of one year in the next contract, then final wealth would have been $(1+r_1)(1+r_2)\ldots(1+r_{40})=(1.14)^{40}$. Obviously, different premia can be estimated from the average return of 34 per cent and the compound return of 14 per cent. Commission reduces these figures by about 1 per cent, but bank interest should be added. As risk-free investments offered an overall compound rate of 9 per cent and margin deposits start at 10 per cent and rarely reach 50 per cent, the investor could surely have averaged an extra 5 per cent in interest. Therefore an annual premium of at least $(14-1+5)-9=9$ per cent appears to have been available, or 29 per cent if the average return is used instead of the compound return. The results support Bodie and Rosansky's opinion that buying and holding commodity futures is an attractive investment. Note that 9 per cent is the historical premium on both UK and US shares according to Dimson and Brealey (1978), while Merton (1980, table 4.7) estimates the US premium to be between 8 and 12 per cent.

A similar analysis for currency futures shows that US investors who bought and sold at half-yearly intervals would have averaged 4.0 per cent per annum from trades less perhaps 0.4 per cent in commission less some bank interest lost because of margin deposits. Any historical premium is thus small, and furthermore the sample means given in table 1 are not significantly different from zero using standard tests. Consequently, passive investment in currency futures cannot be recommended to private investors seeking higher expected returns.

3 Fluctuating standard deviations

Sample variances calculated from disjoint sets of returns are often significantly different; for example, see Merton (1980, table 4.8) for stocks, Labys and Thomas (1975) and Taylor (1982a) for commodities, and Levich (1979) for currencies. For each of the six assets there are substantial differences between the contract standard deviations. Thus the speed at which prices change appears not to be constant. The trading volumes increased with time, particularly for the currencies, but there is not a simple relationship between the standard deviations and the trading volumes.

The appropriate statistical conclusion is that returns are the output from a non-linear stochastic process, which could be stationary. This is explained and proved in section A1 of the Appendix.

It is now convenient to summarize a general statistical approach to the phenomenon of apparent changes in daily standard deviations (Taylor, 1982a). Let

$$X_t = \bar{\mu} + V_t U_t \qquad (1)$$

with $\bar{\mu}$ being the expected return while $\langle X \rangle$, $\langle V \rangle$ and $\langle U \rangle$ are stochastic processes generating returns, standard deviations and standardized returns respectively. Processes $\langle U \rangle$ and $\langle V \rangle$ are constrained by the following.

(a) The U_t have zero means, unit variances and are approximately independent and identically distributed.
(b) The realizations $\langle v \rangle$ of $\langle V \rangle$ are always positive. Given a realization, the conditional standard deviations of the returns are v and hence time-dependent. Returns will appear to have changing standard deviations if $\langle V \rangle$ has suitable autocorrelations and a high coefficient of variation.
(c) Every pair V_s and U_t are independent.

The special case, when $V_t^2 = \sigma^2$ for all t and constant σ^2, will be referred to by the phrase 'constant variance'. Expected returns, $E(X_t)$, are assumed to be constant. The consequences of this in the subsequent analysis are negligible.

4 Price trend models

Trends that slowly incorporate some new information into prices are the popular alternative to the idea of perfect efficiency. Statistical models for trends have been conjectured and tested in previous papers (Taylor, 1980, 1982b). The models are reviewed in this section and claimed to offer a credible description of price behaviour in all six markets. Methods of forecasting future prices are described, and are used to define trading rules in sections 5 and 6.

4.1 *Price trend autocorrelations*

Slow interpretation of any relevant information causes some information to be reflected partially in returns on more than one day. Returns will then be positively autocorrelated. The effect of current information, not reflected in the price, upon future returns should diminish as time progresses, so the autocorrelations should decrease. It is well known that correlations between returns are small. A simple set of small, positive and decreasing autocorrelation functions is used to define the conjecture price trend autocorrelations:

$$\rho_i = Ap^i, \qquad \text{all } i > 0 \text{ with } A > 0 \text{ and } 1 > p > 0. \tag{2}$$

Here ρ_i denotes the correlation between U_t and U_{t+i}, assumed to depend on the time lag i alone. Equation (2) holds for several stochastic processes (Taylor, 1980, section 2). A specific example is presented in section 7.1 below.

Parameter A measures the information not reflected by prices within one day and perfect efficiency would require A to be zero. Parameter p measures the speed at which imperfectly reflected information is incorporated. The average total effect of such information upon returns divided by the effect on the first day equals $(1-p)^{-1}=m$, called 'the mean trend duration' (Taylor, 1980, section 2).

4.2 *Tests of the random walk hypothesis*

Several tests of the random walk hypothesis (H0: $\rho_i = 1$, all $i > 0$) against the price trend hypothesis (H1), defined by equation (2), have already been investigated for London prices, including the commodities' calibration data. New test statistics, which are powerful when price trends define the alternative to random behaviour, were found to reject H0 more often than other statistics. The new tests use

$$T^* = 0.4274\sqrt{n} \sum_{i=1}^{30} 0.92^i R_i \tag{3}$$

and

$$U^* = 0.4649\sqrt{n} \sum_{i=2}^{30} 0.92^i R_i \tag{4}$$

with the R_i being autocorrelations calculated from n observations. The constants 30 and 0.92 are used in equations (3) and (4) to ensure high test power whenever $A \leqslant 0.04$ and $p \geqslant 0.8$ (Taylor, 1982b, section IV). Both statistics are asymptotically normal with mean zero and variance one when H0 is true. If H1 applies, the statistics have positive expected values so H0 is rejected, at the 5 per cent significance level, if the statistics exceed 1.65. When price records are unreliable, U^* is preferable to T^* as errors reduce R_i (Taylor, 1982b, section V). The sample autocorrelations are here calculated from rescaled returns, $\hat{u}_t = x_t/\hat{v}_t$, with $\hat{v}_t$ estimating the effective standard deviation on day t. Further details of the rescaling method are given in section A2 of the Appendix.

Table 4 includes the values of the test statistics and the numbers of positive sample autocorrelations, at lags 1–10 and lags 1–30. The commodity results confirm that London returns are not random, both for the calibration and the test datasets.

All three currency futures did not have random returns during the calibration period, according to the tests at a 5 per cent significance level. No dependence, however, is detected by the tests during the later period for two of the currencies. Movements in the prices of different currencies on the same day are correlated, so the test values are not independent (Taylor, 1982b, Appendix).

A clear majority of the coefficients are positive, as predicted by the price trend hypothesis (see table 4). The observed positive behaviour cannot be explained away by time-dependent expected returns or by the rescaling method, for reasons given in section A2 of the Appendix. A number of other tests were evaluated (defined in Taylor, 1982b, section VIII), and only the test for a peak in the spectrum at frequency zero rejected random behaviour for all the complete datasets.

4.3 Trend parameter estimates

Estimates of the trend parameters, A and $m = (1-p)^{-1}$, have been chosen to optimize the agreement between the observed and theoretical autocorrelations at lags 1–50 (cf. Taylor, 1980, section 5). The estimates are presented in table 4, and also the best A when m is constrained to be 20. It is known that the estimates of A and m

Table 4 Autocorrelation results

	Years	n	T^*	U^*	*Positive r_i* 1–10	1–30	$\hat{A}$	$\hat{m}$	$\hat{A}_{20}$
Complete data									
Cocoa	1971–80	2,412	6.09	5.49	8	22	0.0448	19	0.0436
Coffee	1971–80	2,457	7.02	4.83	10	22	0.0906	7	0.0433
Sugar	1961–80	5,029	7.90	6.58	8	28	0.0378	22	0.0397
Sterling	1974–80	1,718	3.20	2.16	9	23	0.0259	29	0.0306
Deutschmark	1974–80	1,718	4.53	4.41	10	20	0.0397	20	0.0397
Swiss franc	1974–80	1,718	2.59	2.70	10	21	0.0205	40*	0.0262
Calibration data									
Cocoa	1971–6	1,407	4.06	3.40	8	21	0.0440	15	0.0375
Coffee	1971–6	1,450	6.50	4.64	10	23	0.1220	6	0.0523
Sugar	1961–73	3,250	6.52	5.46	9	25	0.0395	21	0.0405
Sterling	1974–8	1,216	3.21	2.20	7	24	0.0295	36	0.0378
Deutschmark	1974–8	1,216	2.37	2.21	10	19	0.0383	9	0.0229
Swiss franc	1974–8	1,216	1.91	1.78	6	16	0.0185	40**	0.0236
Test data									
Cocoa	1976–80	985	3.17	3.02	9	25	0.0397	14	0.0316
Coffee	1976–80	1,005	2.65	1.50	8	19	0.1615	2	0.0245
Sugar	1974–80	1,759	4.43	3.64	7	25	0.0356	23	0.0381
Sterling	1978–80	482	0.23	0.01	6	15	0.0110	6	0
Deutschmark	1978–80	482	3.24	3.26	9	18	0.0685	12	0.0503
Swiss franc	1978–80	482	0.27	0.67	5	14	0.0096	6	0

* Upper limit for m set at 40; overall optima at $m = 64$, $A = 0.0158$

** Ditto with $m = 80$, $A = 0.0165$

are not very accurate. For example, a 95 per cent confidence region for the parameters of the complete sterling data includes the points (0.04, 7), (0.01, 30), (0.04, 30) and (0.02, 100). Consequences of the uncertainty caused by the large confidence regions for users of trading systems are explored in section 7. Commodity futures appear to have shorter trend durations than currency futures, but less information is reflected instantaneously. The sterling futures have smaller estimates than spot sterling prices ($A = 0.034$, $m = 56$; see Taylor, 1980) and are perhaps more efficient.

The observed autocorrelations and estimates of A show that the markets are not perfectly efficient. It might be thought that transaction costs will prevent exploitation of the very low dependence between returns, so that the markets are efficient. However, it will be argued that several positive autocorrelations ρ_i, albeit small, can suffice to make a market inefficient. Sections 5 and 7 will identify sets of trend parameters for which markets are theoretically inefficient, using mathematics and simulation respectively. Afterwards, section 8 presents trading results for the test data, using rules obtained from the theoretical studies.

4.4 *Forecasting equations*

All the trading rules apply results from the statistical theory of optimal linear forecasting, reviewed by Granger and Newbold (1977, chapter 4). Results will be quoted without proof for the special case of returns generated by a stationary, Gaussian process with $E(X_t) = \bar{\mu}$ and var $(X_t) = \sigma^2 = V_t^2$ (also presented in Taylor, 1980, section 6).

At time t, the information in present and past prices, $I_t = \langle z_{t-j}, j = 0, 1, 2, \ldots \rangle$, can be used to calculate expected prices at future times $t+N$, $N > 0$, as follows. First, optimal forecasts $f_{t,i}$ of x_{t+i} can be obtained. There are simple relationships between consecutive forecasts of the next return and between forecasts made for different horizons i:

$$f_{t,1} = \bar{\mu} + q\,(f_{t-1,1} - \bar{\mu}) + (p - q)(x_t - \bar{\mu}) \qquad (5)$$

and

$$f_{t,i} = \bar{\mu} + p^{i-1}(f_{t,1} - \bar{\mu}), \quad i > 1. \qquad (6)$$

In equation (5) the smoothing constant q depends on A and p with $0 < q < p$; section A3 of the Appendix gives the formulae for q and the $f_{t,i}$. Second, the optimal forecasts of $s_N = \Sigma x_{t+i}$ $(i = 1, \ldots, N)$ are simply $g_N = \Sigma f_{t,i}$ $(i = 1, \ldots, N)$. Then, the distribution of $S_N =$

ΣX_{t+i} $(i=1,\ldots,N)$, given the information I_t, is normal with mean g_N and variance $D_N - W_N$, with $D_N = \text{var}(S_N)$ and $W_N = \text{var}(G_N)$. The formulae for D_N and W_N are given in section A3. Finally, the expected values of the future prices Z_{t+N}, condition on I_t, are

$$E(Z_{t+N} \mid I_t) = z_t E(\exp S_N \mid I_t)$$
$$= z_t \exp [g_N + 0.5*(D_N - W_N)]. \quad (7)$$

A useful number is the standardized forecast defined by

$$[g_N - E(G_N)]/sd(G_N) = (g_N - N\bar{\mu})/W_N^{1/2} = h, \quad (8)$$

say, which is independent of N for price trend models. The unconditional distribution of H is normal with mean 0 and variance 1. Given h, and hence g_N, equation (7) still gives the conditional expected prices.

5 Mathematical analysis

It is now assumed that returns are generated by a trend model. Theoretical methods can be used to decide if a pair of trend parameters (A and p) signify an inefficient market, although several assumptions must be made.

5.1 Strategies

An investor's optimal behaviour when futures markets are efficient depends on the expected returns and risks from futures, stocks and other risky assets. In particular, futures will be bought as a long-term investment only if there is a risk premium.

First, consider the investment problem when a premium exists, as provisionally claimed for the London argicultural markets. It is well known that returns from commodity futures are almost independent of stock returns (Dusak, 1973, Bodie and Rosansky, 1980). Therefore an investor with sufficient resources to buy a diversified portfolio should buy and keep both stocks and futures. Bodie and Rosansky (1980) have claimed that adding commodity futures to a portfolio of stocks decreases the standard deviation of annual returns from 19 to 13 per cent without decreasing the expected return. Furthermore, the results in sections 2.4 and 2.5 show that London agricultural futures appear to have similar risks to individual stocks but higher average returns. Thus, to show inefficiencies, an improvement on the 'buy and hold' strategy must be demonstrated.

A trading strategy that gets out of futures when prices are expected to fall is: (a) buy goods worth Q on day 0; (b) sell all the goods on day $t>0$ if the standardized, optimal forecast is less than some number h_0 and put the cash received into risk-free investment for N days; (c) buy goods worth Q again on day $t+N$.

This strategy is less risky than 'buy and hold' because the investor owns risky futures for fewer days. As a mathematical proposition this is certainly true when risk is measured by variance and returns have non-negative autocorrelations. It might, however, appear that trading is a risky activity whereas 'buy and hold' leads to a fairly certain return in the long run: such reasoning is fallacious, since long-term prices are anything but certain when prices are similar to a random walk. Thus the market will be inefficient if the trading strategy increases the expected return, since the risk will simultaneously have decreased.

Second, suppose there is not a risk premium, which appears to be the case for the currency futures. Businessmen might well use futures to reduce risks but it is difficult to believe that private investors would own futures if the market were efficient. To prove inefficient pricing a trading strategy must earn an average return of at least the risk-free interest rate. A strategy intended to earn high returns when the trend is predicted to be substantial is investigated: (a) invest in risk-free assets on day 0; (b) buy or sell, as appropriate, on day $t>0$ if the absolute value of the standardized forecast exceeds a number h_0; (c) on day $t+N$ liquidate the position and revert to risk-free investments. Applying this strategy with part of an investor's wealth is similar to adding a risky asset to a portfolio. The risk will again be less than the 'buy and hold' risk.

5.2 Assumptions

The strategies are evaluated by assuming the following.

(a) Some investors know the stochastic process generating prices; in particular, they know the trend parameters, A and p.
(b) Returns are multivariate normal distributed with means $\bar{\mu}$ and constant variances σ^2.
(c) Departures from the efficient market policy always last a fixed time, N days, whatever the prices during that period.
(d) Brokers are paid cQ in commission when futures worth Q are obtained; this covers the cost of opening and closing the position.
(e) One margin deposit of dQ is made to a broker, who pays no interest on it.

(f) Risk-free investments pay interest on trading days alone, at the rate r per day.
(g) Money is transferred instantaneously between the investor's broker and risk-free account, in either direction.
(h) Taxes are ignored.

All these assumptions are made in order to obtain exact results. The first is optimistic and favours the investor. This is offset, to some degree, by the third assumption, which is clearly sub-optimal.

5.3 *Results when there is a risk premium*

Suppose the 'buy and hold' strategist buys on day 0; let day t be the first day (after day 0) on which the standardized forecast h is less than some number h_0. Then selling at time t and buying the goods back at time $t+N$ increases the expected wealth of an investor (at time $t+N$) if

$$1 + Ndr + (1 + Nr)(z_t - z_0)/z_0 > (1 + c)\, E(Z_{t+N}/z_0 | h). \quad (9)$$

It can then be shown that sufficient conditions for an inefficient market are

$$z_t/z_0 > (1 - d)/(1 - d - c), \quad (10a)$$

$$1 > E(Z_{t+N}/z_t | h) \quad (10b)$$

and

$$(1 + Ndr)/(1 + c) > E(Z_{t+N}/z_t | h) \quad \text{for some } N > 0. \quad (10c)$$

Proofs are given in section A4 of the Appendix. Inequalities (10a) and (10c) ensure the truth of inequality (9), while (10a) and (10b) make sure that trading does not decrease the average interest received after time $t+N$. The left-hand side of (10c) has two terms; Ndr measures the additional interest earned when all the deposit is recovered from the broker, while the divisor $1 + c$ reflects the payment of commission when the futures are rebought. Optimal forecasting theory gives the right-hand term of (10c) as a complicated function of A and p, via equations (7) and (8). It is necessary to choose h_0. This is equivalent to stating the proportion of those days, for which (10a) is true, on which profitable trades can be started. This proportion is an essential part of any definition of market inefficiency and I use 0.05, so that $h_0 = -1.65$.

Inequalities (10b) and (10c) have been tested using constants that are appropriate for UK investors in London agricultural futures during 1982:

$$c = 0.01,\ d = 0.2,\ r = 0.12/250,\ \bar{\mu} = 0.0005,\ \sigma = 0.022.$$

The implied risk-free rate is 12 per cent per annum and the values for $\bar{\mu}$ and σ are overall historical averages obtained from table 3. A minimum risk premium of 8 per cent is implied; it increases as either A or p increases from zero. Note that for these values of c, d and r, (10b) is always true whenever (10c) is true for some $N < 104$.

North-east of the curve $L_1 L_2$ on figure 2, a market is theoretically inefficient when all the assumptions made are valid. All three estimates of A and p for the complete datasets of London prices are in the inefficient region; so too are the calibration estimates. Table 5 shows, for the complete dataset estimates, the values of N giving the largest difference between the two sides of inequality (10c); also the percentage expected price fall for the 'buy and hold' strategy and the extra income and costs for the proposed trading variation, when the standardized forecast is -1.65 and z_t is about z_0.

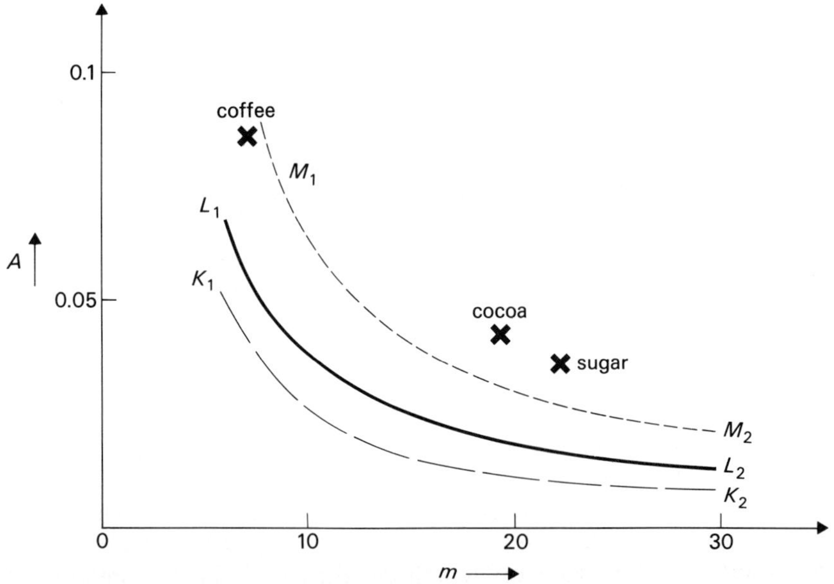

Fig. 2 Examples of inefficient regions when there is a risk premium (section 5.3)

Table 5 Results for trading in the inefficient region based on the complete data set

	Sugar	*Cocoa*	*Coffee*
Best *N*	29	26	11
'Buy and hold'			
Expected price change	−2.9	−2.9	−1.6
Trading			
Extra interest *Ndr*	0.3	0.3	0.1
Less commission *c*	−1.0	−1.0	−1.0
Total	−0.7	−0.7	−0.9
Net gain by trading	2.2%	2.2%	0.8%

Figure 2 also shows the effects on the boundary between efficient and inefficient markets if one constant is changed. When d is 1 (curve K_1K_2) the full value of the goods must be paid to the broker and markets are more likely to be inefficient. Either doubling the commission (to $c = 0.02$) or halving the standard deviation (to $\sigma = 0.011$) increases the amount of autocorrelation consistent with efficient pricing (approximately curve M_1M_2).

5.4 Results when there is not a risk premium

Buying futures when the standardized forecast is h on day t and selling N days later improves on risk-free investments if

$$E(Z_{t+N}/z_t|h) - 1 > c + Nr(c + d). \qquad (11)$$

Inequality (11) states that the gross trading profit must exceed the commission cost plus the interest forfeited on the commission and deposit. It the inequality is true for some $N > 0$ when $h = 1.65$, then the market will be called 'theoretically inefficient'. Constants suitable for US investors in IMM futures have been used:

$$c = 0.002, \quad d = 0.1, \quad r = 0.16/250, \quad \bar{\mu} = 0, \quad \sigma = 0.006.$$

Constant d has been set well above the permitted minimum of about 0.003 and the historical estimates of σ given in table 3 have been averaged to obtain the illustrative value. A risk-free rate of 16 per cent per annum reflects the high interest rates in the United States early in 1982. Large values of N tend to give the best results and an upper limit is required. This has been set at 40 trading days.

North-east of the curve L_1L_2 on figure 3 a market is theoretically inefficient. All the empirical estimates obtained from the complete

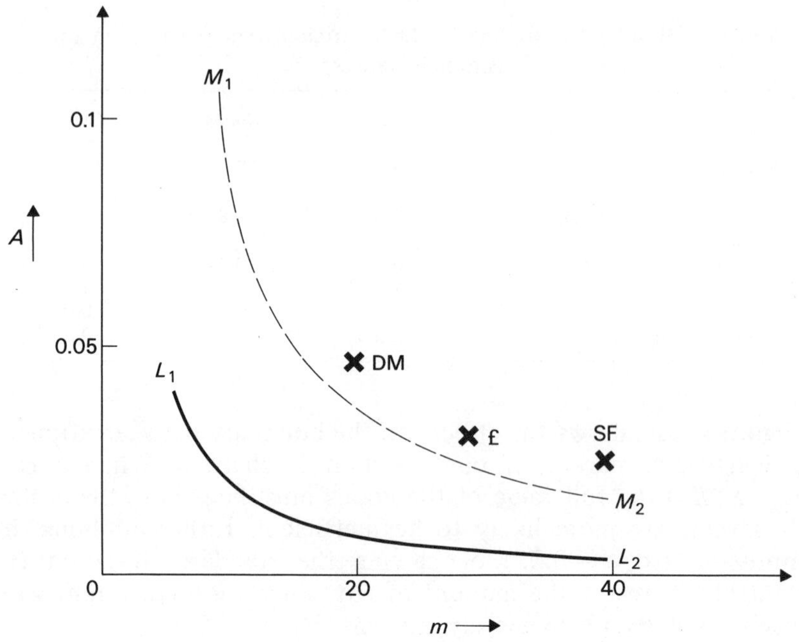

Fig. 3 Examples of inefficient regions when there is no premium (section 5.4)

datasets of IMM prices are in the inefficient region; the same is true of the calibration estimates. Also, using the complete dataset estimates, when N is 40 and $h = 1.65$, trading typically gains 1.8 per cent gross, loses 0.3 per cent in interest and costs 0.2 per cent in commission, making a net gain of 1.3 per cent. Curve $M_1 M_2$ indicates the parameters giving a net gain of 1 per cent. It is seen that, although very small autocorrelations can lead to trading gains, the dependence must be more substantial if the gain is to be valuable.

6 Realistic trading evaluations

The strategies are now made more realistic by improving the rules used to terminate trades. They will be evaluated on simulated prices in section 7 and on real prices in section 8.

6.1 Strategies

The strategies now have two parameters, to control the beginnings and to control the ends of trades. When there is a risk premium, futures are first bought when the (standardized) forecast exceeds h_1. They are subsequently sold if the forecast falls below h_2 and the proceeds are invested in a bank deposit account. Another trade is started when the forecast next exceeds h_1. The 'buy and hold' strategy is evaluated by setting $h_1 = -1{,}000$ and $h_2 < h_1$.

In the absence of a risk premium, trades start when the absolute value of h exceeds h_1 and finish when h is less than h_2 if futures have been bought, or when h is more than $-h_2$ if they were sold. Resources are again invested in a bank between trades. Trades have never been started during the final 15 days. If necessary, trades are concluded on the final (non-delivery) day of a contract.

6.2 Assumptions

The assumptions in section 5.2 are revised to enhance the reality of the results, by reflecting the constraints encountered by investors.

(a) Some investors think they know the structure of the stochastic process $\langle U \rangle$, and possess imperfect estimates of the trend parameters.
(b) Instructions to brokers are made after reading yesterday's closing prices in today's newspapers. Decisions are then evaluated at the next closing price, in effect one day late, as recommended by Jennergren (1975).
(c) All trading quantities are chosen to make the value of the goods bought or sold at the beginning of a trade, denoted Q, equal to the initial capital available for futures trading, denoted C. Keeping Q constant, irrespective of the current price and resources, ensures that the risk of a trading strategy is less than the risk of the 'buy and hold' strategy. Fixing Q at numbers other than C merely selects a different combination of expected final capital and risk. For example, doubling Q will double all the cash flows and so, first, will double the difference between the expected final capital and the wealth from risk-free investments and, second, will double the standard deviation of the final capital. (Note that the number of lots traded will usually not be an integer.)
(d) A broker is paid cQ in commission to start and finish one trade.
(e) An initial margin deposit of dQ is sent to the broker. If the balance with the broker falls below eQ, as a result of the trade losing more than $(d-e)Q$ since the latest margin was sent, then the balance is restored to dQ by sending a further margin deposit. No interest is paid by the broker.

(f) When the broker returns deposits plus trading gains less trading losses there is a delay of D_1 trading days. After the D_1 days, the cash starts to earn interest from the bank.
(g) The bank nominally requires D_2 trading days' notice for withdrawals. It permits immediate withdrawals but then deducts the interest earned on the amount during the preceding D_2 days. The interest rate is R per annum.
(h) Taxes are ignored.

In all subsequent calculations in this paper I have used $D_1 = 3$ and $D_2 = 5$, the current situation for UK investors. The trading constants for all the London commodities have been set at

$$c = 0.01, \ d = 0.1 \ \text{and} \ e = 0.05,$$

for comparison with

$$c = 0.002, \ d = 0.04 \ \text{and} \ e = 0.02$$

for the Chicago currency futures. In both cases further margin deposits are required if half of the original deposit is lost. Interest rates were set in the UK at 10 per cent per annum for simulated prices and the calibration period, increasing to 14 per cent for evaluations on the test data. The US interest rate was taken to be 12 per cent before December 1978 and 16 per cent thereafter.

6.3 *Objectives*

The two parameters of the trading strategies will be chosen to maximize the expected value of a trader's capital at the end of one year, subject to the constraint in assumption (c) above. Note that there is no reason to believe that the derived strategies will then be optimal in a mean/variance or expected utility framework. Neither will they necessarily maximize the probability of correctly rejecting the efficient market hypothesis when it is false.

7 Trading on simulated prices

Prices have been simulated to optimize trading rules and to estimate their expected performance without relying on relatively short historical records. Trend models are again assumed, but now the relationship between the model parameters (A and p) and efficiency can be studied without oversimplifying the stochastic process of prices, the investor's knowledge and the transactions with brokers and banks. In particular, the consequences of uncertainty about the trend model's parameters can be assessed.

7.1 *Stochastic processes*

The product process described in section 3 has been simulated, to give prices $\langle z_t \rangle$ as a realization of

$$Z_t = Z_{t-1} \exp(X_t), \qquad X_t = \bar{\mu} + V_t U_t.$$

Process $\langle V \rangle$ controls the speed at which prices change. It has been supposed that $\langle \log V \rangle$ is Gaussian with means α, variances β^2 and autocorrelations ϕ^i. Thus $\langle \log V \rangle$ is a first-order autoregressive process. Parameters α, β and ϕ have been estimated from data by matching various moments and autocorrelations, using the methods published in Taylor (1982a). Time-dependent standard deviations require minor changes in the formulae for the forecasts and their standardized values, listed in section A3.

Process $\langle U \rangle$ is independent of $\langle V \rangle$ and contains trends. The standardized return U_t equals a trend component T_t plus strict white noise ϵ_t, with $E(T_t) = E(\epsilon_t) = 0$, $\mathrm{var}(T_t) = A$ and $\mathrm{var}(\epsilon_t) = 1 - A$. Component $\langle T \rangle$ follows the basic trend model: $T_t = T_{t-1}$ with probability p, otherwise T_t is independent of all past variables (cf. Taylor, 1980, section 2); the autocorrelations of $\langle T \rangle$ are p^i. Both T_t and ϵ_t have been supposed to have normal distributions.

These processes give X_t the lognormal–normal distribution explored for cotton futures by Clark (1973). The implied kurtosis of the returns is $3 \exp(4\beta^2)$ (Taylor, 1982a, section 6.1). Replacing β by the estimates gives a satisfactory agreement between the predicted kurtoses and the empirical kurtoses listed in table 3.

For each simulated contract, 310 prices are generated by the first 60 of these are used only to obtain initial values.

7.2 *Trading simulated commodity prices*

Prices similar to sugar prices have been simulated using parameters obtained from the calibration data:

$$\bar{\mu} = 3/10{,}000, \ \alpha = -4.25, \ \beta = 0.56, \ \phi = 0.98, \ A = 0.04 \ \text{and} \ p = 0.95.$$

The median, conditional, standard deviation is then $\exp(\alpha) = 0.0143$ and 95 per cent of the conditional deviations are in the range $\exp(\alpha \pm 1.96\beta)$ or 0.0048–0.0429.

Table 6 Summary of annual percentage changes in capital for simulated prices

	Efficient market policy		*Trading strategy*			
	Mean	*St. dev.*	h_1	h_2	*Mean*	*St. dev.*
	%	%			%	%
Parameters based upon						
Cocoa	58.9	61.6	0	−1.8	60.0	59.9
Coffee	43.5	75.9	0	−1.4	49.7	72.5
Sugar	26.3	62.0	0	−1.0	31.7	58.3
Currencies	12.0	0	0.8	−0.3	16.2	10.2

Four sets of 100 contracts have been simulated. The average final capital is almost constant for h_1 between 0 and 0.8 and h_2 between −0.8 and −1.2. Table 6 shows the average capitals and standard deviations for 'buy and hold', and the trading strategy, when the investor correctly estimates A and p, and uses $h_1 = 0$ and $h_2 = -1$. 'Buy and hold' yields a premium of 16.3 per cent and trading adds a further 5.4 per cent to expected capital. As the annual standard deviations are (very approximately) twice the figure for individual stocks, the high premium is not unrealistic.

A large number of contracts need to be simulated for accurate estimates of average final capitals. The estimated standard errors for the averages are the estimated standard deviations divided by 20, i.e. about 3 per cent. The averages for the separate sets of 100 final trading gains show considerable variation: 22, 29, 35 and 41 per cent.

Even if price trend models generate prices, investors must make their decisions using imperfect estimates of A and p. Several sets of 100 contracts have been simulated using different values of A and p to those assumed by the investor. North-east of the curve L_1L_2 on figure 4 the trading strategy based upon $A = 0.04$, $m = 20$, $h_1 = -1$ gives better results than 'buy and hold'. A 95 per cent confidence region for A and p, using calibration prices, is the region $M_1M_2M_3M_4$ (Taylor, 1982a, section 6.6). All the region corresponds to an inefficient market. Thus, if an investor has confidence in the forecasting equations of price trend models, then uncertainty about the parameter estimates is not too important.

Further simulated prices have been obtained using the calibration data for cocoa and coffee to give parameter values: respectively,

$$\bar{\mu} = 14/10{,}000,\ \alpha = -4.18,\ \beta = 0.45,\ \phi = 0.987,\ A = 0.044,$$

$$p = 0.933$$

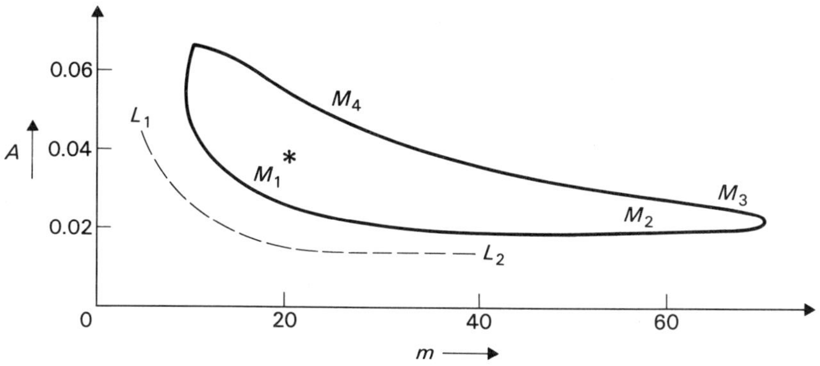

Fig. 4 Inefficient boundary for simulated prices (L_1L_2) and confidence region for sugar prices ($M_1M_2M_3M_4$) (section 7.2)

and

$$\bar{\mu}=11/10{,}000,\ \alpha=-4.39,\ \beta=0.83,\ \phi=0.9,\ A=0.12,\ p=0.833.$$

Table 6 summarizes the optimal results for 400 simulated contracts. Trading is estimated to gain 1.1 per cent per annum for simulated prices based upon past cocoa prices and 6.2 per cent for coffee, when A and p are correctly estimated. The very high average returns during the calibration period cause substantial profits from 'buy and hold' and a greater reluctance to switch from futures, seen in the lower values of h_2.

7.3 *Trading simulated currency prices*

The three confidence regions for the currency trend parameters are large and encompass similar values. Consequently, the estimates for the currencies have been combined and a common trading rule is used for all of them. Currency prices have been simulated for 400 contracts using

$$\bar{\mu}=0,\ \alpha=-5.34,\ \beta=0.46,\ \phi=0.92,\ A=0.028 \text{ and } p=0.95.$$

Trades are started when $|h|>h_1$ and the best values of h_1 are between 0.6 and 1. They are closed for buy trades when h is less than h_2 and the best values are between 0.2 and -0.4. Table 6 summarizes the results for the optimal values $h_1=0.8$ and $h_2=-0.3$, when trading increases the average final capital to 4.2 per cent more than the interest rate. Both the premium from trading and the annual standard deviation are far less than the equivalent figures for stocks.

Results have not been obtained for currency trading with imperfect trend estimates, because the results for real prices do not justify interest in the exercise.

8 Trading results for futures prices

8.1 Calibration prices

Four numbers must be specified to implement the rules: the trend model parameters, A, p, and the decision parameters, h_1 and h_2. All trading results for the calibration prices will be favourably biased, since A and p have been estimated from them. Various values of h_1 and h_2 close to the optima estimated by simulation have been considered, and final choices are made by using the results from both simulated and calibration prices. It would not be a good idea to rely on the calibration results alone, since the averages for a few years often vary haphazardly when small changes are made to h_1 and h_2.

Sugar trading results were much better for $h_1 = 0.4$ and $h_2 = -1$ (trading gains 8 per cent) than for $h_1 = 0$ and $h_2 = -1$ (trading gains nothing), although both values of h_1 were equally good for simulated prices; consequently the final choice made was $h_1 =$

Table 7 Average annual percentage changes in capital

	Efficient market policy	*Trading strategy*			*Trading gains*
	Average	h_1	h_2	*Average*	*Average*
	%			%	%
Calibration data					
Cocoa	61.5	0	−1.6	61.6	0.1
Coffee	52.3	0	−1.6	49.3	−3.0
Sugar	26.2	0.4	−1.0	34.3	8.1
Sterling	12.0	0.8	−0.3	17.6	5.6
Deutschmark	12.0	0.8	−0.3	20.0	8.0
Swiss franc	12.0	0.8	−0.3	21.6	9.6
Test data					
Cocoa	19.5	0	−1.6	20.4	0.9
Coffee	9.0	0	−1.6	9.9	0.9
Sugar	77.3	0.4	−1.0	104.4	27.1
Sterling	16.0	0.8	−0.3	20.9	4.9
Deutschmark	16.0	0.8	−0.3	16.4	0.4
Swiss franc	16.0	0.8	−0.3	12.8	−3.2

0.4. 'Buy and hold' was a very profitable strategy for cocoa and coffee from 1971 to 1976, so it is not surprising that the trading results are uninspiring. The cautious choice $h_2 = -1.6$ was made. Currency trades were consistently more profitable than risk-free investments, and the results could not be improved by slight changes to the parameter values chosen previously.

Table 7 summarises the final choices of h_1 and h_2 and the consequent average gains by trading, if it were somehow possible to select A, p, h_1 and h_2 before seeing the calibration prices. To obtain comparable results for the 'buy and hold' policy, h_1 is set at $-1{,}000$ with $h_2 < h_1$.

8.2 *Commodity results (test prices)*

Table 8 lists the results for each of the 15 contracts in the commodity test datasets. Percentage changes in capital are tabulated

Table 8 Annual results for London futures

	'Buy and hold', with interest		*Trading*	
	Gains	*Days owned*	*Gain*	*Days owned*
	%		%	
Cocoa				
1977	121.8	252	121.8	252
1978	1.9	251	−0.5	192
1979	−17.6	252	−18.0	196
1980	−28.1	250	−21.6	190
Average	19.5		20.4	
Coffee				
1977	−2.5	252	3.6	209
1978	17.7	251	9.4	227
1979	52.2	252	59.8	229
1980	−31.3	252	−33.2	198
Average	9.0		9.9	
Sugar				
1974	535.5	250	537.0	249
1975	−57.4	252	13.5	79
1976	−13.6	254	27.4	153
1977	−20.8	252	5.7	62
1978	−13.2	252	12.8	84
1979	47.5	250	33.7	172
1980	63.2	270	100.9	187
Average	77.3		104.4	
Overall average for 15 contracts	43.7		56.8	

along with the number of days that futures were owned. The efficient market policy, which buys futures and keeps them all year and earns interest on the money not needed for margin deposits, was slightly successful for cocoa but not for coffee. The trading strategy gave marginally better results, which are similar to the efficient market policy because the values of h_2 were extremely low.

The price of sugar soared in 1974, from £90 in December 1973 to £560 at the end of November 1974. 'Buy and hold' consequently recorded a dramatic profit which was almost exactly matched by the trading strategy. Prices then declined so that the trading strategy owned futures for only about 40 per cent of days from 1975 to 1978.

It appears that the sugar market was inefficient. Firm conclusions for the cocoa and coffee markets cannot be given. Any tests in the future would probably use higher values for h_2, as the historical average returns are less than the calibration estimates. Further tests might obtain clearer conclusions.

8.3 *Currency results (test prices)*

Table 7 summarizes the results for currency trading. The gains from sterling deals are almost offset by the losses from trades in Swiss francs. Overall, trading gains an average of 0.7 per cent per annum compared with a bank account. However, a non-trader could probably obtain at least 1 per cent extra interest by investing in a long-term, fixed-interest contract rather than the short-term bank account. Thus the trading results are consistent with efficient pricing.

Table 9 Comparison of the increases in average annual capitals by trading

	Expected increase		*Actual increase*
	Simulated prices	*Calibrated prices*	*Test prices*
	%	%	%
Cocoa	0.7	0.1	0.9
Coffee	5.9	−3.0	0.9
Sugar	5.5	8.1	27.1
Sterling	4.2	5.6	4.9
Deutschmark	4.2	8.0	0.4
Swiss franc	4.2	9.6	−3.2
Average (arithmetic mean of the six figures in the column)	4.1	4.7	5.2

8.4 Expectations and actual outcomes

Table 9 compares the gains actually obtained by trading with the gains expected by analysing the simulated and calibration prices. For all commodities, results are better for test prices than for calibration prices, with the opposite conclusion for the currencies. The final row of the table shows that the average gain by trading for the test contracts is very similar to the averages for the calibration and simulation contracts. This is due mainly to the unexpected high gain from sugar trading.

9 Concluding remarks

Theoretical analysis, by mathematical and simulation methods, shows that very little autocorrelation is required to make a market inefficient. Correlations less than 0.03, between returns, can be sufficient to cause inefficiency, provided that the total of the autocorrelations at all non-zero lags is fairly large. For example, a total of approximately 0.3 suffices for commodity markets to be inefficient.

Empirical analysis, however, is difficult. Many years of prices are required for both the calibration and test datasets if clear conclusions are to be obtained. Furthermore, these datasets must be studied separately. The controversial issue of risk premia in futures markets is crucial when the efficient market policy is defined and a trading rule is constructed for comparison with that policy.

Commodity futures appear to offer investors a risk premium, the prices change at about the same speed as stock prices, and autocorrelation in the calibration years persists into the test years with similar magnitudes. Currency futures, by contrast, do not offer any risk premium, the prices change very slowly compared with other risky assets, and the autocorrelation found among the returns before 1979 may now have disappeared.

Both commodity and currency futures markets have not always reflected freely available information within one day, so the markets are not perfectly efficient. A trading strategy based upon forecasting trends is apparently superior to the 'buy and hold' strategy for investments in sugar futures. The persistent autocorrelation in the cocoa and coffee returns and the minor trading gains for the test years suggest that all three London commodity futures markets could be inefficient. As the sugar gains may have exceeded those expected from the calibration studies by chance, likewise it is not particularly surprising that the cocoa and coffee gains are less than expected. The results from trading currency futures for the two test years are consistent with the hypothesis that the markets are efficient.

Appendix

A1 Non-linear processes

A simple example of a linear stochastic process is strict white noise, defined as a sequence of independent and identically distributed random variables. The general linear process is given by a linear function of the present and past terms from a strict white noise process.

One way to show that the process generating returns is non-linear requires the calculation of squared returns, $s_t = (x - \bar{x})^2$, and their autocorrelations. A detailed description of the method has been published for sugar returns (Taylor, 1982a) and the method is here applied to the complete datasets of all six assets. Each sample autocorrelation between s_t and s_{t+1} exceeds 0.16, whereas those between x_t and x_{t+1} range from 0.02 to 0.07. As linear processes have higher autocorrelations than their squares, it is certain that the returns come from non-linear processes (cf. Granger and Newbold, 1976; Granger and Andersen, 1978).

If each contract had a separate linear process, the method of calculating the autocorrelations of the squares would give similar estimates at all lags. This does not occur; for example, the estimate at lag 1 exceeds those at lags 10 and 20 for every asset.

A2 Rescaled returns

The estimates of v_t used here are calculated from the past returns by

$$\begin{aligned} \hat{v}_t &= 1.253\gamma \sum_{i=0}^{\infty} (1-\gamma)^i |x_{t-i-1}| \\ &= (1-\gamma)\hat{v}_{t-1} + 1.253\gamma |x_{t-1}|. \qquad \text{(A1)} \end{aligned}$$

Similar formulae appear in Taylor and Kingsman (1979), in which it is argued that the best γ is approximately 0.1 (for sugar returns) using maximum-likelihood methods.

Rescaled returns $\hat{u}_t = x_t/\hat{v}_t$ are about equal to $u_t(v_t/\hat{v}_t)$. Their variances are approximately constant, in contrast to non-rescaled returns whose variances are far from constant. Rescaled returns are therefore better data for calculating sample autocorrelations (Taylor, 1980, section 4.3; 1982b, section VI).

The transformation from returns $\langle X \rangle$ to rescaled returns $\langle \hat{U} \rangle$ cannot induce substantial autocorrelation in a random process. If the returns X_t or excess returns $X_t - E(X_t)$ are uncorrelated, it can be shown that the autocorrelations of $\langle U \rangle$ will be less than 0.004 (cf. Taylor, 1980, sections 4.1 and 4.5).

A3 Forecasting formulae

Section 4.4 refers to the optimal forecasts of x_{t+i} made at time t, which minimize the expected squared error, $E(X_{t+i} - F_{t,i})^2$. When the process is linear (and so v_t is constant), they are

$$\begin{aligned} f_{t,1} &= \bar{\mu} + (p-q) \sum_{j=0}^{\infty} q^j (x_{t-j} - \bar{\mu}) \\ &= \bar{\mu} + q(f_{t-1,1} - \bar{\mu}) + (p-q)(x_t - \bar{\mu}) \qquad \text{(A2)} \end{aligned}$$

and

$$f_{t,i} = \bar{\mu} + p^{i-1}(f_{t,1} - \bar{\mu}), \qquad i > 0,$$

with q given by the solution between 0 and 1 of the quadratic equation

$$q^2 - q[1 + (1-2A)p]/[(1-A)p] + 1 = 0.$$

The quantities S_N and G_N referred to in section 4.4 have variances dependent on N, $\sigma^2 = \text{var}(X)$, A and p:

$$\begin{aligned} D_N &= \text{var}(S_N) = \sigma^2\{N + 2mpA[N - m(1-p^N)]\}, \\ W_N &= \text{var}(G_N) = \frac{\sigma^2 Ap(p-q)}{(1-pq)^*[(1-p^N)/(1-p)]^2}. \qquad \text{(A3)} \end{aligned}$$

When forecasting returns from non-linear processes, from section 7 onwards, equations (A2) and (A3) have been modified. In the calculations $\bar{\mu}$ has been ignored and the updating formula for the forecasts of the next return becomes

$$f_{t,1} = (\hat{v}_t/\hat{v}_{t-1})[qf_{t-1,1} + (p-q)x_t] \qquad \text{(A4)}$$

with $\hat{v}_t$ estimating the effective standard deviation on day t by the formula (A1). To obtain the standardized forecast, h has been calculated by

$$h = f_{t,1}/(a\hat{v}_t)$$

with

$$a = 1.064[Ap(p-q)/(1-pq)]^{1/2}. \qquad \text{(A5)}$$

Some further details and empirical evaluations appear in Taylor (1980, section 6).

A4 A mathematical sufficient condition for inefficiency

At time 0, suppose an investor has capital C, buys futures at the price z_0 to deliver Q/z_0 tons at some future date. The investor pays cQ in commission to a broker and sends a further sum dQ as a deposit. The remaining funds are invested in a bank account.

(a) Sell at time $t>0$, when the standardized forecast is h, buy Q/z_0 tons again at time $t+N$. Wealth at time $t+N$ is then

$$(C-cQ-dQ)[1+(t+N)r] \qquad \text{(i)}$$
$$+[dQ+Q(z_t-z_0)/z_0](1+Nr) \qquad \text{(ii)}$$
$$-cQZ_{t+N}/z_0. \qquad \text{(iii)}$$

Term (i) is the original bank balance with interest, (ii) is the money returned by the broker at time t with interest, and (iii) is the commission paid at time $t+N$.

(b) 'Buy and hold' gives wealth at time $t+N$ equal to

$$(C-cQ-dQ)[1+(t+N)r] \qquad \text{(i)}$$

(as before)

$$+dQ \qquad \text{(iv)}$$
$$+Q(Z_{t+N}-z_0)/z_0. \qquad \text{(v)}$$

Term (iv) is the deposit and (v) is the gain or loss from the futures.

Policy (a) has higher expected wealth than (b), after completing business at time $t+N$, if

$$(1+Nr)[d+(z_t-z_0)/z_0]>d-1+(1+c)E(Z_{t+N}/z_0|h)$$

or

$$1+Ndr+(1+Nr)(z_t-z_0)/z_0>(1+c)E(Z_{t+N}/z_0|h). \qquad \text{(A6)}$$

This can be re-written, using $D=z_t/z_0$, as

$$f(D)=[1+Ndr+(1+Nr)(D-1)]/[D(1+c)]>E(Z_{t+N}/z_t|h).$$

Then $f(1)$ is $(1+Ndr)/(1+c)$ and the difference between $f(D)$ and $f(1)$ can be shown to be

$$f(D)-f(1)=(D-1)/D^{*}Nr(1-d)/(1+c).$$

Therefore $D > 1$ implies $f(D) > f(1)$, if $d < 1$. Consequently the conditions,

$$z_t > z_0$$

and

$$(1 + Ndr)/(1 + c) > E(Z_{t+N}/z_t | h) \qquad \text{(A7)}$$

are sufficient to ensure that trading increases the expected wealth after completing business at time $t + N$.

It remains to consider the expected changes in wealth between $t + N$ and the end of the year. The only differences between policies (a) and (b) will arise from different interest payments, if the futures are kept until the end of the year. In the bank at time $t + N$, policy (a) has

$$C + Q(z_t - z_0)/z_0 - cQ - (c + d)\, QZ_{t+N}/z_0$$

while policy (b) has

$$C - (c + d)\, Q.$$

Policy (a) can have less than policy (b) in the bank on average, if the previous conditions are not modified. However, if

$$z_t/z_0 > (1 - d)/(1 - d - c), \qquad \text{and} \qquad 1 > E(Z_{t+N}/z_t | h)$$

and the previous condition (A7) applies, then the average bank interest for (a) is at least the figure for (b).

References

Bodie, Z. and Rosansky, V. I. (1980), 'Risk and Return in Commodity Futures', *Financial Analysts Journal*, 36.

Brown, S. J. and Warner, J. B. (1980), 'Measuring Security Price Performance', *Journal of Financial Economics*, 8.

Cargill, T. F. and Rausser, G. C. (1975), 'Temporal Price Behaviour in Commodity Futures Markets', *Journal of Finance*, 30.

Clark, P. K. (1973), 'A Subordinated Stochastic Process Model with Finite Variance for Speculative Prices', *Econometrica*, 41.

Dimson, E. and Brealey, R. A. (1978), 'The Risk Premium on UK Equities', *Investment Analyst*, 52.

Dusak, K. (1973), 'Futures Trading and Investor Returns: An Investigation of Commodity Market Risk Premium', *Journal of Political Economy*, 81.

Fama, E. F. (1970), 'Efficient Capital Markets: A Review of Theory and Empirical Work', *Journal of Finance*, 25.

Fama, E. F. (1976), *Foundations of Finance*, Oxford.

French, K. (1980), 'Stock Returns and the Weekend Effect', *Journal of Financial Economics*, 8.

Granger, C. W. J. and Andersen, A. P. (1978), *An Introduction to Bilinear Time Series Models*, Göttingen.

Granger, C. W. J. and Newbold, P. (1976), 'Forecasting Transformed Series', *Journal of the Royal Statistical Society*, series B, 38.

Granger, C. W. J. and Newbold, P. (1977), *Forecasting Economic Time Series*, New York.

Jennergren, L. P. (1975), 'Filter Tests of Swedish Share Prices', in E. J. Elton and M. J. Gruber (eds), *International Capital Markets*, Amsterdam.

Jensen, M. C. (1978), 'Some Anomalous Evidence Regarding Market Efficiency', *Journal of Financial Economics*, 6.

Labys, W. C. and Thomas, H. C. (1975), 'Speculation, Hedging and Commodity Price Behaviour: An International Comparison', *Applied Economics*, 7.

Levich, R. M. (1979), *The International Money Market: An Assessment of Forecasting Techniques and Market Efficiency*, Greenwich, Connecticut.

Leuthold, R. M. (1972), 'Random Walks and Price Trends: The Live Cattle Futures Market', *Journal of Finance*, 27.

Merton, R. C. (1980), 'On Estimating the Expected Return on the Market', *Journal of Financial Economics*, 8.

Oldfield, G. S. and Rogalski, R. I. (1980), 'A Theory of Common Stock Returns over Trading and Non-trading Periods', *Journal of Finance*, 35.

Praetz, P. D. (1975), 'Testing the Efficient Markets Theory on the Sydney Wool Futures Exchange', *Australian Economic Papers*, 14.

Praetz, P. D. (1976), 'On the Methodology of Testing for Independence in Futures Prices', *Journal of Finance*, 31.

Taylor, S. J. (1980), 'Conjectured Models for Trends in Financial Prices, Tests and Forecasts', *Journal of the Royal Statistical Society*, series A, 143.

Taylor, S. J. (1982a), 'Financial Returns Modelled by the Product of Two Stochastic Processes: A Study of Daily Sugar Prices 1961–79', in O. D. Anderson (ed.), *Time Series Analysis: Theory and Practice*, vol. 1, Amsterdam.

Taylor, S. J. (1982b), 'Tests of the Random Walk Hypothesis against a Price-trend Hypothesis', *Journal of Financial and Quantitative Analysis*, 17.

Taylor, S. J. and Kingsman, B. G. (1979), 'An Analysis of the Variance and Distribution of Commodity Price-changes', *Australian Journal of Management*, 4.

8

Alternative Strategies for Hedging and Spreading

JACQUES ROLFO AND HOWARD B. SOSIN

1 Introduction

The need or desire to hedge or spread can arise for several reasons. A producer (or middleman) may have inventories of raw materials, work in progress or finished goods, or some combination of the three. He may wish or may be required, perhaps by his bank, to protect the value of his inventory from price fluctuations by selling futures contracts. This would-be hedger has a long position in spot commodities; his problem is to determine the optimal number of futures contracts to sell to protect the value of his inventory from price level changes. Similarly, a manufacturer may wish or be required to establish a profit margin for a future production cycle by 'locking in' the cost of inputs and the value of outputs. One way this can be accomplished is by taking on a 'time spread', that is, by using the combination of a purchase in a near futures contract and a sale in a distant futures contract as a surrogate for the future purchase of inputs and the future sale of outputs. The problem for this would-be hedger is to determine an appropriate position in futures contracts for each of the delivery months.

An optimal hedge is sometimes characterized as the position in futures that minimizes or eliminates risk of absolute price level fluctuations. Cootner (1967) and others point out that, in fact, forming optimal hedging positions depends upon the cost of risk reduction and will be utility-dependent. Cootner stresses that the goal of hedgers is not simply to reduce risk but rather to improve reward-to-risk ratios and to capture economies of scale. The approach suggested by Cootner recognizes that the diversification of production may be infeasible and/or costly owing to economies of scale, costs of entry, learning curves, moral hazards, etc. Further, producers and merchants may have a comparative advantage in the markets in which they produce or deal, and consequently may be willing to assume 'educated' (perhaps non-marketable) risks based upon their knowledge of local conditions. Thus, the pursuit by hedgers of profit-maximizing strategies as described by Cootner is a natural implication of the fact that firms typically do not diversify their primary activity but instead attempt to maximize the monopoly profits attached to specialization. It is the starting point of risk management programmes that aim at reducing the financial uncertainty of the primary activities of firms, and it is also the starting point of this paper.

There are several factors that affect the risk associated with hedging. A producer with random production must contend with quantity risk as well as price risk (see Rolfo, 1980). An analogous situation exists for a manufacturer who is subject to variable labour costs. A hedger located away from a terminal market must bear location risk; a hedger who deals in the cash market in the grade of a commodity not traded in the futures market must bear quality risk; and all these hedgers must bear 'basis risk'.

The 'basis' is defined as futures price minus spot price, or distant futures price minus near futures price. It is the certainty equivalent value of carrying the commodity from one period to another. Keynes (1930), Hicks (1946), Kaldor (1939/40), Blau (1944), Dow (1939/40), Hawtrey (1939/40) and others have identified elements of the basis as physical costs (i.e. handling and processing), monetary costs (financing and insurance), and the 'convenience yield'. The last item is a return obtained (or expected to be obtained) by holders of the commodity (or soon-to-be holders). It is associated with the prevention of stock-out costs caused by locational squeezes. Each element of the basis is to a greater or lesser extent a random variable. Handling and processing costs and the convenience yield may be affected by inventory levels; monetary costs may be affected by inflation. Further, there is the complication of the numeraire. To the extent that the dollar magnitude of elements of the basis are related to the level of the price of the underlying commodity, changes in price levels will affect the magnitude of the basis and the profitability of a hedge (cf. section 2.1).

In this paper we analyse the influence of a stochastic basis on the performance of hedging strategies. We show how potential margin calls and interest rate risk can be explicitly accounted for in designing hedges.[1] We will say that a hedge improves a position when, *ceteris paribus*, the variability of the net change in value of the hedged position decreases. To evaluate the performance of a hedge, a quadratic loss function is introduced as a summary statistic. Section 2 describes the theoretical foundation of a 'traditional' hedging strategy, two industry rules of thumb, and three strategies that are intended to take explicit or implicit account of interest rate and convenience yield fluctuations. Section 3 presents a brief conclusion.

2 Hedging strategies

In the remainder of this paper we focus on the risk of spreading between two futures contracts. We start with a long position in the distant futures contract, either one unit (contract) or a constant dollar amount.[2] The interpretation of a constant dollar hedge is more appropriate, as it abstracts from problems associated with possible heteroskedasticity. Let $F_1(t)$ and $F_2(t)$ be the futures prices at time t of one unit of the commodity for delivery at dates D_1 and D_2, respectively, where the subscript 2 corresponds to a deferred or more distant contract. The values of these two contracts next period (at time $t+1$) are unknown and are described by the distributions $\tilde{F}_1^t(t+1)$ and $\tilde{F}_2^t(t+1)$. This accounts for the fact that futures contracts differ from forward contracts in that they are marked to market on a daily basis. If an agent contracts for future delivery with a forward contract, he establishes a firm price and needs only to worry about having sufficient supplies on hand to meet the contract. Once the initial margin is posted, money does not change hands with price movements, except in the case of extreme price shifts. However, it is often the case that forward contracts are not available, or are too costly (i.e. too large a spread), and so the agent turns to the futures market.

When a futures contract is first established, an initial margin deposit is required. This margin requirement is best viewed as a performance bond, and doesn't really affect the analysis as it can be met with Treasury bills. That is, to the extent that agents can borrow and lend unlimited amounts at the Treasury bill rate, initial margin will be a non-binding constraint. In addition to initial margin, each participant in the futures market is responsible for a maintenance or variation margin that must be paid in cash. That is, at the end of each trading day all futures positions are settled. Thus, if the price rose (fell) from the close of the previous day, cash is transferred to the accounts of the longs (shorts) from the accounts of the shorts (longs).

Hence an analysis of hedging strategies should also take into account potential margin calls.

2.1 *Traditional 'one-to-one' prescription*

Strategy I follows a traditional or 'textbook' prescription. It recommends taking a position in the near futures contract that is equal in size (where size is measured in units of the commodity), but opposite in direction, to the position in the distant contract. One proponent of this strategy, Hieronymus (1971), states:

> Risks are shifted by the process of hedging. To hedge is to take a position in futures equal and opposite to an existing cash position . . . . So long as cash and futures move up and down together, what the hedger makes on the one position he will lose on the other; consequently he will neither gain nor lose from a change in price.

Although Hieronymous's prescription deals specifically with cash and futures, a similar argument can be made for hedging one futures position with another. The *sine qua non* condition for this strategy to be perfectly riskless is that the basis (deferred futures price minus nearby futures price) remains a constant dollar amount. For this strategy, one unit of the near futures contract will be sold for each unit of the distant futures contract that is held long. The distribution of possible changes in the value of the spread is given by relation (1):

$$\tilde{\Delta}_1 = [\tilde{F}_2^t(t+1) - F_2(t)] - [\tilde{F}_1^t(t+1) - F_1(t)]. \qquad (1)$$

2.2 *Industry rule of thumb ≠ 1*

Strategy II is one that is recommended by a major bullion dealer.[3] It recognizes the potential limitation of the one-to-one hedge (caused by shifts in the numeraire), and attempts to eliminate or reduce the basic risk by taking positions of equal dollar amount but of opposite sign in the two futures contracts. Assuming that the strategy always starts by being long one unit of the distant contract, to obtain the same dollar position (of opposite sign) in the near contract, $F_2(t)/F_1(t)$ units will be sold. The distribution of net change in the value of this portfolio is

$$\tilde{\Delta}_2 = [\tilde{F}_2^t(t+1) - F_2(t)] - [F_2(t)/F_1(t)][\tilde{F}_1^t(t+1) - F_1(t)]. \qquad (2)$$

The assumption underlying this approach is that the volatility per dollar invested is the same for all futures contracts, i.e. that potential cash settlements are proportional to initial price levels. This assumption is in contrast to Samuelson's (1965) well-known theoretical result, which suggests that the volatility of futures contracts, in the context of his model, increases as they mature.

2.3 Industry rule of thumb ≠ 2

In strategy III (also used by industry), the price difference between two futures contracts is viewed as a composite cost of storage, part of which is fixed in dollar terms while the remainder, to a greater or lesser extent, is proportional to the price of the contract. This strategy recognizes that a major proportional component of the storage cost, especially for precious metals, is the cost of financing, and explicitly tries to hedge this cost. In taking explicit account of interest costs, this strategy sells $(1 + i_t)$ units of the near contract for each unit held of the deferred contract, where i_t is an implied forward holding period rate of interest at time t. An estimate of the interest rate associated with the interval D_1–D_2 is obtained empirically from the Treasury bill futures market; namely, $i_t(D_1, D_2) = [100/P(t) - 1]$, where $P(t)$ is the true price (i.e. not 100 minus the discount) at time t, of a Treasury bill for delivery at D_1 that matures at D_2. The distribution of change in the value of the hedged position is given by

$$\tilde{\Delta}_3 = [\tilde{F}_2^t(t+1) - F_2(t)] - [100/P(t)][\tilde{F}_1^t(t+1) - F_1(t)]. \qquad (3)$$

To the extent that fixed costs are important in the carry, strategy III would be expected to out-perform strategy II.

2.4 Hedging the interest rate component of the basis in continuous time

Strategy IV recognizes that forward interest rates fluctuate, and that this randomness is related to that of the interest rate implicit in a spread between two futures contracts. It assumes that the price ratio of the two commodity futures contracts is solely a reflection of the forward rate of interest. Let $\tilde{p}^t(t+1)$ be, as of time t, the price distribution for time $t+1$ of the Treasury bill underlying a Treasury bill futures contract that spans the same time period as the spread in the underlying commodity. The holding period return from the Treasury bill is $100/\tilde{p}^t(t+1)$. For strategy IV, the distribution of $\tilde{F}_2^t(t+1)$, is by assumption, identical to $100(\tilde{F}_1^t(t+1)/\tilde{P}^t(t+1))$. This is different from $100[\tilde{F}_1^t(t+1)/P(t)]$ unless distribution $\tilde{P}^t(t+1)$ degenerates into $P(t)$, that is, unless interest rates do not fluctuate. Therefore, hedging one unit of the distant contract with $100/P(t)$ units of the second contract (as in strategy III) is not sufficient to eliminate all price uncertainty.

Strategy IV takes explicit account of interest rate risk, and hedges one unit of the distant contract with n_1 units of the near contract and n_2 units of the Treasury bill futures contract. The spreading (and hedging) problem is to determine simultaneously the numbers of contracts $n_1(t)$ and $n_2(t)$ that minimize or eliminate the volatility of the net change in value of the hedged position,

$$\tilde{\Delta}_4 = [\tilde{F}_2^t(t+1) - F_2(t)] - n_1(t)[\tilde{F}_1^t(t+1) - F_1(t)] - n_2(t)[\tilde{P}^t(t+1) - P(t)] \qquad (4)$$

or, replacing $\tilde{F}_2^t(t+1)$ by $100\tilde{F}_1^t(t+1)/\tilde{P}^t(t+1)$,

$$\tilde{\Delta}_4 = 100[\tilde{F}_1^t(t+1)/\tilde{P}^t(t+1) - F_1(t)/P(t)] - n_1(t)[\tilde{F}_1^t(t+1) - F_1(t)] - n_2(t)[\tilde{P}^t(t+1) - P(t)]. \qquad (5)$$

It will be possible to eliminate the stochastic component of (5),

$$100\tilde{F}_1^t(t+1)/\tilde{P}^t(t+1) - n_1\tilde{F}_1 t(t+1) - n_2\tilde{P}^t(t+1),$$

if $\tilde{F}_1^t(t+1)$ and $\tilde{P}^t(t+1)$ belong to a family of distributions wherein the ratio of two distributions is a linear combination of these two distributions. This result certainly does not hold for normal or log-normal distributions. Consequently, in general, with discrete trading, it is not possible to extract completely the multiplicative uncertainty of $\tilde{F}_1^t(t+1)$ and of the inverse of $\tilde{P}^t(t+1)$ by a linear combination of $\tilde{F}_1^t(t+1)$ and $\tilde{P}^t(t+1)$.

However, the stochastic component of the change in value of the hedged position can be eliminated by recasting this hedging problem in a continuous-time framework. Assume that the stochastic processes for the returns on the distant commodity contracts, dF_2/F_2, and on the Treasury bill futures, dP/P, are given by

$$dF_2/F_2 = m_F\,dt + u_F\,dz_F \qquad (6)$$

and

$$dP/P = m_p\,dt + u_p\,dz_p. \qquad (7)$$

The two variables F_2 and P are assumed to follow diffusion processes where m_F and m_P are the instantaneous expected rates of increase of the two variables, u_F and u_P are the corresponding instantaneous variances, and dz_F and dz_P are standard Gauss–Wiener processes; i.e. the distributions of F_2 and P are lognormal.

Such processes have been widely hypothesized in the literature (see for instance Cox *et al.*, 1978; Feiger and Jacquillat, 1979). Although not explicitly handled, it is of course necessary to assume that the Treasury price process is constrained by a boundary condition because a discount instrument cannot sell above par. Furthermore, to avoid riskless profits, the instantaneous correlation coefficient between the commodity and financial futures contracts is assumed to be zero.

Under these conditions, the dynamics of the product[4] $F_2P/100 = F_1$ are described by

$$d(F_2P)/(F_2P) = (m_F + m_P)\,dt + u_F dz_F + u_P dz_P. \tag{8}$$

The distribution of the change in value of the hedged position is

$$\tilde{\Delta}_4 = dF_2 - n_1 dF_1 - n_2 dF_2. \tag{9}$$

Substituting relations (6), (7) and (8) in (9) yields

$$\tilde{\Delta}_4 = \left[F_2 m_F - \frac{n_1 F_2 P(m_F + m_P)}{100} - n_2 P m_P\right] dt \tag{10}$$

$$+ \left(F_2 u_F - \frac{n_1 F_2 P u_F}{100}\right) dz_F - \left(\frac{n_1 F_2 P u_P}{100} + n_2 P u_P\right) dz_P.$$

Under the assumption that contemporaneous price changes in the commodity and Treasury bill futures are independent, the stochastic components of $\tilde{\Delta}_4$ are eliminated for values of n_1 and n_2 such that the coefficients of dz_F and dz_P are identically equal to zero: namely, $n_1 = F_2/F_1$ (or $= 100/P$) and $n_2 = -F_2/P$. A riskless hedge can be derived in continuous but not in discrete time because the continuous-time framework allows readjustment of the hedge at arbitrarily short intervals, thereby eliminating the problem of multiplicative uncertainty. Note that, with strategy IV, a long position in the deferred commodity futures contract is always combined with a short position in the near commodity futures contract and a long position in Treasury bill futures.

2.5 *Butterfly*

Strategy V is an attempt to immunize the price risk of a unit of the commodity futures contract by going short simultaneously in a nearer and a more distant futures contract, with an average time to delivery on the shorts equal to that of the contract to hedge. Price changes are assumed to be proportional to initial prices, and the weights applied to the short positions are $F_2(t)/2F_1(t)$ and $F_2(t)/2F_3(t)$, where $F_1(t)$, $F_2(t)$ and $F_3(t)$ are the initial futures prices ranked by more distant delivery dates. The distribution of change in value of the hedge is given by

$$\tilde{\Delta}_5 = [\tilde{F}_2^t(t+1) - F_2(t)] - [F_2(t)/2F_1(t)][\tilde{F}_1^t(t+1) - F_1(t)] - [F_2(t)/2F_3(t)][\tilde{F}_3^t(t+1) - F_3(t)]. \quad (11)$$

Note that this strategy is equivalent to applying strategy II (i.e. the industry rule of thumb $\neq 1$) twice, first hedging half a unit of the second contract with a nearer contract, then hedging the second half-unit with a more distant contract. It assumes that the volatility per dollar invested is the same for the three contracts. Another way to view strategy V is that it hedges changes in the interest rate in a commodity spread over one segment of the commodity yield curve by taking on positions in another segment. To the extent that these segments move together, the hedge will be successful. Furthermore, to the extent that interest rates in adjacent segments of commodity yield curves correlate better than contemporaneous segments of the commodity yield curve and the Treasury bill yield curve, strategy V would be expected to out-perform strategy IV.

2.6 *Heuristic strategy to account for interest rate and convenience yield fluctuations*

Under alternative sets of assumptions, strategies I–V yield zero-variance hedges. That is, (strategy I) if the dollar magnitude of the basis is invariant; or (strategy II) if the percentage magnitude of the basis is invariant; or (strategy III) if there is a fixed and a constant proportional basis; or (strategy IV) if there is continuous trading and the fractional basis and the price of futures contracts follow diffusion processes; or (strategy V) if adjacent segments of the commodity yield curve follow the same dynamics, then zero-variance hedges can be formed. Strategy VI takes account of the fact that the above conditions need not prevail because of the existence of market imperfections and convenience yield.

Even if we assume that $F_1 = F_2(P/100 + Y)$ where F_2, P and Y (which is a stochastic term representing both convenience yield and carrying costs) follow diffusion processes, we cannot eliminate all the risk of the hedge. Assume, within a continuous-time framework, that F_1 is equal to $F_2(P/100 + Y)$, where Y includes terms involving the convenience yield and carrying costs. Owing to Y, new terms appear in the change in value of the hedged position. In particular, if Y is assumed to follow a continuous stochastic path similar to those of F_2 and P, there will be a new stochastic term in (4), dz_y, and a new component to the coefficient of dz_F (and also to dt). A proper choice of n_1 and n_2 can still make the coefficient of dz_F and dz_P equal to zero. (Owing to the new terms, these values of n_1 and n_2 are likely to be different from those found for strategy IV). However, because a futures contract on Y does not exist, the stochastic term involving dz_y cannot be eliminated – in general, a zero variance does not exist. For that reason, we define strategy VI in a heuristic way; i.e. we try to incorporate in the parameters of the hedge the various components of uncertainty discussed above, without explicitly stating them.

Strategy VI aims at minimizing a quadratic loss function on the change in value of the hedged position involving a long position in the deferred commodity futures contract and positions in a nearby commodity futures contract and a Treasury bill futures contract.

$$\tilde{\Delta}_6 = [\tilde{F}_2^t(t+1) - F_2(t)] - n_1(t)[\tilde{F}_1^t(t+1) - F_1(t)] - n_2(t)[\tilde{P}^t(t+1) - P(t)] \tag{12}$$

It assumes that the distributions of price relatives, $\tilde{F}_2^t(t+1)/F_2(t)$, $\tilde{F}_1^t(t+1)/F_1(t)$ and $\tilde{P}^t(t+1)/P(t)$, follow a random walk, namely that

$$\tilde{F}_i^t(t+1)/F_i(t) = 1 + \tilde{f}_i, \qquad i = 1, 2 \tag{13}$$

and

$$\tilde{P}^t(t+1)/P(t) = 1 + \tilde{p} \tag{14}$$

where f and p are normally distributed with zero mean. These assumptions are consistent with market efficiency, and have been used extensively in the analysis of stock prices.

The values of $n_1(t)$ and $n_2(t)$, which minimize the variance of the change in value of the hedged position, can be derived and are equal to

$$n_1(t) = \frac{F_2(t)}{F_1(t)}\left[\frac{\operatorname{cov}(\tilde{f}_1, \tilde{f}_2)\operatorname{var}(\tilde{p}) - \operatorname{cov}(\tilde{f}_2, \tilde{p})\operatorname{cov}(\tilde{f}_1, \tilde{p})}{\operatorname{var}(\tilde{f}_1)\operatorname{var}(\tilde{p}) - \operatorname{cov}^2(\tilde{f}_1, \tilde{p})}\right] \tag{15}$$

and

$$n_2(t) = \frac{F_2(t)}{P(t)}\left[\frac{\operatorname{cov}(\tilde{f}_2, \tilde{p})\operatorname{var}(\tilde{f}_1) - \operatorname{cov}(\tilde{f}_1, \tilde{f}_2)\operatorname{cov}(\tilde{f}_1, \tilde{p})}{\operatorname{var}(\tilde{f}_1)\operatorname{var}(\tilde{p}) - \operatorname{cov}^2(\tilde{f}_1, \tilde{p})}\right] \tag{16}$$

where lower-case letters refer to rates of returns.

These coefficients have some interesting properties. In contrast to strategy IV, the signs of $n_1(t)$ and $n_2(t)$ in strategy VI are not unambiguously defined. Note also that $n_1(t)$ and $n_2(t)$ can be interpreted as the hedge ratios prescribed by strategy II (i.e. the industry rule of thumb $\neq 1$, which assumes that the volatility per dollar invested is the same for the two commodity contracts) and the hedge prescribed by strategy IV (which accounts for the randomness of the implied forward interest rate) respectively, adjusted for the covariance effect between price relatives. Ignoring empirical problems associated with estimating the necessary variances and covariances, the performance of strategy VI will always be superior to strategies II or IV. The extent of the improvement should be the greatest for agricultural commodities, where the convenience yield can be a major factor.

3 Conclusion

This paper has analysed the theoretical foundation of six alternative strategies seeking zero-variance hedges. Under alternative assumptions, five of the strategies were shown to produce zero-variance hedges. In particular, if the dollar magnitude of the basis is invariant, then strategy I – a one-unit-to-one-unit traditional hedge – will be riskless. If the percentage magnitude of the basis is invariant, then strategy II – an equal dollar hedge (used and recommended by a major bullion dealer) – will be riskless. If there is a fixed and a constant proportional component to the basis, then strategy III – a hedge based upon forward interest rate levels – will be riskless. If there is continuous trading, a fractional basis that is variable but always equivalent in percentage terms to an alternative interest rate security, and if futures contracts follow diffusion processes, then strategy IV – a cross-commodity hedge – will be riskless. If adjacent segments of a commodity yield curve follow the same dynamics, then strategy V – a butterfly hedge – will be riskless.

However, if one of these sets of assumptions is not satisfied, a zero variance probably cannot be formed. In particular, if the convenience yield is an important factor in the relative pricing of two futures contracts, a riskless hedge need not exist. For this circumstance, we developed a hedging strategy – strategy VI – that explicitly minimizes the variance of hedge results.

Notes

1 Other studies of basis risk and hedging are available; e.g., Johnson (1960), Peck (1975), Rutledge (1970) and Stein (1961).

2 Obviously, the choice of being long or short as a basic position to be hedged is purely arbitrary, as is the choice of which contract – nearby or deferred – to hold fixed and which one to hedge in.

3 This strategy was suggested by Mr Raymond Nessim and is actively used and promoted by Phillip Brothers.

4 A similar approach is followed by Fischer (1978) for the valuation of index bonds, and by Feiger and Jacquillat (1979) for valuation of convertible currency bonds.

References

Blau, G. (1944), 'Some Aspects of the Theory of Futures Trading', *Review of Economic Studies*, 12.

Cootner, P. (1967), 'Speculation and Hedging', *Food Research Institute Studies*, Supplement, 7.

Cox, J., Ingersoll, J. and Ross, S. (1978), 'A Theory of the Term Structure of Interest Rates', Research Paper no. 468, Graduate School of Business, Stanford University, California.

Dow, J. C. R. (1939/40), 'A Theoretical Account of Futures Markets', *Review of Economic Studies*, 7.

Feiger, G. and Jacquillat, B. (1979), 'Currency Option Bonds, Puts and Calls on Foreign Exchange and the Hedging of Contingent-Foreign Earnings', *Journal of Finance*, 34.

Fischer, S. (1978), 'Call Option Pricing when the Exercise Price is Uncertain, and the Valuation of Index Bonds', *Journal of Finance*, 33.

Hawtrey, R. G. (1939/40), 'A Symposium on the Theory of the Forward Market', *Review of Economic Studies*, 7.

Hicks, J. R. (1946), *Value and Capital* (2nd ed.), Oxford.

Hieronymus, T. A. (1971), *Economics of Futures Trading: For Commercial and Personal Profit*, New York.

Johnson, L. L. (1960), 'The Theory of Hedging and Speculation in Commodity Futures', *Review of Economic Studies*, 27.

Kaldor, N. (1939/40), 'Speculation and Economic Stability', *Review of Economic Studies*, 7.

Keynes, J. M. (1930), *A Treatise on Money*, vol. 2, New York.

Peck, A. (1975), 'Hedging and Income Stability: Concepts, Implications and Example', *American Journal of Agricultural Economics*, 57.

Rolfo, J. (1980), 'Optimal Hedging Under Price and Quantity Uncertainty: The Case of a Cocoa Producer', *Journal of Political Economy*, 88.

Rutledge, D. J. S. (1970), 'The Relationship Between Prices and Hedging Patterns in the United States Soybean Complex', PhD dissertation, Stanford University.

Samuelson, P. (1965), 'Proof that Properly Anticipated Prices Fluctuate Randomly', *Industrial Management Review*, 6.

Stein, J. L. (1961), 'The Simultaneous Determination of Spot and Futures Prices', *American Economic Review*, 51.

9

Futures Trading, Risk Reduction and Price Stabilization

DAVID M. NEWBERY

1 Introduction

The May 1976 UNCTAD resolution, calling for an Integrated Programme for Commodities, is the most recent of a long line of attempts to stabilize primary commodity prices. Like most other calls for action, it largely ignores the role that existing institutions, particularly futures markets, might play in achieving its aim, and instead urges the setting up of a Common Fund to finance buffer stocks of suitable commodities. Perhaps one should not be surprised at this apparent official indifference to the role of futures markets, for to the official (and lay) eye the two institutions – buffer stocks and future markets – appear quite incompatible. Buffer stocks are supposed to stabilize prices, while futures markets offer speculators the chance to gamble on fluctuations in prices, an activity that has often been viewed at best as irrelevant, and more often as socially unacceptable. This view has, of course, been criticized by a succession of economists, among them McKinnon (1967), who argued that futures markets so dramatically modify the impact of price stabilization schemes that it was seriously misleading to ignore their presence, as many economists measuring the benefits of price stabilization had done. Newbery and Stiglitz (1981, esp. chapters 3, 12–14) took up this theme and argued that the presence of risk-sharing and risk-reducing institutions such as futures markets can significantly modify the impact of risk-reducing policies such as commodity price stabilization.

The root of the problem is that the economy does not have a complete set of markets, so that the existing markets must typically serve several different functions simultaneously, and none of them quite satisfactorily. In agriculture, markets induce producers to supply commodities that are then allocated among customers. If this were all they had to do, and if they were competitive, they would be efficient. But they also share risk between consumers and producers, and this additional role modifies the efficiency with which the market allocates commodities. If a futures market is introduced, the risk-sharing role is now spread over two markets, and the operation of the spot market will be altered. The effect of price stabilization will thus depend on whether or not there is a futures market.

It is, however, important to distinguish two quite different impacts that futures trading might have on commodity price instability. On the one hand, futures markets may reduce the volatility of spot prices, and so have a directly comparable effect to price stabilization schemes, while on the other hand, they may yield similar (or greater) risk-reducing benefits as those to be derived from commodity stabilization schemes, though in rather different ways. Thus when Streit (1980, pp. 496–9) lists five *a priori* reasons why futures trading may have a stabilizing effect, he is concerned with its effect on price volatility, not on the risk facing producers and traders. It may be useful to list these reasons to contrast this aspect of future markets with the one to be discussed in this paper. First, he argues that futures markets allow information to be diffused more rapidly, and by increasing the speed of market adjustment reduce the size of price changes needed for equilibration. Presumably the argument is that, in the response to information about a rise in future demand, say, producers can now plan to increase future supply and mitigate the future price rise. However, with commodities that are continuously stored, changes in futures prices will have a direct effect on current prices, and hence make them more volatile. One must be careful to distinguish the effect of futures markets in reducing price fluctuations between years, and their effect on price volatility within the year.

The second argument is that futures markets broaden the market for information relevant to the price, and hence reduce forecast errors. Recently, Kyle (1981) has argued in a very elegant paper that it is even beneficial, from the point of view of the informativeness of futures prices, to allow totally uninformed speculations to trade. The argument is, very loosely, that uninformed speculators lose money that informed traders receive as profits. The more uninformed traders there are, the more profits are to be made from acquiring information, and hence the more information will be collected and revealed in the futures price.

Third, futures markets allow traders to choose whether to buy in the spot market (e.g., for storage) or in the futures market. If spot prices rise relative to forecast prices, such traders will shift to the futures market, reducing the pressure on the spot market. This argument seems closely related to the next, which is that futures markets reduce the risk of inter-temporal arbitrage via storage, and hence facilitate this form of price stabilization. This in turn means that disturbances are effectively spread over current and future periods, rather than being concentrated in the present. Finally, futures markets should eliminate cobwebs caused by inefficient or adaptive forecasting methods, and hence reduce endogenous price fluctuations (e.g., Newbery and Stiglitz, 1981, chapter 11).

However, while futures markets may indeed reduce the instability in spot markets, it is not immediately clear why this is beneficial. Since producers are more specialized than consumers, and hence more directly affected by price instability, the relevant question is, how do producers benefit from price stabilization? The standard argument, defended at some length in Newbery and Stiglitz (1981, chapter 3), is that producers are concerned not so much with price risk but with income risk, i.e. with fluctuations in their incomes. The two coincide only if production is certain but prices are risky, so that price fluctuations are the sole cause of revenue and profit fluctuations. In such cases stabilizing prices will indeed stabilize incomes, which, other things being equal, will raise producers' welfare. However, particularly for agricultural products, supply fluctuations are a major source of instability, and stabilizing prices may even increase income instability. Thus, price stabilization schemes are at best an indirect solution to the real problem of income instability, and as such may be inferior to other methods of reducing income risk, such as futures markets.

In order to investigate this possibility, it is necessary to model the risk-reducing options offered by futures markets more formally, for some of the effects to be discussed are too elusive for a verbal account to be convincing. Once we have a satisfactory model of the futures market, we can use it to address a variety of interesting questions. The model that follows is derived and defended more extensively in Newbery and Stiglitz (1981, chapter 13).

2 A model of futures markets

For simplicity we shall consider a futures market in which commodity stockholders and consumers do not trade, so that the only participants are producers and speculators. Following well-established tradition, we assume that agents have constant absolute risk aversion and that prices and quantities are jointly normally distributed. This allows us to use the mean–variance analysis of the standard capital asset pricing model, and gives rise to trading demands in the futures market that are linear in prices, and can therefore be aggregated simply across agents. These assumptions are strong but essential for analytical solutions, and can be defended as second-order Taylor approximation to a presumably more complex reality.

Suppose that the producers are farmers who grow an annual crop. At the time of planting the future weather (and hence output) is uncertain, as is the post-harvest market-clearing price, p. For the moment we shall assume that farmers have no discretion over their planned production (e.g., they devote all their land to the particular crop, and cultivate it using established practice). Their only choice is thus the size of their forward sales, z. If output is $\tilde{q}$, a random variable at the time of planting, and the futures price is p^f, then a farmer's income will be

$$y = \tilde{p}\tilde{q} + z(p^f - \tilde{p}) \tag{1}$$

where any costs and other sources of (non-random) income are omitted as irrelevant in the mean–variance framework. The farmer chooses z to maximize expected utility, which, with constant absolute risk aversion, A, and joint normality of p and q, can be shown (e.g., in Newbury and Stiglitz, 1981, p. 85) to be equivalent to maximizing

$$W = Ey - \tfrac{1}{2}A \operatorname{var} y \tag{2}$$

$$W = Epq + z(p^f - \bar{p}) - \tfrac{1}{2}A[\operatorname{var}(pq) - 2z \operatorname{cov}(p, pq) + z^2 \operatorname{var} p)] \tag{3}$$

where $\bar{p} = Ep$ is the expected post-harvest price. If z can be positive or negative (i.e. if forward purchases are also possible), then the expected utility-maximizing choice of z is

$$z = \frac{\operatorname{cov}(p, pq)}{\operatorname{var} p} - \frac{\bar{p} - p^f}{A \operatorname{var} p}. \tag{4}$$

Speculators, on the other hand, have no risky production or other sources of risky income, and sell z^s forward (or, more accurately, buy $-z^s$ forward) to maximize

$$W^s = z^s(p^f - \bar{p}) - \tfrac{1}{2}A^s z^{s2} \operatorname{var} p$$

$$z^s = -\frac{\bar{p} - p^f}{A^s \operatorname{var} p}. \tag{5}$$

This has the same form as the second term in equation (4), which thus allows us to interpret that as the speculative component, while the first term is the hedging component. In our simple model, the speculators can be persuaded to take a long position (in which they provide the forward purchases that balance the farmers' forward sales) only if p^f is below the expected future price. This normal backwardation provides the risk premium that covers the cost of transferring risk from farmers to speculators.

The hedging component of equation (4) can be simplified for the case in which price and quantity are jointly normally distributed with coefficients of variation σ_p, σ respectively and a correlation coefficient r; for then, as shown in the Appendix,

$$\operatorname{cov}(p, pq) = \bar{q} \operatorname{var} p\,(1 + r\sigma/\sigma_p), \qquad \bar{q} \equiv Eq \tag{6}$$

so that, for farmers,

$$z = \bar{q}\,(1 + r\sigma/\sigma_p) - \frac{\bar{p} - p^f}{A \operatorname{var} p}. \tag{7}$$

For equilibrium in the futures market total forward sales must be equal to total forward purchases, or net sales must be zero. In the absence of any other agents this implies that the sum of the sales of farmers and speculators must be zero, or, if all agents share common beliefs about $\bar{p}$, var p,

$$0 = \Sigma(z + z^s) = (1 + r\sigma/\sigma_p)\,\Sigma\,\bar{q} - \frac{\bar{p} - p^f}{\operatorname{var} p}\,\Sigma\left(\frac{1}{A} + \frac{1}{A^s}\right) \tag{8}$$

If average total production is $\bar{Q}$, then the bias in the futures market, or the extent of normal backwardation, is

$$\bar{p} - p^f = \alpha\bar{Q}(1 + r\sigma/\sigma_p) \operatorname{var} p \tag{9}$$

where α is a measure of the degree of risk aversion displayed by the market as a whole:

$$\frac{1}{\alpha} = \Sigma\left(\frac{1}{A} + \frac{1}{A^s}\right). \tag{10}$$

In particular, if any agent i is risk-neutral, so that $A^i = 0$, then $\alpha = 0$ and the market will be unbiased. Equation (9) can now be used with (7) to solve for the size of farmer i's involvement in the futures market:

$$z^i = \bar{q}^i(1 + r\sigma/\sigma_p)\left(1 - \frac{\alpha\bar{Q}}{A^i\bar{q}^i}\right) = \beta(1 + r\sigma/\sigma_p)\,\bar{q}^i \tag{11}$$

where

$$\beta \equiv 1 - \frac{\alpha \bar{Q}}{A^i \bar{q}^i} \tag{12}$$

is a measure of the extent to which the farmer is more risk-averse than average (A^i/α) and more exposed to risk than average ($\bar{q}^i/\bar{Q}$). If all farmers are identical and there are no speculators, $\beta = 0$, while if there is one risk-neutral speculator, so that $\alpha = 0$, then $\beta = 1$. In between, if there are n farmers and m speculators, all equally risk-averse, then, for an average farmer

$$\beta = 1 - \frac{n}{n+m} = \frac{m}{n+m}.$$

The term β can also be thought of as the extent to which the farmer is able to share the risk with other agents in the economy. The larger is the number of speculators, the more the farmer is able to transfer risk to them, and the more heavily he is willing to be involved in the futures market. The less risk-averse speculators are, the smaller will be α and the more willing they will be to accept the farmer's risk, and, again, the more the farmer will be willing to trade these risks in the futures market.

There is another way of looking at the farmer's futures trade. Define a new parameter γ

$$\gamma \equiv \frac{\alpha \bar{Q}}{A^i \bar{q}^i} = 1 - \beta. \tag{13}$$

Then γ is the fraction of the forward sale that is speculative, and γz^i is equal to the second, speculative term in equation (4) or (7). The riskiness of a farmer's income after he has chosen his optimal forward sale is measured by its variance, and, substituting for z in the last term of equation (3), is

$$\operatorname{var} y^f = \left[\operatorname{var}(pq) - (1-\gamma^2) \frac{\operatorname{cov}^2(p, pq)}{\operatorname{var} p} \right]. \tag{14}$$

The first term is evaluated in the Appendix:

$$\operatorname{var}(pq) = \bar{p}^2 \bar{q}^2 [\sigma_p^2 + 2r\sigma_p\sigma + \sigma^2 + (1+r^2)\sigma^2\sigma_p^2] \tag{15}$$

while

$$\frac{\operatorname{cov}^2(p, pq)}{\operatorname{var} p} = \bar{p}^2 \bar{q}^2 [\sigma_p^2 + 2r\sigma_p\sigma + r^2\sigma^2] \tag{16}$$

Since the term in equation (16) is positive, the riskiness of the farmer's income is an increasing function of γ, his willingness to speculate. If he were solely interested in using the futures market to reduce his income risk, then he would set $\gamma = 0$, and take a solely hedging position.

The more willing the farmer is to take a speculative risk, the larger will be γ and his remaining income risk, but provided $\gamma < 1$, access to the futures market unambiguously reduces his income risk. With this framework we can now examine the risk-reducing role of the futures market in special cases.

3 The risk-reducing role of a futures market

3.1 Pure demand risk

If production is non-stochastic, but prices vary (perhaps because income varies, or supplies of competitive or complementary products vary), then $\sigma = 0$ and equation (14) simplifies to

$$\text{var } y^f = \gamma^2 \bar{q}^2 \text{ var } p. \tag{17}$$

Clearly, if the farmer chooses, he can set $\gamma = 0$ and completely hedge the income risk by selling his entire crop forward. And if the market is unbiased, so that $p^f = \bar{p}$, then he will choose to do so. If, however, the market is biased and the farmer is less than infinitely risk-averse, he will choose to bear some of the risk in exchange for the risk premium implicit in the bias.

3.2 Pure supply risk

In this case, production is stochastic, and the demand schedule is non-stochastic. Prices will fluctuate in response to fluctuations in supply, and the correlation coefficient between price and quantity, $r = -1$. For a farmer who does not speculate, and sets $\gamma = 0$,

$$\text{var } y^f = 2 \text{ var } p \text{ var } q \tag{18}$$

and the coefficient of variation of income, σ_y, is

$$\sigma_y = \sqrt{2}\, \sigma_p \sigma$$

which will typically be rather small (less than 10 per cent). More precisely, if ϵ is the elasticity of demand, so that $\sigma_p = \sigma/\epsilon$, then the ratio of income risk with and without a futures market (when $\text{var}\, y = \text{var}\, pq$) is, from (14) and (15),

$$\frac{\text{var}\, y^f}{\text{var}\, y} = \frac{\sigma^2}{\frac{1}{2}(1-\epsilon)^2 + \sigma^2}.$$

For typical UNCTAD 'core' commodities, $\epsilon = 0.5$, $\sigma = 0.2$, this will be quite small (25 per cent).

These two examples show that the futures market can provide substantial income risk insurance, though at a cost (the premium implicit in the normal backwardation). It is therefore interesting to compare the efficacy of futures markets to that of price stabilization schemes. This in turn requires specifying the form that the price stabilization scheme will take. The one most popular with international agencies is the 'band width rule', which specifies the upper and lower intervention prices that will be defended by the agency selling from or buying into its stockpile. Various writers have demonstrated that this is a very expensive way of achieving a given degree of price stabilization because of the large stocks required to defend the price band (Goreux, 1978; Newbury and Stiglitz, 1981, chapter 30), that it is potentially vulnerable to speculative attack (Salant, 1979) and that it is manipulable by producers with market power (Newbery, 1981). It also provides less price risk insurance than a futures market, since prices will still vary between the upper and lower intervention points, which may typically be at 5–7 per cent above and below the mean price.

The efficient stockpiling rule, on the other hand, is the same as the competitive arbitrage rule, in which stockholders buy until they have driven current and expected futures prices sufficiently close together that the expected capital gains just cover the interest and storage costs (Newbery and Stiglitz, 1981, chapter 30). It does not eliminate all price fluctuations, but it does reduce them, perhaps substantially, and at a much lower cost than the band width rule. It is the kind of price stabilization that is naturally complementary to a futures market; for, being a competitive rule, it can be decentralized, with each stockholder being guided in his stocking decision by the information revealed on the futures market, which at the same time provides hedging services. While this form of price stabilization reduces farmer's price risk, it does not eliminate it, and they will still wish to trade in the futures market (at least if the cost, or the premium, is not too high).

There is another form of price stabilization that would be infeasible for an international price stabilization agency, but is feasible and popular with individual governments or marketing boards. In this, the agency announces a price at the start of the season, and buys the entire harvest at this price. Of course, there is no guarantee that this announced price will equal the post-harvest world market-clearing price, and as a result the agency may make a profit or a loss, but the presence of a world market means that it can sustain this announced price without having to worry about the matching of global demand and supply, which an international agency would have to worry about. Moreover, there is no need to carry stocks in order to achieve this form of price stabilization. Since it offers complete price stability, and since it would eliminate the need for a local futures market,[1] it is logical to compare it with the alternative of a futures market.

4 Domestic market board price stabilization and futures markets

The best insurance the futures market can offer requires setting $\gamma = 0$ in equation (14), in which case the remaining income risk after optimally hedging on the futures market is, from (14)–(16),

$$\operatorname{var} y^f = \bar{p}^2 \bar{q}^2 \sigma^2 [1 - r^2 + (1 + r^2)\, \sigma_p^2] \tag{19}$$

where again r is the correlation coefficient between price and quantity. If the market board sets its buying price at $\bar{p}$ (or p^f, which will be close to $\bar{p}$), the farmers' income risk will be

$$\operatorname{var} y^s = \bar{p}^2 \bar{q}^2 \sigma^2. \tag{20}$$

The marketing board will offer superior income insurance only if

$$r^2 < \frac{\sigma_p^2}{1 - \sigma_p^2}. \tag{21}$$

Newbery and Stiglitz (1981, chapter 20) have analysed data for six of UNCTAD's core commodities for 14 developing countries, which were either large exporters of these commodities or for which the commodities were major exports, for the period 1951–75. Define the critical value of the correlation coefficient to be

$$\rho = \surd [\sigma_p^2 / (1 - \sigma_p^2)].$$

Then this figure can be computed for the six core commodities chosen. The only problem is defining the appropriate measure of price instability. Two measures are presented below (see table 1). The first is the coefficient of variation (CV) of detrended real prices,

Table 1 Measures of price instability and critical correlations, 1951-75

	σ_p (1)	ρ (2)	σ_p^e (3)	ρ^e (4)
	%	%	%	%
Cocoa	31	33	27	28
Coffee	15	15	15	15
Cotton	26	27	15	15
Jute	20	20	16	16
Rubber	20	20	20	20
Sugar	58	71	33	35

Sources: col. (1), Newbury and Stiglitz (1981, table 29.4, col. 3); col (3), Newbury and Stiglitz (1981, table 20.1, col. 3); col. 4, the critical correlation coefficient using σ_p^e.

σ_p; the second is a measure of the uncertainty about the future price p_t^e, at date $t - 1$ (i.e. the previous year), defined by the equation

$$p_t^e = a + bp_{t-1}.$$

The forecast errors were found by regressing p_t on p_{t-1} and then calculated as the standard deviation of the residuals deflated by mean p_t, σ_p^e.

The next step is to regress price on quantity for each of the countries and commodities, in order to find the value of the correlation coefficient r. The results, to one significant figure, are given in table 2, grouped into cases where the correlation is high enough to make futures markets unambiguously better, and cases where market board stabilization may be preferable.

Several comments are in order. First, if the maintained hypothesis is one of no correlation between supply and price, then table 2 is somewhat more favourable to the case for futures markets than is statistically warranted. Moreover, some of the reported correlations are positive, which suggests a supply response to demand shifts, a feature that as yet our model has not accommodated, and which will require separate investigation. Finally, by choosing developing countries that are important producers, the sample is biased towards countries with high correlation coefficients. Most smaller countries will presumably have a lower correlation between their supply and world price.

This analysis suggests a useful taxonomy. Countries are small if they have little influence on the world price of the commodity, in which case they are likely to have a low correlation coefficient

Table 2 Comparison of actual with critical correlation coefficients

	r	ρ	ρ^e
High-correlation cases			
Ghana, cocoa	−0.7	0.3	0.3
Nigeria, cocoa	−0.7	0.3	0.3
Brazil, coffee	−0.4	0.2	0.2
Mexico, coffee	0.3	0.2	0.2
Egypt, cotton	−0.6	0.3	0.2
Mexico, cotton	−0.6	0.3	0.2
Thailand, jute	0.4	0.2	0.2
Malaysia, rubber	0.8	0.2	0.2
Thailand, rubber	0.7	0.2	0.2
Low-correlation cases			
Brazil, cocoa	0.3	0.3	0.3
Colombia, coffee	−0.1	0.2	0.2
Ivory Coast, coffee	0.0	0.2	0.2
Sudan, cotton	−0.3	0.3	0.3
Brazil, cotton	−0.1	0.3	0.2
Bangladesh, jute	−0.0	0.2	0.2
Nigeria, rubber	0.2	0.2	0.2
Sri Lanka, rubber	0.1	0.2	0.2
Mauritius, sugar	0.2	0.7	0.4
Philippines, sugar	0.1	0.7	0.4
Brazil, sugar	−0.3	0.2	0.4

Source: r: Newbury and Stiglitz (1981, table 20.4, col. 5).

between price and supply. (They may have a higher correlation coefficient if they occupy the same climatic region as most producers, but if the bulk of the crop is grown in a sufficiently small region to experience the same climate, then production is likely to be quite concentrated anyway.) For these countries, marketing board price stabilization needs further study. Countries are large if they have significant influence on the world market price, in which case they will experience a higher correlation between price and supply. Table 3 shows that there are quite a few cases in which countries are large as far as particular commodities are concerned. For these countries it may be misleading to assume that they behave competitively, either on the spot or futures markets.[2] Consequently, in section 7 below we study the way in which oligopolistic countries exploit their market power, not only in the spot market, but also in the futures market.

However, before we can satisfactorily analyse these two cases it is necessary to relax the assumption that farmers have no choice over output. While in principle it is possible to solve fully for the choice

Table 3 Shares of individual countries in world trade of commodities, averages, 1977-79

Country	*Product*	*Percentage*
More than 50%		%
USA	Maize	73
Philippines	Coconut oil	71
Bangladesh	Jute	70
Malaysia	Palm oil	69
Argentina	Linseed oil	62
Australia	Wool (greasy)	60
Malaysia	Copra	55
Malaysia	Rubber	51
25-50%		
USA	All cereals	49
Brazil	Sisal	42
USA	Wheat	39
Malaysia	Tin	36
Morocco	Phosphate rock	34
Senegal	Groundnut oil	29
USA	Cotton	29
Tanzania	Sisal	28
India	Tea	27
Saudi Arabia	Oil	26
Guinea	Bauxite	25
Canada	Barley	25
Cuba	Sugar	25

Sources: Commodity Trade and Price Trends, World Bank, 1981; FAO Trade Yearbook, 1979

of output as well as the level of futures trade, given the form of the production function, at this stage we are concerned mainly with qualitative results. Fortunately, these are readily available and are intuitively fairly obvious.

5 The supply response induced by different market structures

Suppose that output after the harvest depends multiplicatively on the weather ($\tilde{\theta}$) and the level of inputs, x:

$$q = \tilde{\theta} f(x) \qquad E\theta = 1, \qquad \text{var}\,\theta = \sigma^2.$$

In the absence of a futures market, the farmer will choose x at the start of the crop year to maximize expected utility:

$$W = E[p\theta f(x) - wx] - \tfrac{1}{2}A \text{ var } [p\theta f(x)] \tag{22}$$

where w is the price of the input, x. This yields as the first-order condition.

$$(Ep\theta - Af \operatorname{var} p\theta)\, f'(x) = w. \tag{23}$$

The first term in brackets is the action certainty equivalent price, $\hat{p}$, i.e. the price that, in the absence of uncertainty, would lead the farmer to choose the same action, or level of inputs, x).

$$\hat{p} = Ep\theta - Af \operatorname{var} p\theta. \tag{24}$$

If, however, the farmer has access to a futures market, then he can simultaneously choose his inputs and forward sales, and in this case he maximizes

$$W = E[p\theta f(x) - wx - z(p - p^f)] - \tfrac{1}{2}A \operatorname{var}(p\theta f - zp). \tag{25}$$

This time the action certainty equivalent price is

$$\tilde{p}^f = Ep\theta - A[f \operatorname{var} p\theta - z \operatorname{cov}(p\theta, p)] \tag{26}$$

where z is the optimal futures trade, satisfying (4) or (11). Suppose now that a futures market is introduced into an otherwise unstabilized market, and that it has no effect on the beliefs or information about future prices. If it had no effect on the post-market-price distribution, then, from (24) and (26),

$$\hat{p}^f - \hat{p} = Az \operatorname{cov}(p\theta, p) = A\beta f \frac{\operatorname{cov}^2(p\theta, p)}{\operatorname{var} p} \tag{27}$$

substituting from (11). In this case the futures market unambiguously increases the action certainty equivalent price, which, other things equal, will induce a supply response, and thus will lower the average spot price.

A useful way to summarize this result is the following: any institutional change that lowers income risk to producers will induce an increase in supply.

6 The costs and benefits of market board stabilization for small countries

The simplest case to consider is one in which the futures market is unbiased, so $p^f = \bar{p}$, and there is zero correlation between the small country's output and the world price. (More precisely, farmers and the government act as though this is the case. In most cases of low correlation it would be difficult to reject the hypothesis of zero correlation on the evidence available.) If farmers are free to hedge on the futures market, their action certainty equivalent price will be, from (26),

$$\hat{p}^f = \bar{p}[1 - A\bar{p}f\sigma^2(1 + \sigma_p^2)] \tag{28}$$

and their welfare will be

$$W^f = \bar{p}q^f - wx - \tfrac{1}{2}A(\bar{p}q^f)^2\sigma^2(1 + \sigma_p^2) \tag{29}$$

where

$$q^f = q(\hat{p}^f) = f(x)$$

is expected output, a function of $\hat{p}^f$. If the government now announces $\bar{p}$ (i.e. p^f) at the start of the crop year, the farmers now face less income risk; their utility is

$$W^s = \bar{p}q^s - wx - \tfrac{1}{2}A(\bar{p}q^s)^2\sigma^2. \tag{30}$$

This time their action certainty equivalent price is

$$\hat{p}^s = \bar{p}(1 - A\bar{p}f\sigma^2) > \hat{p}^f, \tag{31}$$

and planned supply is

$$q^s = q(\hat{p}^s) > q^f.$$

The proportionate increase in expected supply if the elasticity of supply is η is

$$\frac{\Delta q}{q} = \eta\frac{\Delta p}{\bar{p}} = \bar{R}\eta\sigma^2\sigma_p^2 \tag{32}$$

where $\bar{R} = A\bar{y}$ is the coefficient of relative risk aversion at mean income, a dimensionless measure of risk aversion with a probable value in the range 0.5–2.0 (Newbery and Stiglitz, 1981, chapter 7). For plausible values of σ (0.1–0.4) and σ_p (0.1–0.3), if the elasticity of supply is 1, the increase in supply is likely to be small (less than 2 per cent, probably much less than 1 per cent). The proportionate increase in producers' welfare of switching from the futures market to a guaranteed price are

$$\frac{\Delta W}{\bar{p}\bar{q}} = \tfrac{1}{2}\bar{R}\sigma^2\left(\frac{2\Delta q}{\bar{q}} + \sigma_p^2\right) \simeq \tfrac{1}{2}\bar{R}\sigma^2\sigma_p^2, \tag{33}$$

or roughly half as much as the supply response (for unit supply elasticity). Thus, although for small countries a guaranteed price offers increased income insurance, the gain is very slight and the induced supply response also small.

The costs of the policy are twofold. First, the marketing board now bears the price risk, though it can lay off a significant part on the world futures markets. In an unbiased uncorrelated market, the board will hedge the whole of the expected crop. Its income will be

$$Y = Q\theta(\tilde{p} - \bar{p}) + Z(p^f - \tilde{p}) \qquad p^f = \bar{p}, Z = Q = \Sigma q$$

$$Y = Q(\tilde{p} - \bar{p})(\theta - 1). \tag{34}$$

If the marketing board also has constant absolute risk aversion A^b, then its welfare will be, since $EY = 0$,

$$-\tfrac{1}{2}A^b\bar{p}^2Q^2\sigma^2\sigma_p^2$$

and, relative to the average revenue of the crop, will be

$$-\tfrac{1}{2}\bar{R}^b\sigma^2\sigma_p^2. \tag{35}$$

Clearly, unless the marketing board is (relatively) less risk-averse than the farmers, there is no gain in transferring the risk from the farmers to the board. The country as a whole will gain only to the extent that this risk shifting is advantageous. (There may be additional benefits from pooling risk if farmers have imperfectly correlated risk, for then the coefficient of variation of the total harvest will be lower than that of each individual farmer.)

The second cost is potentially more serious. So far we have assumed that the farmer makes only one input decision at the start of the crop year, at which time the only available information is the expected price (or its reflection, the futures price, or the guaranteed price). If, however, the farmer has some subsequent influence over output (weeding, fertilizing, spraying, etc.) that is price-sensitive, and if information about the past harvest price changes during the crop year (as reflected in changes in the futures price), then a guaranteed price will generate inefficiencies, since in general it will differ from the current best estimate of the post-harvest price, and will hence induce an inappropriate choice of inputs. Had the farmer hedged on the futures market, he would continue to be interested in maximizing the (utility of) profit from his crop at the post-harvest price, and so would continue to monitor the forecast or futures price and adjust inputs. Since the benefits of the guaranteed price are so low, it is very likely that forgoing the option of making adjustments to the initial plan will not be worth this extra benefit.

Thus, to conclude, while there may appear to be a case for guaranteed prices as opposed to trading on futures markets in small (i.e. uncorrelated) countries, the benefits of the price guarantee are so small that they will most certainly be outweighed by the costs of additional inflexibility they introduce.

7 Manipulation of futures markets by large countries

Consider the case in which a dominant producer of a commodity confronts a competitive fringe of price-taking countries who also supply the commodity. Suppose also that, in order to exercise market power, the dominant producer markets through a marketing board, and is able to restrict supply either directly, or indirectly by paying a low domestic producer price. Suppose also that, as a result, the country can behave in an essentially risk-neutral manner (e.g., because the risks are assumed by the marketing board, which has access to the international capital market and so can even out income fluctuations). Producers in the other countries will typically be risk-averse in the absence of any institutions to provide income insurance. If a futures market is now established, then the fringe producers will be able to hedge their risk and will, as shown above in section 5, unambiguously increase their supply and drive down the price. Since we have argued that the dominant producer is risk-neutral, he gains no insurance benefit from the futures market, but he will be harmed by the induced increase in fringe supply. One would therefore expect the dominant producer to be hostile to the introduction of futures markets.

If, however, futures markets are introduced, and they affect the trading environment facing the dominant producer, he will typically have an incentive to manipulate the futures market to increase his overall profits. (By manipulation, we mean using trading strategies that are not just designed to hedge risk or speculate on price movements. If the dominant producer is risk-neutral he will have no hedging motive for trading anyway.) This manipulation can take three forms. First, as a large agent, he may be able to exercise market power in the futures market quite independently of his activities as a producer. His power will, however, be limited by the willingness of other agents to arbitrage prices, and since entry is relatively easy into this market, his power is likely to be small. It is perhaps worth remarking that a large speculator can exercise market power in two different ways. He can influence the futures price, and hence induce a supply response, and thus has a direct and indirect impact on the volume of futures trading. The direct response is consequent on the change in the futures price, the indirect response comes via a change in supply, which affects the spot price and hence the volume of futures trading. This effect persists even if producers know exactly what trading strategy the large speculator is following. The second way relies on producers and other traders not knowing what strategy the large speculator is following, in which case, if he knows how they forecast futures prices, he can systematically induce them to make errors and lose money to the large speculator. This form of manipulation has been studied by Hart (1977), and relies on being able to mislead other agents. In this paper we assume that all agents hold rational expectations, so that this second route is not available to the large speculator.

The second way on which the dominant producer can advantageously manipulate the futures market is to change the futures price, and hence, via a change in the action certainty equivalent price, to induce a supply response by the fringe that increases the dominant producer's profits. If, for example, he can lower the futures price, this will reduce fringe supply and increase his sales price. However, this is not costless, as he may lose on his futures trading activities, and the extent to which this strategy is profitable requires a careful cost–benefit calculation.

Finally, he may be able to destabilize the futures market and thus reduce its risk-reducing advantages for the fringe, and hence their supply. If, for example, there is a close correlation between fringe supply and the spot price, then it would pay the dominant producer to reduce this correlation by, for example, introducing noise into his own supply. His problem is to find a cheap way of doing this.

Elsewhere (Newbery, 1981) we argued that, if the price elasticity of demand falls[3] with price, then the dominant producer will have a comparative advantage in storage. In the presence of a futures market it will pay him to randomize his storage decisions somewhat to introduce some additional price variability, provided other producers cannot observe his storage decision. (If they could, then their uncertainty about the future spot price is reduced, though they still will not know the dominant producer's storage decision next year.)

While the first and third motives seem reasonably clear-cut, the second needs further study to see if there is an additional reason (i.e. over and above the first reason) for manipulating futures markets.

We find that, regardless of the source of risk, the dominant producer does have an incentive to manipulate futures markets beyond the level he would have chosen as merely a large risk-neutral speculator with no production. We shall demonstrate this by examining two polar cases – pure supply and pure demand risk – within the simple linear model described above. While the exact form of market manipulation is, of course, sensitive to the specification of the model, the result that manipulation is profitable is clearly robust.

7.1 *Futures market manipulation with correlated supply risk*

This model is an extension of the one presented in Newbery and Stiglitz (1981, section 13.4, p. 190). Individual fringe producers, subscripted i, experience multiplicative risk, so that their output is

$$\theta q_i, \qquad E\theta = 1, \qquad \text{var } \theta = \sigma^2.$$

All fringe producers have the same production function, with planned output q, a function of inputs, x:

$$q_i = \sqrt{2\lambda_i x} \tag{36}$$

If the input price is unity, this has the property that planned supply is a linear function of the action certainty equivalent price. Aggregating over all fringe producers gives

$$Q = \Sigma q_i = \lambda \hat{p} \tag{37}$$

where $\hat{p}$ is the action certainty equivalent price. The dominant producer likewise faces the same multiplicative risk, and produces $q\theta$, where q is his planned output. Demand is non-stochastic and linear, so price p satisfies

$$p = a - b(q + Q)\,\theta \tag{38}$$

$$\text{var } p = \bar{p}^2\sigma^2/\epsilon^2$$

where ϵ is the elasticity of demand at the mean price, $\bar{p}$. Since price and total supply are perfectly negatively correlated and, by assumption, jointly normally distributed,

$$\text{cov }(p, p\theta) = (1 - \epsilon) \text{ var } p, \quad \text{var } p\theta = [(1 - \epsilon)^2 + 2\sigma^2] \text{ var } p. \tag{39}$$

Fringe traders will sell z forward, where

$$z = q(1 - \epsilon) - \frac{\bar{p} - p^f}{A \text{ var } p}, \qquad q = f(x) \tag{40}$$

and their hedged income will be

$$y = p\theta f(x) - z(\bar{p} - p^f) - wx. \tag{41}$$

Their action certainty equivalent price $\hat{p}$ is, ignoring terms in σ^4,

$$\begin{aligned} \hat{p} &= Ep\theta - (1 - \epsilon)(\bar{p} - p^f) \\ &= (1 - \epsilon)p^f + \epsilon\bar{p}(1 - \sigma^2/\epsilon^2) \end{aligned} \tag{42}$$

and their collective planned supply will be

$$Q = \lambda\hat{p} = \lambda(1-\epsilon)\,p^f + \lambda\epsilon(1-\sigma^2/\epsilon^2)\,\bar{p}. \tag{43}$$

The dominant producer plans to produce q, and sell S forward in the futures market to depress future prices and hence $\hat{p}$ and Q. Equilibrium in the futures market requires

$$S + \Sigma z_i = 0 = S + Q(1-\epsilon) - \frac{\bar{p} - p^f}{\operatorname{var} p}\,\frac{\Sigma^1}{A_i}. \tag{44}$$

Define α to be a measure of the risk aversion of the market, as in (10), and let $v = \operatorname{var} p$, so that

$$\alpha v \equiv \frac{\operatorname{var} p}{\Sigma^1/A_i}. \tag{45}$$

Then

$$S + Q(1-\epsilon) = \frac{1}{\alpha v}(\bar{p} - p^f). \tag{46}$$

Substitute for Q from (43):

$$S = \left[\frac{1}{\alpha v} - \lambda(1-\epsilon)\,\epsilon(1-\sigma^2/\epsilon^2)\right]\bar{p} - \left[\frac{1}{\alpha v} + \lambda(1-\epsilon)^2\right]p^f.$$

Define new parameter γ, ϕ:

$$\phi = \frac{1}{\alpha v} + \lambda(1-\epsilon)^2 \tag{47}$$

$$\gamma\phi = \frac{1}{\alpha v} - \lambda(1-\epsilon)\,\epsilon(1-\sigma^2/\epsilon^2) \tag{48}$$

so

$$S = \phi(\gamma\bar{p} - p^f)$$

or

$$p^f = \gamma\bar{p} - S/\phi. \tag{49}$$

Then, from (43),

$$Q = \lambda\psi\bar{p} - \frac{\lambda(1-\epsilon)}{\phi}S \tag{50}$$

where

$$\psi = \epsilon(1-\sigma^2/\epsilon^2) + \gamma(1-\epsilon). \tag{51}$$

The average market price $\bar{p}$ is found by taking the expectation of (38):

$$\bar{p} = a - bq - bQ = a - bq - b\lambda\psi\bar{p} + b\lambda(1-\epsilon)\,S/\phi$$

so

$$\bar{p} = \frac{a - bq + b\lambda(1-\epsilon)\,S/\phi}{1 + b\lambda\psi}. \tag{52}$$

The dominant producer's objective is to maximize profits from production and future market manipulation. His expected profit is

$$y = qEp\theta - wx - S(\bar{p} - p^f)$$

$$y = q\bar{p}(1 - \sigma^2/\epsilon) - wx - \alpha vS[S + Q(1-\epsilon)], \qquad q = f(x) \tag{53}$$

from (46). The last term can be written as

$$-\alpha vS\left\{S + (1-\epsilon)\lambda\psi\left[\frac{a - bq + b\lambda(1-\epsilon)\,S/\phi}{1 + b\lambda\psi}\right] - \lambda(1-\epsilon)^2 S/\phi\right\}$$

$$= -\alpha vS\left\{\frac{(1-\epsilon)\lambda\psi(a - bq)}{1 + b\lambda\psi} + S\left[1 - \frac{\lambda(1-\epsilon)^2}{\phi(1 + b\lambda\psi)}\right]\right\}.$$

The dominant producer's profit-maximizing choice of x satisfies

$$\frac{\partial y}{\partial x} = \frac{\partial y}{\partial q} f' - wx = 0,$$

and his marginal revenue (action certainty equivalent price) is

$$\frac{\partial y}{\partial q} = \left[\frac{a - 2bq + b\lambda(1-\epsilon)\,S/\phi}{1 + b\lambda\psi}(1 - \sigma^2/\epsilon)\right] + \frac{\alpha vbS(1-\epsilon)\lambda\psi}{1 + b\lambda\psi}. \tag{54}$$

The key point to notice here is that the producer's choice of inputs depends on his scale of activities in the futures market. His choice of forward sale satisfies

$$\frac{\partial y}{\partial s} = 0 = \frac{q(1 - \sigma^2/\epsilon)\,b\lambda(1-\epsilon)}{\phi(1 + b\lambda\psi)} - \alpha v\left\{\frac{(1-\epsilon)\lambda\psi(a - bq)}{1 + b\lambda\psi}\right.$$

$$\left. + 2S\left[1 - \frac{\lambda(1-\epsilon)^2}{\phi(1 + b\lambda\psi)}\right]\right\}. \tag{55}$$

Again, the dominant producer's choice of futures sale is not independent of his planned level of production, q; and hence his activities in the futures market are not just those of a large speculator.

It is easy to see what happens as the number of speculators in the futures market increases, or their risk aversion falls, reducing the size of $\bar{p} - p^f$. In this case the parameter α falls and in the limit goes to zero. Then, as

$$\alpha \to 0, \quad \gamma \to 1, \quad \alpha v\phi \to 1, \quad \psi \to 1 - \sigma^2/\epsilon,$$

all the terms in S in expression (54) vanish, and the dominant producer's supply decision is then independent of his future sales, since he no longer is able to influence the futures price independently of the spot price.

To summarize, if all producers face correlated supply risk, then the dominant producer will benefit from manipulating the futures market not just by an extent of his market power in the futures market, but by using that power additionally to influence the profits he earns on this production.

7.2 *Futures market manipulation with pure demand risk*

Suppose that the spot price fluctuates because of variations in demand, and that all supply is non-stochastic. Thus, with linear demand

$$\tilde{p} = \tilde{a} - b(q + Q), \qquad Ea = \bar{a}. \tag{56}$$

(There is no difficulty in having b random.) With pure demand risk, futures markets offer perfect income insurance (though agents may also wish to speculate), and it is easy to use the mean–variance model to show that in such cases the action certainty equivalent price is equal to the futures price. This is, however, a special case of a general result, due to Danthine (1978, p. 82), which can be restated using the present notation. If $U(y)$ is the utility of income y, then producers choose inputs x, and forward sales z, to

$$\max_{x,z} EU[\tilde{p}^f(x) - wx - z(\tilde{p} - p^f)]. \tag{57}$$

The first-order conditions are

$$f'EU'p = wEU'$$
$$EU'p = p^f EU';$$

hence

$$p^f f'(x) = w, \tag{58}$$

and p^f is the action certainty equivalent price. If the production function takes the same form as in the previous section, then

$$Q = \lambda p^f. \tag{59}$$

The futures sales of the fringe will be collectively

$$\Sigma z = Q - \frac{1}{\alpha v}(\bar{p} - p^f)$$

where αv is defined in (45). If the dominant producer sells S forward in the futures market, then equilibrium requires that

$$S + \Sigma z = 0 = S + Q - \frac{1}{\alpha v}(\bar{p} - p^f). \tag{60}$$

Substitute for Q from (59):

$$p^f = \frac{\bar{p} - \alpha v S}{1 + \alpha v \lambda}. \tag{61}$$

Hence

$$Q = \frac{\lambda(\bar{p} - \alpha v S)}{1 + \alpha v \lambda}. \tag{62}$$

From the demand schedule, substituting for Q,

$$p = a - bq - \frac{b\lambda(\bar{p} - \alpha S)}{1 + \alpha\lambda v}$$

$$\bar{p}\left[\frac{1 + (\alpha v + b)\lambda}{1 + \alpha v \lambda}\right] = a - bq + \frac{\alpha v b \lambda S}{1 + \alpha v \lambda}. \tag{63}$$

The dominant producer's expected profits are

$$y = \bar{p}q - wx + S(p^f - \bar{p}). \tag{64}$$

The last term can be written (from (60)) as

$$-\alpha v S(S + Q) = \frac{\alpha v S(S + \lambda \bar{p})}{1 + \alpha v \lambda}.$$

Marginal revenue for the dominant producer is then

$$\frac{\partial y}{\partial q} = \frac{a - 2bq + \alpha v b \lambda S/(1 + \alpha v \lambda)}{\xi} + \frac{\alpha v S \lambda b}{\xi(1 + \alpha v \lambda)} \tag{65}$$

where

$$\xi = \frac{1 + (\alpha v + b)\,\lambda}{1 + \alpha v \lambda}. \tag{66}$$

Again, we see that the dominant producer's input decision depends on the size of his sales in the futures market. His choice of futures sales is given by

$$\frac{\partial y}{\partial S} = 0 = \frac{avb\lambda}{(1 + \alpha v \lambda)}\, q - \frac{\alpha v(\lambda \bar{p} + 2S)}{1 + \alpha v \lambda} - \frac{\alpha v S \lambda}{(1 + \alpha v \lambda)^2}\,\frac{\alpha v b \lambda}{\xi}. \tag{67}$$

Again, the dominant producer's choice of futures sales depends on his planned level of production, and hence shows that his trading activity is not just that of a large speculator. All that is required for this result is that the dominant producer's profit be not additively separable in S and q; and, since prices depend on S and q, it is most improbable that profits would be so separable, except perhaps in a linear model such as those discussed here. Since even in a linear model manipulation is profitable, the result must hold generally.

8 Conclusion

Futures markets offer better insurance to producers than price stabilization schemes except when the producer has a very low correlation between his output and the world price. In this case, however, a price guarantee scheme operated by a domestic marketing board offers such a small improvement in income insurance that such benefits will almost certainly be offset by costs of operating such a scheme. These costs are not limited to the management and operating costs (e.g., preventing smuggling), but include the inefficiency of confronting producers by an inefficient predictor of the market price, and hence inducing inappropriate input decisions.

Although government intervention (via a marketing board) seems unattractive for small price-taking countries, it will be attractive to large producers, since this intervention can take the form of restricting supply to increase the spot price, and, more interestingly from our point of view, of manipulating the futures market. Large producers benefit from making the futures market less attractive to small producers, and hence increasing their risk and reducing supply. One way to do this is to reduce the correlation between price and supply, by introducing noise into their own supply. Another way might be to make the futures market itself noisier by random speculation (and, of course, if possible, by misleading other speculators in a way that causes them to lose money). In addition to making the market riskier, the large producer may find it attractive to manipulate the futures market in a predictable way to increase his profits.

We showed that, regardless of the source of the risk, large producers had an incentive to manipulate the futures market to induce an advantageous (to them) fringe supply response. The policy implications of this are interesting. Since futures markets are valuable to competitive producers and vulnerable to manipulation, it is desirable to encourage as much competitive speculation on these markets as possible to limit the ability of large producers to manipulate the forward premium, $\bar{p} - p^f$. We showed that, as the futures market became more risk-neutral (i.e. as more agents entered to share the risk), so the scope for manipulation diminished, to the advantage of the competitive producers.

Appendix: Properties of joint normal distributions

If x and y are jointly normally distributed about the origin with SDs σ_1, σ_2 and correlation coefficient ρ, then write this

$$N(0, 0, \sigma_1^2, \sigma_2^2, \rho).$$

The moment generating function (m.g.f.) is

$$M(t_1, t_2) = \exp\left[\tfrac{1}{2}(\sigma_1^2 t_1^2 + 2\rho\sigma_1\sigma_2 t_1 t_2 + \sigma_2^2 t_2^2)\right]$$

and then

$$\mu_{rs} = Ex^r y^s = \text{coefficient of } \frac{t_1^r t_2^s}{r!s!}$$

in the expansion of the m.g.f. Therefore

$$\mu_{11} = \rho\sigma_1\sigma_2; \quad \mu_{22} = (1 + 2\rho^2)\,\sigma_1^2\sigma_2^2; \quad \mu_{12} = \mu_{21} = 0.$$

To evaluate $Ep\theta$, var $(p\theta)$, cov $(p, p\theta)$, write

$$p = \bar{p}(1 + x), \quad \theta = 1 + y$$

$$Ep\theta = \bar{p}E(1 + x)(1 + y) = \bar{p}(1 + \mu_{11}) = \bar{p}(1 + \rho\sigma_1\sigma_2)$$

$$\text{var}\,(p\theta) = \bar{p}^2 E(1 + x + y + xy - 1 - \rho\sigma_1\sigma_2)^2.$$

$$\text{var}\,(p\theta) = \bar{p}^2[\sigma_1^2 + 2\rho\sigma_1\sigma_2 + \sigma_2^2 + (1 + \rho^2)\,\sigma_1^2\sigma_2^2]$$

$$\text{cov}\,(p, p\theta) = \bar{p}^2 Ex(x + y + xy - \rho\sigma_1\sigma_2).$$

$$\text{cov}\,(p, p\theta) = \bar{p}^2(\sigma_1^2 + \rho\sigma_1\sigma_2).$$

Notes

1 It may require the banning of trade on external futures markets in order to preserve different domestic and world prices.

2 Of course, if these countries have been manipulating prices, then the recorded correlations may be lower than they would have been in the absence of manipulation, for reasons given below. There may thus be more opportunities for manipulation than these crude data suggest.

3 Strictly speaking, falls sufficiently fast. It will with, e.g., a linear demand schedule.

References

Danthine, J. P. (1978), 'Information, Futures Prices, and Stabilizing Speculation', *Journal of Economic Theory*, 17.

Goreux, L. M. (1978), 'Optimal Rule of Buffer Stock Intervention', International Monetary Fund Research Department, mimeo DM/78/7, Washington.

Hart, O. D. (1977), 'On the Profitability of Speculation', *Quarterly Journal of Economics*, 91.

Kyle, A. S. (1981), 'Market Structure, Futures Markets, and Price Formation', mimeo, Princeton University.

McKinnon, R. I. (1967), 'Futures Markets, Buffer Stocks, and Income Stability for Primary Producers', *Journal of Political Economy*, 75.

Newbery, D. M. G. (1981), 'Commodity Price Stabilization in Imperfectly Competitive Markets', Development Research Center Discussion Paper no. 32, World Bank, Washington DC.

Newbery, D. M. G. and Stiglitz, J. E. (1981), *The Theory of Commodity Price Stabilization*, Oxford.

Salant, S. W. (1979), 'The Vulnerability of Price Stabilization Programs to Speculative Attack', mimeo.

Streit, M. E. (1980), 'On the Use of Futures Markets for Stabilization Purposes', *Weltwirtschafliches Archiv*, 116.

10

The Swap Market and its Relation to Currency Forward and Futures Markets

BRENDAN BROWN

1 Introduction

In discussion of the equilibrium relation between interest rates in different currencies, the forward exchange rate and the spot exchange rate, different authors have highlighted various possible channels of arbitrage. Most of these have involved quadrangular comparisons between the cost of dealing directly in one of the markets and the cost of dealing indirectly in the other three. Yet in practice, arbitrageurs in the exchange market study triangular rather than quadrangular opportunities. Covered arbitrage operations between deposit markets occur wholly within the triangle formed by the swap and deposit markets in the two given currencies. The swap market is a corner of a second triangle, formed from the spot, swap and outright forward markets, and arbitrage opportunity may also arise here. The quadrangular arbitrage opportunities can arise if and only if unexploited opportunities exist in each of these two triangles.

In the triangle formed from the swap and deposit markets, one corner – called here the 'dominant corner – should be the focus of arbitrage activity. For if an arbitrage opportunity were to exist at a non-dominant corner, then an even larger opportunity would exist at the dominant corner. Indeed, in all examples of triangular arbitrage, whether between deposit and swap markets, or between various associated futures markets, one corner of the triangle is dominant and triangular arbitrageurs should concentrate their operations there. The dominant corner is where the least liquid of the three markets is situated, for here the arbitrageur can make a relatively favourable comparison between the costs of effecting a deal indirectly by combining two transactions at the other corners and the costs of dealing directly.

The swap market is linked intimately by the operations of triangular arbitrageurs not only to the deposit markets but also to the spot and outright forward markets. The swap market plays an essential role in the generation of liquidity in the outright forward market. This is due to the scope for dealers to manufacture outright forward quotes by arbitraging with the spot and swap markets in foreign exchange. Market-makers in the currency futures markets do not share the advantage of their forward market counterparts in having direct access to the swap market.

Confusion about the swap market and its role in covered arbitrage between deposit markets has often handicapped the discussion of whether official intervention should be concentrated in the spot or forward markets.[1] Intervention in the forward market is equivalent to a combination of spot and swap market intervention. Swap market intervention weakens the influence of spot market intervention on the spot rate, and to an extent that is an increasing function of the degree of the currency's inconvertibility. However, in a highly restricted currency market, spot intervention is especially efficacious; a central bank can engineer here a squeeze on the spot market similar in nature to those against which regulators of organized futures markets are constantly on guard.

2 The currency swap market

The swap contract provides for a simultaneous spot and forward transaction. In a swap deal, two currencies are exchanged in the spot market, and simultaneously they are exchanged in the opposite direction in the forward market. For example, a customer effecting a swap transaction in dollars against marks with his bank could sell \$100,000 spot for marks and simultaneously buy back \$100,000 against marks for delivery in three months. The swap rate is a price difference – it is the premium or discount at which the parties agree to reverse the spot deal at a given date in the future. Swap dealing is very common in exchange markets and there is a much greater volume of swap than of outright forward transactions.

Swap transactions often have their source in a commercial hedging operation. For example, consider the exchange risk of a German corporation that has committed itself to an export of specialist capital goods, with delivery to be effected 18 months from now, and with the sale price fixed in US dollars for an amount of $10 million. The corporation can reduce its exposure to exchange risk by selling dollars forward against marks; it can enter into either only one forward contract, with a maturity date 18 months from now, or into a succession of short-term contracts (e.g., with three-month maturities), rolling each maturing contract into a new one. The corporation effects the roll-over by dealing in the swap market, buying US$10 million spot (to fulfil the obligation to deliver dollars under the maturing forward contract) and selling $10 million three months forward, both against marks.

A swap transaction is fundamentally a borrow-and-lend transaction. To illustrate this, consider in greater detail the combined transaction of selling US dollars spot against Deutschmarks and re-buying simultaneously dollars forward against marks. Under the spot transaction, dollars are paid out and marks received; under the forward leg of the transaction, dollars are received while marks are paid out. If we divide the transactions into two sets by currency rather than time, we have (from the viewpoint of the person swapping dollars into marks) a mark cash inflow now, followed by a mark cash outflow three months later; in addition, there is a dollar cash outflow now followed by a dollar cash inflow three months later. The pattern of mark cash flows is the same as for a mark-denominated three-month borrowing. The pattern of dollar cash flows is the same as for a three-month dollar loan.

The swap market is one corner of two important market triangles, where a 'market triangle' is defined as a set of three markets in which it is possible to effect the equivalent of a transaction in any one by dealing in the other two. The two market triangles are those formed from the spot/outright, forward/swap and swap/deposit markets respectively. As an alternative to buying marks three months outright forward against dollars, a transactor can buy marks spot and swap the marks into dollars for three months. As an alternative to swapping marks into dollars, he can borrow dollars and lend marks. Thus, liquidity in the outright forward market is supported by that in the spot and swap markets, and liquidity in the swap market is supported by that in the mark and dollar deposit markets.

3 The currency futures market

In the currency futures market, as found on Chicago's International Monetary Market (IMM), floor traders (in particular, we are considering here those that maintain two-way quotes) are not themselves market-makers in the swap, spot and deposit markets. This contrasts with the traditional outright forward market in which banks participate: a bank that is an important market-maker in the outright forward market will almost certainly be also a market-maker in the spot, swap and deposit markets. The comparative 'isolation' of the futures market floor trader is a handicap to the creation of a high level of liquidity in the currency futures market. A floor trader with an imbalance in inventory, unlike his forward market counterpart, cannot encourage a simultaneous offsetting adjustment in spot and swap inventory positions. Either the imbalance must be offset by trading with the IMM, or the trader can 'lay off' his position with a bank in the outright forward market. Costs would be incurred in this latter type of transaction.

Organizers of currency futures exchanges have been aware of the key role that arbitrage between their own exchange and the traditional forward market plays in the generation of liquidity. The IMM has a special class of member, called a class B member, which specializes in arbitrage between the IMM and the forward market. The class B member is exempt from margin requirements, and furthermore the clearing house of the exchange guarantees his credit to the banks. Therefore these small members (small by commercial standards) are able to get a line of credit with a specific bank to do the arbitrage in foreign exchange.

If banks, which are themselves market-makers in the outright forward, spot and swap exchange markets, also held seats in and traded on the floor of the IMM, then they would be better placed to seize arbitrage opportunity than the present floor traders using the class B facility. When the latter can see an arbitrage opportunity, the bank market-maker with its lower order of costs could surely see an even bigger opportunity. But in the first ten years of the IMM's existence, US banks have shown great reluctance to participate directly in the futures market. Collectively, large market-making banks may have an interest in not promoting the liquidity of the IMM, which would help it capture a larger share of total foreign exchange business; but it is difficult to explain at the level of an individual bank why at least some banks should not have entered directly into arbitrage between the futures and forward markets.

Despite the handicap of having no direct link to the swap market, the currency futures market has succeeded in winning business away from the forward market. By having standardized contract sizes and maturity dates, the futures market has an advantage compared with the forward market in the creation of liquidity, but only in one very narrow section of the maturity spectrum. The IMM has proved capable of creating liquidity only for one or two positions (maturities) simultaneously, and for no more than three months ahead. In the outright forward market, the swap (and indirectly the deposit) market and spot market become growingly important with length of the contract in the creation of liquidity, as common hedging business is concentrated in the 0–3-month maturity range. The IMM, with no direct link to the swap, spot and deposit markets, cannot quote competitively for the low-volume business in quoting for far-distant delivery dates.

The comparatively short maturity of the active IMM currency futures contract makes the IMM an unsatisfactory vehicle for speculators wishing to assume a position for long periods (three months or more). Long-term contracts on the IMM do not enjoy a liquid market; rolling over short-term contracts as part of a long-term strategy involves a series of swap transactions (effected just prior to the maturity of the current futures contract), and the futures market – with no access to the deposit markets – is ill-equipped to handle these.

4 Interest rate parity relationships

There are five distinct markets that are potentially relevant to covered arbitrage operations between deposit markets in two currencies (named here for simplicity Swiss francs and US dollars). These are:

(a) the spot exchange market, where francs are exchanged against dollars for immediate delivery (interpreted in practice as two business days ahead);
(b) the outright forward exchange market, where francs are exchanged against dollars for delivery at a given date in the future;
(c) the swap exchange market, where francs are bought (sold) spot and simultaneously sold (bought) forward against dollars;
(d) the deposit market in francs;
(e) the deposit market in dollars.

4.1 Conventional quadrangular covered arbitrage

Most discussions in the economics literature about the possibility of covered interest arbitrage have ignored the existence of the swap exchange market and have explored the following possible channels of arbitrage:

(a) borrow dollars, sell dollars spot for francs, lend francs and buy dollars forward against francs, where the maturities of all contracts (other than the spot) are identical;
(b) lend dollars, buy dollars spot against francs, borrow francs, and sell dollars forward against francs.

(The sets of transactions under each of (a) and (b) are termed two-way arbitrage in that the arbitrageur starts from a zero net position.)

(c) one-way channels of arbitrage (in a one-way arbitrage transaction, the arbitrageur considers whether it is cheaper to deal directly in one market, or indirectly by putting together deals in other markets):
  (i) instead of buying francs forward outright against dollars, borrow dollars, sell these spot for francs, and lend francs;
  (ii) instead of selling francs forward outright against dollars, borrow francs, sell these spot for dollars, and lend dollars;
  (iii) instead of lending francs, sell the francs spot for dollars, lend dollars, and buy francs forward against dollars;
  (iv) instead of borrowing francs, borrow dollars, sell the dollars spot for francs, and sell francs forward against dollars;
  (v) instead of lending dollars, sell the dollars spot for francs, lend francs, and sell francs forward;
  (vi) instead of borrowing dollars, borrow francs, sell the francs spot for dollars, and sell dollars forward.

4.2 Triangular arbitrage operations

The ignoring of the swap market in foreign exchange has been unfortunate, for it has led to covered arbitrage operations being treated as quadrangular rather than triangular. In practice, only three markets are involved – two deposit and one swap – rather than all four of the spot, outright forward and two respective deposit markets. The nature of the relationship that should hold between deposit and swap rates in market equilibrium – where there is no triangular arbitrage opportunity – is given in inequalities (1)–(6) below, in which the symbols should be interpreted as:

E, three-month dollar loan rate (expressed at a three-month rate);
e, three-month dollar deposit rate;
D, three-month franc loan rate;

d, three-month franc deposit rate;
F, number of francs per dollar that the bank quotes to a customer buying dollars three months from the present;
f, number of francs per dollar that the bank quotes to a customer wishing to sell dollars, say, three months from the present;
S, number of francs per dollar that the bank quotes to a customer wishing to buy francs in the spot market;
s, number of francs per dollar that the bank quotes to a customer wishing to sell dollars in the spot market;
C, discount below a reference spot price (francs/dollar) at which the bank offers to buy dollars forward from a customer to whom the bank sells simultaneously spot;
c, discount below a reference spot price (francs/dollar) at which the bank offers to sell dollars forward to a customer from whom the bank buys simultaneously spot.

(F, f are outright forward exchange rates; S, s are spot exchange rates; and C, c are swap exchange rates.)

The six inequalities are derived as conditions excluding the following arbitrage opportunities.

Franc deposit corner

(1) An investor with francs could, as an alternative to placing these directly in a three-month deposit, obtain a franc deposit indirectly by swapping the francs into dollars (selling francs spot for dollars and selling the same number of dollars three months forward for francs), investing the dollars in a three-month deposit, and selling the interest receivable on the deposit outright forward for francs (the interest is not covered under the swap transaction). The condition that no arbitrage opportunity exists from taking the second indirect route compared with the first direct one may be expressed symbolically as

$$(S - C) + ef < S(1 + d). \quad (1)$$

(2) As an alternative to borrowing francs directly for three months, an investor can obtain franc finance indirectly by borrowing three-month dollars, swapping these into francs, and covering the interest payment on the dollar loan in the outright forward market. The market equilibrium condition of zero arbitrage opportunity may be expressed as

$$(S - C) + EF > s(1 + D). \quad (2)$$

Franc/dollar swap corner

(3) As an alternative to swapping francs into dollars as one transaction in the swap market (selling francs spot for dollars and selling the same number of dollars simultaneously forward for francs), a trader can borrow dollars for three months, lend the equivalent number of francs (using s as the exchange rate), and buy dollars against francs in the outright forward market to cover the interest on the dollar borrowing. The market equilibrium condition of zero arbitrage is

$$(s - C) + EF > (1 + d)\,s. \qquad (3)$$

(4) As an alternative to swapping dollars into francs as one transaction in the swap market (selling dollars spot for francs and buying the same number of dollars forward simultaneously for francs), a trader can lend dollars for three months, borrow the equivalent number of francs (using S as the exchange rate), and sell dollars against francs in the outright forward market to cover the interest on the dollar deposit. The market equilibrium condition of zero arbitrage is

$$(S - c) + ef < (1 + D)\,S. \qquad (4)$$

Dollar deposit corner

(5) As an alternative to placing dollars directly in a three-month dollar deposit, the investor could swap the dollars into francs (selling dollars spot for francs and buying back the same number of dollars forward), lend francs and cover in the outright forward market the franc interest plus surplus principal of the franc deposit that would remain after buying back the dollars forward against francs as the final leg of the swap transaction. The market equilibrium condition of zero arbitrage is

$$(s - c) + eF > s(1 + d). \qquad (5)$$

(6) As an alternative to borrowing dollars directly for three months, the borrower could finance himself in francs and swap these into dollars, buying francs in the outright forward market to cover interest on the franc loan plus the shortfall of franc principal after repayment with the francs bought against dollars under the outright forward contract that is the final leg of the swap transaction. The market equilibrium condition of zero arbitrage is

$$(S - C) + Ef < S(1 + D). \qquad (6)$$

In sum, there are three pairs of possible arbitrage opportunities, at the franc deposit, franc/dollar swap, and dollar deposit corners respectively of the desposit/swap market triangle in franc/dollars. Inequalities (1)–(6) express the conditions that arbitrage opportunity should not exist; (1) and (2) refer to the franc deposit corner, (3) and (4) to the franc/dollar swap corner, and (5) and (6) to the dollar deposit corner.

4.3 Dominant corners

It can be shown that, if arbitrage opportunity were to exist in the deposit/swap market triangle, it would always be greatest at one given corner, which may be called the 'dominant corner'. Indeed, if arbitrage is efficient, then arbitrage should only ever occur at the dominant corner. This proposition about dominance in the franc deposit/swap triangle may be derived from inequalities (1)–(6). Compare first arbitrage profit at the franc deposit market corner and the franc/dollar swap corner. Arbitrage profit (positive or negative) derivable from the transactions behind inequality (4) less that behind inequality (1), $P_{4,1}$, is given in equation (7) below:

$$P_{4,1} = (C - c) - S(D - d). \qquad (7)$$

Thus arbitrage profit from a (4)-type set of transactions is greater than from a (1)-type set if $(C - c)/S$ is greater than $D - d$, implying that the swap market is more illiquid than the franc deposit market. A similar conclusion applies to the comparison of arbitrage profit from a (3)-type set of transactions with a (2)-type, as in equation (8) below:

$$P_{3,2} = (C - c) - s(D - d). \qquad (8)$$

We do not need to compare arbitrage profit of a (1)-type with a (3)-type, or a (2)-type with a (4)-type, because these arbitrage opportunities are mutually exclusive.

Similar results would follow from comparing arbitrage profit at the franc deposit corner with that at the dollar deposit corner and then the latter with arbitrage profit at the swap market corner. The conclusion would emerge that arbitrage opportunity at the corner where liquidity is least (i.e. where bid–offer spreads are greatest) would dominate arbitrage opportunity elsewhere. In the swap/deposit market triangle, the swap market is likely to be the least liquid corner, and the dollar deposit market the most liquid corner. Arbitrage profit cannot exist at the dollar deposit corner without a greater profit existing at the franc deposit corner and an even greater profit existing at the franc/dollar swap corner.

Owing to the intersection of the swap/deposit market triangle in francs/dollars and the spot/swap/outright forward market triangle in francs/dollars at their common swap market corner, which is the dominant corner of the first but not of the second triangle, quadrangular arbitrage opportunities can emerge sometimes. Instead of buying francs against dollars in the outright forward exchange market, the transactor may find it cheaper to buy francs against dollars in the spot market and swap the francs into dollars; rather than undertaking the latter transaction, he may find it cheaper to borrow francs and lend dollars. But the quadrangular arbitrage opportunity can exist if and only if arbitrage is available in each of the two intersecting triangles. Market participants do not risk sacrificing quadrangular arbitrage opportunity if they monitor only market triangles, and indeed this is how they operate in practice.

5 Triangular arbitrage generalized

The discovery that one corner – the swap market – is dominant in the swap/deposit market triangle, may be generalized. Where three markets form together a triangle, the arbitrageur should concentrate his attention on one corner that proves to be dominant. The dominant corner is the market where bid–offer spreads are the greatest, or where liquidity is least. This proposition is demonstrated symbolically for two further situations of triangular arbitrage, one for the spot exchange markets and one for the financial futures markets. Triangular arbitrage opportunity does not exist in the currency futures market, for all trading there is against the US dollar. Even in the conventional spot exchange market with banks as market-makers, triangular arbitrage opportunity is rare, given the prevalence of quoting rates in non-dollar exchange markets by simply combining two rates from dollar exchange markets.

5.1 Triangular arbitrage in spot currency markets

Consider triangular arbitrage between the spot exchange market in marks/dollars, florins/dollars and marks/florins, in each of which independent market-making is found. In market equilibrium, the following three pairs of conditions, describing the absence of one-way arbitrage opportunities, must be fulfilled at the mark/florin, florin/dollar and mark/dollar market corners respectively:

(A) *Mark/florin pivot*

$$(1)\ E_{fl/DM} \times e_{DM/\$} < E_{fl/\$}$$
$$(2)\ e_{fl/DM} \times E_{DM/\$} > e_{fl/\$}$$

(B) *Florin/dollar pivot*

$$(3)\ E_{fl/\$} < F_{fl/DM} \times E_{DM/\$}$$
$$(4)\ e_{fl/\$} > e_{fl/DM} \times e_{DM/\$}$$

(C) *Mark/dollar pivot*

$$(5)\ E_{DM/\$} \times e_{fl/DM} < E_{fl/\$}$$
$$(6)\ e_{DM/\$} \times E_{fl/DM} > e_{fl/\$}$$

where $e_{fl/DM}$, $E_{fl/DM}$ are the bank's offer and bid rate of florins against marks; $e_{fl/\$}$, $F_{fl/\$}$ are the offer and bid rate of florins against dollars; and $e_{DM/\$}$, $E_{DM/\$}$ are the offer and bid rate of marks against dollars.

In practice, bid–offer spreads are least in the mark/dollar exchange market and greatest in the mark/florin market. It can be shown that pair (A) dominates (B), and that by extension (B) dominates (C). For arbitrage profit in (1) less arbitrage profit in (4), $A_{1,4}$ can be expressed as

$$A_{1,4} = e_{DM/\$}(E_{fl/DM} - e_{fl/DM}) - (E_{fl/\$} - e_{fl/\$}). \qquad (10)$$

And, given the lower level of liquidity in the florin/mark market than in the florin/dollar market, $A_{1,4}$ can be seen to be greater than zero. Thus, if an arbitrage profit can be derived from selling dollars for marks and marks for florins rather than dollars directly for florins, a larger profit can be derived from selling florins for dollars and dollars for marks than for selling florins directly for marks. Similarly $A_{2,3}$ is positive.

5.2 *Triangular arbitrage in deposit markets*

Consider, next, triangular arbitrage between the three-month and six-month deposit markets and the three-month forward 91-day certificate of deposit (CD) futures market. In market equilibrium the following three pairs of conditions, describing the absence of one-way arbitrage opportunities, must be fulfilled:

(A) *Six-month money market pivot*

$$(1)\ 1 + {}_0r_6 > (1 + {}_0r_3)(1 + {}_3r_6)$$
$$(2)\ 1 + {}_0R_6 < (1 + {}_0R_3)(1 + {}_3R_6)$$

(B) *Three-month forward 91-day CD pivot*

$$(3)\ (1 + {}_3r_6)(1 + {}_0R_3) > (1 + {}_0r_6)$$
$$(4)\ (1 + {}_3R_6)(1 + {}_0r_3) < (1 + {}_0R_6)$$

(C) *Three-month money market*

$$(5)\ (1 + {}_0r_3)(1 + {}_3R_6) > (1 + {}_0r_6)$$
$$(6)\ (1 + {}_0R_3)(1 + {}_3r_6) < (1 + {}_0R_6)$$

where ${}_0r_3$, ${}_0R_3$ are lending and borrowing rates in the three-month money market; ${}_0r_6$, ${}_0R_6$ are lending and borrowing rates in the six-month money market; and ${}_3r_6$, ${}_3R_6$ are lending and borrowing rates in the three-month forward 91-day CD market.

Arbitrage at corner A concerns the possibility of lending (borrowing) three-month money, and buying (selling) a 91-day CD three months forward, rather than lending (borrowing) six-month money. Arbitrage at corner B concerns lending (borrowing) six-month money and borrowing (lending) three-month money rather than buying (selling) a three-month forward 91-day CD. Arbitrage at corner C concerns lending (borrowing) six-month money and selling (buying) a three-month forward 91-day CD rather than lending (borrowing) three-month money.

Suppose the liquidity of the three-month money market is greatest and that of the futures market in 91-day CDs is least. Then consider arbitrage profit potential in A compared with that in B. Arbitrage profit underlying (4) compared with (1), $A_{4,1}$, is given in

$$A_{4,1} = (1 + {}_0r_3)({}_3R_6 - {}_3r_6) - ({}_0R_6 - {}_0r_6). \tag{10}$$

Given the orders of liquidity described, $A_{4,1}$ is positive. Similarly, arbitrage profit in (2) dominates that in (3). (A) is the dominant corner of the arbitrage triangle. It is the transactor in the CD futures market rather than that in the three-month or six-month money markets, who should monitor continuously the possibility of arbitrage profit.

6 Official intervention in the swap/deposit market triangle

In the discussion of covered interest arbitrage in the first section of this paper, the absence of impediments to arbitrage was assumed. But in practice, many central banks place restrictions on triangular arbitrage between the deposit and swap markets. The placing of restrictions is not the only type of official operation in the swap market. Central banks may enter the swap market as a direct buyer or seller, either for the sole purpose of influencing the domestic interest rate, or to effect, together with spot intervention, the equivalent of outright forward market intervention.[2, 3] The effects of outright forward intervention should be distinguished according to whether or not arbitrage is permitted freely in the deposit/swap market triangle.

6.1 Forward intervention in 'convertible' currency

Intervention in the outright forward market is in effect equivalent to intervention in the spot market and simultaneously in the swap market. For example, if the Swiss National Bank wished to buy francs in the three-month outright forward market, it would effect the transaction by buying francs (against dollars) in the spot market, and swapping francs into dollars over three months (i.e. selling francs spot for dollars and buying them back three months forward). This procedure is followed because the three-month outright forward market is usually illiquid compared with the swap and spot markets.

Forward intervention in itself has no effect on reserves of the banking system and so should be considered as one of a family of sterilized intervention tactics that can be used by the authorities in the exchange market. Whether a central bank prefers to sterilize the effect on bank reserves of its intervention in the spot exchange market by effecting swaps (thus translating spot into forward intervention) rather than by operating in the domestic credit market depends on which method of sterilization has least counter-influence on the spot exchange rate.

As illustration, we compare here sterilization in the three-month swap market with that in the three-month domestic credit (or Treasury bill market). The two are not of identical effect. Whereas most studies show that covered arbitrage is almost perfect between euro-deposit markets and the swap market, such is not the case between domestic deposit markets and the swap markets. Significant marginal convenience yields usually exist on domestic deposits compared with euro-deposits.[4] In the Swiss example, swap intervention depresses the three-month euro-franc interest rate to a greater extent, and the three-month domestic franc interest rate to a lesser extent, than does intervention in the three-month domestic franc market. If international capital flows are more sensitive to the euro- than to the domestic franc rate – a hypothesis supported by the observation that a particularly large proportion of investors in the euro-markets have an 'international approach' to money management – then the swap intervention would in consequence weaken the spot rate of the franc to a greater extent than would the credit market intervention. Thus, swap intervention has the disadvantage, compared with credit market intervention, of more seriously undermining the influence of intervention in the spot exchange market on the spot exchange rate.[5]

Next, compare sterilization in the three-month credit market with sterilization in the longer-term credit markets, say that for one-year bills. A one-year bill is equivalent to a three-month bill plus positions in three three-month bill futures contracts with delivery months respectively three, six and nine months forward. Both types of sterilization have a similar influence on conditions in the three-month credit market, but significantly different influences on the mentioned futures markets. What non-similarity exists in influence on the three-month credit market is due either to some holders of cash who would respond to a fall in both the spot and three-month forward three-month interest rate but not just to the spot three-month rate by switching out of bills into cash (and so draining reserves from the banking system), or to entrepreneurs who would not undertake extra investment projects in response to a fall in just the spot three-month interest rate but would in response to a fall in both the spot and three-month-forward three-month interest rate. In the franc example, intervention in the one-year market depresses term interest rates for periods of from three months to one year by significantly more than does intervention in the spot three-month market. The depression of these longer-term rates reduces demand for francs in the spot exchange market and so sterilization in the long-term credit markets reduces the effectiveness of spot intervention by more than does intervention in the short-term credit markets.

6.2 Effectiveness of forward market intervention in 'inconvertible' currency

The most common inconvertibility for currencies of advanced industrial countries is the type in which restrictions cover only the making of foreign investments by domestic residents and the borrowing of the national money by foreigners. Arbitrage cannot occur directly between the swap market and the relevant domestic deposit markets. But there are several channels of indirect arbitrage, which are illustrated below for the situation in which the discount on the three-month forward franc quoted in the swap exchange market is greater than the interest rate differential between domestic franc and euro-dollar deposits (both for three-month maturities):[6]

(a) Non-residents may swap domestic francs into dollar deposits; this arbitrage flow is limited by the growth in marginal convenience yield on domestic deposits as these are run down.
(b) Non-residents may lag payment for imports from France (the issuer of francs in this example), and buy francs forward rather than spot. Their gain – both from obtaining the forward discount on the franc and from interest on their increased liquid balances – should be greater than the exporter's loss of interest earnings on domestic franc deposits owing to their being run down to finance the extension of credit. (Presumably the exporter passes on the cost by disallowing some discount for early settlement; but the cost will be measured by reference to domestic interest rates.)
(c) Domestic residents may delay repatriation of export receipts, investing them for a short time in, say, the offshore dollar market, sell the receipts forward for francs rather than spot, and run down their domestic franc liquidity.
(d) Domestic residents may try to accelerate their payment for imports invoiced in foreign currency, buying foreign exchange spot rather than forward, running down their domestic franc liquidity, and hoping to obtain a settlement discount from the supplier together with a saving of the premium on the price of forward compared with spot foreign exchange that will exceed the loss of interest on domestic liquidity. The settlement discount should reflect interest rates on the freely convertible currency used to denominate the supplier's invoice.

In very tightly regulated currencies, arbitrage channels (a)–(d) are in principle all blocked. Non-resident deposits are not convertible (and non-resident speculation occurs exclusively in the forward market); export invoices are denominated in 'specified' foreign currencies; domestic residents may not advance payment for imports. In such currencies, intervention in the spot market is very effective. A purchase of francs there drives up the spot price of the franc, while its forward discount widens sharply (as the forward rate continues to be depressed by bearish sentiment). In a convertible currency, and to a lesser extent in partially inconvertible currencies, this widening would ignite arbitrage flows of francs from the forward into the spot market, either directly or via channels (a)–(d) above, weakening the force of intervention there.[7] In an inconvertible currency arbitrage is blocked, and the central bank, by bidding for more francs than are presently supplied from commercial sources, can name its price. A classic bear squeeze is the result.[8]

As in section 6.1, two alternative methods of sterilizing the influence on bank reserves of intervention in support of the franc in the spot exchange market can be compared, but now where the franc is partially inconvertible:

(i) swapping francs for dollars over a three-month maturity (selling francs spot and simultaneously buying them forward);
(ii) buying three-month Treasury bills in the domestic market.

The comparison is made for a partially inconvertible currency.

As illustration, suppose that the franc is at a forward discount to the dollar, and that domestic franc interest rates are below covered parity with dollar rates. On impact, policy (i) narrows the forward discount on the franc, and by more than the fall in domestic franc interest rates under the influence of banks adjusting to the increased supply of reserves, assuming that the demand for reserves (which are non-interest-bearing) is not very inelastic with respect to interest rates. But the narrowing of the forward discount on the franc is held in check, first, by arbitrage flows via channels (a)–(d) above (in the reverse direction to that previously described); and, second, by the public taking open long and short positions in the spot and forward exchange markets, respectively, as they respond to the fall in the value of the spot franc, and rise in value of the forward franc, that correspond to the narrowing of the swap margin. Elasticity of demand in the spot market with respect to the spot exchange rate is provided by traders being ready to delay or cancel an intended purchase of spot francs should the franc/dollar rate fall. Distinct from arbitrageurs, these traders do not match their delayed purchase in the spot market with the simultaneous assumption of a forward position.

Arbitrage flows through the four channels are of lower elasticity with respect to the swap rate than are arbitrage flows of any form (including straight financial arbitrage) in the example of a fully convertible currency. In the latter, the counter-party to the central bank's swap intervention would be the banks. As the central bank swapped francs into dollars, the forward discount on the franc would narrow and banks could gain from borrowing dollars and lending francs rather than swapping francs into dollars to meet customers' orders to swap dollars into francs. As franc interest rates fell, banks would increase their demand for reserves, given that these are non-interest-bearing, and in the new equilibrium interest rates would have fallen to equate banks' demand for reserves with their increased supply. In a currency that suffers from inconvertibility, and where domestic interest rates are substantially below covered parity with dollar rates, swap market intervention would not quickly trigger the arbitrage described. Instead, a greater proportion of the official swap intervention in a partially inconvertible currency must be offset by the public taking open positions in the spot and forward market than in a fully convertible currency. Thus the forward discount on the franc narrows by more, the forward value of the franc rises by more, and the spot value of the franc falls by more, the greater is the extent of restriction on arbitrage – direct or indirect – between swap and deposit markets. Indeed, intervention in the forward market (equal to spot intervention plus an equal swap operation) is powerless to influence the spot rate where arbitrage flows are blocked, and where demand in the spot exchange market is not perfectly inelastic; the only possible counterpart to the official swaps are bear speculators in the outright forward exchange market and official purchases of francs in the spot market.

Policy (ii) brings downward pressure on the three-month interest rate. If arbitrage flows between the domestic deposit and swap markets can occur, albeit only to a limited extent, then the forward discount on the franc comes under narrowing pressure. The pressure is less, being indirect, than under policy (i), and so the forward franc strengthens to a lesser extent in the outright forward market. In turn, less downward pressure is exerted on the franc in the spot exchange market. In sum, policy (ii) is less undermining than policy (i) of the effectiveness of official intervention in the spot exchange market. Policy (ii)'s relative advantage increases with the degree to which the currency is restricted. It is somewhat paradoxical that intervention in the outright forward market – or, equivalently, spot intervention together with sterilization in the swap markets – has been characteristic of central bank policy in countries where the currency is not fully convertible.[9]

7 Conclusion

In contrast to the conventional analysis of covered arbitrage between currencies, only three rather than four markets are found here to be involved – the two deposit markets and the swap exchange market. Thus, covered arbitrage opportunities belong to a general class of arbitrage described as 'triangular'. One corner of the triangle is usually dominant, in that efficient arbitrage there precluded arbitrage opportunity at any other corner, but not conversely. The dominant corner is the most illiquid of the three markets. Another example of triangular arbitrage – that between the spot, swap and outright forward exchange markets – is of particular importance to the creation of liquidity in the forward exchange market. Currency futures markets, in contrast to forward markets in currency, are somewhat isolated from swap and spot markets, and so are handicapped in the generation of liquidity. Organizers of currency futures markets have tried to compensate for this handicap by encouraging arbitrage between their own market and the traditional markets.

Official intervention in the forward exchange markets is equivalent to intervention in the spot exchange market plus an equal value operation in the swap market that has the effect of sterilizing any influence of spot support on the reserves of the banking system. Arguments in favour of forward intervention are in effect in favour of sterilizing spot intervention via operations in the swap market rather than in one of the domestic credit markets. The difference between the alternative methods of sterilization is greatest where the domestic currency is subject to severe exchange restrictions. Here, swap operations undermine almost entirely the influence of spot intervention on the spot exchange rate.

Notes

1 For a survey of the literature on the interest rate parity theorem, see Kohlhagen (1978).
2 See Day (1976) for a discussion of forward intervention as an alternative to exchange restrictions.
3 See Pardee (1980) for an account of recent forward operations.
4 See Aliber (1978). Marginal convenience yield includes such factors as potential saving of transaction costs from using the domestic banking system.
5 If, however, offshore deposits are subject to zero reserve requirements in contrast to domestic deposits, swap intervention by decreasing the demand for offshore compared with domestic deposits (by narrowing the interest rate differential) may create a shortage of reserves, pushing up the general level of franc interest rates.
6 For example, suppose three-month domestic franc interest rates, three-month euro-dollar rates, and the three-month forward discount on the franc, all expressed at annual rates, were 15, 12 and 6 per cent.
7 Technically, the arbitrage described impacts on the swap market, narrowing the forward discount on the franc. In turn, the firming of the outright forward rate stimulates bears to take short positions in the forward market,

which the banks match by offsetting deals in the swap and spot markets. The latter transmits selling pressure into the spot market.

8 See Yaeger (1966) for an account of the famous bear squeeze effected by Russia's Minister of Finance, Count Witte, in 1894. Russian agents in Berlin bought forward large volumes of ruble notes – more than were in circulation outside Russia; then export of ruble notes from Russia was banned and short-sellers were squeezed.

9 See Einzig (1975) for a history of intervention in the forward exchange markets. One prominent example was the heavy purchases of forward sterling by the Bank of England in 1964–67, during a time when exchange restrictions were being tightened.

References

Aliber, R. Z. (1978), 'Monetary Independence under Floating Exchange Rates', *Journal of Finance*, 33.

Brown, B. D. (1979), 'A Clarification of the Interest Rate Parity Theorem', *European Economic Review* 12.

Day, W. H. (1976), 'The Advantages of Exclusive Forward Exchange Rate Support', *IMF Staff Papers*, 23.

Einzig, P. (1975), *A Dynamic Theory of Forward Exchange*, London.

Kohlhagen, S. (1978), *The Behaviour of the Foreign Exchange Markets – A Critical Survey of the Economic Literature*, New York.

Pardee, S. E. (1980), 'Treasury and Federal Reserve Foreign Exchange Operations: Interim Report', *Federal Reserve Bulletin*, December.

Yaeger, L. B. (1966), *International Monetary Relations*, New York.

11

Inventive Activity in Futures Markets: A Case Study of the Development of the First Interest Rate Futures Market

RICHARD L. SANDOR and HOWARD B. SOSIN

1 Introduction

In early 1972 the research department of the Chicago Board of Trade (CBT) began work on an interest rate futures contract. It was to have been a simple revision of a wheat contract, to have taken less than 12 months to develop and market, and to have required a research budget totalling less than $100,000. Three and one half years, 23 or so drafts and approximately $250,000 in research and development costs later, the Government National Mortgage Association (GNMA) futures contract was born.

Almost six years have passed since the GNMA contract started trading. By almost any yardstick it has been a successful contract. For example, consider table 1, which presents monthly volume and open interest figures for the GNMA contract and for the wheat contract (a traditional standard of success). It is particularly noteworthy that during 1978 the GNMA contract actually surpassed the 'venerable' wheat contract in open interest – a supremacy it has maintained. In addition, on several occasions when measured daily, GNMA volume has exceeded wheat volume.

Other measures of success can be reported. For example, it is estimated that the CBT has received annual exchange fees that are a significant multiple of research and development costs. Also, the contract generates tens of millions of dollars annually in commissions for the brokerage community. Furthermore, the success of the GNMA contract has encouraged the development of additional interest rate futures contracts, most notably the Treasury bill futures on the International Monetary Market of the Chicago Mercantile

Table 1 Monthly volume and open interest for the GNMA contract and the wheat contract, 1975–81

	Volume of sales Number of contracts			*Month-end open interest Number of contracts*	
	GNMA	*Wheat*		*GNMA*	*Wheat*
1975			*1975*		
October	6,240	231,876	October	1,277	44,508
November	8,423	192,041	November	1,166	39,970
December	5,462	144,130	December	1,325	36,271
1976			*1976*		
January	8,299	169,516	January	1,708	33,163
February	6,159	279,715	February	1,679	41,331
March	7,487	294,334	March	1,610	40,573
April	8,033	257,692	April	1,902	34,245
May	10,179	224,194	May	2,395	36,704
June	11,953	351,670	June	3,452	45,282
July	10,611	359,285	July	3,873	47,432
August	11,729	245,639	August	3,364	45,440
September	12,568	234,539	September	3,624	46,761
October	12,552	236,067	October	4,560	54,047
November	13,937	201,030	November	4,413	52,093
December	15,030	120,146	December	5,182	45,889
1977			*1977*		
January	23,982	115,338	January	6,680	44,009
February	21,745	161,916	February	6,506	47,602
March	25,944	177,632	March	8,820	40,608
April	20,026	138,675	April	11,043	39,317
May	29,626	119,496	May	13,219	36,597
June	32,226	169,225	June	15,242	40,028
July	34,642	164,748	July	18,787	41,533
August	61,807	124,638	August	16,645	41,624
September	36,875	155,419	September	16,211	48,199
October	45,363	147,905	October	18,709	49,640
November	43,398	196,320	November	18,772	47,379
December	41,787	149,484	December	20,719	49,026
*1978**			*1978*		
January	48,423	138,838	January	20,386	45,870
February	46,723	142,650	February	19,624	40,139
March	57,065	225,906	March	20,254	36,112
April	57,241	236,762	April	24,004	32,979
May	60,141	212,563	May	27,480	38,646
June	75,178	224,368	June	33,503	32,629
July	73,578	226,648	July	39,424	37,990
August	109,207	262,308	August	43,558	48,188
September	96,119	204,227	September	41,621	51,188
October	110,982	252,011	October	54,366	48,348
November	108,950	254,312	November	60,017	48,070
December	109,602	175,541	December	62,722	37,271

Table 1—*continued*

	Volume of sales Number of contracts			*Month-end open interest Number of contracts*	
	GNMA	*Wheat*		*GNMA*	*Wheat*
1979			*1979*		
January	89,762	177,724	January	62,380	39,007
February	79,818	174,659	February	63,473	39,021
March	68,057	160,977	March	63,011	34,695
April	82,029	131,945	April	62,831	37,445
May	99,752	219,164	May	68,479	35,193
June	111,767	375,695	June	73,339	50,043
July	76,997	386,390	July	70,644	51,727
August	95,274	361,113	August	75,015	60,516
September	164,451	369,943	September	77,049	63,952
October	164,932	542,739	October	71,019	56,812
November	157,853	371,587	November	76,330	57,506
December	180,349	310,139	December	88,982	57,374
1980			*1980*		
January	170,046	412,788	January	65,917	55,892
February	155,505	443,220	February	54,748	53,320
March	156,282	379,412	March	46,082	44,504
April	190,271	418,295	April	55,462	42,832
May	219,729	410,792	May	60,609	42,690
June	248,385	402,287	June	71,853	54,000
July	161,990	667,205	July	67,575	69,089
August	151,597	389,877	August	63,145	69,141
September	133,939	510,193	September	67,076	75,262
October	204,955	543,968	October	83,191	88,557
November	206,546	429,286	November	98,488	84,023
December	318,735	412,035	December	115,161	70,109
1981			*1981*		
January	179,779	370,991	January	97,020	58,214
February	159,941	301,891	February	97,135	47,299
March	186,458	346,908	March	99,837	42,335
April	202,296	266,867	April	105,712	41,964
May	211,400	280,022	May	107,513	48,598
June	188,538	434,825	June	121,010	56,613
July	162,031	473,645	July	133,860	64,876
August	156,233	411,054	August	116,583	65,891
September	189,848	366,637	September	115,429	67,450

* On a daily basis GNMA volume exceeded wheat volume on several days during 1978 including eight days in December.

Exchange and the Treasury bond contract on the CBT.[1] Finally, it led to the creation of two entirely new commodity exchanges – the American Commodities Exchange, a subsidiary of the American Stock Exchange (no longer in existence); and the New York Futures

Exchange, a subsidiary of the New York Stock Exchange – and encouraged financial futures trading at Commodities Exchange, Inc. (COMEX) the Mid-American Exchange and in London (yet to open).

The GNMA contract that began trading in 1975 and the one that trades today retains much of the character of an agricultural commodity futures contract. That is, it balances the diverse interests of cash and futures markets participants, and potential longs and shorts. Alternatively stated, the key considerations in designing this contract were a desire to obtain active participation of floor traders combined with use by the trade and speculators. Participation by these parties insures a liquid market, helps to provide an inexpensive hedging vehicle, and promotes convergence between cash and futures prices. The contract was also designed to reflect the regulatory environment and the traditions of the CBT.

This paper traces the development of the GNMA futures contract from first draft to final product. The evolution of the provisions of the contract is of interest as it provides insights into the 'art' of contract design and information that may be useful in evaluating the potential of the many proposals for futures contracts that are currently pending at the Commodity Futures Trading Commission. Section 2 describes the CBT's decision to write a futures contract on GNMAs; section 3 analyses the evolution of the provisions of the contract; section 4 discusses initial liquidity and floor permits; section 5 provides a description of the regulatory environment; and section 6 presents a summary and conclusion.

2 Why GNMAs?

The first question to be resolved is why a 'grain' exchange in the Mid-West would be interested in interest rate futures. In fact, by 1972 labelling the CBT as simply a grain exchange would be a misnomer. As a response to the decrease in trading volume that occurred in the early 1960s, the CBT and many other exchanges initiated programmes of product diversification. Thus, by 1972, in addition to the grains, the CBT was trading futures on steer carcass beef, live choice steers, iced broilers, silver and plywood.[2]

At the time of the development of the interest rate futures contract, the CBT was also considering futures on other commodities, including sugar, coal and reinsurance.[3] The focus on interest rate futures at the Chicago Board of Trade coincided with the establishment of a research department at the exchange and the 'credit crunches' of the late 1960s and early 1970s that severely affected financial institutions. The idea of using an interest rate futures market as a vehicle for shifting mortgage interest rate risk seemed worth pursuing.[4]

Having focused on mortgage interest rate futures,[5] it was necessary to choose a deliverable instrument. A paper by the authors[6] illustrated that individual mortgages were extremely difficult to 'grade' or 'standardize' because factors such as neighbourhood and borrower ratings play significant roles in the interest rate assigned to individual mortgages. The search for a trading standard led to an analysis of the recently developed GNMA market. This 'commodity' appeared to satisfy the homogeneity criterion that has been identified with successful futures contracts. In addition, a variety of other desirable criteria, including price variability, an open spot market, competitively determined prices and a pattern of forward contracting that was unreliable, appeared to exist.

2.1 What are GNMAs?

GNMAs are securities that are backed by pools of Federal Housing Association (FHA) and Veterans' Administration (VA) mortgages organized by pool originators (mortgage bankers, savings and loan associations, etc.). The mortgage-backed certificate programme was initiated in 1970. Any mortgage lender authorized to make FHA and VA loans can put together a pool. The contents of the pool must be approved by the Government National Mortgage Association (GNMA). Once approval has been obtained, GNMA guarantees the pool by pledging the full-faith and credit of the US government, thus insuring timely payment of both interest and principal. Thus, a purchaser of a GNMA certificate is assured prompt payment of interest, amortization and any prepayments that may occur. To the owner of a certificate, a default is indistinguishable from a prepayment, as GNMA provides the principal and interest lost in the default and disburses it to the holders of the certificate. The reduced credit risk associated with mortgages resulting from the pooling operation has encouraged investment in mortgages by pension funds and insurance companies and has dramatically aided the liquidity of the secondary mortgage market.

3 The evolution of the provisions of the GNMA futures contract[7]

A futures contract traded on an organized exchange is an agreement to buy or sell a specific quantity and quality of a commodity at a specific price on a specific date in the future. In addition to these provisions, a futures contract specifies minimum price increment ('tick size'), intra-day maximum price variation (price limits), delivery procedures, position limits of traders and trading hours, and provides authorization to specify delivery months.

The first draft of the GNMA futures contract was written in May 1972. It called for delivery of $250,000 (face amount) of 6½ per cent GNMAs with a 4 per cent tolerance. (Thus, the face amount to be delivered could range from $240,000 to $260,000.) To be eligible for delivery the GNMAs were required to satisfy a seasoning criterion – to have an issue date no less than 45 days prior to the date of delivery and no more than two years prior to the date of delivery of the futures contract. The minimum price increment tick size was established at 0.01 per cent of par, or $25 per contract; the trading limit was set at 0.5 per cent of par above or below the previous day's settlement price, or $1,250 per contract. No position limit was established; trading hours and delivery months were not specified. As described in the remainder of this section, each of the provisions of this contract was to undergo substantial revision.

3.1 Contract size

While other conditions for a successful futures contract may be debatable, all would agree that price variability is key. The original contract size was set to allow a variability in dollars relative to initial margin that was commensurate with the variability in dollars relative to initial margin that existed for CBT grain futures contracts. While not originally specified, it was always implicit that the original margin was to be set at a level that was consistent with the grain contracts at the CBT ($500–$1,000 in 1972). A $250,000 contract size was chosen after an analysis of the historical variability of the spot GNMA market.[8]

With initial margin size fixed, there is a trade-off between contract size and variability. Obviously by making the contract size large enough any variability can be achieved. However, a problem exists; the larger the contract size the less feasible it becomes for speculators and/or spreaders to make or take delivery.[9] The CBT has a long tradition of trading 'spreadable' commodities.[10] Members of the CBT floor community are familiar with the concept of carrying charges between delivery months and the risks and returns of spreads. Hence, the relatively large contract value ($250,000 face value as opposed to $10,000–$50,000 for the grains) met with resistance by members of the exchange. Fortuitously, economic uncertainty came to the rescue. By the time subsequent drafts of the contract were written, movements in interest rates were such that, when translated into price fluctuations, a $100,000 contract size appeared adequate. $100,000 was still in excess of the size of existing grain contracts, but was more in range.[11] This contract size still exists today.

3.2 Minimum price movements 'tick size'

Arguments for the creation of a futures contract include: (a) that it will provide a hedging vehicle that is less expensive than existing vehicles (i.e., short sales, etc.), and/or (b) that it may reduce the costs of participating in the cash market (i.e., reduce spreads). In early 1971 the dealer bid–ask spread on GNMAs was as large as two full points (2 per cent of value). As the GNMA cash market matured (and as volume increased), spreads decreased but still remained large relative to spreads in other markets. By mid-1971 the spread was between 1 and 1½ points; during 1972 it narrowed to 1 point and was sometimes slightly less.[12] The CBT felt that an active futures market could further reduce these spreads.[13]

The original tick size (i.e., minimum price movement) set by the CBT was $25 or 0.01 per cent of the original $250,000 contract value – considerably less than the bid–ask spread in the cash market. It was, however, considerably larger than the tick size in the grains, which was 1/8 cent per bushel (5,000 bushels per contract) or $6.25. When the contract size was changed to $100,000 the tick size remained 0.01 per cent of the contract value, which then translated into movements of $10.00 per contract – an amount consistent with movements in the grain markets.

A glance in the newspaper reveals that futures prices are typically quoted in price increments that are consistent with the practices in the cash market – hence 1/8 cent per bushel in the grains and dollars per hundredweight in the meats. This observation was made to the CBT research staff in reference to the GNMA contract. It led to the adoption of 1/64 cent, or $15.625 per $100,000 contract, as the tick size in one of the early drafts of the GNMA contract.

It is important to realize that the tick size is also the minimum return to market makers of 'scalpers'. That is, in the early 1970s grain traders made a 1/8 cent-per-contract ($6.25) market.[14] The larger the tick size, the larger the return to the market-maker, *ceteris paribus*. To encourage market-makers to enter the GNMA pit, thus promoting liquidity, it was decided that the dollar-per-contract tick size should exceed that of the grains, and therefore the GNMA tick size was subsequently increased to 1/32 cent, or $31.25 per $100,000. This was the tick size when the market opened and is still the tick size today.[15]

3.3 Daily price limits

Unlike stock or stock options markets, futures markets have daily limits on the size of a possible price increase or decrease.[16] These are usually rationalized as providing time for the market to 'cool off' and for the clearing house to collect and disburse funds.[17] Daily limits can be changed at the discretion of the exchange and/or by established rules ('elastic limits'). While most exchanges do not have analytical rules, changes typically occur as the volatility of futures prices changes. To be consistent with other futures contracts, a price limit was established for the GNMA contract. The first draft of the contract called for a limit up or down of ½ point ($1,250 per $250,000 contract). This limit initially was maintained when the contract size was changed to $100,000. Here ½ point translated to $500, which was also the daily limit on the grains (i.e., 10 cents per bushel). Prior to the opening of trading in 1975, the GNMA daily limit was increased to ¾ point ($750 per contract), consistent with the higher levels of volatility in interest rates observed between 1972 and 1974. The contract opened with the ¾ point limit; however, the limit has been raised and currently stands at 2 points.[18]

3.4 Position limits

To prevent 'concentration' or 'congestion' during delivery, and/or attempts to corner a market, exchanges typically impose position limits on traders. In view of the size of the GNMA cash market (there were $4 billion outstanding in 1972), early versions of the contract called for position limits of 300 contracts ($300,000,000). By the time the contract started trading the cash market had grown considerably (in 1975 there were $30 billion outstanding) and the position limit was raised to 600 contracts. (It is interesting to note that the position limit on soybeans at that time was also 600 contracts.) At the time of writing (1981) the cash market is approximately $80 billion; there is no position limit.

3.5 *The deliverable grade and delivery instrument*

Perhaps the most difficult issue to be resolved in writing the contract was the question of deliverable grade and delivery instrument.

The first draft of the contract called for certificate delivery (the actual delivery of the GNMAs) of 6½ per cent GNMAs (and only 6½ per cent GNMAs).[19] 6½ per cent was the GNMA coupon rate that prevailed in 1972. However, as time passed and interest rates fluctuated, significant quantities of GNMAs appeared that carried different (higher) coupons. To increase the deliverable supply, thus reducing the threat of a corner, the exchange felt it would be desirable to find a way to allow all GNMAs to be delivered regardless of coupon. The first solution that the research department came up with was called 'certificate delivery with yield maintenance' and was based upon a 6½ per cent coupon. That is, on the delivery day of each maturing GNMA futures contract there would be a settlement price for $100,000 face amount of the standard grade (6½ per cent) GNMAs. From this price one could compute an implied yield to maturity. This was done under the assumption that the underlying GNMA pool would have a 12-year life – the assumption of the cash market. $100,000 face amount of GNMAs with coupons other than 6½ per cent could then be delivered in lieu of the standard grade. The price to be paid by the long for the cash instrument would be the discounted value of the $100,000 face of the issue being delivered; the discount rate to be applied was the yield to maturity established on the 6½ per cent coupon GNMAs.

As time passed and interest rates changed, and the various early drafts of the contract came and went, this certificate delivery with yield maintenance procedure persisted. It was modified somewhat in early 1974, when, to reflect an increase in interest rates, the 8 per cent coupon replaced the 6½ per cent coupon as the standard guide. In fact, certificate delivery might have remained the delivery procedure[20] had it not been for the strong tradition of spreading on the CBT and the fact GNMAs are 'wasting assets'. That is, mortgage payments by individuals represent payment of interest and repayment of principal, and therefore the holder of a GNMA receives both interest and principal monthly – hence the name 'pass-through' that is attached to GNMAs. Furthermore, defaults or prepayments are also passed through to the holder of the GNMA. Thus $100,000 face value of GNMAs will 'waste away' over time. In particular, it is entirely possible that $100,000 face value of GNMAs received as delivery on one futures contract (say, the March contract) may not be deliverable on a subsequent contract (say, the June contract) owing to wastage.

The wasting issue implies that a speculator or spreader who takes delivery on a GNMA futures contract may not be able to redeliver the commodity and may be forced to liquidate an 'odd lot' in the cash market. The cash market may well be one in which he has neither expertise nor credit arrangements – he would be at a disadvantage to regular traders in the cash market and might be a distress seller. *Ceteris paribus*, the wasting problem would be expected to lead to less liquid markets (reduced floor participation). Bid–ask spreads would be expected to reflect a return for the risk associated with wastage, and would be larger than bid–ask spreads in non-wasting commodities.

The problem of balancing the interest of the longs and the shorts and/or the interests of the trade with those of the floor members is not a new one. For the CBT the issue has been particularly important in the development of both soybean meal and plywood futures contracts. For these contracts, rather than physical delivery, delivery is accomplished with a shipping certificate that represents a call on production. In the grains, delivery is accomplished with a warehouse receipt – a truck does not deliver grain to your door.[21]

The GNMA 'due bill'[22] grew out of this heritage; it was a combination of a warehouse receipt and a shipping certificate. It gave the long a call on GNMAs but did not force him to take delivery of the underlying commodity until and unless he wanted to. However, a problem developed. In plywood, the commodity did not have to be produced until the certificate was exercised (in fact, not until a fixed time interval thereafter). However, the short side of a GNMA contract making delivery typically has the underlying GNMAs and would want to get rid of them. Unlike the grains, where, when storing the commodity, the long must pay storage costs, GNMAs, when stored, pay out interest and principal. Thus the due bill had to pay the long for the use of his funds.

All of these considerations resulted in the following preliminary structure for 'due bills'. GNMA delivery was to be accomplished with due bills. The long would pay the settlement price for the due bill (all other discrepancies having been settled through the daily marking-to-market procedure of the exchange). The due bill would be collateralized with GNMAs. The short would be charged with the responsibility of maintaining the collateral (i.e., increasing it when wastage occurred). At any time in the future the long would have the right to tender the due bill and to receive the underlying GNMAs. In the interim between delivery and tendering he would receive $667 per month – the monthly interest payment from an 8 per cent perpetuity.

So far so good – at least for the long. He could now take delivery of the due bill, carry it until the next delivery month, and redeliver it. All wasting was removed. However, the wasting risk now resided with the short. True, he was probably better equipped to handle it than the long – but he certainly wouldn't bear risk without compensation. That is, what incentive was there for a short to create a due bill? To handle this problem, the interest rate on the perpetuity was reduced from 8 to 7.62 per cent ($635 per month). The differential was a reward for bearing wasting risk and could be viewed as a servicing fee. In fact, the magnitude of the servicing fee was set to be consistent with the servicing fee paid to mortgage bankers who serviced the mortgages underlying a GNMA pool.

One problem remained.[23] Suppose a long tendered his due bill and 'called' for the underlying GNMAs. If the short were required to deliver $100,000 face of 8 per cent coupon GNMAs, then delivery would have been unambiguous. However, for the sake of liquidity, it was desirable to let the short deliver other coupons as well. Thus the question was, what price should the short get for his underlying GNMAs and the allowed $2\frac{1}{2}$ per cent variation in quantity?[24] It could have been based on yield maintenance calculations; however, at what yield? The yield could have been based on the settlement price on the date the due bill was created; however, the problem with this procedure is that due bills would not be homogeneous – each delivery month would cause the creation of new bills. A multiplicity of due bills (all deliverable) would complicate the determination of what was cheapest to deliver, and would have increased basis risk. Alternatively, the yield could have been set at the time the due bill was cancelled. However, due bills may be cancelled at any time (and not necessarily just when a futures contract is maturing). This latter procedure would have required the use of a spot price/yield to fix the price of the due bill. Unfortunately, generally accepted and publicly available spot prices did not and do not exist. Therefore this procedure was not feasible.

Once again, in searching for the solution to a contract design problem, the research staff turned to the grain contracts. In the

Table 2 Quantities of GNMAs to be delivered at various interest rates

Stated interest rate on GNMA (%)	*Conversion factor*	*8% par equivalent balance ($)*	*Range of principal balance providable for GNMAs of various interest rates 2½% tolerance range ($)*
$6\frac{1}{2}$	1.121233	112,123.30	109,320.22 – 114,926.38
7	1.078167	107,816.70	105,121.28 – 110,512.12
$7\frac{1}{4}$	1.058201	105,802.10	103,174.60 – 108,465.60
$7\frac{1}{2}$	1.038062	103,806.20	101,211.04 – 106,401.36
$7\frac{3}{4}$	1.018675	101,867.50	99,320.81 – 104,414.19
8	1.000000	100,000.00	97,500.00 – 102,500.00
$8\frac{1}{4}$	0.982198	98,219.80	95,764.30 – 100,675.30
$8\frac{1}{2}$	0.965018	96,501.80	94,089.25 – 98,914.35
9	0.931677	93,167.70	90,838.51 – 95,496.89
$9\frac{1}{4}$	0.916031	91,603.10	89,313.02 – 93,893.18
$9\frac{1}{2}$	0.900322	90,032.20	87,781.39 – 92,283.01
$9\frac{3}{4}$	0.885609	88,560.90	86,346.88 – 90,774.92
10	0.871460	87,146.00	84,967.35 – 89,324.65
$10\frac{1}{4}$	0.857143	85,714.30	83,571.44 – 87,857.16
$10\frac{1}{2}$	0.843289	84,328.90	82,220.68 – 86,427.12
$10\frac{3}{4}$	0.830450	83,045.00	80,968.87 – 85,121.13
11	0.817439	81,743.90	79,700.30 – 83,787.50
$11\frac{1}{4}$	0.804829	80,482.90	78,470.83 – 81,284.65
$11\frac{1}{2}$	0.793021	79,032.10	77,319.55 – 81,284.65
$11\frac{3}{4}$	0.781250	78,125.00	76,171.87 – 80,078.13
12	0.769724	76,972.40	75,048.09 – 78,896.71
$12\frac{1}{4}$	0.758534	75,853.40	73,957.06 – 77,749.74
$12\frac{1}{2}$	0.747664	74,766.40	72,897.24 – 76,635.56
$12\frac{3}{4}$	0.736920	73,692.00	71,849.70 – 75,534.30
13	0.726744	72,674.40	70,857.54 – 74,491.26
$13\frac{1}{4}$	0.716846	71,684.60	69,892.48 – 73,476.72
$13\frac{1}{2}$	0.707214	70,721.40	68,953.36 – 72,489.44
$13\frac{3}{4}$	0.697350	69,735.00	67,991.62 – 71,478.38
14	0.688231	68,823.10	67,102.52 – 70,543.68
$14\frac{1}{4}$	0.679117	67,911.70	66,213.91 – 69,609.49
$14\frac{1}{2}$	0.670578	67,057.80	65,381.36 – 68,734.25
$14\frac{3}{4}$	0.661888	66,188.80	64,534.08 – 67,843.52
15	0.653595	65,359.50	63,725.51 – 66,993.49
$15\frac{1}{4}$	0.645507	64,550.70	62,936.93 – 66,164.47
$15\frac{1}{2}$	0.637450	63,745.00	62,151.38 – 65,338.63
$15\frac{3}{4}$	0.629921	62,992.10	61,417.30 – 64,566.90

Table 2—*continued*

Stated interest rate on GNMA (%)	*Conversion factor*	*8% par equivalent balance ($)*	*Range of principal balance providable for GNMAs of various interest rates 2½% tolerance range ($)*
16	0.622084	62,208.40	60,653.19 - 63,763.61
16¼	0.614753	61,475.30	59,938.42 - 63,012.18
16½	0.607441	60,744.10	59,225.50 - 62,262.70
16¾	0.600601	60,060.10	58,558.60 - 61,561.60
17	0.593472	59,347.20	57,863.52 - 60,830.88
17¼	0.586941	58,694.10	57,226.75 - 60,161.45
17½	0.580131	58,013.10	56,562.77 - 59,463.43
17¾	0.573888	57,388.80	55,954.08 - 58,823.52
18	0.567376	56,737.60	55,319.16 - 58,156.04

grains, delivery calls for one particular grade. However, at the option of the seller, and at fixed differentials established by the exchange, other grades may be delivered. This procedure was adopted in the GNMA contract. Specifically, it was decided that $100,000 market value of GNMAs had to be delivered under the assumption that the interest rate was 8 per cent.[25] Thus, more than $100,000 face of 6½ per cents and less than $100,000 of 9 per cents could be delivered. The actual coupon or combination of coupons that were delivered was left to the seller's option (the tradition of the grain trade). Table 2 presents the quantities that had to be delivered.[26] Clearly, a short would choose the coupon whose market value deviated the most from the payment he was to receive (the settlement price).[27] He would deliver the cheapest GNMA just as in the grain trade people deliver the grade that has the most distorted price.[28]

Due bill delivery was in the final draft of the GNMA contract and is still there today. It is complicated and cumbersome. It appears to cause difficulties for both the longs and the shorts. It is in that sense fair, and may be the reason it has been successful.

4 Initial liquidity

Integral to the success of the GNMA contract was the manner in which liquidity was developed. It was decided that additional floor memberships were necessary to provide speculative interest in the contract, as commission houses usually do not encourage their customers to speculate in new contracts. 'Trading permits' were authorized in GNMAs and 37 were issued in October of 1975. Permits were granted to non-members authorizing them to execute trades in GNMAs (and only GNMAs) as principal and as broker for others. The fees for a permit were $5,000 for the first six months, $5,000 renewal for the second six months, and $1,500 for each quarter thereafter. Permits were to be outstanding for only three years. However, in 1977, as more financial futures contracts came on board, the CBT felt it was necessary (and desirable) to expand its membership further, and thus 'financial instrument' memberships were created. Permit holders were given the opportunity to purchase these memberships for $25,000, which gave them trading privileges in all the new financial futures contracts. In addition, a total of 100 of new financial memberships were created and sold at $30,000 each.[29] While this membership expansion was highly controversial at the time, it was very successful and is now an established practice in the development of new contracts at the CBT (and other exchanges). Permits have been issued for commercial paper, certificate delivery GNMA, Treasury debt contracts, gold, iced broilers and plywood.

5 Regulation

Discussions of the birth of this industry must include comments on the role of regulation. During the initial stages of research the regulatory environment for interest rate futures was uncertain. The Commodity Exchange Authority, an agency of the Department of Agriculture, was empowered to regulate futures, but only futures on agricultural commodities, and then only the 'regulated' commodities. Early in the design of the GNMA contract, the Federal Home Loan Bank Board expressed interest in regulating a futures market in actual mortgages. In fact, their office drafted a bill that was to have been submitted to Congress. The purpose of the proposed 'Residential Mortgage Securities Act' (drafted in 1972) was to transfer the regulatory responsibility over mortgages and mortgage transactions from the Securities and Exchange Commission to the Federal Home Loan Bank Board (FHLBB). The counsel to the Chicago Board of Trade worked with the Federal Home Loan Mortgage Corporation to insure that futures contracts in GNMA mortgages would also fall under the jurisdiction of the FHLBB.

During this same period the Commodity Exchange Act of 1936 was under review by Congress, and a new regulatory agency for the futures industry, the Commodity Futures Trading Commission (CFTC), was proposed. Under the old Act, commodities were designated as regulated and non-regulated (essentially, storables and non-storables). Thus, GNMAs were not defined as commodities under the old Act. When the new Act was being proposed, the Chicago Board of Trade (along with the Federal Home Loan Bank Board, other exchanges, firms and individuals) was instrumental in presenting the definition of a 'commodity' that would insure an unambiguous regulatory environment.[30] The definition of 'commodity' under the Commodity Futures Trading Act of 1974 was expanded to include 'all services, rights, and interests in which contracts for future delivery are presently or in the future dealt in'. The Act also gave exclusive regulatory jurisdiction over such commodities to the CFTC.

The CFTC became effective in April 1975, and the GNMA contract was the first futures contract to be approved by the Commission. The new contract was scheduled to begin trading on 20 October 1975. On the Friday before the contract was to open the SEC contacted the Chicago Board of Trade, attempting to block trading. The SEC stated that a GNMA was a security and that the CBT had not applied to the SEC for approval prior to trading. None the less, the contract started trading on the following Monday and on Tuesday the Chicago Board of Trade met with SEC and CFTC lawyers. It became clear to the SEC that the CEA Act of 1974 gave the CFTC, and not the SEC, regulatory jurisdiction over the GNMA contract and any subsequent financial futures contracts. However, the jurisdictional battle between the SEC and the CFTC was far from over, and still goes on today as the regulatory turf for commodity options is being debated.

6 Summary and conclusions

The GNMA contract was an innovation in the futures markets. It marked the beginning of a new complex of futures contracts that currently rivals many of the traditional futures complexes in volume and open interest. The GNMA mortgage market was an excellent candidate for experimenting in a new futures complex. It offered an active cash market, competitively determined price, an inadequate secondary market, great price variability and a homogeneous trading instrument. These qualities offered many similarities to the traditional grain contracts and thus allowed the design of similar contract specifications including contract size of $100,000, tick size of $31.25, daily limits of $2,000 and a delivery instrument consisting of a receipt backed by GNMA certificates. In fact, the contract was intentionally designed as a bastard of traditional agricultural contracts in order for it to gain acceptance in that established futures arena and to diminish regulatory difficulties.

The due bill (CDR) delivery mechanism of the GNMA contract is cumbersome and intimidating to many users. However, the liquidity of the contract is indicative of its success and use by commercial and speculative interests alike. Volume averages 12,000–15,000 contracts per day with open interest at 70,000 contracts. And the success of the GNMA contract is measured not only by its own growth but also by the contracts (some successful, some not) that have evolved from it, including Treasury bonds, Treasury notes and bills, commercial paper, certificates of deposit and other contracts not yet trading such as euro-dollar CDs, various stock and portfolio index contracts and options on futures. The GNMA futures contract paved the way for a new era in the futures industry and provided a new tool in financial management.

Notes

1 It is interesting to note that 25 per cent of the volume of the world's oldest and largest futures market, the Chicago Board of Trade, now comes from its interest rate futures complex.

2 For further details of innovation in futures markets see Sandor (1973).

3 See Goshay and Sandor (1973).

4 While research was going on at the CBT, independent research on mortgage futures was being conducted at the Federal Home Loan Bank Board under the direction of Tom Bomar. See Bomar (1975).

5 Other interest rate futures markets could have been pursued (e.g., Treasury bonds and Treasury bills) and were considered. The GNMA contract was chosen as the first contract in an interest rate complex because the concept enjoyed an enormously favourable response from the 'trade' (the savings and loan associations and mortgage bankers) and from the relevant regulators (see section 5). Interest rate futures were entirely new concepts and therefore it was essential to have this diverse support. Furthermore, the potential size of the market persuaded members of the exchange that the research required was worth pursuing.

6 See Sandor and Sosin (1975).

7 Several authors have discussed the importance of contract provisions on the success of a futures contract. For an early example, see Powers (1967).

8 Less than two years of spot GNMA price data existed at the time the contract was initially written. Thus, the statistical techniques used to determine contract size were necessarily relatively *ad hoc.*

9 The Treasury bill futures market on the IMM calls for delivery of $1 million, which rules out delivery for most individual speculators. However, it does not appear to have hampered the success of the contract.

10 A commodity is 'spreadable' if storage costs are small relative to contract value; that is, if it is feasible to deliver on a future contract, take delivery, store the commodity and redeliver on another contract. Note that prohibitive storage costs (i.e., for live cattle) do not preclude the action of spreading in futures; they do however increase the risk of the activity as arbitrage boundaries are dramatically increased. This theme of spreadability will reappear when the delivery question is subsequently tackled.

11 When soybeans went to $12.90 per bushel in 1973 the contract value reached $64,500.

12 The source of this spread information is 'Mortgage-Backed Securities Reports', Washington, DC, and discussions with industry participants.

13 In fact, the threat of spread reduction caused trade representatives to be somewhat uncooperative with the exchange. Imagine going to a dealer and saying, 'Hi, I'm from the Chicago Board of Trade – I'm here to narrow your spreads.' The point here is that trade reluctance is not sufficient reason to abandon a prospective futures contract.

14 Hence the adage, 'Buy at 1/8th and sell at 1/4th.'

15 It is interesting to note that the tick size in grains was later increased to 1/4 cents or $12.50 per contract.

16 Note that a similar limit can be imposed on stocks, as stock exchanges can choose not to open a stock or to discontinue trading.

17 The 'cooling off' notion, or the prevention of 'excess speculation', has been modelled. See Goldman and Sosin (1979).

18 Daily price limits on grains have also been increased.

19 There were additional restrictions concerning the seasoning of the issue. Specifically, pools had to be between 45 days and two years old. These restrictions were later dropped, allowing delivery of all GNMAs with a term of 12 years or more – the practice of the cash market.

20 GNMA contracts on other exchanges, ACE (when it existed) and COMEX (and the new contract on the CBT), use a delivery procedure that is based upon yield maintenance – none of these contracts is successful.

21 It is interesting to compare the plywood contract on the CBT with the lumber contract on the CME. The former delivers with a shipping certificate while the latter delivers with railroad cars of lumber. Both seem to work.

22 'Due bill' is a term used on Wall Street – it is a receipt for securities due the owner and not a call on securities. It was really a misnomer, and subsequent to the introduction of the contract the name was changed to 'collateralized deposit receipt' (CDR).

23 There were others. For instance, banks were supposed to hold the GNMAs for an escrow fee. Most banks – in fact, all but one bank – were initially reluctant to participate. It was only because one particular bank viewed due bill escrowing as an entry vehicle into other commodity business that the escrowing programme succeeded.

24 It should be noted that the allowed delivery variance was consistent with the practice in the cash market, where it is needed to allow for possible prepayments and the lack of a continuum of odd-lot sizes. The size of the tolerance was changed from 4 to $2\frac{1}{2}$ per cent to be consistent with the prevailing practice in the cash market.

25 Hence, in an 8 per cent interest rate environment there is in fact yield maintenance.

26 Thus, for the sake of simplicity, yield maintenance at par was chosen. This had the added attraction of providing significantly less work for the depository bank in monitoring collateral for the purpose of ensuring that any due bill was always collateralized by $100,000 of 8 per cent GNMAs at par or the equivalent. Simplicity also dictated that equivalency be effected by alterations of the principal amount of GNMAs having coupons other than 8 per cent. Non-standard unit sizes are possible in GNMAs because principal can easily vary owing to procedures at GNMA and the fact that there is continuous variation in principal as a result of paydowns. The choice of settling the variation of $2\frac{1}{2}$ per cent above or below $100,000 in cash also resulted from an effort to seek simple solutions.

27 In fact, it is more complicated because of the $2\frac{1}{2}$ per cent tolerance in the quantity delivered. The differential (or tail) is settled in cash at par value – not at market value (who is to set the market value?). This procedure leads to games of the 'tail', where it is desirable to choose the deliverable instrument so as to maximize the tail (or the cash settlement). This can lead to the delivery of combination of coupons rather than just a single coupon.

28 Ignoring the tailing problem (see n. 27), it typically has been advantageous to deliver the highest available coupon.

29 Financial instrument memberships have traded at prices in excess of $150,000.

30 See the Commodity Exchange Act as amended 30 September 1978, section 1.3. As indicated in Bomar (1975), it is interesting to note that Phillip Johnson, the current chairman of the CFTC, was instrumental in drafting regulations that defined futures contracts to include contracts on GNMAs.

We would like to dedicate this paper to David Alhadef, Thomas Bomar and Anthony Frank for their intellectual support and guidance. Without their help there might not have been interest rate futures markets in the United States. We would also like to thank Fred Arditti, Tom Coleman, Marilyn Grace, Kani Tamir and Lester Telser for their valuable comments and discussions.

References

Bomar, T. (1975), 'Trading Mortgage Interest Rate Futures', *Federal Home Loan Bank Board Journal*, September.

Goldman, M. and Sosin, H. (1979), 'Information Assimilation, Market Efficiency and the Frequency of Transactions', *Journal of Financial Economics*, 7.

Goshay, R. and Sandor, R. (1973), 'An Inquiry into the Feasibility of a Re-insurance Futures Contract', *Journal of Business Finance*, 5.

Powers, M. (1967), 'Effects of Contract Provisions on the Success of a Futures contract', *Journal of Farm Economics*, 49.

Sandor, R. (1973), 'Innovation by an Exchange: A Case Study of the Development of the Plywood Futures Contract', *Journal of Law and Economics*, 16.

Sandor, R. and Sosin, H. (1975), 'The Determinants of Mortgage Risk Premiums: A Case Study of the Portfolio of a Savings and Loan Association', *Journal of Business*, 48.

12

The Establishment of an Interest Rate Futures Market: The Experience of the Sydney Futures Exchange

DAVID J. S. RUTLEDGE

1 Introduction

The general question of the preconditions necessary for the introduction and success of a futures contract has been examined from a number of viewpoints in the economic literature.

In its earliest form this literature focused on the conditions to be satisfied by a commodity as a prerequisite for it to be the basis of a successful futures contract. Thus for many years textbooks on agricultural marketing listed such characteristics as storability, fungibility, competitive physical markets and so on as the prescribed conditions. The experience of the past twenty years has required many of these lists to be substantially revised.

A second approach, adopted most notably by Working (1977c) and Gray (1966), was to study the institutional characteristics of futures markets themselves rather than the commodities traded thereon. Arising from their analysis were several conclusions relating to requirements for a successful market: first, the need for contract specifications to favour neither buyer nor seller; second (but related to the first point), the pre-eminent need for the futures contract to attract hedging participation; third, the need for speculative participation to be attracted into the market. Clearly, these three requirements are closely interrelated. The work of Gray and Working in these area has left its mark even today in CFTC Guideline 1. It is worth noting in passing that Gray and Working essentially concluded that, if a futures contract is attractive to hedgers, speculative participation will tend to 'come out of the woodwork' to service hedgers, requirements; in other words, that hedging need is the first criterion to be satisfied. Their conclusions might require modification in the light of development of the precious metals markets, where trade participation is far less significant than speculative participation, and in the light of certain of the financial instrument markets, where speculative interest apparently developed at a considerably faster rate than did hedging interest, at least in the early stages of trading.

The most recent contributions to the literature in this area are those of Sandor (1973) and Silber (1981), who examine the question in the context of competitive pressures on commodity exchanges to innovate.

In each of the foregoing instances, empirical work has related almost exclusively to futures markets in the United States. This is hardly surprising, in view of the fact that that country is unquestionably the citadel of futures trading. Yet these markets have developed, albeit on a more modest scale, in a variety of countries outside the United States. They have a long and honourable history in the United Kingdom, and have made a significant, if less enduring, impact on the economics of a number of other countries.

The past decade has seen a resurgence of interest in futures markets in both Europe and Asia, partly as a response to sharply increased commodity price volatility, and partly as an attempt to emulate the remarkable growth in activity in US markets. The structure of economies in which new futures contracts have been launched are diverse, ranging from the United Kingdom to Singapore, from Australia and Canada to Hong Kong and Japan. This diversity raised the question as to whether the paradigms of market innovation developed in the United States are appropriate internationally, and it is to this question that the present paper is in part directed.

In particular, I shall attempt to place the operation of the Sydney Futures Exchange in its institutional setting and to describe the development of the interest rate futures contract (which was, incidentally, the first such contract launched outside the United States) on that Exchange.

It is hoped that this description, although rather journalistic in style, will draw out a number of institutional differences between futures trading in Australia and, say, the United States and, second, that it may be of interest to those who will be closely watching the introduction of financial futures contracts in London later this year.

2 History of futures trading in Australia

Prior to the Second World War, financial markets in Australia were largely undeveloped. Aside from banks, the only significant financial firms or corporations were stockbrokers, life insurance companies and pastoral houses. Secondary markets in debt instruments were largely non-existent. Without a broadly based infrastructure of financial markets, the economic environment was hardly conducive to the introduction of commodity futures markets.

This situation has changed progressively over the past 35 years. Additionally, the early postwar period saw an easing of government controls over commodity markets including several in which Australia was a participant. This was particularly so in the case of wool, which was at the time Australia's major source of export revenue. During the 1950s wool prices fluctuated violently, and the Australian wool industry's interest in futures was whetted by the opening in 1953 of a wool tops futures market in London. It should be remembered that, at that time, the Australian economy was still closely linked to that of the United Kingdom.

For a number of reasons, notably that Australian merchants were dealing in greasy wool rather than wool tops and that difficulties arose in communications and coping with time differences, a consensus developed within the Australian wool trade as to the desirability of developing a greasy wool futures market within Australia. The barriers to the operation of a futures exchange in Australia were essentially those arising from ignorance of the purpose and functioning of futures markets on the part of the community generally and the government in particular.

Government approval was required because of controls then existing over foreign exchange dealings. European, Japanese and North American wool interests would not use the futures market in the absence of an assurance that funds relating to futures transactions could be readily transferred. It is worth noting that, although foreign exchange controls have been considerably liberalized since the 1950s, they remain today a major restriction on the further development of futures trading in Australia.

After considerable lobbying, the required assurances relating to bona fide wool hedging transactions were given by the Australian government in November 1959. The Sydney Greasy Wool Futures Exchange (SGWFE) was founded shortly thereafter and trading commenced in May 1960.

In two very significant respects the new Exchange emulated UK institutional arrangements rather than those of the United States: namely, in membership structure and clearing house arrangements.

At the US exchanges, membership is vested in individual persons. They may be guaranteed by firms or corporations and may, in turn, confer membership privileges on the firm or corporation of which they are a director, partner or employee. Only individual members are allowed to trade on the exchange floor. For this reason, depending on the size of the exchange, the number of members of US exchanges ranges from several hundred to as many as nearly 1,500.

At the UK exchanges, primary membership (known as 'floor membership') is granted only to firms or corporations. Each floor member may place a number of its employees on the floor to trade. Hence the number of floor members at any UK Exchange is typically far fewer than the number of members of a US Exchange. As recognition of the need to attract trade house (i.e. hedging) participation, most UK markets have also created associate memberships, holders of which are entitled to a concessional commission or brokerage rate but are not permitted to trade on the floor.[1]

One consequence of the UK market membership structure is that it does not provide for 'locals' or 'scalpers', the importance of which has been discussed by Working (1977a, 1977b) and Gray (1966), *inter alia*. Although some floor members may engage in a certain amount of 'market-making' activity, there can be little doubt that the lack of locals is a major factor in explaining the lower levels of activity on UK futures markets than on their US counterparts.

Presumably because of the close financial links between Australia and the United Kingdom in the 1950s, the SGWFE developed its membership structure on the UK model. At the commencement of trading in 1960 there were 15 floor members, all with strong wool trade (though not necessarily futures) orientation. Associate membership was created at the Exchange's inception and rapidly grew to number 114, mostly comprising firms in the wool trade both in Australia and overseas.

The second important respect in which Australian practice followed that of the United Kingdom rather than the United States was in the arrangements for clearing the market. All the US exchanges either act as their own clearing house or are cleared by an affiliated clearing organization made up of the larger exchange members. On the other hand, the London markets (and a number of others around the world) are cleared by a completely independent clearing house, ICCH. The founders of SGWFE decided that the UK practice was preferable. Until 1969 the market was cleared by an Australian organization (Australian Development Clearing House); since that time ICCH has cleared the Sydney market.

With these major institutional decisions made, the SGWFE developed very much along the London model for its first ten years. It quickly developed into the world's pre-eminent wool futures market,

Table 1 Trading volume in contracts, by commodity, on Sydney futures exchange, 1960–81

	Wool	*Cattle*	*Gold*	*BAB*	*Currency*	*Other*	*Total*
1960	19,042						19,042
1961	32,891						32,891
1962	28,536						28,536
1963	82,034						82,034
1964	130,703						130,703
1965	77,446						77,446
1966	62,271						62,271
1967	66,597						66,597
1968	56,330						56,330
1969	37,055						37,055
1970	65,074						65,074
1971	44,807						44,807
1972	103,284						103,284
1973	186,011						186,011
1974	152,416						152,416
1975	87,024	1,446					88,470
1976	98,156	2,158					100,314
1977	61,739	1,829					63,568
1978	28,108	6,036	30,359				64,503
1979	75,493	49,937	136,545	2,259		1,550	265,784
1980	173,308	184,214	229,846	16,859	6,881	160	611,268
1981	66,660	198,688	125,016	28,031	32,407	2,994	453,796

with the support of wool trade interests internationally. It attracted relatively little public speculative participation, and, probably for this reason, was subjected to no government regulation apart from the indirect supervision of the Reserve Bank of Australia.

The slump in wool prices of the late 1960s and early 1970s, accompanied by more aggressive wool support price schemes by the government, sowed the seeds for the developments of the late 1970s. The decline in wool futures activity at that time (table 1) prompted the SGWFE to consider other possible contracts.

By 1972 the Exchange was seriously examining the introduction of futures contracts in live cattle and in foreign currencies; the need to diversify had been clearly perceived. In October of that year the Exchange changed its name to Sydney Futures Exchange (SFE).

A cattle contract was launched in 1975 but its delivery specifications were found to be wanting. It was not until these were substantially modified that the cattle contract came to be actively traded. The introduction of the cattle contract posed a major question to the Exchange, namely the appropriateness of the credentials of the then floor members for trading in commodities other than wool. A number of floor members had developed into predominantly 'futures commission merchant' operations and were able to extend their activities into cattle without difficulty. Nevertheless, none had significant meat trade involvement. This issue was addressed by the Exchange selling 'from Treasury' a floor membership to a firm with strong meat trade ties. The pattern was nevertheless established whereby the existing floor members, to a large degree, would shoulder the burden (and reap the reward) of servicing new contracts. This approach stands in contrast to the London markets, where new terminal markets are created for new commodities, each with its own group of floor members.

A gold futures contract was introduced in 1978 and boneless beef and interest rate contracts in 1979. During this period a number of new floor members, with involvement in the investment banking, currency and money market area, were admitted, bringing the number of floor members to 26. From the viewpoint of the Exchange, the gold contract was introduced at a most fortuitous time, as it proved to be the most active contract traded in 1979 and 1980. For the first time in the Exchange's history the general public began to trade futures to a significant extent, and this in turn aroused the interest of government regulatory agencies.

During 1980 currency futures contracts (specifying cash settlement rather than physical delivery) were introduced, and in 1981 a second livestock contract (fat lambs) and a silver contract were added.

Throughout the period 1960–80 the number of floor members fluctuated from the original 15 to a low of 11 and subsequently to the present figure of 26. The number of associate members has grown to approximately 400.

It seems clear that the Sydney Futures Exchange has enjoyed a considerable degree of natural protection, arising first from the size of the domestic market and second from the fact that this market is rendered essentially 'captive' by virtue of Reserve Bank limitations on Australian residents speculating in overseas futures markets. Thus the process of innovation has been driven predominantly by the need to list a sufficiently diverse set of commodities to sustain the floor membership throughout the cycle of commodity prices.

3 The development of the Australian money market[2]

As indicated in the previous section, Australian financial markets were largely undeveloped prior to the 1940s, with short-term 'instruments' being essentially restricted to fixed deposits with banks. Progress during the period to 1959 was slow, with the rapidly growing hire purchase companies issuing debentures as a means of attracting funds and with the development of an infant secondary market in government debt.

A great impetus to the development of a robust financial sector came in 1959 with the creation by the Reserve Bank of an 'Official Short-term Money Market'. The Bank designated a number of 'authorized dealers' to whom it agreed to provide lenders-of-last-resort facilities provided that the composition of the dealer's assets satisfied certain criteria. The official market plays an important role in the implementation of monetary policy by the Reserve Bank.

During the 1960s the major growth in money market activity came in the 'unofficial' sector, first with the growth of an inter-company market for funds and subsequently with the development of a commercial bill market. The traditional commercial bill, akin in some respects to a 'bankers' acceptance' in the United States, was the 'trade bill'. The major development of the 1960s was the development of 'accommodation finance bills', a discount security, and of an active secondary market in these instruments. A major class of such bills are 'bank-accepted bills', in which the party agreeing to pay out the face value of the bill on maturity is a bank. We shall return to bank-accepted bills in the next section of the paper.

Since the 1960s the major features of the Australian money market have been, first, the very rapid growth in the commercial bill market and, in the past few years, the development of markets in promissory notes and negotiable certificates of deposits.

Each of these three instruments is a short-term instrument with a typical term to maturity of 90–180 days. Further out on the yield curve, say from two to five years, the secondary market is restricted to government and semi-government debt, and these markets become increasingly thin as the term to maturity increases.

4 Development of the bank bill futures contract

As the previous section has indicated, the Australian money market by the late 1970s had developed to the point where an interest rate futures contract could realistically be considered for introduction. At the SFE, interest in such an innovation was undoubtedly reinforced by the successful introduction of the GNMA and Treasury bill futures contracts in Chicago.

A committee was established at the Exchange in mid-1978 to study this question. Its members were either representatives of Exchange member firms with strong money market ties or individuals with detailed knowledge of this market in their own right. Included on the committee were representatives of a number of firms who at that time were not members of the Exchange. The following major points required the committee's consideration:

(a) On which instrument should the contract be based?
(b) On what term to maturity of the underlying instrument should the contract be based?
(c) Subordinate to the first two points, but nevertheless important, were questions relating to contract size, delivery procedures, delivery centres, delivery window and the precise nature of deliverable paper.

As previously noted, by far the most active secondary money market instruments are those at the short end of the yield curve. Additionally, there has been a marked trend for corporate borrowings in Australia to become shorter in recent years. For these reasons the committee concluded that a short-term instrument would be the most appropriate on which to base a futures contract. The available alternatives were Treasury notes, bills of exchange, certificates of deposit and promissory notes.

The Reserve Bank's selling method for Treasury notes was not conductive to the development of a futures contract in these instruments. Furthermore, Australian government tax policy encourages many financial institutions to hold government securities in their portfolios when they otherwise would not choose to do so; this gave rise to concern as to the 'adequacy of deliverable supply', a phrase that was haunting US exchanges at that time.

The remaining candidates were all based on private rather than government debt. The choice among them was based on the need to use a highly homogeneous instrument, readily tradable on description, so that holders of long positions could stand for delivery, if they wished, with confidence. On this criterion the 'bank-accepted bill of exchange', commonly called 'bank bill' or BAB, was selected by the committee.

In legal terms, a bill of exchange has two essential characteristics (Seidler, 1981):

(a) it is an unconditional order in writing, addressed by one person (the drawer) to another person (the drawee);
(b) it requires the drawee to pay a sum of money, either on demand or at a definite future time to the payee (who may be the drawer himself or some other person) or to bearer.

There are three parties to a bill: the drawer, the acceptor and the endorser. These respective functions have been summarized as follows (Australian Merchant Bankers Association, 1981, p. 16).

The acceptor
By accepting the bill the acceptor undertakes to pay to the person presenting the bill (called the holder in due course) the face value of the bill. On payment of the bill the acceptor retires the bill. Where the acceptor is the initial providor of the credit he will, by arrangement on the maturity of the bill, require the borrower to place him in funds of an amount equivalent to the face value of the bill.

The drawer
The drawer engages that the bill will be accepted and paid according to its tenor, and if it is dishonoured he will compensate the holder or alternatively any one of the endorsers for the outlay of funds.

The endorsers
Each endorser can demand payment in the case of dishonour from any preceding endorser, the drawer and the acceptor.

Although commercial bills are short-term instruments, being typically drawn for 90, 120 or 180 days, they have come to play a crucial role in medium-term borrowing by the Australian corporate sector. In recent years it has become increasingly common for a corporation wishing to borrow for, say, three years to do so under what is known as a 'bill facility' for that period.

Under such a facility the corporation may draw down, say, 180-day bills from a bank or finance house with the pre-arranged ability to 'roll-over' this position every six months for the next three years. The rate applying to each roll-over would be the market discount rate for bills on the date of roll-over. In these circumstances a futures market in bills provides the opportunity for the borrower to fix the roll-over rate in advance if he so desires.

Next to be addressed was the question of the term to maturity of the deliverable instrument. Bank-accepted bills are typically drawn, as noted above, with a term to maturity of 90, 120 or 180 days – the most commonly employed are 90 and 180 days. For these reasons, and because a futures contract on a 90-day bill can be used to cover 180-day positions while the opposite is not the case (see, for example, Stigum, 1978), it was decided to base the futures contract on 90-day bank bills. A window of 85–95 days was set for bills to be deliverable.

Bank bills are typically traded in multiples of $A100,000, and the committee decided to recommend a contract size of $A500,000. This appeared to be a satisfactory compromise, being large enough to be of use to hedgers yet small enough that the original margin (called the 'deposit' in the United Kingdom and Australia) would be low enough to attract the speculator.

The financial standing of a bank-accepted bill is, in the last analysis, dependent upon the financial strength of the accepting bank. For this reason the definition of deliverable bills was restricted to those accepted by one of the six major trading banks. The contract specifications provide for the Exchange to vary the list of 'approved acceptors' from time to time.

With regard to delivery months, it was clear initially that June should be listed as a traded month because the Australian financial year closes on 30 June and money markets in June are particularly volatile. This, taken with the implicit 90-day cycle in the deliverable instrument itself, led to the delivery months being March, June, September and December. In addition, to facilitate hedging use of the market, the spot and next five calendar months were listed as delivery months.

The remaining aspects of the contract specifications had to do primarily with the delivery process itself. Bank-accepted bills are negotiated instruments, and discussions with industry representatives soon revealed that the delivery process would have to involve the physical passing across of the bills by the deliveror to the clearing house in return for immediate payment by bank cheque, together with a similar exchange between the clearing house and the party taking delivery. This process is greatly complicated by virtue of the fact that each bill contains certain signatures whose validity must be checked. In addition, the overall conformity of the bill with the Bill of Exchange Act must be verified.

In order to accomplish the various checks, all deliveries are set to occur on a single day in each delivery month, two days after the last day of trading. Parties with open short positions at the close of trading are required to notify the clearing house of the details of the bills that will be delivered. This prior notification greatly expediates the settlement process on the day of delivery.

Although this procedure no doubt sounds rather cumbersome, it has been shown to work. Deliveries against the September 1981 contract totalled 260 contracts or $A130 million worth of bills, a significant figure by Australian standards. Nevertheless, the general area of deliveries remains a difficult one for the Exchange and the clearing house, largely because the BAB futures market is the first exposure that most Australian money market participants have had to the concept of futures trading. Many of those who are accustomed to the highly personalized nature of the money market, where one deals to a significant extent on the basis of trust, have difficulty in accepting the more rigid impersonal nature of transfer of title to paper by way of delivery against futures.

The committee made its final recommendation to the SFE Board in June 1979. The contract specifications were approved by the

Table 2 Development of bank bill futures market

Calendar month	*Trading volume (all delivery months)*	*Month end open positions (all delivery months)*	*Deliveries ($m)*
1979			
Oct.	350	209	
Nov.	1,224	658	
Dec.	693	595	
1980			
Jan.	868	678	15.0
Feb.	798	664	4.5
Mar.	1,279	615	5.5
Apr.	2,542	1,061	6.5
May	2,756	1,056	1.0
June	1,409	1,013	64.5
July	1,693	777	4.5
Aug.	880	756	5.5
Sept.	1,299	737	52.5
Oct.	1,051	909	4.0
Nov.	953	800	3.0
Dec.	1,360	761	41.5
1981			
Jan.	1.642	968	33.0
Feb.	1,397	1,144	13.5
Mar.	2,415	1,179	42.5
Apr.	2,369	1,112	11.5
May	3,084	1,032	17.0
June	3,683	1,109	27.5
July	1,159	1,500	–
Aug.	2,720	1,688	13.5
Sept.	2,018	1,147	130.0
Oct.	2,329	1,265	–
Nov.	2,846	1,673	3.5
Dec.	2,598	1,416	50.0
1982			
Jan.	5,274	2,344	31.0
Feb.	6,834	2,694	8.0

Board and circulated to all floor members. A meeting was held between the committee and floor members in August 1979, resulting in a number of variations to the contract specifications, notably the decision to quote price on an index rather than yield basis. The BAB By-Laws were approved on 25 September 1979 and trading commenced in October.

The evolution of the BAB market in terms of volume and open interest is portrayed in table 2. The upward trend in both series reflects the learning process, while fluctuations around the trend reflect changes in the condition of the money market from time to time. For the first 12–18 months of the market's existence participation was largely restricted to money market dealers. There was little involvement by corporate borrowers or lenders as a means of hedging future borrowings or by investment of funds. At the same time there was relatively little speculative participation, probably because those floor members with a traditional base of speculative clients were unfamiliar with the operation of the short-term money market.

The increase in trading activity and open positions in recent months can be attributed to higher yields in the short-term money market, which in turn have attracted the interest of the corporate hedger and the speculator.

As noted above, the delivery system has been shown to function adequately, a critical ingredient for a futures contract to succeed. Deliveries have tended to represent 4 or 5 per cent of contracts traded in each delivery month, which conforms to the norm for futures contracts generally.

5 Experience since the contract launching

It is of course true that the only measure of success of an innovation, in the form of the introduction of a new futures contract by an exchange, is the extent of trading activity it generates. By this criterion the BAB contract on the Sydney Futures Exchange would, I assess, be judged a moderate success. Considerable insight can also be gained by examining the nature and extent of variations, if any, in contract specifications after the commencement of trading. These variations are, on the one hand, an attempt by the Exchange to improve the contract specifications and, on the other, a reflection of the attitudes of market users.

Amendments to the BAB contract specifications since October 1979 have in fact been of only a minor nature. They have involved, first, a variation of listed delivery months; second, an addition to the list of approved accepting banks; and, third, minor variations in the delivery procedure.

In early 1981 the delivery month schedule was amended by the addition of the sixth calendar month from spot. The purpose of this amendment was to facilitate the hedging of physical bill 'roll-overs' 180 days in advance. In fact, this facility has not been greatly used. As can be inferred from the last column of table 2, trading activity has been concentrated heavily in the regular cycle of calendar quarters – March, June, September, December – with little activity in the 'off' months. It is worth noting too that the BAB market has attracted relatively little spread trading. On Comex, for example, which has a similar pattern of 'regular' and 'off' delivery months, the liquidity in the 'off' months is largely provided by spreading. The paucity of such trading on the Sydney Futures Exchange is of course partly a reflection of the absence of locals on the Sydney floor.

The second change of significance occurred in early 1980, with the addition of a further name to the list of approved acceptors. This may appear a trifling issue, but is is one that has presented a problem for the Exchange. The money market in Australia is not as well integrated geographically as that of the United States. In particular, there are a number of so-called 'state banks', which operate only within the borders of one state and whose acceptances are not widely traded outside that state. These banks have been eager to have their names added to the list of approved acceptors for the BAB futures contract. The pressure for this to occur is similar in many ways to that for additional delivery centres to be designated in the more traditional futures contracts. The Sydney Futures Exchange has resisted this pressure on the grounds that its inquiries in the physical bill market suggest that state bank acceptances, particularly when located 'out-of-state', may trade at a yield premium to those of the trading banks who operate on a national scale. This places the Exchange in the unfortunate role of being perceived as rating the quality of bills accepted by different banks.

The remaining modifications to the contract specifications have been of a relatively minor nature in connection with the mechanics of delivery. The fact that the contract has developed steadily over a two-and-a-half-year period with only minor modifications to the contract indicates that the contract development process was thoroughly undertaken. Aside from the growth of trading activity itself, a most encouraging development has been the influx of new associate members, attracted by the BAB contract. This has included all the major

Australian banks, several of whom have set up futures brokerage operations for their own clients in the interest rate area.

A final point of interest relates to 'exchange-for-physicals' (EFP) transactions. EFP transactions, which facilitate basis trading, were introduced on to the SFE only in September 1981. While they have not yet been widely used in any of the Exchange's markets, they have been employed in the BAB market, indicating that bill futures traders are examining the possibilities of basis. Price relationships between bank-accepted bills and other short-term instruments such as bank-endorsed bills, promissory notes and certificates of deposit are such that the BAB futures market can be used to cover positions in these instruments, particularly by using the EFP facility.

6 Prospective developments in interest rate futures in Australia

Having successfully launched one interest rate futures market, it is hardly surprising that the Sydney Futures Exchange has been examining the possibility of introducing further such contracts. Pressure to do so has come from the membership, who perceive the general trend to be away from traditional commodity futures and towards financial futures, and from hedge-users of the present market, who are now coming to appreciate the potential role to be played by these markets in risk management. From the viewpoint of the Exchange, a further benefit of such a development would be the arbitrage business generated for the BAB market.

In considering the introduction of a new contract it has been generally accepted that it should be based on an instrument of longer term to maturity than the present 90-day bill contract. Attention has focused on the two- to five-year area of the yield curve. Hedge positions of a term less than two years can be taken by an appropriate combination of BAB futures positions. Beyond five years, the secondary market in interest-bearing securities is very thin and not of sufficient depth to support a futures market. Based on discussions with as many interested parties as possible, the Financial Instruments Committee of the Exchange has indicated a tentative preference for two years, the reasons being:

(a) a more active secondary cash market;
(b) the fact that at this term there is a possibility of attracting significant participation from the official short-term money market;

(c) the fact that a two-year contract, with delivery months listed 24 months forward, would effectively provide for the covering of cash positions as far out as four years.

Having settled on a contract in this area, the choice of the nature of the underlying instrument is virtually automatic, as the only active cash markets are in government debt, known as 'Commonwealth bonds'. A major question is that of deliverable supply, the adequacy of which depends largely on the window selected for deliverable paper.

The outstanding obstacle confronting the introduction of a two-year bond contract lies in the provisions of securities legislation in Australia. Government bonds are defined in this legislation to be securities, and furthermore the statute is framed in such a way that a futures contract that calls for delivery of a security is itself a security. The consequences of this situation are quite severe and would involve, among other things, the registration of the Sydney Futures Exchange as a stock exchange, restrictions on 'short selling' of bond futures, and registration of futures brokers as 'securities dealers'. Commercial bills do not fall within the Act's definition of 'security', so that the BAB futures contract is not subject to these restrictions.

It seems clear that futures contracts were not in the minds of the legislators when the Act was drafted. Nevertheless, futures contracts based on such instruments as government bonds clearly fall within its terms, and their introduction at present is therefore effectively precluded. This subject is presently a matter of discussion between the Exchange and the authorities.

The other major innovation underway in relation to interest rate futures at the Sydney Futures Exchange is in connection with options. Options on futures contracts have been traded on certain of the Sydney Futures Exchange markets for several years. Since 1 March 1982 options have been traded on BAB futures. This makes the Sydney Futures Exchange the first exchange in the world on which options on financial instrument futures can be traded.

Because options on futures contracts are still rather novel instruments, they perhaps warrant some attention in their own right.

7 Options

Options are a widely used instrument with applicability in many areas of commerce. They have reached the highest degree of sophistication in the 'stock options' area as best exemplified by trading on the Chicago Board Options Exchange.[3]

In the area of commodities, options are occasionally employed in physical commodity transactions, and a form of option known as a 'privilege' was traded on the Chicago Board of Trade until they were banned some 50 years ago. Options on futures contracts have been traded in London for many years under rules promulgated by ICCH. A rather different kind of option trading on futures contracts was launched on a pilot basis in the United States in late 1982.

Unlike futures contracts, which create an obligation to give or take delivery in the future, options give the buyer (also known as the 'taker' of the option) the right, but *not* the obligation, to give or take delivery. Correspondingly, the seller or grantor of the option enters into an obligation conditional on the exercise of the option by the taker. Options to take delivery are known as 'call options', those to give delivery as 'put options', while options that give the taker the right either to give or take delivery are known as 'double options'. Options on futures contracts, if exercised, create a new futures contract with the taker and grantor on opposite sides.

In return for granting an option the grantor receives a price, known as the '*premium*', which is paid by the taker regardless of whether he exercises or abandons the option. Where options are traded on futures exchanges the premium is determined competitively in the same way as the price of a futures contract.

The theory of option pricing is in itself a major topic and will not be discussed here (see Breeden, 1980; Smith, 1976). Similarly, recently there have been undertaken a number of important empirical studies on this subject to which the reader is referred (for example Hoag, 1978). Rather, it is the purpose of the following brief discussion to indicate the potential commercial role of options.

Options have rather different risk characteristics to futures contracts. In particular, the liability of the taker is limited to the amount of the premium, whereas in a futures contract both parties to the contract have unlimited liability. As a result options are a particularly useful tool for hedgers subject to both price and quantity uncertainty.

To illustrate this proposition consider the following two simple illustrations.

Example 1: Options on currency futures. Consider the example of a manufacturer competing for an export order denominated in a foreign currency. On the one hand, he could base his bid on the current (forward) rate quoted in the foreign exchange market. However, in the period intervening between the submission of bids and the awarding of tenders, the foreign exchange market may move against him, possibly erasing his profit margin. One approach to hedging this risk would be to take cover in the appropriate currency futures market. However, this strategy would fail in the event that his bid was unsuccessful, for then he would have an open futures position showing a profit or loss in its own right. This is a reflection of his 'quantity uncertainty'; at the time the cover is required the exporter does not know whether he will gain the order. On the other hand, the exporter could take a put option over the appropriate currency futures contract and by so doing limit the extent of his loss to the premium that he pays for the option. At the same time, the cost of the premium could be incorporated in the overall quote. If the bid is successful the option would be exercised; if not, the option would be allowed to expire at no additional cost.

Example 2: Options on interest rate futures. The principles of hedging by way of options on interest rate futures apply in essentially the same way as those illustrated in the above example. Consider, for example, the case of a corporate treasurer required to prepare a case for his board on whether or not to undertake a particular capital project. This decision will of course depend, *inter alia*, on the cost of funds. If interest rates are volatile, they may increase between the time at which the proposal is developed and that at which it is finally approved to such an extent that it is not justified. In this case the risk could be hedged by taking a put option on the appropriate interest rate futures contract, and building the premium into the cost of the project.

It has been suggested by some writers, notably Gemmill (1981), that the distinction between options and futures is illusory in the sense that options are formally equivalent to futures contracts overlaid with appropriate stop-loss orders. In a formal sense this equivalence is indeed valid, but in practice it may not be. In particular, stop-loss orders may not be executed because the market may move too quickly; thus the potential liability cannot be fixed as the difference between the stop-loss price and the current market price.

Finally, it should be noted that the commodity options recently introduced in the United States differ in a number of important respects from those presently traded in Sydney and London. The latter do not involve a set of 'striking prices' at which options are traded; rather, the price on the options is that currently prevailing in the futures market. Most importantly, in the London/Sydney style of option it is not possible to offset an option position by the assumption of an equal and opposite position, whereas this is a feature of the new US 'exchange traded' option. On this latter point it should be noted that the London/Sydney option does not detract from liquidity in the underlying futures market, while some commentators have conjectured that this will be a consequence of the US experiment.

The success of option trading on interest rate futures, both in Australia and in the United States, remains to be seen. Their potential for providing a commercially useful hedging medium for borrowers and lenders is very great indeed.

8 The regulatory environment

The question of market regulation may not appear to be directly pertinent to the subject of this paper. However, it is arguable that the nature and extent of market regulation can influence the process of innovation – the involvement of the CFTC in the process of contract market designation certainly appeared to hamper introduction of new contracts on US exchanges during the period 1977–81. This section briefly describes the regulatory environment within which the SFE operates and draws some very tentative conclusions about the effect of this environment on the process of innovation.

Market regulation involves two distinct aspects: first, regulation of brokers' activities to protect the public participant in the market, and second, market surveillance to prevent manipulation and other forms of price distortion which detract from the commercial utility of the futures market.

Throughout the brief history of the Sydney market, the emphasis has been on self-regulation rather than on control by a statutory authority. Until the late 1970s the predominant function of the Exchange's regulations was to govern the operations of the market-place, and very little attention was paid to the relationship between an exchange member and his client. This is hardly surprising when it is remembered that general public participation in the Sydney Futures Exchange markets was only limited prior to that time.

The impetus for change came with the development of public interest in the gold market in 1978 and the subsequent gyrations in that market. Two large futures brokers experienced financial difficulty during that period, and, inevitably, the attention of regulators charged with protecting the public was aroused. The result was a state government rather than Australian government statute, the Futures Market Act, which was passed into law in late 1979.

The primary provision of this Act, aside from exempting futures contracts from gaming and betting legislation, was to give the state government supervisory powers over the Sydney Futures Exchange and, in particular, to give it such powers over the Exchange's own regulations. In other words, the thrust was to require the Exchange to develop an effective set of regulations with the role of the government being to monitor the efficacy of the self-regulation process. Within this framework the Exchange has completely rewritten its own regulations, with particular emphasis on the question of client protection. The new regulations took effect on 1 February 1982.

The question that comes to mind is whether or not the previously inadequate regulations (in terms of the broker–client relationship) had a negative impact on the early growth of the BAB futures market. As already noted, the early growth of the contract in Sydney, even in proportionate terms, was a good deal slower than in the United States. No doubt the lack of locals was a major contributor to this. However, when it is remembered that the potential hedge-users of this contract are the medium to large corporations, banks and other financial institutions, it would appear to be a reasonable conjecture that the lack of prudential control over futures brokers may have acted as a disincentive to use the market. This is particularly so when taken in conjunction with the general lack of understanding of futures markets that prevailed among such firms.

Surveillance of the Sydney Futures Exchange markets, in terms of monitoring of market positions and related activities, rests on the shoulders of the clearing house. It is in this area that the benefits of an independent clearing house are most pronounced. The question of the optimal degree of government involvement in market surveillance and associated regulatory activities in the United States, particularly in financial futures markets, has been thoroughly canvassed elsewhere (Cagan, 1981; Froewiss, 1981; Struble, 1981). In Australia these issues have not arisen, largely because the interest rate futures market is based on private rather than government debt. Although it is an interested observer of the futures market, the reserve bank has, as yet, expressed no interest in involving itself in market regulation. This would presumably change if a government bond contract were to be introduced.

Returning to the relationship between innovation and regulation, two conclusions can be drawn in the context of the Sydney market. First, the process of development of the bank bill contract was not impeded by regulation. Second, it is possible that the speed of adoption of market use by the corporate sector was impeded by a lack of regulation.

9 Summary and conclusion

This paper has attempted to describe the introduction of a new futures contract on to a small futures exchange in an economy that is relatively insulated from many of the competitive pressures operating among the major exchanges of the world.

The primary conclusions are as follows.

(a) Because of the natural protection enjoyed by the Sydney Futures Exchange, the innovative process has been driven more by the Exchange's need to diversify, rather than by any competitive pressure as such.
(b) The membership structure of an exchange may be a more important factor in determining the success of a new contract than has been generally recognized, in its role in generating both hedging and speculative participation.
(c) Absence of local traders impedes the development of new contracts, as it is in the early days of a new contract's life that their market-making' role is particularly important.
(d) It is conjectured that lack of adequate prudential control over futures brokers may impede the development of new contracts, particularly in the financial futures area.

In broad terms, the experience of the Sydney Futures Exchange in introducing the BAB contract is consistent with the Working–Gray hypothesis that both hedging and speculative participation are required for a futures market to develop to a viable level.

As a concluding comment, it should be noted that the possibility exists that the Australian government's position on foreign exchange control may change during the next two or three years. Any relaxation of the current policies would remove much of the protection presently enjoyed by the Sydney Futures Exchange. At the same time, bearing in mind the international time zone in which the Sydney market operates, such a change in policy would open the Sydney Futures Exchange to more foreign participation than is presently possible. Under a less stringent regime of foreign exchange control, the Sydney Exchange would be subject to a radically different set of competitive pressures than those that presently prevail. This would of course provide a fascinating testing ground for the general theories referred to in the opening section of this paper.

Notes

1 These comments on UK Exchange membership structure do not apply to the new London International Financial Futures Exchange, which opened in September 1982 and which has modelled itself more along US lines.

2 This discussion is necessarily very brief. More detail can be found in Wilson (1973) and Securities Institute of Australia (1981).

3 A comprehensive review of these markets may be found in the 'Report of the Special Study of the Options Markets to the Securities and Exchange Commission' (US Congress, 1978).

References

Australian Merchant Bankers Association (1981), *Bills of Exchange and Promissory notes*, Melbourne.

Breeden, D. T. (1980), 'Futures Markets and Commodity Options', Columbia University, Center for Study of Futures Markets, Working Paper no. 20.

Cagan, P. (1981), 'Financial Futures Markets: Is More Regulation Needed?' *Journal of Futures Markets*, 1.

Froewiss, K. C. (1981), 'Comment', *Journal of Futures Markets*, 1.

Gemmill, G. (1981), 'The Choice Between Options and Futures Contracts', *Investment Analyst*, 55.

Gray, R. W. (1966), 'Why Does Futures Trading Succeed or Fail? An Analysis of Selected Commodities', in *Futures Trading Seminar*, vol. III, Madison, Wisconsin.

Gray, R. W. (1978), 'Commentary', *International Futures Trading Seminar*, vol. V, Chicago.

Hoag, J. W. (1978), 'An Introduction to the Valuation of Commodity Options', Columbia University, Center for Study of Futures Markets, Working Paper no. 19.

Sandor, R. L. (1973), 'Innovation by an Exchange: A Case Study of the Development of the Plywood Futures Contract', *Journal of Law and Economics*, 16.

Securities Institute of Australia (1981), *Money Market Lecture Notes*, Sydney.

Seidler, R. L. (1981), *Legal Aspects of Bills of Exchange*, paper presented to 1981 Congress of the Institute of Chartered Accountants, Sydney.

Silber, W. L. (1981), 'Innovation, Competition and New Contract Design in Futures Contracts', *Journal of Futures Markets*, 1.

Smith, C. W. (1976), 'Option Pricing: A Review', *Journal of Financial Economics*, 3.

Stigum, M. (1978), *The Money Market: Myth, Reality and Practice*, Homewood, Illinois.

Struble, F. M. (1981), 'Comment', *Journal of Futures Markets*, 1.

US Congress (1978), Report of the Special Study of the Options Markets to the Securities and Exchange Commission, Washington DC.

Wilson, J. S. G. (1973), 'The Australian Money Market', *Banca Nazionale del Lavoro Quarterly Review*, 104.

Williams, J. C. (1980), 'The Economic Function of Futures Markets', PhD dissertation, Yale University.

Working, H. (1977a), 'Price Effects of Scalping and Day Trading', reprinted in *Selected Writings of Holbrook Working*, Chicago.

Working, H. (1977b), 'Tests of a Theory Concerning Floor Trading on Commodity Exchanges', reprinted in *Selected Writings of Holbrook Working*, Chicago.

Working, H. (1977c), 'Economic Functions of Futures Markets', reprinted in *Selected Writings of Holbrook Working*, Chicago.

13

Regulating Futures Markets: A Review in the Context of British and American Practice

GORDON T. GEMMILL

1 Introduction

Both the Reagan administration and the government of Mrs Thatcher are committed to reducing the role of government in the day-to-day operation of markets of all kinds. From this viewpoint, self-regulation by associations of traders appears to be both cheap and effective. In Britain there is already little governmental regulation of financial markets, but a number of recent failures of investment trusts and commodity funds is pushing government to introduce more, and not fewer, rules to protect investors. The Bank of England is nominally responsible for the surveillance of futures trading in the United Kingdom, but it has no statutory powers in this regard. The Bank used to be able to remove access to foreign exchange from a recalcitrant broker of futures and hence had some leverage, but the lifting of exchange controls in 1979 changed this. New 'memoranda of understanding' between the Bank and the futures markets may be expected in 1983, which will at least provide the Bank with the degree of power it had before 1979. Such memoranda are voluntary and not statutory agreements. By contrast, American securities markets have a comprehensive set of laws which limit their powers of self-regulation. For futures markets the regulations are embodied in the Commodity Futures Trading Act of 1974, which also established the Commodity Futures Trading Commission (CFTC) to supervise the rules. Prior to the existence of the CFTC, the Commodity Exchange Act (CEA) of 1936 had set the rules for agricultural markets in domestic products but had not affected the international and non-agricultural markets in New York (metals, cocoa, coffee and sugar). The Department of Agriculture was responsible for supervising the CEA.

The purpose of this paper is to examine the objectives and instruments of governmental regulation as applied to futures markets and to contrast the results of the seemingly *laissez-faire* attitude of the Bank of England with the interventionist approach of the CFTC. The paper is in five sections. Section 2 makes some general observations about the way in which regulation is effected in Chicago and New York versus London. Different approaches to regulation could result from: a difference in the products traded, a difference in the composition of the players (e.g. more speculative in the United States), or merely the inertia of historical forces. These possibilities are examined as well as the hypothesis that the advent of regulation in New York in 1975 drove trade away to the benefit of London markets. Section 3 discusses the scope and limitations of regulation as applied to futures markets in the United States and United Kingdom and its economic rationale. Section 4 is concerned solely with the regulation of corners and squeezes. There appears to have been little economic analysis of these phenomena, although such analysis might be expected to be a prerequisite to designing rules. Recent events in the silver and tin markets suggest that such analysis is timely. Hypotheses concerning the susceptibility of different products to manipulation and the frequency of such events are tested empirically. Section 5 contains a summary with conclusions. The general hypothesis on which this paper attempts to cast some light is one often propounded by traders on both sides of the Atlantic: 'that statutory regulation of futures markets is designed to mollify an ill-informed public, has no economic benefit to society and tends to disrupt normal business, thus imposing costs arbitrarily upon traders.'

The economics of regulating futures markets does not lend itself to a particularly formal treatment. In this regard it is similar to industrial economics with its loosely defined structure–conduct–performance paradigm. With the present state of knowledge one is not able to specify formal models that can be used to derive the impact of alternative rules. The closest to this approach that has been achieved so far is the work of Telser (1981). He developed a static equilibrium model of a futures market to demonstrate that raising margins, everything else held constant, would increase the variance of prices because of the resulting fall in liquidity. Telser's approach is very useful if one wants to argue that margins should be kept as low as possible in normal circumstances, but it is not helpful or even applicable in conditions of a squeeze, when a monopolist is able to make price deviate from the normal equilibrium. For these reasons this paper is largely descriptive in character.

2 The players, the rules and the umpires

2.1 British rules

Every futures market practises self-regulation in the interest of its members. The institutions of the market consist of an exchange with a governing committee and a clearing house. In London, the weakness of governmental control has resulted in relatively strong market committees and a powerful and independent clearing-house. The International Commodities Clearing House (ICCH) (which is owned by a group of six banks including the four largest) is responsible for clearing all the major non-metal markets. The London Metal Exchange (LME) does not clear through the ICCH or any other clearing system, but maintains a principal's contract for which the security depends on the solvency of the two parties to a trade. On the LME there are therefore no margins between ring members. The aggregate position of each member is however monitored, and variation margins (of less than 100 per cent) may be imposed once a member exceeds his allowable open interest, the latter depending on the capitalization of his company. There is also a compensation fund to take over any difficulties in relation to short-run liquidity following a default by a ring member.

Under its 'memoranda of understanding' the Bank of England had the right to ask for certain information from each London futures market, and this continues on a voluntary basis. It receives data on ICCH members' positions once a week direct from the clearing house and data on the main LME ring members' positions by a survey once a month. Positions are classified into 'trade' and 'non-trade' (i.e., speculative) categories. The Bank has through time established what could be called the normal proportions of these two categories, and if there is a large change it raises the matter with the committee of the relevant exchange. When the Bank last reported on the effectiveness of this operation (Bank of England, 1978), it claimed to have been instrumental in averting congestion in the May 1976 zinc contracts and in cocoa and coffee for March and September 1977 respectively. The Bank also intervened to avoid widespread liquidity problems arising from the 1967 devaluation of the pound. Companies that had not moved their money out of sterling, either because they had not foreseen this event or because they followed the Bank's exhortations not do so so, were in difficulties. A company that had purchased commodities in foreign currency and hedged in sterling-denominated futures faced a windfall loss of 10 per cent – market prices anticipated the devaluation of 14 per cent by only a 4 per cent premium. Since these companies were playing the game according to the government's rules (in the country's interest), it is hardly surprising that the Bank felt obliged to tide them over, with loans that totalled only £3.5 million. In sum, the Bank's position is one of merely being informed of what is happening in order to prod the exchanges into regulating themselves; it has no power of direct intervention.

One of the arguments used by the Bank in support of the present informal (non-statutory) approach is that writing down the rules would invite the players to find loopholes. Without any rules the Bank can use its 'discretionary' powers. If the players in the game accept that the Bank has such powers, then the Bank is clearly in a very powerful position: it not only decides on the rules, but can change them in the middle of the game. The absurdity of this position has recently been demonstrated in relation to the banking sector. The Hong Kong and Shanghai Bank wished to take over the Royal Bank of Scotland. The Bank of England opposed this 'foreign' take-over because it would be difficult informally to control the new conglomerate, thus weakening the pursuit of monetary policy. While the Bank was able to prevent this take-over, via the Monopolies Commission ruling that it was not in the public interest, the case has demonstrated that the discretionary powers of the Bank are usable only if not challenged. The emperor has no clothes, but this does not matter so long as everybody acts as if the emperor has clothes.

2.2 US rules

As earlier stated, the CFTC has a clear-cut statutory basis for regulation. The CEA of 1936 already provided powers to: (a) set speculative limits; (b) place daily price limits; (c) establish reporting requirements; and (d) register certain trading professionals. Amendments in 1968 gave the power to: (e) compel exchanges to enforce their own rules. The CFT Act of 1974 provided more resources and extra powers to: (f) license traders; (g) vet new contracts, which must be 'in the public interest'; (h) adjust the number of delivery points; (i) act to restore 'orderly trading'; and (j) make regular investigations. When it began work in 1975, the CFTC immediately brought the New York international markets into its regulatory net. During its seven years of existence the Commission has brought cases for manipulation, imposed position limits, delayed new contracts, and closed markets temporarily for 'disorderly trading'. The Commission does not have the power to impose minimum (initial) margins, although such authority was debated in 1974 and is again being sought in the hearings on the future of the CFTC in 1982.

The information upon which the Commission judges that a squeeze is imminent is the daily report, which is required from traders whose positions exceed a given level. Such reported trades are divided into hedging and speculative categories. The CFTC may request further information on the beneficial owner of any outstanding contracts. This brings it into conflict with foreign traders, who may refuse to reveal their clients, sometimes arguing that their national laws do not allow such disclosure.[1] To overcome this impasse the CFTC has proposed that foreign traders must have domestic agents in the United States from whom information can be obtained, otherwise such foreign-held contracts will be closed out. The CFTC currently does not seem likely to push this particular proposal, since there appears to be a larger loophole in its domestic control system, whereby small, non-reporting positions may be built up and coordinated by a single speculator (e.g., the Hunt silver case).

2.3 British and US comparisons

Now that the powers of intervention have been outlined, it is interesting to look at the evidence that regulation by the CFTC has driven trade from New York to London. As early as 1892, US traders were arguing that regulation of American futures markets would merely benefit foreign commodity exchanges (Cowing, 1965, p. 13). New York and London have comparable markets for cocoa, coffee and sugar (among other products). The hypothesis is that after 1975, when governmental regulation of these markets began, there was a shift in activity to London. One way to test this is to observe the ratio of London-to-New York turnovers in these products before and after 1975, which is done in figure 1.

The figure does not support the view that there was a sudden flight of trading from New York to London after 1975. Cocoa shows a long-term trend towards London from the mid-1960s, which was reversed quite dramatically after 1978. The explanation is a change in the New York contract in that year which allowed delivery of West African as well as South American cocoa and a shift from a 30,000 lb unit to 10 metric tons. Sugar shows a drift towards New

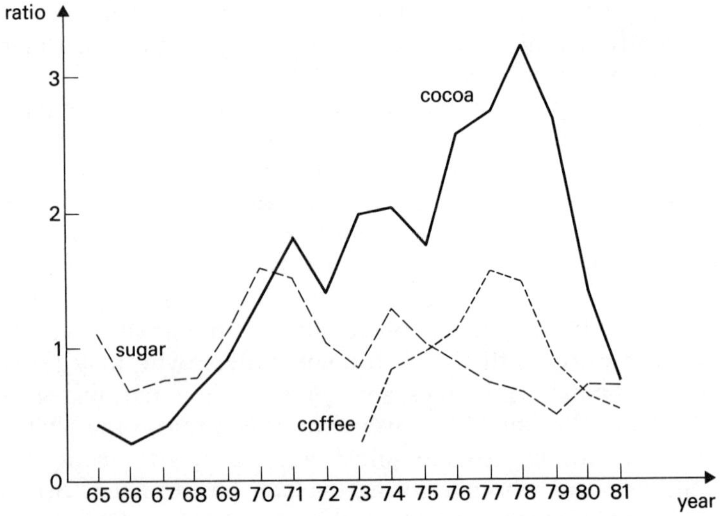

Fig. 1 Ratio of UK to US volumes

York from 1970, which traders suggest is the result again of a preferred contract. Until 1979 the London contract had c.i.f. delivery and the New York contract f.o.b. delivery. Coffee shows a trend towards London from 1973 to 1977/78 and a trend towards New York thereafter. The coffee price reached a peak in mid-1977 and Latin American producers attempted to support it by buying, and taking delivery on, futures contracts on London and New York from mid-1977 to mid-1980 (see Greenstone, 1981). The New York Coffee and Sugar Exchange and the CFTC in November 1977 declared an emergency in the December contract when three Latin American traders held 75 per cent of the long open position. There was no such emergency in London, but discussions were held with the producers' agents in order that delivery could be facilitated in the September 1977 contract. It does appear that the actions of the CFTC resulted in producers switching some of their trading to London in 1978. When a further limitation on trading was imposed by the New York Exchange at the request of the CFTC in the December 1979 contract, there does not seem to have been much shift towards London. In London the coffee contract is for robusta, while in New York it is for arabica. London has attempted several times to introduce an arabica contract, denominated in dollars, but with no success, despite the existence of the CFTC. It appears, in sum, that the CFTC has had little detrimental impact on coffee volumes in New York, just as for cocoa and sugar.

A recurrent theme among traders in London is that more overt regulation is required in the United States because the composition of the players is different. Viewed from London, the American game is highly speculative, with many small players. Government feels that it needs to do something to protect the interests of the latter, who are remarkably ill-informed; hence the existence of the CFTC.

There are no data with which to judge the proportion of small speculators in London futures markets. *A priori*, one would expect fewer small speculators in London because the tax treatment of commodity gains and losses is less liberal than in the United States. Other forms of gambling, such as off-track betting on horses, are more readily available in Britain than in the United States, and the tax treatment of gains from betting are more favourable than for gains on futures (maximum of 8 per cent as compared with a minimum of 30 per cent). Another plausible reason for more small speculation in the United States is simply that higher American incomes have a positive influence on the demand for speculation.

Another consensus view in London concerning the American markets is that much of the volume is composed of day-trading by small operators on the market floor who have hired seats to 'try their luck'. There are no 'locals' on the London markets, and access to the club is not possible by simply hiring a seat.[2] The above consensus view can be tested by reference once again to cocoa, coffee and sugar in New York and London. The higher the proportion of day trades, the higher should be the ratio of volume to open interest.

Table 1 Volume and open interest, cocoa, coffee and sugar in New York and London, 1979 and 1980 (million tonnes)

		New York			*London*		
Product	*Year*	*Volume*	*Open interest*	*Ratio*	*Volume*	*Open interest*	*Ratio*
Cocoa	1979	3.159	1.214	2.282	8.389	1.660	5.060
	1980	4.566	0.879[a]	5.194	6.474	1.640	3.949
Coffee	1979	7.651	2.282	3.353	6.840	2.271	3.013
	1980	15.427	2.538	6.089	5.524	1.940	2.848
Sugar	1979	90.599	32.066	2.825	44.270	8.921	4.963
	1980	181.709	45.296	4.012	126.851	15.402	8.236

[a] Calculated under the assumption that open interest was divided between 30,000 lb and 10 tonne contracts in proportion to volume in the two contracts

Source: Futures Industry Association Commodity Yearbook, ICCH Ltd

Table 2 Major products traded in Chicago, New York and London, 1981*

	Chicago	New York	London
Cattle	/	/	–
Cocoa	–	/	/
Coffee	–	/	/
Copper	–	/	/
Cotton	–	/	–
Financial instruments	/	/	–
Gasoil	–	/	/
Gold	/	/	–
Lead	–	–	/
Orange juice	–	/	–
Pork bellies	/	–	–
Potatoes	/	/	/
Rubber	–	–	/
Silver	/	/	/
Soyabeans	/	–	–
Sugar	–	/	/
Tin	–	–	/
Wheat	/	–	/

* This list is not exhaustive

Table 1 gives this ratio for New York and London in 1979 and 1980 for the three products; it is in all cases between 2 and 8. For cocoa and coffee the London ratios exceed those in New York for 1979, but not for 1980. For sugar the London ratio substantially exceeds the New York ratio in both years. The hypothesis that day-trading is more prevalent in New York than in London is therefore not generally supported.

The most plausible reason for the existence of greater regulation on American futures markets is that it derives from the mixture of products traded. Chicago has markets predominantly for US domestic (agricultural and financial) products, while New York has markets for international products for which the United States is not a major producer. London has significant markets only for international products. Table 2 lists some of the major products traded in the different cities in 1981. The difference in product-mix can be explained quite simply: it is a function of agricultural policy. The Common Agricultural Policy of the EEC raises and stabilizes the domestic prices of most temperate agricultural products. The result is that price risks are small and the demand for hedging is correspondingly small. Prior to joining the EEC (in 1972), Britain already had futures markets in grains (which still trade successfully), but the size of other markets and the influence of the marketing boards were such that futures trading in other domestic products was not initiated. Continental Europe's farm vote and stable prices have stifled the development of futures trading in any other temperate products with the exception of potatoes. American farm policy, by contrast, has seldom completely stabilized prices, although on occasion it has temporarily had that effect.

The agrarian (farm) movement was powerful in the United States in the late nineteenth century, and the Hatch Bill of 1893, which would have taxed futures markets out of existence, narrowly failed to gain the necessary three-quarters vote in the House. The 'progressives' of the 1920s and 1930s, who continued the agrarian tradition in a more sophisticated form, eventually succeeded in enacting their desired anti-speculative legislation: the Securities and Exchange Act for stock markets (1934) and the Commodity Exchange Act for futures markets (1936). The later US legislation, such as the Commodity Futures Trading Act of 1974, which created the Commodity Futures Trading Commission (CFTC), really just continued the theme that speculation should be controlled but not taxed out of existence (which would have been un-constitutional).[3]

Farmers in both Europe and America effectively control farm policy and have 'captured' the EEC Commission and the US Department of Agriculture respectively. The SEC and the CFTC are the results of a long agrarian history in which the 'small guy' in a distant location attempts to defend himself from the manoeuvres of the 'city-slicker'. A parallel exists in the suspicion of today's developing countries about the mechanisms of price determination on futures markets that are located in the industrial nations. Since Europe has never had significant domestic agricultural futures markets, there has never been the demand for regulation that has existed in the United States.[4]

3 Scope, limitations and rationale of regulation

Having determined that farm policy probably led to the more interventionist approach to regulation in the United States as compared with Britain, we now turn to the reasons for and against regulation as practised. As stated in the introduction, a review of the economics of manipulation will be held over for the next section.

The reasons for regulation may be grouped under three headings: regulation of natural monopoly; control of externalities; and public relations. The reasons against regulation also come under three headings: restriction on the evolution of markets; the possibility of evasion of the rules, rendering them ineffective; and blundering application of the rules by the regulator.

3.1 Natural monopoly

It has been argued by a former chairman of the CFTC that there are 'powerful scale economies in operational technology, liquidity and product acceptance, as well as from the quasi-governmental rulemaking powers with which an exchange is imbued' (Stone, 1981, p. 118). There are really two arguments here. First, a successful contract has liquidity and hence low transactions costs. This makes it difficult for another exchange to compete on the same contract, and attempts to do so (e.g., New York Futures Exchange) have failed. Any monopoly rent is reflected in the price of a seat. Second, there are economies of scale in running an exchange and particularly in running a clearing-house. American exchanges have subsidiary clearing operations, but in London the ICCH has a virtual monopoly and also has an interest in the clearing houses in Paris, Hong Kong, Sydney, Kuala Lumpur and Bermuda.

Neither of these arguments is very strong. If an exchange tries to exploit its monopoly it soon finds that forward markets are close substitutes for futures and business drifts away. The seemingly trivial differences that distinguish a successful contract from a failure (see Silber, 1981) tend to support this view. The monopoly argument for regulation is stronger in London than in New York. In London the seats on some markets (particularly the LME) are not bought and sold and there is no method of appeal against rejection of an application for membership. The monopoly in clearing of ICCH is also considerable. However, competition between London and New York limits the rent earned by exchange members, and they, in turn, bargain with ICCH. The CFTC approach to regulating exchanges' monopoly power is to limit the number of contracts being traded through the use of an 'economic purpose test'. To gain approval, a contract must have a heding rationale and/or a price discovery function. It seems absurd to limit the number of contracts in this way, as there is likely to be less competition between exchanges as a result. In London the Bank of England has essentially no overt control on new contracts nor any policy on exchange monopoly.

3.2 Externalities

Three kinds of externality result from futures trading. The first is outright fraud. The possibilities here include: brokers contra-trading against customers; clients' money being converted from one purpose to another and not being traceable if the broker goes bankrupt; and the sale of 'naked' options or futures at unrealistic prices to ill-informed customers. The CFTC has attempted to regulate each of these frauds, whereas there is very little regulation in London. The methods of regulation in the United States include: licensing of brokers; a requirement that funds of customers be segregated from those of a broker; and a partial ban on option trading (this was relaxed in 1982). The lack of regulation in London is the result of the very small 'retail' trade in futures or options. Nevertheless, the recent failures of a commodity investment house (M. L. Doxford) and similar events in the securities market have led to a report that is highly critical of investor protection in the futures markets.[5] It is better for the government to investigate malpractices than for exchanges to do so themselves, because there can then be no question of a conflict of interest.

The second externality of futures trading is manipulation of prices by a monopolist. This is the most important externality, which will be reviewed, in detail, later.

The third externality is moral hazard. Government has an obligation to prevent a financial collapse. Knowing that the government will provide a safety-net encourages traders to take greater risks. Government therefore has a right to constrain such risk-taking. The obvious example here is the loan of $1.1 billion to the Hunt brothers in March 1980, which was engineered by the Federal Reserve in order that the Hunts could pay their debt to various commission houses which otherwise would have been insolvent (see CFTC, 1981). A main reason why the system of margins proved inadequate at that time was that silver had been used by the commission houses as collateral for loans to margin long futures positions in silver. As the spot and futures markets fell, there was therefore a doubling of the level of required margin-call. This kind of 'imprudent' banking could occur equally well in New York or in London under present regulations, but in both cities the central bank would be likely to intervene.

3.3 Public relations

The 'capture hypothesis' of regulation holds that the regulator has such close contact with those being regulated that he unwittingly becomes a defender of the latter's interest against the much less easily identified 'public interest'. A plausible reason for regulation is then that the public becomes aware that a regulator exists, which is comforting, while the traders are able to use the regulator as a buffer between themselves and the public. It is difficult to judge whether the CFTC falls in this mould. Nevertheless, the lack of retail futures sales in the United Kingdom may reflect the lack of a regulator, since the larger traders know that the impact of a scandal on them would be greater than the benefits from finding many new, small customers.

3.4 *Evolution of markets*

The argument that regulation will stifle new developments, which has recently been repeated by Cagan (1981), is an old one. Early in this century Justice Oliver Wendell Holmes put it thus: 'legislators and courts have generally recognised that the natural evolutions of a complex society are to be touched only with a very cautious hand . . .' (quoted by Cowing, 1965, p. 253). The CFTC has certainly delayed new developments, via its system of approval for new contracts (Silber, 1981). My judgement is that simple risk aversion has had an even greater impact on the evolution of futures markets in London: few new developments occur there that have no precedent in Chicago or New York. The battles over new American contracts are therefore of great value to the London markets in arguing the need for new markets, the latest example being the belated introduction of financial futures in London in 1982.

3.5 *Evasion of rules*

As earlier stated, the Bank of England might argue that to write down the rules invites evasion. Among the most important of the weapons in the control of corners and squeezes that the CFTC or an exchange may deploy is the imposition of position limits. However, a determined manipulator would find it relatively easy to evade such limits. First, he could open many small, non-reporting accounts with many brokers.[6] Second, he could utilize a foreign-based broker whose laws do not permit the divulgence of a client's name.[7] The existence of markets in London that compete with those in New York may limit the ability of the CFTC to enforce position limits. As was earlier demonstrated, however, regulation after 1975 does not seem to have driven trade to London, so either the regulation was not harsh or evasion was easy.

3.6 Blundering application of rules

If a regulator has little understanding of the functioning of futures markets he is likely to use his power to close markets or declare emergencies at inappropriate moments. The CFTC has advised exchanges to allow trading only for liquidation in particular contracts when it believed a squeeze to be imminent (e.g., coffee in December 1977, wheat in February 1979 and silver in December 1979 and March 1980). Most traders would maintain that no 'emergency' existed. A more clear-cut example of 'blundering regulation' was the closure of the French sugar market in 1974 (see Simon, 1977). In December 1974 the clearing house in Paris (CLAM) had failed to collect sufficient securities to meet its obligations as the price of sugar fell. It urged the exchange, run by the Compagnie de Commissionaires Agrees (CCA), to declare *force majeure.* The CCA agreed, knowing that some of its major members held long positions that were likely to be in default. The regulator, the French Ministry of Commerce, agreed to closure and a rule was activated under which settlement of contracts occurred at the average price of the previous 20 days – much to the advantage of the longs. The row that ensued resulted in almost no trade in sugar in Paris for two years. Simon (1977) argues that the clearing house was to blame, but the lack of knowledge of the Ministry of Commerce about futures markets was also instrumental.[8]

4 Manipulation of prices

Manipulation involves the use of a dominant position in a market in order to distort prices from the equilibrium that otherwise would have resulted. Although the Commodity Exchange Act of 1936 and the CFT Act of 1974 did not define manipulation, they did make it a felony, punishable by a fine of up to $100,000 or imprisonment for up to five years or both. The courts have successfully prosecuted cases of manipulation in the United States that involved a squeeze of the shorts by the longs, i.e., a 'long squeeze'.[9] Such cases were based on the fact that: (a) the squeezer controls the long futures position; (b) the squeezer also controls deliverable supply; and (c) the squeezer deliberately exacts an artificially high price in the fulfilment or liquidation of the futures contracts. In a legal analysis of such manipulation, McDermott (1979) denies that a squeeze can be recognized merely from former prices – conditions change so rapidly that former prices are an ineffective guide to what current prices 'should' be. He proposes a definition of a squeeze as 'A trader's buying or threatening to take delivery of what [he] has already bought or owns'. A long trader may prevent or hinder a short trader from delivering by: (a) almost simultaneously buying the same commodity more than once; (b) threatening to take delivery of the same commodity more than once; or (c) buying what he already owns.

Squeezes are of two kinds. First, there is the general squeeze, which attempts to manipulate the cash market. The existence of a futures market is not necessary for such a squeeze, but may facilitate it. Second, there is the futures market squeeze, in which profits are made only at the expense of participants in the futures market while in the cash market only the price of the deliverable quality of the commodity is affected. The Commodity Futures Trading Act does not distinguish between these two squeezes. Indeed, the Act does not limit the CFTC to regulating only futures markets but could be deemed to include cash markets as well (Hieronymus, 1977).

General squeezes are merely a special kind of destabilizing speculation. The literature suggests that they will be profitable only if: (a) they create a bandwagon effect, so that losses are passed on to the unwitting followers; or (b) the market is so dominated by the manipulator that he (alone) faces an elasticity of demand smaller than minus unity; i.e., a cartel is formed. The relevance of futures markets to such squeezes is that they provide a means whereby cash market purchases may be made without the identity of the purchaser or his intention to take delivery being divulged at the outset. It is therefore convenient, and probably more profitable, to initiate a general squeeze via futures contracts.[10] That is what happened (intentionally or not) in the silver market in 1979–80, and it appears to have happened in the tin market (in London) in 1981–82. The coffee-producing nations squeezed their market in 1977–78 and the cocoa producers in 1977, using futures contracts on which delivery was taken.

The question to be posed is whether the regulation of futures markets can affect such general squeezes. The actions of the New York Commodity Exchange (COMEX) with respect to silver in 1979–80 at the instigation of the CFTC included raising initial margins, imposing position limits, and allowing trading only for liquidation. All of these actions reduce the open interest and force a squeezer either to quit or to take his squeeze into the cash market, where the costs are higher owing to the absence of trading on margins.

Although the Hunts were forced to accept delivery of silver in November 1979, owing largely to the actions of COMEX, the peak in the market did not come until 17 January 1980, and the Hunts failed to meet their margin call only on 27 March 1980. Nevertheless, the COMEX actions probably speeded up the chronology. Had the Hunts' and other speculators' actions been concentrated in London (on the LME), it is doubtful that any exchange action would have occurred. In the February 1982 tin squeeze the committee of the LME declared that the spot prices could not exceed the settlement prices for one day ahead by more than £120 per tonne, i.e., a three-month premium in excess of £10,000 on a spot price of £9,000! This action probably averted a default, while keeping the market open, and it may have also accelerated the eventual outcome merely by making public the imminent squeeze. Had such a squeeze occurred on a non-metal London market, ICCH would no doubt have imposed special deposits on any large position-holder and accelerated events just as on COMEX above, but not made the position public.[11]

A general squeeze can be intiated via futures only if there is a large open interest for that product relative to world supply (annual production plus stocks). Table 3 lists this 'speculative ratio' for some markets (approximately), as well as a second ratio of volume of futures to world supply (this latter because the LME gives no open interest data). The table has an open interest speculative ratio ranging from 2 per cent for wheat to 121 per cent for silver. Cocoa and coffee have ratios of 119 and 77 per cent respectively, not far behind silver. The volume-based speculative ratios range from a low of 14 per cent for rubber to a high of 2,668 per cent for silver. Silver's nearest rivals are soyabeans (1,111 per cent) and cocoa (529 per cent). While the table demonstrates the huge volumes of trading in silver, it does not suggest that silver is significantly more susceptible to a squeeze initiated via futures than, for example, cocoa. The implication is that, if position limits are to be used to prevent such general squeezes, such limits should apply equally to all markets.

The futures squeeze is a relatively minor incident when compared with the general squeeze. As short squeezes are very rare, we will be concerned only with long squeezes. The analytics of a long squeeze are as follows. In the final days of a contract a time is reached after which it is impossible to put stocks into a deliverable position. In other words, the deliverable supply is then fixed. The long squeezer holds futures contracts and deliverable stocks such that some part of his long futures can be delivered only with his own stocks or with the stocks he will own. He has effectively bought, or threatens to

Table 3 Speculative ratios for various products, 1980

Product	Annual production (1)	Stocks (2)	Average open interest[f] (3)	Turnover (4)	Ratio (3)/[(1) + (2)]	Ratio (4)/[(1) + (2)]
	(million tonnes)				%	%
Cocoa	1.5	0.6	L1.6	6.5	119	529
			N0.9	4.6		
Coffee	4.8	0.9	L1.9	5.5	77	368
			N2.5	15.5		
Copper	9	2.5	L0.2[c]	5.8	6	184
			N0.5	15.4		
Cotton	14	5	9.7	56.5	51	297
Lead	4	—	—	2.7	—	68
Rubber	9	2	—	1.5	—	14
Silver[d]	430[a]	360[b]	L27[c]	586	121[d]	2,668[d]
			N929	20,495		
Soyabeans	96	48[e]	C18.7	1,600	13	1,111
Sugar	90	40	L15.4	127	47	238
			N45.3	182		
Tin	0.25	—	—	0.29	—	116
Wheat	420	55	C8.5	738	2	155
Zinc	6	—	—	1.8	—	30

[a] Million troy oz.
[b] Visible.
[c] Assuming same ratio to volume as on COMEX.
[d] All data for 1979, as more representative.
[e] Beginning of year, USA.
[f] L = London, N = New York and C = Chicago Board of Trade.

Sources: ICCH Commodities Yearbook, 1980/81; ICCH; LME; Commodity Yearbook, 1981; Futures Industry Association.

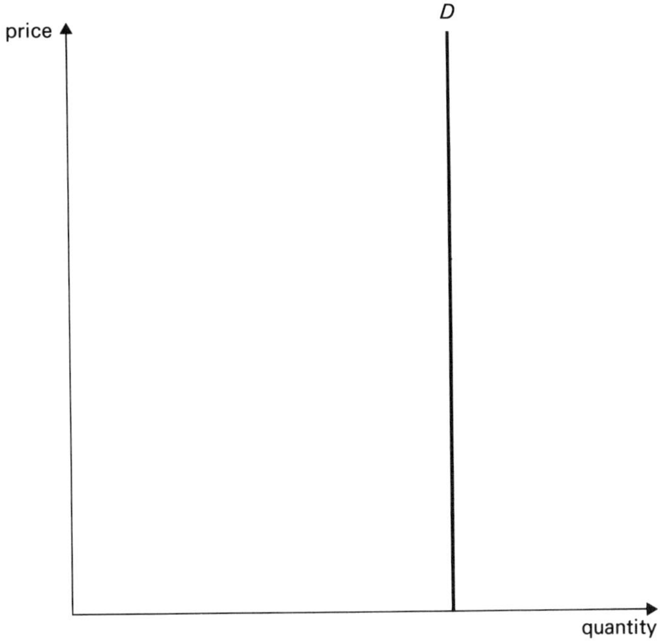

Fig. 2 Demand for stocks or long futures by shorts

buy, the same commodity twice. The demand curve of the shorts is completely inelastic, as in figure 2, and the squeezer can choose that price at which he settles.

It is a little more realistic to consider that supplies may still be made deliverable, but at a very high cost. For example, in 1955 the New York Mercantile Exchange potato contract called for delivery in 100lb bags. The shorts, who were squeezed in the May contract, had to re-pack from 50lb to 100lb bags to meet the delivery conditions, at extra cost. Another famous example is the so-called Leiter corner of 1894, in which Joseph Leiter was squeezing Philip Armour in the Chicago wheat market, but Armour successfully delivered by extraordinary effort, including dynamiting frozen waterways (Hieronymus, 1977). The supply curve of non-squeezer stocks therefore has a positive slope, as in figure 3.

Another more realistic assumption would be that, at some price, the shorts prefer to default than to pay the long squeezer immediately. They may not win by doing this, but at least they delay their losses

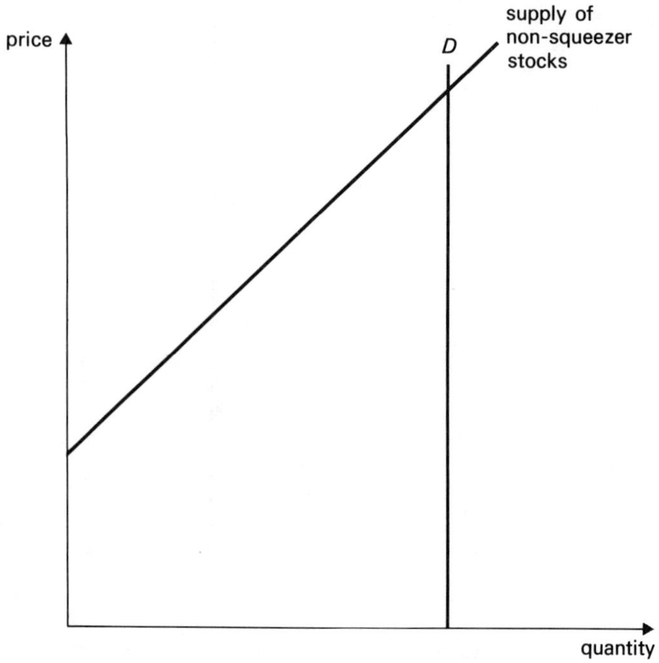

Fig. 3 Supply of stocks and demand for stocks or futures

until the exchange settles the inevitable dispute over payments. This implies that the demand-for-stocks curve has a negative slope at high prices, as shown in figure 4. As an example, default occurred on about half of the May 1955 potato contracts cited above. To maximize his revenues, the long squeezer must then determine the price at which excess demand for stocks and futures has unitary elasticity, such as P^* in figure 4. At that price no defaults occur, Q_1, non-squeezer stocks are delivered, and the shorts buy $(Q_2 - Q_1)$ futures from him.

The futures squeeze may undoubtedly be very profitable, but it is not easy to accomplish. It cannot result in large public losses because it is, of necessity, short-lived and does not affect the cash market price except for the deliverable quality. The regulatory approach to this manipulation is to impose limits on speculative holdings (in the United States) and to raise margins on the longs if they try to hold large positions into the final days of a contract (in the United States and the United Kingtom). Paul *et al.* (1981) have considered these two possibilities in the context of the potato

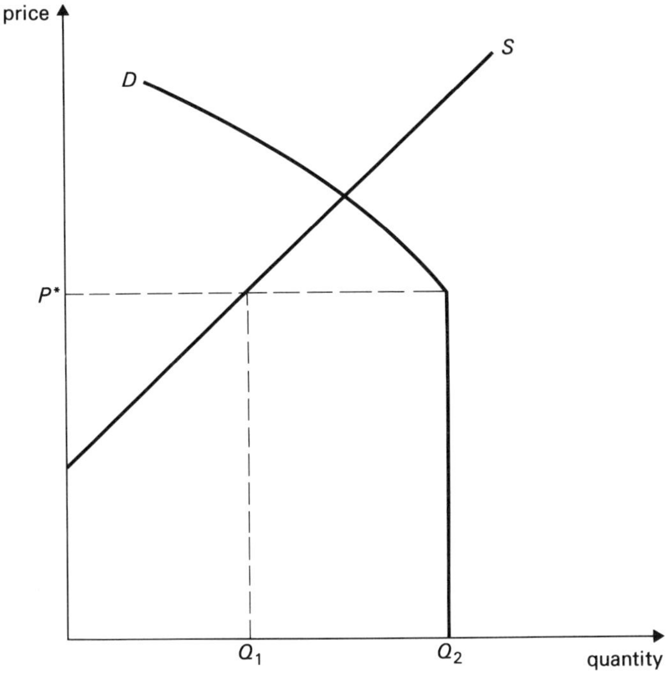

Fig. 4 Supply of stocks and demand for stocks or futures

market default of 1976 and find neither ideal. Position limits existed on potato speculators, but might have also been imposed on hedgers. Such limits need to reflect the deliverable supply and not be a single, inflexible number. With regard to margins, they suggest that raising them could prove inequitable, an argument that is difficult to follow since this would occur only in the last days of a contract. The market-traders' view would probably be that those who hold on to the end of a contract can expect to be periodically hurt by a squeeze.[12] However, squeezes become more difficult if the contract allows a wide variety of locations and qualities for delivery. But the problem with broadening the contract is that it becomes weaker in terms of hedging effectiveness owing to greater basis risk (with respect to quality and location). Yet another alternative would be to use cash settlement according to a formula, as suggested by Paul *et al.* (1981) for potatoes and as already practised on some financial futures markets.

While evidence from prices alone is not sufficient to demonstrate a futures squeeze, the narrowing (widening) of the basis between

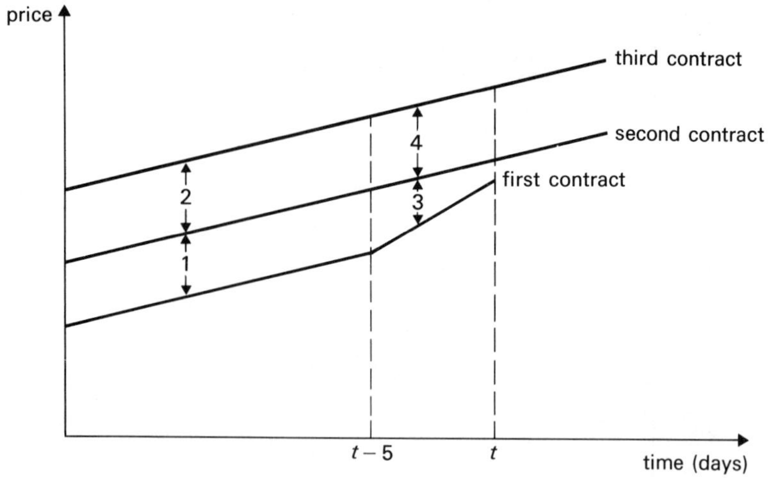

Fig. 5 Basis behaviour as contract matures

the maturing future and the next (second) contract month relative to the basis between the latter and the third contract month is a necessary condition for a long (short) squeeze. Diagrammatically, in figure 5 one may establish the normal relationship between basis 1 and basis 2 over a period and then compare the actual basis 3 with that which would be expected given basis 4, using simple proportions.[13]

This method of analysis was used on all maturing contracts in London for cocoa, coffee and sugar for the period March 1974–December 1979.[14] The basis 1–basis 2 relationship was established in the first part of a month and deviations from expected basis 3 were found for the last five days of a contract. For comparative purposes, the changes in bases in months which contracts did not mature were similarly analysed. The distributions of deviations of basis 3 from expected basis 3 are given in table 4. A negative value for the deviation represents a rise in price of the maturing contract, hence an intended or unintended long squeeze. As would be expected, the delivery-month distributions have wider tails than the non-delivery-month distributions, demonstrating some unexpected price movements in maturing contracts. Beginning with cocoa, there are two delivery-month outliers, one short squeeze in March 1974 and one long squeeze in September 1977. The deviations in both cases exceed 8 per cent. For coffee there are also two possible outliers, but they are in the 6–8 per cent range. They represent a short squeeze in January 1979 and a long squeeze in March 1979.

Table 4 Deviation of basis between nearest and second-nearest contract from expected basis (percentage of price)

	Number of contracts in class[a]					
	Cocoa		*Coffee*		*Sugar*	
Deviation %	*D* %	*ND* %	*D* %	*ND* %	*D* %	*ND* %
>10	1					
8 to 9.99	0					
6 to 7.99	0	1	1			
4 to 5.99	3	1	2	1		
2 to 3.99	6	1	4	3		2
0 to 1.99	10	19	10	19	15	14
−2 to −0.01	6	16	13	10	11	20
−4 to −2.01	2	1	3	1	1	3
−6 to −4.01	1		1	1	1	1
−8 to −6.01	0		1		0	
−10 to −8.01	1				0	
<−10					1	
Total	30	39	35	35	29	40

[a] D is a delivery-month; ND is a non-delivery molnth.

For sugar there is only one outlier, a deviation of more than 10 per cent for August 1976, representing a long squeeze. Whether any of these was a real squeeze is difficult, at present, to judge. However, the analysis suggests either: (a) that the incidence of squeezes – a possible 5 out of 94 contracts – is not large; or (b) that regulation by ICCH is effective.

5 Summary and conclusions

This review has attempted to examine the economics of regulating futures markets in general and the reasons why the approach to regulation in the United States is so different from that in the United Kingdom. In London the powers of the Bank of England are limited to surveillance and advice, although the Bank stands ready to prevent a financial collapse emanating from the futures markets, as evidenced by its assistance after the 1967 devaluation. In the United States the CFTC has statutory power to intervene in markets when there is 'disorderly trading'. The powers of the CFTC are limited by the ease with which position limits may be evaded and by the possibility that trade could migrate from New York to the equivalent markets in London. An analysis of cocoa, coffee and sugar markets did not, however, support the view that the advent of the CFTC in 1975 had caused any such migration. An analysis of the volume-to-open interest ratios for these markets in London and New York also rejected the view that New York's markets are heavily populated by day-traders while London has larger 'trade' participation and hence a lower ratio. It appears that US agricultural policy, which allows prices to fluctuate and so futures markets for farm products to thrive, explains the existence of statutory regulation in the United States. The agrarian movement culminated in the establishment of the SEC and the Commodity Exchange Commission, forerunner of the CFTC, in the 1930s. By contrast, stable prices in Europe have given farmers little interest in futures trading and hence no demand for regulation.

The arguments for regulation are all weak, except with respect to protection of the public from fraud and the prevention of manipulation. To the extent that there are more small speculators in the United States, a visible regulator of these markets is important both to protect these individuals from fraudulent traders and to shield traders from angry invididuals who have made losses. The primary weapon at the CFTC's disposal in controlling manipulation – position limits – may easily be evaded, and the secondary weapon – raising initial margins – is used by exchanges in both the United States and the United Kingdom. The analysis of manipulation suggested that there is a danger of futures markets being increasingly used to initiate general cash market squeezes. There seems little that can be done to prevent this, since position limits are evadable. Ordering trade to be for liquidation only, or putting on heavy initial margins, effectively closes down a market and forces the manipulator into the cash market. Such actions at least bring forward the demise of the squeeze. An analysis of open interest and volume relative to supply for various products did not identify some products as being more 'squeezable' via futures trading than others.

A futures squeeze is a delicate operation in which the manipulator must carefully judge the likelihood of default by the squeezed participants and also the supply of available stocks. An analysis of 94 contracts for cocoa, coffee and sugar in London from March 1974 to December 1979 could identify only five possible squeezes, suggesting that regulation by ICCH is effective, and/or that squeezes are not frequent.

In sum, given the ineffectiveness of regulation in the United States except at the 'retail level', it is doubtful whether traders are more heavily regulated in the United States than in the United Kingdom. The efforts of government to regulate in the United States have merely led to the substitution of governmental regulation for self-regulation, and not to a greater level of regulation in total.

Notes

1 The most publicized such case concerned a Swiss trader, Wiscope. See Greenstone (1981) for a review.
2 The London International Financial Futures Exchange, which opened in autumn 1982, is an exception to this pattern.
3 See Cowing (1965).
4 This statement has an exception. In 1896 the German Reichstag passed a bill that required exchange speculators to register. Fewer than 400 actually registered, and the trade moved to France, England and Holland. The bill was enacted at the instigation of farmers, but was repealed as a failure in 1908 (Cowing, 1965, pp. 105–6).
5 'The present weakness, as I see it, is that self-regulation of the Exchanges and the surveillance of the Bank of England are directed towards the efficient running of the markets and the protection of members in their dealings *inter se* on the Exchanges, and not towards the protection of investors – the ultimate clients on whose behalf they are dealing. Rules banning practices unfair or detrimental to the latter are hardly to be found; nor are there compensation provisions for their protection' (Gower, 1982, pp. 126–7).
6 This occurred in the silver boom.
7 For example, Wiscope of Switzerland, in rèlation to coffee in 1977 (see Greenstone, 1981), and Banque Populaire Suisse in relation to silver in 1980 (see CFTC, 1981).
8 It should be noted that the clearing house, CLAM, was liquidated; that function is now performed by a completely new company in Paris.
9 The use of the term 'long squeeze' for such a situation is perhaps slightly confusing, as it is sometimes called a 'short squeeze'. Hieronymus (1977) uses the term 'long manipulation' for a long squeeze.
10 The assumption here is that the futures market is more liquid than the cash market, so that the (absolute value of the) price elasticity in the futures market is greater than in the cash market.
11 It is an interesting question whether public announcement is as effective a control mechanism as the private imposition of extra deposits.
12 A famous example of large players was the case of Bunker Hunt versus Cook Industries in May 1976 soyabeans, in which Cook was the loser; see Morgan (1979).
13 Somewhat similar analyses have been made by Cagan (1981) for Treasury bills, by Johnson (1957) for coffee and by Islam (1966) for cotton.
14 Data courtesy of ICCH Ltd.

The comments of participants at the Conference on Futures Markets, European University Institute, Florence, 11–13 March 1982, and of participants at seminars at the City University and London Business Schools are gratefully acknowledged.

References

Bank of England (1978), 'Surveillance of the Commodity Markets', *Bank of England Quarterly Review*, 18.

Cagan, P. (1981), 'Financial Futures: Is More Regulation needed?', *Journal of Futures Markets*, 1.

Commodity Futures Trading Commission (1981), *Report to Congress*, 29 May 1981.

Cowing, C. B. (1965), *Populists, Plungers and Progressives*, Princeton, New Jersey.

Gower, L. L. B. (1982), *Review of Investor Protection*, London.

Greenstone, W. D. (1981), 'The Coffee Cartel: Manipulation in the Public Interest', *Journal of Futures Markets*, 1.

Hieronymus, T. (1977), *The Economics of Futures Trading for Commercial and Personal Profit*, 2nd ed., New York.

Islam, T. (1966), 'Cotton Futures Markets in India: Some Economic Studies', PhD thesis, University of London.

Johnson, C. L. (1957), 'Price Instability, Hedging and Trade Volume in the Coffee Futures Market', *Journal of Political Economy*, 65.

McDermott, E. T. (1979), 'Defining Manipulation in Commodity Futures Trading: The Futures Squeeze', *Northwestern University Law Review*, 74.

Morgan, D. (1979), *Merchants of Grain*, London.

Paul, A., Tomek, W. and Kahl, C. (1981), *Performance of Futures Markets: The Case of Potatoes*, US Department of Agriculture Technical Bulletin no. 1636.

Silber, W. L. (1981), 'Innovation, Competition and New Contract Design in Futures Markets', *Journal of Futures Markets*, 1.

Simon, Y. (1977), *Bourses de Commerce et Marchés à Terme de Marchandise*, Paris.

Stone, J. M. (1981), 'Principles of the Regulation of Futures Markets', *Journal of Futures Markets*, 1.

Telser, L. G. (1981), 'Margins and Futures Contracts', *Journal of Futures Markets*, 1.

Yamey, B. S. (1968), 'Cotton Futures Trading in Liverpool', in P. T. Bauer and B. S. Yamey, *Markets, Market Control and Marketing Reform*, London.

Index